19

The Year Everything Changed

Rob Kirkpatrick

Skyhorse Publishing

For Toni and Robbie

New Introduction Copyright © 2019 by Rob Kirkpatrick

Copyright © 2011 by Rob Kirkpatrick

All Rights Reserved. No part of this book may be reproduced in any manner without the express written consent of the publisher, except in the case of brief excerpts in critical reviews or articles. All inquiries should be addressed to Skyhorse Publishing, 555 Eighth Avenue, Suite 903, New York, NY 10018.

Skyhorse Publishing books may be purchased in bulk at special discounts for sales promotion, corporate gifts, fund-raising, or educational purposes. Special editions can also be created to specifications. For details, contact the Special Sales Department, Skyhorse Publishing, 555 Eighth Avenue, Suite 903, New York, NY 10018 or info@skyhorsepublishing.com.

www.skyhorsepublishing.com

10 9 8 7 6 5 4 3

Paperback ISBN: 978-1-5107-4307-6
eBook ISBN: 978-1-5107-4314-4

Library of Congress Cataloging-in-Publication Data is available on file.

Printed in the United States of America

ACKNOWLEDGMENTS

I want to thank my editor, Ann Treistman, for her enthusiasm in championing this title and for her great work on this book. Ann is a throwback in the best sense of the word, an editor who advocates for her authors and involves herself in every aspect of the books she publishes. Thanks also go to her assistant, Kathleen Go, for her valuable suggestions, and to copyeditor Melissa Hayes for her close reading. Last but not least, many thanks go to my agent, Joy Tutela, for her generous time and wise counsel.

CONTENTS

SELECTED TIMELINE

JANUARY

Ted Kennedy voted
Majority Whip in Congress.

Black students
take over Swarthmore College
administration building.

Dusty in Memphis
released.

1—2—3—4—5—6—7—8—9—10—11—12-13·14—15

Ohio State defeats
USC 27–16
in the Rose Bowl.

Trial of
Sirhan Sirhan
begins.

Led Zeppelin releases
debut album.
New York Jets upset
the Baltimore Colts 16–7
in Super Bowl III.

Supreme Court rules on Tinker v. Des Moines
Independent Community School District.

28—27—26—25·24·23—22—21—20—19—18—17—16—15

MARCH

Apollo 9 launches.

I Am Curious (Yellow)
screened for the first time in
America.

1—2—3—4—5—6—7—8—9—10·11—12—13—14—15

Mickey Mantle retires from baseball.
Jim Morrison of the Doors
allegedly exposes himself during a concert
in Miami, Florida.

Black students stage
armed standoff
during Parents Weekend at
Cornell University.

30—29—28—27—26—25—24—23—22—21—20—19·18—17—16

Organization Us gunmen kill Black Panthers John Huggins and Bunchy Carter in Los Angeles.

Santa Barbara oil slick.

16-**17**-18—19-**20**-21—22—23—24—25—26—27—28-**29·30**-31

New York City chemistry teacher Frank Siracusa attacked and set on fire by three black students. Richard Nixon inaugurated as nation's thirty-seventh president.

The Beatles give "rooftop" concert in London.

FEBRUARY

The Boeing 747 takes its maiden flight. "Lindsay's Blizzard" hits NYC.

14-13—12—11—10-**9**-**8**-7—6—5—4—3—2—1

Vito Genovese dies in prison in Springfield, Missouri.

10,000 University of Wisconsin-Madison students protest National Guard presence following demonstration.

Dwight D. Eisenhower dies.

16-**17**-18—19—20—21—22—23—24—25—26—27-**28**-29-**30**-31

Operation Breakfast commences.

Gun battle between Detroit police and New Republic of Africa members.

APRIL

New York City police arrest twenty-one Black Panthers on conspiracy charges.

Harvard Student Strike.

15-**14**-13—12—11—10-**9**-8-**7**-6—5-**4**-3-**2**-1

North Korean MiG shoots down a U.S. Navy EC-121 reconnaissance plane.

Supreme Court rules on *Stanley v. Georgia*.

Dr. Denton Cooley performs the first artificial heart transplant.

MAY

1 — 2 — 3 — 4 — 5 — 6 — 7 — 8 — 9 -**10**-11 — 12 — 13 -**14·15**——————

Neil Young and Crazy Horse release
Everybody Knows This Is Nowhere.

"Zip to Zap."   James Rector is killed during
the People's Park riots.

Stonewall riots begin.

The Grateful Dead
release *Aoxomoxoa.*

Gate-crashers and demonstrators
are combated by riot squads
at the Denver Pop Festival.

SDS splits in two during
its national convention;
the Weathermen organization is born.

The Wild Bunch
premieres in Los Angeles.

30 — 29 -**28·27**-26 — 25 — 24 — 23 -**22**-21-**20**-19 -**18·17**-16——————

Cuyahoga River catches on fire.

Jimi Hendrix headlines
Newport Pop Festival in
Northridge, California.

Oh! Calcutta!
opens in New York City.

JULY

Zodiac Killer kills one
and seriously injures another
in Vallejo, California attack.

Mets pitcher Tom Seaver
takes a perfect game
into 9th inning against
first-place Chicago Cubs.

Easy Rider premieres
in New York City.

1 — 2 -**3**-**4**-5 — **6**-7 — 8 — **9**-10 — 11 — 12 — 13 -**14**-15——————

Brian Jones found dead
in his pool in Sussex, England.

Led Zeppelin, Jethro Tull, and Sly & the Family Stone
play the Newport Jazz Festival in Rhode Island.

Hurricane Camille
hits the coast of Mississippi.

Arlo Guthrie
Alice's Restaurant premieres.

31 — 30 — 29 — 28 — 27 -**26**-25 — 24 — 23 — 22 — 21 -**20**-19 -**18·17**-16——————

Medium Cool
premieres in New York City.

Woody Allen stars in
Take the Money and Run.

American forces emerge victorious in
the Battle of Hamburger Hill.
Alex Rackley is killed by members of
the New Haven Black Panthers.

Midnight Cowboy
premieres in New York City.

16 — 17 · **18** - 19 · **20** · 21 — 22 — **23** - 24 · **25** · 26 — 27 · **28** · 29 — 30 — 31

Apollo 10 launches.   The Who releases *Tommy*,   Sergio Leone's
the first "rock opera."   *Once Upon a Time in the West*
released in the U.S.

JUNE

15 — 14 — 13 — 12 · **11** - 10 — 9 — 8 — 7 — 6 — 5 — 4 — 3 — 2 — 1

True Grit with John Wayne premieres.

Mary Jo Kopechne
perishes in
Chappaquiddick incident.

Man walks on the moon.

Mets manager Gil Hodges pulls
leftfielder Cleon Jones
off the field in the middle
of an inning during doubleheader loss.

16 — 17 · **18** · **19** · **20** · 21 — 22 — 23 — 24 — **25** · 26 — 27 — 28 — 29 · **30** · **31**

Ted Kennedy pleads guilty to
leaving the scene of an accident,
delivers televised speech on
Chappaquiddick incident.

The Zodiac Killer mails letters
with coded messages to the editors of
the *San Francisco Chronicle*,
San Francisco Examiner,
and *Vallejo Times-Herald*.

AUGUST

U.S. soldiers mutiny during a battle
in the Song Chang Valley in
South Vietnam.

Iggy Pop and the Stooges
release their debut album.   Atlantic City Pop Festival.

15 - 14 — 13 — **12** - 11 — 10 — **9** — **8** — **7** — 6 — **5** — **4** — 3 — 2 — **1**

The Manson Family strikes again,
killing Leno and Rosemary LaBianca.
San Francisco Chronicle publishes
solution to the Zodiac Killer's message.

Atlanta International Pop Festival.

"This is the Zodiac speaking . . ."

Woodstock Music and Art Fair
in White Lake, New York.

"Helter Skelter":
Manson Family murders at
the home of Sharon Tate and
Roman Polanski.

SEPTEMBER

Lieutenant William Calley
formally charged for his role
in the My Lai massacre.

LOOK WHO'S NO. 1!
Mets sweep doubleheader with
Expos to vault into first place for
first time in franchise history.

1—2—3—4—5—**6**—7—**8**—9—**10**-11—12—13—14—15

Police raid the Black Panther breakfast
in Watts, California.

The first message is sent via the ARPANET,
predecessor of the Internet.
Judge Julius Hoffman orders
defendant Bobby Seale bound and gagged
during the Chicago 8 trial.

The Mets defeat the Orioles
to win the World Series.

31—30-**29**-28—27—26—25—24—23—**22**-21—20—19—18—17—**16**

Led Zeppelin II is released.

NOVEMBER

Richard Nixon delivers his
televised "Silent Majority" speech.

Seymour Hersh breaks
story of the My Lai massacre.

1—2—**3**—4—5—6—7—8—9—**10**-11—**12**-13—14—**15**

Sesame Street debuts on the
National Educational Television network.

Nearly half a million people
participate in the Mobilization Rally
in Washington, D.C.

Curt Flood declares his intentions
to challenge baseball's reserve clause and
file as free agent.

31-30—29—28—27—26—25-**24**-23—22—21—20—19—18—17—16

Jimi Hendrix and the Band of Gypsys
perform at New York's Fillmore East.

Bob & Carol & Ted & Alice premieres at the New York Film Festival.

"Chicago 8" trials begin. The Mets clinch National League Eastern Division.

The Zodiac Killer attacks Cecelia Shepard and Bryan Hartnell at Lake Berryessa.

16 **17** 18 19 20 21 22 **23 24** 25 **26 27** 28 **29** 30

Butch Cassidy and the Sundance Kid hits screens in limited release.

The Beatles release *Abbey Road*. *The Brady Bunch* debuts on ABC's Friday night lineup.

Love, American Style debuts on ABC.

OCTOBER

War protesters stage nationwide Moratorium.

Baltimore Orioles sweep Minnesota Twins; Mets sweep Atlanta Braves.

15 14 13 12 **11** 10 9 **8** 7 **6** 5 4 3 2 1

The Zodiac Killer murders San Francisco taxi driver Paul Stine.

"Days of Rage" commence in Chicago.

Strategic Arms Limitation Treaty (SALT) talks between the United States and the Soviet Union commence in Helsinki, Finland.

CBS Evening News airs interview with Vietnam veteran Paul Meadlo on his role in My Lai.

16 **17** 18 **19 20** 21 22 23 **24** 25 26 27 **28** 29 30

Apollo 12 lands on the moon's Ocean of Storms.

Cleveland Plain Dealer publishes photos of the My Lai incident. Members of Indians of All Tribes seize Alcatraz Island.

The Rolling Stones release *Let It Bleed*.

DECEMBER

The Rolling Stones headline the ill-fated free concert at the Altamont Speedway.

15 14 13 12 11 10 9 8 7 **6** 5 **4** 3 2 1

Black Panther Party leaders Fred Hampton and Mark Clark are killed during a raid by Chicago police.

INTRODUCTION TO THE 2019 EDITION

In June 2018, archaeologists performed an excavation of the hillside at the original Woodstock Music and Art Fair site. They rolled back squares of grass and sifted through sod, unearthing shards of glass bottles and pull tabs from aluminum cans (the now-banned bane of bare feet once immortalized as the "pop top" Jimmy Buffet stepped on in "Margaritaville"), all valuable finds as the workers look to determine the original surface level and stage location of the festival. (The bottom of the hillside was regraded in the 1990s to accommodate a temporary stage for an anniversary concert.) Aerial shots from that storied weekend in August 1969 can't be relied upon to determine the precise location of the original stage or its light and speaker towers. But archaeologists now think they've identified the spot where the wooden "Peace Fence" in front of the stage and the chain-link fence on the side of the stage met, which will enable the group to match historic photos to estimate the location and dimensions of the stage. The excavation project will help the Museum at Bethel Woods in planning walking routes for the fiftieth anniversary of Woodstock.[1]

In writing this introduction for the tenth anniversary edition of this book—to publish for the fiftieth anniversary of 1969—it occurs to me that the original hardcover of this book has become a time capsule itself. *1969: The Year Everything Changed* was published in 2009, a year that many Americans had looked to hopefully, if perhaps naively, as a year of transformative change. But in the decade since then, rather than achieving a "post-racial" America, we have only seen our divisions grow deeper.

As the Sixties came to an end, Diana Ross announced she was leaving the Supremes to go solo. Her recording of the soul anthem "Someday We'll Be Together" was open to multiple interpretations—was it about a romantic reunion? the future of the Supremes? civil rights unrest? the Vietnam War?—all of which spoke to a universal yearning for togetherness.

I've always been fascinated with what pop culture can reveal about our society. We can look back to two "controversial" television specials from late 1969 that spoke to social schisms that still resonate today.

On November 30, Simon and Garfunkel ruffled feathers with their special, *Songs of America*, which aired on CBS. Directed by Charles Grodin, the hour-long program was about as overtly political as Dion's hit song from the previous year, "Abraham, Martin, and John." Rather than making straightforward statements, *Songs of America* simply showed clips of many newsmakers of the day, interspersing scenes of American landscapes, pollution, and social unrest with B-movie clips and footage of Howdy Doody, Mickey Mantle, Lenny Bruce, and Harry Truman playing piano. The duo's forthcoming single, "Bridge Over Troubled Water," which would go on to win the Grammy Awards for Record of the Year and Song of the Year, was unveiled to viewers accompanied by visuals of John and Bobby Kennedy, Martin Luther King, Jr., and Cesar Chavez. AT&T, the original sponsor, reportedly pulled out over objections that too many dead Democrats had made the cut.

With a new sponsor in the beauty product company Alberto Culver, *Songs of America* aired with an introduction by veteran actor Robert Ryan. He explained to viewers: "These two young men have attained a tremendous following among the youth of America with their lyrical interpretation of the world they live in. We think you will find the next hour both entertaining and stimulating." Youth culture was still gaining acceptance at the end of the decade, and this "statement" from two twenty-eight-year-olds from Queens had to be prefaced, pre-emptively defended. "The starry-eyed optimism that had taken hold of America during the mid-Sixties didn't just die in 1969," recalls writer Bud Scoppa, "it was ripped to shreds." During the first commercial break, a million viewers got up and changed the channel.[2]

In the ensuing decades, youth culture has gained more and more control over the marketplace, its voice more and more accepted as the shaper of society. But some factions remain suspicious of young people with opinions. Our nation experienced yet another gun-related tragedy on Valentine's Day 2018 when a former student opened fire on students and staff of Marjorie Stoneman Douglas High School in Parkland, Florida. In the dark aftermath of that day, teenagers from the school emerged as reluctant leaders of a national movement, gaining prominence while speaking passionately and with authority about their experiences and the need to have responsible gun regulations in America. Many observers welcomed the emergence of this new, refreshing segment of the political discourse. But right-wingers and Trumpeteers objected, asking what right these young survivors had to speak up and say anything.

The comparisons between Nixon and Trump are inevitable in the cynicism and deception both Republican presidents brought to the White House. As historians charge Nixon with a treasonous act in conspiring to delay Vietnam peace talks during his '68 campaign, Trump will be haunted by his many alleged connections to Russian interests and his open praise of foreign dictators. Yet even with all his faults, we must remember that Nixon established the EPA and was sympathetic to such ideas as single-payer health care and a universal income. Such things make the architect of Watergate and secret bomber of Cambodia seem downright progressive when compared to the agenda of the current administration.

On December 7, the Fifth Dimension appeared on *The Ed Sullivan Show* and sang a medley of "A Change Is Gonna Come" and "People Got to Be Free" along with lines from the Declaration of Independence. The juxtaposition was too much for some viewers. As one newspaper editorial later recalled, "Believe it or not, the lyrics of 'The Declaration' were controversial at the time, considered an anti-government, anti-President Nixon protest. At the time, statements like 'a long train of abuses and usurpations, pursuing, invariably the same object, evinces a design to reduce them under absolute despotism' hit home for war protesters."[3]

One might say the notion of the nation's founding document being controversial has found its twenty-first century incarnation in the "take a knee" protest movement started by NFL quarterback Colin Kaepernick. Conservatives have interpreted this expression of protest as "disrespecting the flag" or "disrespecting the military." The former charge seems to fetishize the flag at the expense of the ideas it symbolizes—including the freedom of speech and expression—while the latter assumes the national anthem is for the military only and not for every American citizen. Much as baseball's Curt Flood risked ostracization among MLB circles when he challenged the sport's reserve clause, Kaepernick has found himself out of the league and at the center of a collusion case against the NFL as many fans, team owners, and even the White House have condemned him.

Writing about a year that people lived through can be dicey. People are protective of their memories, and they want your retelling of the times to resemble their experiences, their nostalgia.

One criticism I've heard of this book was of my "liberal perspective." Others said I paid too much attention to sports: namely, the twin triumphs of New York's underdog Jets and Mets. Not everyone is a sports fan, but not everyone need be a fan to appreciate how certain teams and stories transcend the culture. As I began to write this new introduction, I opened the *New York Times* and saw two such stories: one on the NFL anthem protests and one on the New York Yankees' plans to commemorate the fiftieth anniversary of the Stonewall Riots of 1969. Much as the Yankees had been slow to follow as Major League Baseball became integrated, the MLB club was also the last one to launch an LGBT initiative. As recently as 2010, Yankees fans had greeted opposing teams' fans with a homophobic chant to the tune of "YMCA." The announcement spoke to the changing times in professional sports and a breaking down of the macho stereotype previously forced upon athletes and fans alike.[4]

✻ ✻ ✻

Today, as funding for public education and health care is in the sights of the president and the congressional GOP, we can look back to a memorable exchange on the floor of the Senate that helped shape children's lives for years to come. On May 1, 1969, Fred Rogers (known to children and former children for generations since as "Mr. Rogers") appeared before the United States Senate Subcommittee on Communications, chaired by John Pastore, to argue against proposed cuts in funding for the Corporation for Public Broadcasting. "I'm very much concerned, as I know you are, about what's being delivered to children in this country," Rogers told Pastore. "We deal with such things as the inner drama of childhood. We don't have to bop somebody over the head to make drama on the screen. We deal with such things as getting a haircut, or the feelings about brothers and sisters, and the kind of anger that arises in simple family situations, and we speak to it constructively."

Pastore initially appeared skeptical, but three minutes into Rogers's speech, the senator seemed visibly won over. Rogers continued: "I give an expression of care every day to each child, to help him realize that he is unique. I end the program by saying, 'You've made this day a special day by just being you. There's no person in the whole world like you, and I like you just the way you are.' And I feel that if we in public television can only make it clear that feelings are mentionable and manageable, we will have done a great service for mental health. I think that it's much more dramatic that two men could be working out their feelings of anger, much more dramatic, than showing something of gunfire."

Pastore said, "Well, I'm supposed to be a pretty tough guy, and this is the first time I've had goosebumps in the last two days."

To put the ball over the goal line, Rogers recited lines from a song in his show: "What do you do with the mad that you feel?"

"I think it's wonderful. I think it's wonderful," the senator said. Referring to the funding in question, he added, "Looks like you just earned the twenty million dollars."[5]

Since the original publication of *1969: The Year Everything Changed*, everything has changed for me, too. I got married. My wife, Toni, and I had a son, Robert IV. My first Father's Day as a father also was my first without one, as my father had passed away at the age of eighty-seven. His grandson now watches *Daniel Tiger's Neighborhood*, the animated spinoff from the late Fred Rogers's land of Make-Believe.

I take frequent jaunts with my wife and son to the Berkshires, shunning extravagant vacations for the all-American tradition of the modest, family road trip. On the way through New York's Columbia County, we take scenic Route 11A, which a sign demarcates as recipient of the "NATIONAL BEAUTY HIGHWAY AWARD 1969." The sign reminds me of the billboard that used to call out to young, hirsute types during the counterculture era: BEAUTIFY AMERICA: GET A HAIRCUT.

Among the mountains of western Massachusetts, we often visit the town of Stockbridge, where we found the deconsecrated church featured in the film *Alice's Restaurant*, now home to the Guthrie Center. Walking along Stockbridge's main drag, we pass by the site of Alice's old restaurant, though we have yet to find a time when it is open. Sometimes you can't get anything you want.

During part one of our honeymoon, which we took in the Catskills, we drove through winding back roads to West Saugerties and found the salmon-colored bungalow known as Big Pink, where Bob Dylan and the Band had their landmark recording sessions. Big Pink is a rental now, though neighbors had posted a sign at the beginning of a long, narrow entrance road to discourage trespassers. It seems some residents today feel the same about tourists as Bob Dylan began to feel about people coming to check out the Woodstock "scene" back then.

Songs from the Big Pink sessions wound up on an unauthorized vinyl collection known as *The Great White Wonder*, which began to circulate in 1969 and became the first widely popular rock bootleg. Another bootleg from later that year, *Live'r Than You'll Ever Be*, collected smuggled recordings from the notorious 1969 Rolling Stones tour and became so successful that it was reviewed in *Rolling Stone* magazine. The underground "enterprisers" of the day led to the torrent trading sites of today. One friend, a dedicated Deadhead, names a Fillmore West show from February 1969 as his pick for the band's most essential download.

❋ ❋ ❋

The story of this book's long, strange trip to market is an interesting one. Another publisher had originally signed me to a contract, but that publisher went through a series of management changes and began to cancel contracts. When they introduced a "partial delivery" stage that wasn't in my contract, I felt something was amiss. I returned my advance and told them to rip up our contract. I strongly believed the story of 1969 would have an audience. Two other publishers agreed and made offers on the book, and I accepted one. I moved twice and worked long, full-time days at the same time I wrote the book in your hands.

1969

Getting a book published is merely the first step to getting it to you, dear reader. Stores need to order the book before you can buy it. Alas, one major account initially passed on the book altogether. This alone can doom a book to poor sales. But then *USA Today* columnist Craig Wilson called me for an interview and wrote a wonderful, two-page story on the book *1969* and the year 1969 that ran on the front page of the "Life" section. That account then decided to stock the book. When that stock sold out, they re-ordered more stock. And so did the other accounts.

Appearances followed on *CBS Sunday Morning* with Mary Calvi in New York City, on the WGN-TV superstation with Antwan Lewis, with Nick DiGilio on WGN FM radio, and many others. The Freemont Street Experience organization generously flew me out to Las Vegas for their "Summer of '69" celebration and invited me on stage to hold up my book for hundreds of people to see as the great Fifth Dimension sat huddled at stage side, waiting to perform for the crowd. A Los Angeles theater producer contacted me to let me know he was staging a play partially inspired by my book. I appeared as a commentator in the History Channel documentary *Sex in '69: The Sexual Revolution in America*. The book was translated into Chinese. Ken Burns and Lynn Novick included *1969: The Year Everything Changed* in the bibliography of the companion book to their documentary, *The Vietnam War*. Five years after publication, my book became an Amazon bestseller on the eBook general list.

To paraphrase John Sebastian during his tripped-out Woodstock performance, this ride has been the mind-fucker of all time. I feel vindicated in my belief that 1969 was a uniquely memorable, culturally cataclysmic year in American history.

—Rob Kirkpatrick, October 2018

PROLOGUE: REVOLUTION, APOCALYPSE, AND THE BIRTH OF MODERN AMERICA

"It was a year of extremes, of violence and madness as well as achievement and success."

—*Barry Miles, Hippie*

For a year that had so many amazing, startling, and culture-defining moments—the year that perhaps defined the era more than any other—it's hard to believe that no one had yet written a book about 1969.

Nineteen sixty-eight, with its assassinations and riots, seems to have lasted in the collective consciousness as the year that embodies the turbulent late sixties. And, indeed, there is a veritable glut of books on 1968; as one customer reviewer wrote on Amazon, "The statement that 1968 was a year like no other has now become almost a cliché." (One colleague even jokingly suggested I call this book *1969: The Year After the Important Year.*) Turn the calendar over from 1968, though, and one finds a twelve-month period that is unparalleled in American history.

Humankind hurtled through air and space in 1969, the year of the moon landing and the inaugural flight of the 747. It marked the beginning of the age of Nixon and the Silent Majority, and it saw the effective end of Camelot with the Chappaquiddick incident. It was when American forces began the covert bombing of Cambodia and fought the Battle of Hamburger Hill, when the American people lost their innocence with the discovery of the My Lai massacre, and when they came together in the Moratorium and the Mobilization.

It was the year when America got undressed—figuratively and literally—on screen, onstage, and outdoors. Nineteen sixty-nine was the height of the Sexual Revolution, with *Portnoy's Complaint* and *Oh! Calcutta!* and *Midnight Cowboy* and *I Am Curious (Yellow)* and *Bob & Carol & Ted & Alice* all speaking to the changing climate of morality and social taboos. It was the year of the commune, the year of nudity onstage, and the year of the outdoor music festival— highlighted by the generation-shaping Woodstock. It also revealed the dark side of the counterculture with Charles Manson and the Altamont Speedway Concert.

Musically, it was a year of firsts. The Stooges and MC5 released the first punk records, while Led Zeppelin's first two albums and U. S. tour launched heavy metal in America. Miles Davis propelled jazz into a new age with the seminal rock-fusion classic *Bitches Brew*, while King Crimson set the mold for progressive rock with *In the Court of the Crimson King*. The Grateful Dead's *Aoxomoxoa* and the Allman Brothers' debut release gave us the initial offerings of jam band music and Southern rock. The Who debuted the rock opera *Tommy*, and Crosby, Stills & Nash and Blind Faith appeared on the scene as rock's first supergroups. The Rolling Stones reached their creative peak, and, with their 1969 U. S. tour, assumed the mantle of Greatest Rock 'n' Roll Band in the World.

Broadway Joe and the Jets scored an upset for the ages that cemented the merger of the AFL and NFL and led to the network deal for *Monday Night Football*. Tom Seaver and the Amazin' Mets staged baseball's biggest miracle. The year saw baseball's future with the designated hitter, an experiment introduced that spring, and even more controversial, Curt Flood's challenge to the sport's reserve clause in seeking to become baseball's first free agent.

The FBI declared war on the Black Panther Party, and the Weathermen declared war on America. The Stonewall Riots inspired the birth of the Gay Rights movement, and the Indians of All Tribes' seizure of Alcatraz Island began the Red Power movement. The Santa Barbara Oil Slick, the Cuyahoga River fire, and People's Park gave impetus to the Ecology movement. It was the year when the Revolution came to the suburbs, and when they paved paradise and put up a parking lot.

In a single year, America saw the peaks and valleys of an entire decade—the death of the old and the birth of the new—the birth, I would argue, of modern America.

❈ ❈ ❈

For those who first came into consciousness in the beginning of the 1970s, as I did, there was a sense of the country having just gone through an enormous upheaval—a paradigm shift that the generation before us had witnessed first hand, through which we had emerged as if through the other side of the looking glass. It was like arriving at a production of *Hamlet* near the end of Act V: Hamlet lay poisoned on the ground, the bodies of courtiers lay around him, and as Fortinbras did, you wondered how things had gotten to that point. With this book, I set out not just to tell the story of 1969 in America, but also to examine the *zeitgeist*—literally, the "time spirit"—of this iconic, tumultuous, cataclysmic year. As Theodore Roszak wrote in *The Making of a Counter Culture*, "that elusive conception called 'the spirit of the times' continues to nag at the mind and demand recognition, since it seems to be the only way available in which one can make even provisional sense of the world one lives in."[1]

In reviewing the popular culture of the day, notions of the apocalypse appear with surprising frequency. I found references to the end-times not just in news stories on the armed takeover of Cornell University or the Days or Rage or the first Strategic Arms Limitation Talks, but also in reviews of Jefferson Airplane's *Volunteers* and Sam

Peckinpah's *The Wild Bunch*, in the work of artist Ron Cobb, the chaos at the Altamont Free Concert, even in the fiction of John Cheever. The decade was one of the most turbulent in the history of the United States, and as it came to an end, an early form of millennial anxiety seemed to grip the country. The end of things was very much on the collective American mind at the end of the sixties.

But the sixties no more ended in 1969 than they began in 1960. As is implied by the bookend works of Jon Margolis's *The Last Innocent Year: America in 1964—The Beginning of the "Sixties"* and Andreas Killen's *1973 Nervous Breakdown: Watergate, Warhol, and the Birth of Post-Sixties America*, the sixties was not so much a period of ten years as it was a less distinctly defined period of cultural and social change during which America tuned in, turned on, dropped out, grew up, woke up, blew up.

In telling the story of America in this incredible year, I looked to re-create the experience of living through this pivotal time. Accordingly, I've divided the narrative into four parts, each roughly corresponding to the seasons. Within each of these parts, I group thematic chapters that are built around central events from those seasons. One of the pleasant surprises in writing this book was the ways in which these chapters emerged "organically"—e.g., stories of the sexual revolutions of springtime, the flowering of the counterculture in the summer, the apocalyptic standoffs at year's end. Life does not happen in neat and orderly ways, as if following a timeline, but the story of 1969 is one that develops in dramatic tension, builds to a climax, and concludes in its December denouement.

—Rob Kirkpatrick, October 2008

I. WINTER'S CHILDREN

The rain is gone,
the sun shines on us,
the splendid, radiant, torturous sun of Winter.

—Ursula K. LeGuin,
The Left Hand of Darkness

1. NIXON'S COMING

The inauguration of the nation's thirty-seventh president marks an increasing rift in America, while his secret bombing of Cambodia sinks the United States deeper into the quagmire of the Vietnam War.

He stood on the steps of the Capitol overlooking the crowd of people that had assembled on this cold, gray, windy January day, undoubtedly thinking back with a sense of warm vindication on the path that had brought him there.

In college, Richard Nixon had been, if not a big man on campus, at the very least an active member of campus life—a member of the football and debating teams as well as a student thespian with handsome looks and thick, wavy hair. Yet even then there had been a darker side to him. Classmates remembered Nixon as a loner with streaks of meanness, even paranoia. Hailing from a modest, middle-class, Quaker family, he would carry a lifelong suspicion of those with privileged backgrounds.

He had risen to prominence in politics—first in Congress, then as the nation's vice president under a beloved war hero. But when his time came to run for president, it seemed as if events had conspired against him to steal away his destiny. He had performed well in the first nationally televised presidential debate—indeed, in sheer rhetorical points, had performed *better* than his opponent, the charismatic John F. Kennedy. Yet a relentless campaign schedule coupled with an extended hospital stay had left him looking gaunt and haggard. Wearing a five o'clock shadow, and with the glistening of perspiration underneath his now-receding hairline, Nixon appeared less competent than his opponent, whose handsome and youthful features and composed cadence seemed to give him a more "presidential" pedigree. While the majority of those who listened to the debate on the radio believed the former vice president had won, most of those who watched it on television thought his opponent did. When Kennedy proceeded to emerge from the bitter campaign with the narrowest of victories—thanks in large part, it would later emerge, to backroom dealings orchestrated by father Joe—distrust of the system grew even greater within the mind of the vanquished candidate. When he returned to his adopted home state and lost the gubernatorial race, he told the press they wouldn't have him to kick around anymore.

Yet it wasn't long before Nixon was eyeing a return to the White House. Next time, he promised himself, things would be different.

It almost wasn't. The younger brother of his former nemesis was waiting in the wings—a popular candidate in Robert F. Kennedy, who galvanized a growing peace movement while carrying the torch for his slain sibling. But then destiny stepped in. The younger brother, like his older brother before him, was felled by an assassin's bullet. In the ensuing convention, the political party of these two fallen brothers fell apart before the nation's eyes.

This time, Nixon had emerged victorious. And so on this day, he stood on the Capitol steps, ready to address the nation that had once rejected him.

His wife of twenty-eight years stood beside him, holding not one but two family Bibles, both open to Isaiah 2:4: "They shall beat their swords into plowshares, and their spears into pruning hooks; nation shall not lift up sword against nation, neither shall they learn war anymore."[1] He raised his right hand and took the oath of office. Then Nixon addressed the nation for the first time as president: "I ask you to share with me today the majesty of this moment. In the orderly transfer of power, we celebrate the unity that keeps us free," he said. "Each moment in history is a fleeting time, precious and unique. But some stand out as moments of beginning, in which courses are set that shape decades or centuries. This can be such a moment."

The nation—*his* nation, now—was at the nexus of a dizzying technological revolution. "Forces now are converging that make possible, for the first time, the hope that many of man's deepest aspirations can at last be realized. The spiraling pace of change allows us to contemplate, within our own lifetime, advances that once would have taken centuries. In throwing wide the horizons of space, we have discovered new horizons on earth."

Yet the nation was also at war, fighting battles against an enemy in a far-off land—and, in a sense, against itself on its own streets. The new president continued:

> For the first time, because the people of the world want peace, and the leaders of the world are afraid of war, the times are on the side of peace. . . . The greatest honor history can bestow is the title of peacemaker. This honor now beckons America—the chance to help lead the world at last out of the valley of turmoil, and onto that high ground of peace that man has dreamed of since the dawn of civilization. If we succeed, generations to come will say of us now living that we mastered our moment, that we helped make the world safe for mankind.

Nixon spoke in the traditional rhetorical mode of newly sworn-in presidents—shunning specifics in favor of grand generalities, while adding a sacred tone reminiscent of the verse found in the Bible on which he'd taken his oath just moments before:

> We have found ourselves rich in goods, but ragged in spirit; reaching with magnificent precision for the moon, but

falling into raucous discord on earth. We are caught in war, wanting peace. We are torn by division, wanting unity. We see around us empty lives, wanting fulfillment. We see tasks that need doing, waiting for hands to do them. To a crisis of the spirit, we need an answer of the spirit.

He spoke of the nation's deepening schism, addressing the partisan passions in which he had been both the loser and, now, the winner:

In these difficult years, America has suffered from a fever of words; from inflated rhetoric that promises more than it can deliver; from angry rhetoric that fans discontents into hatreds; from bombastic rhetoric that postures instead of persuading. We cannot learn from one another until we stop shouting at one another—until we speak quietly enough so that our words can be heard as well as our voices.

Thus, Richard M. Nixon became president of the United States at the beginning of what would become one of the most pivotal years of the twentieth century.

❉ ❉ ❉

During the inaugural parade, the new president encountered the extremes that would mark much of his term. A float from the group "Up with People" sent good vibes to the onlookers lined up in their winter coats. Cheering crowds greeted him for the first few blocks as the presidential motorcade proceeded on its way from the Capitol building to Nixon's new home on Pennsylvania Avenue. But as the parade reached 13th Street, a double line of police struggled to keep back a group of war protesters, who threw sticks, stones, cans, and bottles at the presidential limousine while chanting, "Four more years of death!" and "Ho, Ho, Ho Chi Minh, the NLF is going to win." One protester brandished a sign that mocked Nixon's '68 campaign slogan: NIXON'S THE ONE—THE NO. 1 WAR CRIMINAL. Some demonstrators spit at the police. Others took the small American flags that had been distributed by local Boy Scouts and burned them. It was the first time in the nation's history that an inauguration parade had been so marred.[2]

But as the limo rounded the corner onto 15th Street, the atmosphere changed. Onlookers assembled in front of the Washington Hotel and the Treasury Building applauded the new chief executive. Nixon ordered the sunroof opened so that he could stand and wave to the people—his people.

❀ ❀ ❀

In their groundbreaking 1969 book, *The Peter Principle: Why Things Always Go Wrong*, Dr. Laurence J. Peter and Raymond Hull sought to explain why organizations in both the public and private sectors contained so many incompetent people. Examining case studies of "occupational incompetence" as a "universal phenomenon," Peter discovered a commonality: an employee who had been "promoted from a position of competence to a position of incompetence." The recurring pattern revealed was of the employee who had performed competently at his or her given position and was then rewarded with a promotion to a position of greater responsibility. Following this pattern, the employee rises through the ranks and inevitably reaches a position for which he or she is no longer competent; there, the employee plateaus, remaining at the position of incompetence. Thus was born the Peter Principle: "In a Hierarchy Every Employee Tends to Rise to His Level of Incompetence."

After having served as a United States congressman for six years and vice president for eight, the American voting pubic had "promoted" Nixon to the highest office in the land, one that would instantly test his competency as chief executive. As Nixon entered the White House in January 1969, more than 500,000 American soldiers were stationed in Southeast Asia as part of U. S. involvement in the Vietnam War. Although he never mentioned Vietnam by name in his inaugural address, the underlying focus of his address was clear. In his campaign for the American presidency, Richard Nixon had resurrected his career. Described as the "new Nixon," he had defeated incumbent vice president Hubert Humphrey by portraying himself as the proverbial law-and-order candidate and attacking the Democratic administration's handling of the war in Southeast Asia. In the words of his speechwriter, William Safire, Nixon had "hammered away" at the fact that there was "no end in sight" to the war.[3]

In Vietnam, enemy forces—both the North Vietnamese Army (NVA) and the insurgent National Liberation Front (NLF), or Vietcong—were proving relentless, and as more and more American families sent their sons to the far side of the globe to fight against an enemy that posed no threat of attack on American soil, popular support for U. S. involvement in the war was declining. In 1968, antiwar protests had led to televised scenes of violence from the streets of Chicago during the Democratic National Convention, and the disproportionate number of soldiers from urban areas throughout America fueled racial unrest during the "long, hot summer." As the calendar turned to January 1969, the Vietnam War was, as Safire would write, "the bone in the nation's throat."[4]

Nixon's chief of staff, H. R. Haldeman, later wrote about a conversation that he'd had with Nixon on the campaign trail about Nixon's plan to end the war. "I call it the Madman Theory, Bob. I want the North Vietnamese to believe I've reached the point where I might do anything to stop the war. We'll just slip the word to them that, 'for God's sake, you know Nixon is obsessed about Communism. We can't restrain him when he's angry—and he has his hand on the nuclear button'—and Ho Chi Minh himself will be in Paris in two days begging for peace."[5] In the transition period between Election Day and inauguration, he'd vowed, "I'm not going to end up like

LBJ, holed up in the White House afraid to show my face on the street. I'm going to stop that war. Fast."[6]

Yet during the final stages of the campaign, Nixon had done his best to thwart Lyndon Johnson's last-ditch efforts to forge a truce with North Vietnam and the insurgent National Liberation Front. The Nixon camp had passed word to South Vietnamese president Nguyen Van Thieu through Anna Chennault, widow of famed World War II pilot Claire Chennault, that if Saigon stalled participation in the Paris peace talks, Johnson's planned bombing halt would lose its effect and help swing the election away from vice president Humbert H. Humphrey and toward Nixon. If he were elected, Nixon indicated, the United States would negotiate more firmly in the interest of Saigon. Thieu, a Machiavellian figure who was coping with both an aggressing neighbor to the north and growing schisms within his own country, effectively sabotaged Johnson's negotiations with Hanoi and helped Nixon win a very close election in November 1968.

Before he officially took office, Nixon had told Henry Kissinger to prepare a report on North Vietnamese Army presence in Cambodia, which bordered the Vietnamese nations on the west. In February, Kissinger reported back that not only were North Vietnamese Army forces using the Ho Chi Minh Trail to aid their operations against South Vietnam, but that they also had established a headquarters in the "fish hook" area of the nation, northeast of Tay Ninh in South Vietnam, in anticipation of a major offensive to be launched from Cambodian territory.[7]

Four days later, Communist forces launched an offensive against targets throughout South Vietnam, effectively violating the truce that Johnson had struck with Hanoi at the end of 1968. American personnel suffered nearly 900 casualties within two weeks.[8] While aboard Air Force One en route to Europe, Nixon issued an order to commence covert bombing missions against North Vietnamese forces in Cambodia. But before the order could be carried out, both

Secretary of Defense Melvin Laird and Secretary of State William Rogers expressed their reservations to the president. Laird told Nixon he felt it would be difficult to keep Cambodian strikes secret from the American public; Rogers concurred. Nixon, who feared how the country would react to knowledge of missions that seemed to expand the scope of the war, went against his instincts and rescinded his order.

Nixon was asked at a news conference on March 4 if the American people would allow the war to continue for a span of "months and even years." "I trust that I am not confronted with that problem, when you speak of years," he responded. "I think the American people will support a President if they are told by the President why we are there, what our objections are, what the costs will be, and what the consequences would be if we took another course of action."[9]

Ten days later, as the enemy offensive continued, Nixon sent a message to Hanoi—and to his own nation—saying, "It will be my policy as President to issue a warning only once, and I will not repeat it now. Anything in the future that is done will be done. There will be no additional warnings."[10]

The president called Kissinger the following day to tell him that he was ordering a strike against Cambodian targets, and this time, he said, "State is to be notified only after the point of no return." Remembering that he had allowed his mind to be changed once before, he added, "The order is not appealable," and then hung up. He called Kissinger back minutes later and told him he wanted "No comment, no warnings, no complaints, no protest . . . I mean it, not one thing to be said to anyone publicly or privately without my prior approval."[11]

Kissinger convinced Nixon to meet with Laird and Rogers in the Oval Office on March 16, to at least give the appearance of asking for their counsel. Laird favored going public; Rogers opposed the mission altogether. But Nixon had made up his mind. "I have ordered the bombing to begin as soon as possible," he told them. "Tomorrow, if the weather is good enough." It was to be kept secret from Congress and the American people.[12]

As the early morning hours of March 17 broke in Washington, U. S. forces commenced Operation Breakfast, the first stage of a planned three-part "Menu" against Vietnamese forces in Cambodia. Sixty B-52 bombers, flying in waves of three, rained bombs onto the Cambodian countryside three miles inside the border. Pilots hit ammunition and fuel depots and recorded seventy-three "secondary explosions." Early reports indicated the mission was a success. Haldeman would record in his diary that Nixon and Kissinger were "really excited," and that the following day Kissinger was "beaming."[13]

But the early reports of success turned out to be exaggerated. The B-52 crews misinterpreted the "secondary explosions" and mistakenly concluded that enemy units in the area had been disabled. When a Daniel Boone Special Forces unit was sent in for mop-up duty, it ran straight into VNA forces and was massacred. A second unit was ordered to go in, but its soldiers mutinied rather than walk headlong into the slaughter.[14]

Nixon later wrote in his memoir that Operation Breakfast "was the first turning point in my administration's conduct of the Vietnam War." Although the strike had not achieved its goals, it steeled Nixon in his resolve to end the war—on his terms. Nixon had been a virulent anti-Communist since his days in Congress, and many historians would argue that his obsession with Communism was no calculated bluff. Historian Jeffrey Kimball argues that the bombing of targets in Cambodia was "transformed by Nixon into a demonstration of his will."[15] Operation Breakfast signaled the start of a balancing act for Nixon, one in which he would begin to bring troops back home while at the same time escalating the war in Southeast Asia.

Three days after the initial bombing of Cambodia, Nixon told his cabinet that the war would be over by the following year.

2. Something in the Air

A "virus of dissent" plagues the nation as the battle lines are drawn between the Right and the New Left.

In its first issue of the year, *Time* magazine looked back on the calendar year that had just passed into the history books:

> Mankind could be thankful at least that at no time in 1968 did the superpowers come close to an irreconcilable conflict. Yet nations around the world were confronted with a new kind of crisis: a virus of internal dissent. The spirit of protest leaped from country to country like an ideological variant of Hong Kong flu. Protest marches, sit-ins and riots attacked every kind of structure, society and regime.[1]

The "virus of internal dissent" plagued many American cities in 1968. From the violence on the streets of Chicago to the student takeover of Columbia University to the rioting in black neighborhoods following the assassination of Martin Luther King, scenes of urban unrest made news headlines throughout much of the year. But outside the cities, there was a sense that quiet, rural, and suburban America was sheltered from the majority of the unrest. By the end of 1969, this would no longer be true. "Lock up the streets and houses," went one Top 40 hit, "Because there's something in the air." Beginning in early January, as students returned from winter break, college campuses throughout the nation became the

11

battleground of the American culture wars. While student activism of past years was founded largely on the principles of civil disobedience, by the end of the decade the mode of campus protest had become increasingly violent. On the campus of San Francisco State, a picket by members of the Third World Liberation Front, which sought the establishment of a "Third World college" and the hiring of more minority faculty, led to twenty-five incidents of arson, three bomb explosions, and 150 arrests. The following month, student demonstrators at Cal-Berkeley armed themselves with their own billy clubs and fought with campus police.[2] Like an epidemic, indeed, student unrest spread to campuses throughout the nation in the first two months of the year—from California to Wisconsin, from Duke and Swarthmore to Rutgers, Brandeis, and the City College of New York. *Time* dubbed the semester the "Spring of Discontent,"[3] while *Newsweek* observed that newspapers had "started carrying front-page summaries of building seizures and general disruptions, much like baseball box scores."[4]

For decades, such institutions of higher learning had stood as symbols of intellectual and cultural havens. But universities were now seen as symbols of the establishment, and as students returned to their campuses for spring semester, radical groups within these institutions looked to take over the reins of power.

❈ ❈ ❈

On January 16, Courtney Smith walked from his home on the campus of Swarthmore College to Parrish Hall, home of the school's admissions office. Wearing the Ivy League tweeds fashionable among northeastern academia, the fifty-two-year-old college president and former Rhodes Scholar at Oxford walked quietly, carrying a heavy burden. For the past week, life at the tiny Quaker college located just outside Philadelphia had been disturbed in a way not seen in its entire 105-year history. Forty members of the Swarthmore

Afro-American Students Society (SASS) had occupied the admissions office in Parrish, demanding that the school increase not just its enrollment of black students but also the presence of blacks in its administration.

There was more than a measure of cruel irony in the crisis that Smith now faced. Swarthmore's president had a reputation for being somewhat of a progressive. While serving at a naval training station at Pensacola, Florida, during World War II, he had fought to get gym and beach facilities for black sailors. As a college administrator, he had earned the reputation of an integrationist, and in his tenure at Swarthmore, black enrollment had increased from practically 0% to 5%.[6]

Yet just before Christmas, black campus activists had sent a mocking holiday greeting to Smith that presented him with a rigid set of demands: the admission of "risk" students and the provision of support for said students, a black assistant dean of admissions, and a black counselor to advance a "black perspective" on campus. As political science department chair J. Roland Pennock later recalled, "He was confronted with non-negotiable demands and rhetoric that did great offense to him. . . . This hurt him bitterly. But he never let himself be moved to anger despite the affront to his standards of civility."[6]

Smith tried to mediate the situation between the activists and college trustees. When the students' demands were not met, they forced their way into the administration's offices on January 9 and took over the building. They would remain encamped in Parrish for the following week, defying the administration.

The events on the Swarthmore campus had taken their toll on Smith. As he climbed a flight of stairs in Parrish Hall on the morning of January 16, Smith's heart gave out, sending him collapsing to the floor. A college physician was summoned but he was unable to find a pulse in Smith's body. The school's president had expired— literally, one could say without much hyperbole, from a broken heart suffered amid the turmoil of early 1969.

News spread quickly around the campus. In an era of contentious relationships between university administrations and student bodies, Smith had been a rarity—a popular college president. Upon hearing of his death, groups of students sat outside Parrish in the winter air, mourning his passing.

Out of respect for Smith, or perhaps simply wishing to avoid drawing the ire of a mourning student body, SASS abandoned the admissions office—but not their demands. They issued a statement that paid tribute to Smith but nevertheless maintained an indictment of white society: "We sincerely believe that the death of any human being, whether he be the good president of a college, or a black person trapped in our country's ghettos, is a tragedy."[7]

The outbreak of black student protest announced a new phase in both civil rights goals and strategy. Now, the protesters sought not only equal rights within the social structure but equal opportunity to shape the social structure. Black student unions throughout the nation looked to act as agents of change within the institutions that trained the nation's future leaders, seeking not only higher admissions of blacks in "white" schools, but more representation among the faculties and administrations of these schools. It was no longer sufficient for blacks to study Eurocentric history while training to work as cogs in the machines of white corporate society; they wanted to rebuild the machinery. As Charles Hamilton, department chair of political science at Roosevelt University, said, black students would no longer allow themselves "to be made into little middle-class black Sambos."[8]

Black student groups staged occupations to take symbolic control of the seats of power on college campuses. At The City College of New York, 200 black and Latino students occupied the administration building, broke into President Buell Gallagher's office, and, in a gesture of class-war defiance, helped themselves to his private stock of liquor. Queens College was closed for two days after students demanded a white administrator be removed from a program for 700 students from low-income areas. Sixty-five black students at Brandeis seized a building that housed the campus computers and telephone switchboard. University of Illinois-Urbana-Champaign students employed different ways of disrupting campus functions, including demonstrating in the driveway of university president David Henry, placing a barrage of phone calls to tie up the campus telephone lines, and booking phantom appointments with officials in order to keep them occupied. At the University of Chicago, sixty students occupied the school's six-story administration building to protest the sociology department's decision not to rehire assistant professor Marlene Dixon, an active member of the radical New University Conference. Across town at Roosevelt University, black students took over classes in literature, political science, and psychology and delivered Afrocentric lectures. In Durham, North Carolina, sixty to seventy members of the Afro-American Society at Duke University seized the ground floor of the administration building to demand a black studies program on par with northern Ivy League programs, and to push for a campus ban on the old nineteenth-century blackface minstrel song, "I Wish I Was in Dixie."[9]

This string of black student activism created growing fear among mainstream white society. Juan Cofield, a leader of the Black Student Movement at the University of North Carolina, presciently predicted, "The outcome [of black activism] will be determined by how the whites react. They'll probably try to repel this, like they've repelled other black demands over the century. If they do, this will become quite a violent situation. Black people are much more united now, and they're not willing to put up with the same old treatment."[10]

Takeovers at the University of Chicago and at the City College of New York ended without fanfare when they were essentially ignored by the administrations. But many university officials, such San Francisco State University president S. I. Hayakawa, only fanned the flames of campus dissent in 1969. Known for his hard-line approach, Hayakawa said,

> [T]he real issue is not violence but the radical-directed assault on academic freedom. . . . What is really happening is that we're witnessing the rise of an arrogant elitist student movement, the overwhelming majority of whom are from wealthy families and attending the fashionable and expensive universities. In fact, we are now beginning to undergo in the United States what has already occurred in the underdeveloped countries, where the university students consider themselves an elite with a mission to improve the lot of the vast majority of poverty-stricken and illiterate peasants, if necessary by rebelling against the system and overthrowing it.[11]

When met with resistance, demonstrations often turned into full-scale riots. At Duke University, the Afro-American Society students who had occupied the ground floor of the administration building eventually left the building peaceably, passing by police as they vacated by way of Campus Drive. It seemed as if trouble had been avoided, but as the police staked out the empty building, approximately 2,000 white students came by to check out what the police were doing. At some point, objects—the police would claim they were rocks; the students would claim they were crumpled-up pieces of paper—were hurled at policemen. A ninety-minute brawl broke out, with police wielding their clubs and spraying tear gas at the students. Twenty-five students were sent to the hospital to be treated for injuries. The Duke student body led a three-day boycott of classes in protest.

On February 7, after 500 black students at the University of Wisconsin-Madison issued demands to school chancellor Edwin Young, who refused to give in, 600 students, most of them white, demonstrated at the Field House during a basketball game against Big Ten rival Ohio State. One hundred police officers were called in, but most of the campus was reportedly "apathetic to the demonstration." Then, just as the protest seemed to be losing momentum, Madison's mayor asked governor Warren Knowles to send in the National Guard. Nine hundred troops arrived that night. This only served to galvanize the students against authority. By the middle of the following day, the demonstration had grown, numbering between 4,000 and 5,000 protesters. Another 1,000 guardsmen were sent in. Student rebels blocked traffic and taunted the National Guard. The guardsmen teargassed the students, battling them on the streets and over the hills of the campus grounds. That night, nearly 10,000 students marched to the state capitol in protest.[12]

To officials on both coasts, the nation's campuses had become a collective battleground. State University of New York (SUNY) Stony Brook president John Toll had a "student protest shelter" built for himself across campus that came equipped with red carpet, Xerox machines, and space for up to four secretaries. Students at SUNY Purchase still hear stories today of how the campus's concrete mall was designed so as to allow for the presence of tanks in case student demonstrations necessitated military intervention.

Out west, S. I. Hayakawa had to be escorted each morning on his way to work by Mill Valley police down Highway 101 to the Golden Gate Bridge, where California Highway Patrolmen took over. California's governor, future president Ronald Reagan, was one of the most outspoken critics of both student demonstrators and of university officials whom, he claimed, coddled the demonstrators. Reagan gave voice to what many in conservative America had started to feel about the outbreak of student violence on campus when he announced, "This is guerrilla warfare."[13]

In the first six months of 1969 alone, there were at least eighty-four bombings, attempted bombings, or acts of arson reported on college campuses. Twenty-seven incidents of bombings and attempted bombings were reported in the nation's high schools.[14]

In February, the Supreme Court issued a ruling in *Tinker v. Des Moines Independent Community School District*, which had originated from the December 1965 suspension of three high school students who had worn black armbands to school in protest of U. S. military action in Vietnam. In a 7–2 decision authored by Justice Abe Fortas, the Warren Court reversed the Eighth Circuit Court decision and found that the students' act of donning black bands was protected as free speech under the First Amendment. The school administration had taken the stance that, since one student from one of the Des Moines public high schools had been killed in Vietnam, the students' symbolic act might incite "something which would be difficult to control" among the friends of that student. However, the Supreme Court found that upholding the rights of the students to wear the armbands did not pose a substantial threat to school discipline.[15] Nonetheless, to teachers from the Old School, the message was clear: They were no longer in charge.

The increasing violence in the cafeterias and hallways of urban high schools seemed to reinforce this message. An assistant principal in Washington, D.C. was shot and killed while attempting to stop three students from robbing the school bank. Just outside New Haven, Connecticut, seven high school students in Hamden were arrested after participating in a race-inspired cafeteria brawl. In San Francisco, a riot squad of police was ultimately called in to disperse students from the grounds of Mission High School after six days of violence between blacks and Latinos.

In New York City schools, tensions between whites, blacks, and Latinos yielded weekly episodes of violence. The *Village Voice* described the situation at Franklin Lane High School, located on the border of the Queens and Brooklyn boroughs: "Every day there is a riot on the subway or a fight in the bathroom or an arrest in the halls or a brawl in the cafeteria or a suspension of more black students. . . . Lane is a time bomb, and everyone—blacks, whites, teachers, Board of Ed—admits it could explode any day. Yet no one has marshaled the power or imagination or trust to head off the disaster."[16]

The most extreme incident took place on January 20 when a rock was thrown through the window of chemistry teacher Frank Siracusa's classroom. Siracusa went to investigate and was confronted by three black students on a stairwell. They punched and kicked him, sprayed him with lighter fluid, and set him on fire. Officials closed the school for several days, and when it reopened, it was with fifty New York City policemen stationed on school grounds. Tensions grew between whites and blacks. A few months later, black students took down an American flag from one classroom and replaced it with a flag from the pan-African movement. When school officials took it down, hundreds of black students ran through the halls in protest.

In March, two hundred black students in Brooklyn's Eastern District High School wreaked havoc throughout the school, breaking furniture and shattering glass partitions in hallways and classrooms. Days later, they set fires throughout the school and forced it to close down. Riots also occurred at Morris High School in the Bronx; Samuel Tilden, Bushwick, and Erasmus Hall high schools in Brooklyn; and in George Washington High School in Manhattan, where blacks battled not only with whites but also with the school's Dominican population.[17] In a report to mayor John Lindsay, the High School Principals Association of New York City concluded: "Disorder and fears of new and frightening dimensions stalk the corridors of many of our schools."[18]

❊ ❊ ❊

In the winter of 1969, the Curtis Publishing Company announced that the February 8 issue of the *Saturday Evening Post* would be its last. Since the turn of the century, the *Post* had been an institution of front-porch America, editorially preaching conservative American values while entertaining small-town, middle-class America with interviews of Hollywood stars and the fiction of such twentieth-century masters as Jack London, Joseph Conrad, Thomas Wolfe, Scott Fitzgerald, and William Faulkner. In its eulogy of the weekly magazine, *Newsweek* reminisced that "a generation of boys delivered it door to door through the leafy streets of small-town [and] rural America," and noted that its oversized format had even helped determine the size of mailboxes. The magazine had perhaps been best known for it cover artists, which included N. C. Wyeth, John Falter, and, most famously, Norman Rockwell, who provided covers for the *Post* on a semi-regular basis for more than four decades. "Rockwell's paintings were supposed to mirror the America that read the *Post*," *Newsweek* commented. "But more and more the reality wasn't there anymore—if it ever was."[19] As Rockwell himself said in the spring of 1969, "I used to reflect the country's mood in my work, but now the questions are so bitter—and nothing is clear cut."[20]

By the end of the 1960s, the nation had grown increasingly fractured, and the fabric of American society had begun pulling at the seams. Over winter break in January, 800 delegates for Students for a Democratic Society (SDS) had met at its national convention at the University of Michigan in Ann Arbor, and, by a margin of only twelve votes, passed a resolution for a Revolutionary Youth Movement (RYM) designed to step up its radicalism and take its revolutionary initiative into the nation's high schools. Bernardine Dohrn, an SDS officer and a leader of the RYM faction, argued that American high schools were ". . . baby-sitting jails. They are used to trap people into the Army, into stupid colleges to train for jobs they don't want. They are oppressive."[21]

The twenty-seven-year-old Dohrn, a former high school cheerleader who had graduated with a law degree from the University of Chicago, was representative of the growing Revolutionary Youth Movement faction—well-educated, clean-cut, hailing from white, middle-class, or upper-middle-class neighborhoods, committed to social revolution. Whereas the SDS of past years had forged social change through tactics of civil disobedience and nonviolent protests, the more radical members argued that such methods had yielded—what? Assassinations, an escalating war, imperialist aggression, a "law and order" president. "There's no way to be committed to nonviolence in the middle of the most violent society that history's ever created," declared Dohrn, a thin, white, attractive brunette who served as an outspoken member of the organization. "I'm not committed to nonviolence in any way."[22]

Princeton undergraduate Clarence "Chip" Sills was another poster boy for the New Left. Sills had come to Princeton from Ascension Academy, a Catholic prep school in affluent Alexandria, Virginia, as the epitome of the All-American student (student council president, captain of the wrestling team, editor of the school paper), and had been accepted into Princeton ROTC. Four years later in 1969, the twenty-two-year-old senior philosophy major had dropped out of ROTC, exchanging his short hair and preppie clothing for long hair and a leather jacket. In 1967 Sills had headed west to Haight-Ashbury to experience the Summer of Love. "You know the first thing I saw after riding that hot motorcycle for 36 hours?" he mused. "Five kids beating up an old man and taking his wallet. That's what our society does to people." Disillusioned with the "hippie" scene as well as the machines of conventional society, he joined the Princeton chapter of the SDS, and, as the chapter's "internal education secretary," had helped lead a campus-wide protest to get Princeton to divest itself of businesses with investments in South Africa. Sills then participated in the RYM initiative by going to high schools with the aim of "radicalizing" future college students.[23]

The SDS national convention in Ann Arbor magnified the rift between the RYM (pronounced *rim*) and the Progressive Labor (PL) faction, which, according to Kirkpatrick Sale, saw the RYM as a ploy to "undercut their influence in SDS and take away their exclusive identification with working-class politics." The PL favored the building of political power within the working class through its Worker Student Alliance caucus, while the RYM sought to enlist students to fight against U. S. imperialism worldwide. PLers, explains Sale, thought the RYM "placed too much emphasis on youth and the 'phony' youth culture, and suggested that youths themselves would make the revolution; it ignited more of the old resistance politics of street violence, leading to dangerous 'wild-in-the-streets' attitudes."[24]

Newsweek recounted the scene at Ann Arbor, saying, "The meeting had all the trappings and rhetoric of the New Left. Young radicals filled hour after hour arguing about a 'workers' revolution' and 'class consciousness.' Slouched in dungarees, fatigue jackets, sweatshirts and boots, they understandably hissed disapproval of The Beatles' antirevolutionary 'Revolution' blaring from a big jukebox in the corner of the dormitory snack bar." The more radical convention participants filled the meeting hall with chants of "Ho Ho Ho Chi Minh" and "Two-Four-Six-Eight, Organize and Smash the State."

"The movement is coming to a turning point," said Dennis Sinclair, the former campaign manager for Eldridge Cleaver of the Black Panthers. "SDS is either going to become a mass-based political organization or a sort of revolutionary cadre, who feel they're the vanguard of the future and are not concerned with building a movement." National secretary Mike Klonsky added, "I see a lot of people in this movement hardening their positions."[25]

And so it was in the United States in 1969. Positions hardened, forces for change radicalized, reactionary forces dug in their heels, and the cultural divide grew ever wider.

3. THE NEW SOUNDS

Debut albums from the MC5, Iggy and the Stooges, and Neil Young and Crazy Horse, as well as Led Zeppelin's first U. S. tour, signal new directions in the American music scene.

Elvis Presley had spent a good deal of time in the Sixties acting (sort of) in a string of cheesy movies, and he had scored just one Top Ten hit in the past five years. Presley had become a relic of rock 'n' roll past, a pop icon whose fan base was now comprised more of youngish housewives than of young girls. December 1968 had seen NBC's broadcast of Presley's much-celebrated comeback special. Simply titled *Elvis*, the program had featured Presley, dressed in a black leather suit, performing a concert-in-the-round for a small but highly receptive crowd. The '68 television special had reintroduced him to the country at large and had helped to reestablish his relevancy in popular culture. Following the special, manager "Colonel" Tom Parker wanted to get his legendary client back in the studio right away to record his next record.

Memphis was fast replacing Nashville as the center of the recording universe, and Chips Moman's American Sound Studios had produced more than a hundred hit singles with leading pop, R&B, and soul artists. Dusty Springfield had headed there to record tracks for her classic record, *Dusty in Memphis*. (Ironically, Springfield had redubbed her vocals in New York.) Released in January 1969, the album had the white, London-born singer seemingly channeling

Aretha Franklin on lush hits like "Son of a Preacher Man" and "I Don't Want to Hear It Anymore." Across town at Ardent Studios, Isaac Hayes and his backing band the Bar-Kays cut the seminal 1969 album *Hot Buttered Soul*. The album's four epic grooves—the twelve-minute rendition of "Walk on By," the nine-and-a-half-minute "Hyperbolicsyllabicsesquedalymistic," "One Woman," and a nearly nineteen-minute jaunt through "By the Time I Get to Phoenix"—showed the R&B genre moving away from the Motown sound and toward sly and sexy seventies funk.

With a legion of first-class session musicians assembled, Team Presley entered Moman's studio on January 13. "He was in his prime," pianist Bobby Wood remembered.[1] That evening, Elvis and the band ran through its first song, "Long Black Limousine," the melodramatic tale of a girl who leaves the country behind and heads for the big city, only to return in a hearse. Producer and author Ernst Jorgensen recalls that "when Elvis selected it as his first number at the session, he brought to it a sense of loss and desolation, a kind of anger that seemed driven by an almost personal identification with the subject of the song. . . . the passion in his voice has few counterparts in his recorded work."[2]

The performance set the tone for one of the most prolific sessions of Presley's career, perhaps the most prolific since his original sessions with Sam Phillips at Sun Records over on Union Avenue in 1953. Over the next ten days, Presley and the band laid down tracks for such songs as "In the Ghetto," "Don't Cry Daddy," "Rubberneckin'," and in the early-morning hours of January 23, a song that was previously recorded by its author, Mark James, called "Suspicious Minds."

"We've done some hits, haven't we, Chips?" a pleased Elvis said to the studio head at the end of the session.

"Maybe some of your biggest," Moman told him.[3]

Presley returned in mid-February for another six days of recording, this time laying down such tracks as "Kentucky Rain," "Only the Strong Survive," and "Any Day Now." The King of Rock 'n' Roll had never sounded as good, or as sincere—not even when his nick-name had really meant something. The American sessions would produce three Top Ten singles for Presley in 1969: "In the Ghetto," "Don't Cry Daddy," and his first number-one record in more than seven years, "Suspicious Minds." "Kentucky Rain" would chart in 1970, completing a renaissance for Presley.

While Presley was logging his second session at American, Bob Dylan was immersing himself in the traditional Nashville sound at the Columbia Music Row Studios over six days that February. Having grown tired of being labeled as the voice of his generation, Dylan was looking to record material that would lead not to reintroduction but to reinvention. "I had been anointed as the Big Bubba of Rebellion, High Priest of Protest, the Czar of Dissent, the Duke of Disobedience, Leader of the Freeloaders, Kaiser of Apostasy, Archbishop of Anarchy, the Big Cheese," he writes in *Chronicles, Volume One*. "Horrible titles any way you want to look at it. All code words for *Outlaw*."[4]

The sessions for *Nashville Skyline* were steeped in country music culture, with session work of guitarist Charlie Daniels, Peter Drake's steel guitar, and guest appearances by Carl Perkins and Johnny Cash. Dylan sang with a low and relaxed, plaintive and almost mournful voice, a style that would shock listeners—a "previously unheard gentle croon" that was "disarming upon first listen," Stephen Thomas Erlewine describes.[5] Along with *The Gilded Palace of Sin*, the first The Flying Burrito Brothers (released in February 1969), *Nashville Skyline* would help establish the genre of country rock. The album reached the Top Five, and "Lay, Lady, Lay," a song originally intended for John Schlesinger's *Midnight Cowboy* but completed too late for use in the film, would reach number one on the Billboard Hot 100.

The year in music, however, would be remembered neither for Presley's swan song nor Dylan's Nashville dirge. It was the end of the decade, the nation was changing, and the politics of dissent had come to Middle America. The revolution needed a soundtrack, and the popular music of 1969 captured the sense of imminent upheaval in American culture. On one of the top-selling albums at the beginning of 1969, the Rolling Stones spoke of "the sound of marching, charging feet" and the time being right for a "palace revolution." Jefferson Airplane would sing of the "volunteers of America" and chant "Got a revolution!" Even the pop group The Lovin' Spoonful, now without singer John Sebastian, released an album called *Revelation: Revolution '69*, with the lyrics, "I'm afraid to die but I'm a man inside and I need the revolution." As the one-hit wonder group Thunderclap Newman sang on "Something in the Air," "the revolution's here, and you know it's right."

In a year of revolutionary music, the MC5 were the most self-consciously radical. Originally formed in Detroit (the "MC" stood for Motor City) and managed by White Panther Party leader John Sinclair, the group had moved to Ann Arbor shortly after the King assassination. There, they formed an urban commune with ten other residents in an eighteen-room house on Fraternity Row. On the cover of *Rolling Stone*'s first issue of 1969, MC5 lead singer Rob Tyner was shown in a billowy satin shirt and all his white-man's-Afro glory. At the time of the story, a decision was pending on an appeal to a recent possession charge against Sinclair, who'd been arrested after giving a joint to a narc. Eric Ehrmann, the scribe of the piece, wrote:

> John Sinclair was one of those cats who brought the forces together, and if he is sent to jail, Detroit will burn once again. There are more politicized hippies in Detroit and its surrounding areas who have helmets, gas masks, teargas and homemade Mace along with other ordnance paraphernalia than any other city currently in insurrection. While the guerrillas wait in hiding, their band the MC-5 helps them get money by playing political benefit concerts.[6]

The group offered a raucous mix of sex and revolution that made for great headlines. Even before their debut album, *Kick Out the Jams*, was released in January 1969, "they had been the most publicized group in the history of American rock," said Elektra Records publicist Danny Fields.[7] The same week as the *Rolling Stone* cover story, a *Time* review of the band's concert at New York's Fillmore East celebrated the MC5's brand of sonic anarchy, from the carnally charged "I Want You Right Now," in which Tyner "writhed on the floor in sexual postures," to the cover of bluesman John Lee Hooker's "Motor City Is Burning," with Tyner yelling, "All the cities will burn . . . You are the people who will build up the ashes."[8]

MC5 was just as much a political statement of revolution and anarchy as it was a group of performers—or at least that was its shtick. "I guess you could say our thing is a condemnation of everything that is false and deceitful in our society," John Sinclair boasted. In the classic *Please Kill Me: The Uncensored Oral History of Punk*, Legs McNeil and Gillian McCain describe the 5's politics as, "a midwesternized version of anarchy. Tear down the walls, get the government out of our lives, smoke lots of dope, have lots of sex and make lots of noise."[9] In his book on *Kick Out the Jams*, Don McLeese says, "The MC5 weren't just a band; they were a movement, the musical vanguard of the militant White Panther Party. In order to embrace this music, you apparently had to commit to the destruction of Western civilization as we knew it." In the album's liner notes, Sinclair declared, "The MC5 is totally committed to revolution, as the revolution is totally committed to driving people out of their separate shells and into each other's arms."[10]

Kick Out the Jams, recorded live at Detroit's Grande Ballroom, touches off with an introduction by band associate Brother J. C. Crawford, who incites the crowd: "I wanna hear some revolution . . . Brothers and sisters, the time has come for each and every one of you to decide whether you are going to be the problem or you are going to be the solution!" Just before the band breaks into the title track—a blitz of dueling guitar-fuzz from Wayne Kramer and Fred "Sonic" Smith and proto-punk rage—Tyner yells, "And right now . . . right now . . . right now . . . it's time to . . . *kick out the jams, motherfuckers!*"

Tyner's invocation was taken as a "shout-out" by the street activist group that went by the name Up Against the Wall Motherfuckers. They followed the band to dates in Boston and New York City and caused riots with crowds and promoters by insisting that music of the revolution should be free. Through guilt by association, the MC5 were effectively banned from concert halls on both coasts by promoters Bill Graham and Don Law. In April, the magazine that had helped feed the MC5 hype machine just three months earlier panned the album. In his first published review, a young Lester Bangs wrote in *Rolling Stone* that *Kick Out the Jams* sounded like "a bunch of 16 year olds on a meth power trip [and] a ridiculous, overbearing, pretentious album."

Soon thereafter, Bangs would do a 180 after seeing the band perform in Detroit, saying, "now I completely and finally understand why so many people lose their cool and objectivity over this band. . . . THERE IS NO BETTER BAND ANYWHERE!" But two weeks after Bangs's initial review, Elektra had dropped MC5 from its label. By then, the band's reputation had boomeranged against the MC5 in some corners. Hudson's, the leading department store in downtown Detroit, refused to stock the album. In response, the band took out a full-page ad in the *Argus*, an Ann Arbor underground newspaper, which declared, "KICK OUT THE JAMS, MOTHERFUCKER! And kick in the door if the store won't sell you the album on Elektra. FUCK HUDSON'S."[11]

❄ ❄ ❄

After Elektra had sent Fields to scout MC5 in 1968, he ended up signing the group's opening act, as well. Also hailing from the Ann Arbor music scene, Iggy and the Psychedelic Stooges were known primarily for the antics of their wild frontman, one James Newell Osterberg, who took the stage name of Iggy Pop. Pop's early performing style was a unique mix of hippie affectations and the confrontational style of the Theater of Cruelty—he would smear food across his chest, cut himself with glass, and flash his penis at the crowd. The band played a handful of fierce street anthems, though they frequently stretched their songs into extended avant-garde pieces through solos and improvisation, sometimes even using household appliances such as a blender or vacuum cleaner to create walls of feedback.

Elektra Records president Jac Holzman pondered this new challenge. Not only did he have to find a way to capture the energy of The Stooges (who dropped the "Psychedelic" part of their name) on vinyl, but as he remembered later, the band "could barely play their instruments." Added to that, when the band showed up for its sessions at the Hit Factory in New York, they arrived armed with just the five songs they were using as performance pieces: "1969," "I Wanna Be Your Dog," "We Will Fall," "Ann," and "No Fun."[12]

"You guys got more material to do an album, right?" Holzman asked guitarist Ron Asheton. Asheton assured Holzman they did; then he and Pop dashed back to their room at the Chelsea Hotel. Asheton came up with some riffs, Pop wrote some quick lyrics, and in a couple of hours they had three more songs for the sessions: "Real Cool Time," "Not Right," and "Little Doll."[13]

Holzman paired The Stooges with producer John Cale, formerly a member of the Velvet Underground, and the band clashed with their new studio mate. Asheton remembered, "We were used to playing on 10, and he's saying, 'No, that's not the way it's done!'"[14] The guitarist told punk historian Legs McNeil:

> We couldn't play unless it was high volume. We didn't have enough expertise on our instruments; it was all power chords. We had opened up for Blue Cheer at the Grande, and they had like triple Marshall stacks, and they were so loud it was painful, but we loved it. . . . That was the only way we knew how to play. So Cale kept trying to tell us what to do, and being the stubborn youth that we were, we had a

sit-down strike. We put our instruments down, went in one of the sound booths, and started smoking hash.[15]

Band and producer worked out their differences. The record, simply titled *The Stooges*, arrived with much less fanfare than did MC5's *Kick Out the Jams*, but its effect on the American rock scene would be more lasting. *AllMusic Guide*'s Mark Deming writes that, "While the Stooges had a few obvious points of influence—the swagger of the early Rolling Stones, the horny pound of the Troggs, the fuzz-tone sneer of a thousand teenage garage bands, and the Velvet Underground's experimental eagerness to leap into the void—they didn't really sound like anyone else around when their first album hit the streets in 1969."[16]

The album's leadoff track, "1969," sets a tone for a new sound and a new time. Asheton starts out with a few bars of psychedelic wah-wah pedal, but, as if to drive home the fact that the days of Flower Power are long gone, the band steps right into a street-pounding rhythm that's as fierce as it is simple. "It's another year for me and you / Another year with nothing to do," Pop sings, summing up the attitude of disaffected youth without hot fun in the summertime to look forward to.

"*The Stooges* didn't so much connect with the music that came before it, rather, it dragged rock 'n' roll down to the car wash and scrubbed it up one side and down the other," writes Detroit music critic Brian Smith,[17] From the angst anthem "No Fun" to the sado-masochistic fantasy of "I Wanna Be Your Dog" to "Real Cool Time"—a musical come-on that comes across as something between a promise and a threat in the hands of Pop, who infuses the lyrics with sexual aggression ("What do you think I wanna do? / That's right")—the debut Stooges disc helped set the mold for the punk movement that would follow. Although the album barely broke the

U. S. charts, with it and subsequent albums *Fun House* and *Raw Power*, the band wrote the blueprint for future generations of punk rock. Music writer Greg Prato argues that "every single punk band of the past and present has either knowingly or unknowingly borrowed a thing or two" from Iggy Pop and The Stooges.[18]

What The Stooges were to the formation of punk, Neil Young and Crazy Horse and their *Everybody Knows This Is Nowhere* album were to cowpunk, grunge, and everything in between. A Canadian singer-songwriter who had come to California and formed the short-lived psychedelic folk-rock group Buffalo Springfield, Young found a new sound—one of many in his notoriously eclectic career—when he hooked up with a six-piece country-rock outfit from Los Angeles going by the name of The Rockets.

"No one remembers exactly how Neil Young stumbled upon the Rockets," says biographer Jimmy McDonough. But when they got together, The Rockets laid down a perfect backdrop against which Young could bring out a new, big, loud guitar sound courtesy of "Old Black," a 1953 Gibson Les Paul guitar fed through a 1959 Fender Deluxe amp, which he first used on *Everybody Knows*. He sat in with The Rockets for a gig at the Whisky a Go Go, and he later invited the core rhythm section of the group—guitarist Danny Whitten, bass guitarist Billy Talbot, and drummer Ralph Molina—to a jam session in Topanga. Soon afterward he booked studio time in Hollywood for himself and his three new musical soul mates, who would take the name Crazy Horse. "Everybody thought San Francisco music was druggy," said aficionado Charlie Beesley. "Crazy Horse was *really* druggy—bleary, laid-back, stoned. Nobody played that slow."[19]

The resulting album was recorded over two sessions in early 1969, one in January and a second in March. The first session in January yielded the album's standout tracks: "Cinnamon Girl," which opened with nearly two minutes of Young's distorted Old Black fuzz before the first words are sung; the country-tinged title track; and two deliberately paced guitar epics, the nine-minute "Down by the River" and ten-minute "Cowgirl in the Sand." Atop the Crazy Horse druggy backbeat, Young's tortured guitar riffs made no pretense of technical virtuosity but simply burn both figuratively and literally; legend has it that he wrote the two songs while delirious with fever. One reviewer would write: "He draws out notes with a sound that might remind one of a man taking his own blood with a knife."[20] In these early, epic songs, the one-time folk singer summoned a sound that captured the ominous static energy of the calm before an approaching electrical storm. Looking back on the *Everybody Knows* sessions, producer David Briggs said, "These guys didn't act like they were in the studio, they acted like it was the end of the world."[21]

On January 30, 1969, The Beatles climbed onto the roof of the Apple building in London and played into the air overlooking Burlington Gardens. It was to be their last public performance as a group. After releasing the beautifully erratic White Album, the onetime Fab Four had struggled to gel as a band during their ill-fated sessions that month for the planned *Get Back* album. A group of songs from the sessions would be collected in *Let It Be*, which appeared in 1970 as the last album of new material released by the group. But their true swan song would come in the masterwork of *Abbey Road*, released in the U. S. in the fall of 1969. The album contained versions of songs that The Beatles had attempted in the *Get Back* sessions, along with studio takes from their last sessions together as a group. *Abbey Road* produced such lasting classics as "Here Comes the Sun," "Oh! Darling," and the number-one single, "Come Together," which John Lennon wrote for Timothy Leary's unsuccessful gubernatorial campaign in California that year. The record became a double-sided hit when the flip side, George Harrison's "Something," reached number three.

While *The Beatles* (the "White Album") and *Beggars Banquet* sat at the top of the American album charts that winter, the top-selling classical recording music was Walter Carlos's *Switched-On Bach*, an album comprised of selections from Johann Sebastian Bach that Carlos, a twenty-nine-year-old composer and musician from Rhode Island, played entirely on Moog synthesizer—the first album of that distinction. Not only was the juxtaposition of classical material with modern music technology unique enough to propel the album to become the first classical work to sell a half-million copies, but it also went a long way toward popularizing an instrument that would become integral to popular music in the ensuing decades.

Many audiophiles condemned the work, dismissing it as a novelty that trivialized "serious" music. It drew raves from others, such as famed Canadian pianist Glenn Gould, who called it "the record of the year . . . no, the decade."[22] *Switched-On Bach* was so enormously influential in the field of electronic music that it spawned multiple knockoffs. Carlos himself released a successful follow-up later in the year, *The Well-Tempered Synthesizer*, with Moog performances of works by Bach, Monteverdi, Handel, and Domenico Scarlatti. Soon, the Moog company was inundated with orders, and the synthesizer would become a staple of modern pop and rock music.

Carlos's venture into electronic music was an apt representation of how the musical landscape was about to change. Miles Davis flirted with fusion and electronic music on his 1969 releases *Filles de Kilimanjaro* and *In a Silent Way*. The day after Jimi Hendrix's legendary performance at Woodstock, Davis, who himself had been influenced by Hendrix's innovative guitar work, was recording tracks for the album that jazz aficionados would point to as the musical equivalent of *Ulysses* and *Guernica*.

With a legion of musicians who would go on to fame of their own, including Chick Corea and Herbie Hancock, and future members of Weather Report and the Mahavishnu Orchestra, Davis laid down tracks in the now-legendary three-day session that would provide the majority of material for the *Bitches Brew* double album: "Pharaoh's Dance" and "Bitches Brew" (at twenty and twenty-seven minutes, respectively), "Spanish Key," "John McLaughlin," "Miles Runs the Voodoo Down," and "Sanctuary."

Twenty years after Davis had ushered bebop into the realm of cool jazz with *Birth of the Cool*, *Bitches Brew* arose like a postmodern *Rite of Spring*, revolutionizing jazz once again for future generations of emulators. Having already pioneered modal jazz, Davis established loose guidelines for the other musicians in the session, giving them the tempo, modal framework, and brief descriptions on the overall mood of the song. Within this structure, improvisation formed the bridge from one section to the next. Melodies were only hinted at, emerging in abstract phrases, while rhythm *became* the melody.

"It's hard to overstate the importance of *Bitches Brew*," writes critic Paul Tingen. "It is one of the seminal albums that shaped Western music culture in the second half of the 20th century, dividing it into a 'time before' and a 'time after.'"[23]

The improvisation, syncopation, and rhythmic grooves of jazz and jazz fusion drifted into the rock scene, spawning what would one day be labeled the "jam band" movement. At the center of the movement was the Grateful Dead, who in 1969 released the acoustic/psychedelic opus *Aoxomoxoa* (with the classic "St. Stephen") and also their first live album, *Live/Dead*, which captured its classic performance of "The Eleven," a song in 11/8 signature time. Meanwhile, the Allman Brothers Band, who formed in Jacksonville, Florida, in March 1969, would take jamming into the arena of hard rock. The band's signature sound derived from Greg Allman's down-home vocals and organ melodies, along with the dueling guitars of brother Duane Allman and Dickey Betts—often sustained over ten- or twenty-minute solos in concert. Their self-titled debut album, released in November, sold modestly but featured future concert highlights in "Dreams" and the angry blues-rock epic "Whipping Post" (which also begins in 11-beat time). With its lyrical solos and harmonics, the band's swampy, jam-heavy brand of blues rock set the mold for the Southern rock genre that would take off in the seventies.

❊ ❊ ❊

Much as the British invasion of the early 1960s had revolutionized American pop music, groups from the far side of the Atlantic once again transformed the music scene in 1969. The Beatles' *Abbey Road* pointed the way to the progressive rock movement with the fugue-inspired climax of "I Want You (She's So Heavy)," the Beethoven chord progression played backward on "Because," along with the suite of song fragments that conclude the B-side, culminating in "The End." But *In the Court of the Crimson King*, the debut from King Crimson, was perhaps the most influential recording among the progressive rock or "art rock" genre. With the name of both band and album alluding to Lucifer in his realm in Hell, the record's innovative mix of hard rock, jazz improvisation, symphonic music, and lofty lyrical concepts, not to mention song lengths ranging from six to twelve minutes, helped established a blueprint for Album Oriented Radio. The self-titled 1969 debut from Yes as well as Jethro Tull's second album, *Stand Up*, further propelled the movement away from psychedelia and toward classically inspired virtuosity in the realm of hard rock.

But the biggest thing to come over from Britain in 1969 was not the heavily packaged orchestrations of progressive rock. Instead, it was the electric explosiveness of heavy metal as first witnessed on the January release from the late-sixties version of a Fab Four, Led Zeppelin.

Heavy metal had existed, at least in name, since the 1968 hit "Born to Be Wild," on which Steppenwolf sang of "heavy metal thunder," and certainly acid-rock power trios like Cream and the Jimi Hendrix Experience paved the way for the electrified blues of heavy metal. But it was Led Zeppelin who took things to the next level, adding not just volume but a sexualized *sturm und drang* that spoke to music fans at the end of the decade, post–Flower Power. Even the cover of the group debut album *Led Zeppelin*—a rendering of the fiery *Hindenburg* crash over Ocean County, New Jersey, in May 1937—announced the onset and *onslaught* of something big and new. As *Rolling Stone*'s Greg Kot wrote, "The image did a pretty good job of encapsulating the music inside: sex, catastrophe and things blowing up. . . . Jimmy Page's guitar pounces from the speakers, fat with menace; John Bonham's kick drum swings with anvil force; Robert Plant rambles on about the perils of manhood. Hard rock would never be the same."[24]

The band's eight-song debut drew heavily on the classic blues: "You Shook Me," "I Can't Quit You Baby," and "How Many More Times" borrowed from original songs by such bluesmen as Willie Dixon, J. B. Lenoir, and Albert King. Even Plant's echoing of Page's guitar riffs with his sexualized wails updated the call-and-response from early American roots music. Other songs ranged from the steel-string, Eastern raga acoustics of "Black Mountain Side" to the amped-up traditional folk song "Babe I'm Gonna Leave You," to the raucous and relentless "Communication Breakdown," driven by a rapid-fire downstring riff that punk legend Johnny Ramone would later credit as inspiring his own technique. And then there was the album-concluding "Dazed and Confused," an ominous and blistering acid-rock attack featuring Page's virtuoso guitar solos and demonic atmospherics created by his taking a cello bow to his guitar, played atop John Paul Jones's creeping bass line.

When Led Zeppelin played its first set on North American soil at the Denver Auditorium Arena on December 26, 1968, it did so as an unbilled opening act for the psychedelic band Vanilla Fudge. Critics were slow in accepting Led Zeppelin's brand of pop music—many took issue with Zeppelin's uncredited "borrowing" of the blues, and others objected to the in-your-face baseness of the sound—but young fans responded to this new, harder, bluesier foursome. Led Zeppelin was something American audiences had never seen: Page, the gangly and brooding virtuoso; Plant, all beanpole and blond locks, shrieking the white man's blues infused with Flower Power sexuality; Jones on bass, the quiet Zep; and Bonham, playing like an angry Keith Moon equipped with the hammer of Thor. Led Zeppelin played a total of one hundred dates in North America during three stretches in 1969, and by the end of the year had established itself as a headline act in its own right.

In between tour dates, the group logged time at studios in Los Angeles, New York, and London to record their sophomore record. Jimmy Page acted as producer once again, but this time Led Zeppelin worked with veteran sound engineer Eddie Kramer, who had done all three albums with the Jimi Hendrix Experience. Because of the tour's blitzkrieg schedule, Led Zeppelin could only enter the studio for short periods of time, so they focused primarily on reworking some of the classic blues, soul, and rock 'n' roll songs that they were playing onstage at the time.

Led Zeppelin II, released in October 1969, showed the band focusing its heavy metal guitar attack. Page used overdubbing to create a layered guitar attack and cleverly miked John Bonham's drums for maximum percussive effect. Meanwhile, Robert Plant emerged as a lyricist with a mix of blues sex euphemisms ("Squeeze my lemon 'til the juice runs down my leg"), overstated romance, and Tolkienesque fantasies that proved especially conducive to pubescent testosterone. While the band still "borrowed" lyrics liberally from blues legends—Willie Dixon on "Whole Lotta Love," Howlin' Wolf on "The Lemon Song," and Sonny Boy Williamson on "Bring It On Home"—Page was moving away from verse-chorus structures toward songs based around extended guitar solos. The virtuosity shown on songs like "Heartbreaker" set the mold for generations of aspiring guitarists. Similarly, "Moby Dick" provided a spotlight for Bonham, and in its live incarnations (which got ever longer as the band's concerts became bigger and bigger spectacles) brought the rock drum solo out of free-jazz jams and into the realm of muscular, showstopping exhibitionism.

The album also yielded Led Zeppelin's first (and ultimately biggest) hit single. "Whole Lotta Love" opens the album with an echoing riff and then moves into a reworking of Muddy Waters's "You Need Love." With its ninety-second interlude marked by Page's theremin solo and Plant's orgasmic cries, the thunder-and-lightning attack of Bonham and Page, and Plant's nods to Willie Dixon's "Shake for Me" and "Back Door Man," the song was unlike anything that had ever played on AM radio. "Whole Lotta Love" climbed all the way into the Top Five, a surprising feat for an album-oriented rock band. Off the strength of the hit single and the band's relentless touring in 1969, *Led Zeppelin II* became the top-selling album in America, the first of six number-one albums for the group within the span of a decade.

In the words of music writer Stephen Thomas Erlewine:

> Led Zeppelin was the definitive heavy metal band. It wasn't just their crushingly loud interpretation of the blues— it was how they incorporated mythology, mysticism, and a variety of other genres . . . More than any other band, Led Zeppelin established the concept of album-oriented rock, refusing to release popular songs from their albums as singles. In doing so, they established the dominant format for heavy metal, as well as the genre's actual sound.[25]

Ads trumpeted led zeppelin—the only way to fly, and young kids across the country hopped on board that year. So did a whole slew of hard rock and heavy metal bands that followed in their footsteps, creating a subculture for fans who liked their music louder, faster, bigger, heavier, *more*.

4. Super Jets

Joe Namath's guaranteed Super Bowl victory helps the AFL-NFL merger take off.

In 1969, the modern era of air travel was ushered in with the unveiling of the Boeing 747 airplane. Dubbed the world's first "jumbo jet," the 747 was the first wide-body commercial aircraft. Two and a half times the size of Boeing's 707 craft, with a fuselage 225 feet long and a tail six stories high, the new 747 could cruise at 625 miles per hour while transporting more than 400 passengers and 3,400 baggage items. Its trademark "hump" on top of the fuselage created more lounge and seating area.

The 1960s had seen a boom in air travel, and while rivals Lockheed and McDonnell Douglas focused on wide-body, three-engine "tri-jets," Boeing focused its energies on developing a giant passenger plane for client Pan Am, which ordered twenty-three passenger planes and two freight planes in 1966. Initially, Boeing did not even have a factory large enough to assemble the new model, so it built a massive assembly plant near Everett, Washington, that was big enough to house forty-three football fields. With the company mortgaging its future on the new plane, workers soon dubbed "The Incredibles" worked around the clock so that the planes could be delivered to Pan Am by the 1970 deadline.

The maiden test flight of the 747 occurred on February 9, 1969, and in November, the plane was unveiled to American and European press eager to see the future. While it was initially thought that the 747 would eventually be rendered obsolete by the new supersonic jets (such as the Anglo-French *Concorde*, which made its first voyage on March 2), the 747 would prove much more fuel-efficient, setting the standard for air travel into the 1970s and well beyond.[1]

Humankind was reaching for the sky and beyond as never before. On January 10, *Apollo 8* astronauts Frank Borman, James Lovell, and William Anders were celebrated as conquering heroes with a ticker-tape parade in New York City. Two days after the parade in the Big Apple, the astronauts were honored guests at a certain pro football game played at the Orange Bowl in Miami, in which the man dubbed "Broadway Joe" would lead his team to victory and give New Yorkers reason to cheer again.

The New York Titans began playing in 1960 as part of the upstart American Football League, a competitor to the established National Football League. After three years, the team took on new owners and a new name—the Jets, a testament to the modern era of travel and technology. The new name was fitting in a league that had established a reputation for playing a higher-scoring and more freewheeling brand of football that featured more passing than did its conservative counterpart.

But the idea of a championship game had not yet been wholeheartedly embraced by the football community. The first AFL-NFL World Championship in 1967 had not sold out, and NBC later recorded over its broadcast tapes of the game, erasing the footage forever. Prevailing wisdom held that the caliber of AFL play was still far inferior to that of the NFL, and that the NFL Championship Game was actually the true "world championship." In the first two AFL-NFL games, Vince Lombardi's Green Bay Packers had defeated the 1967 AFL Champion Kansas City Chiefs and the 1968 AFL Champion Oakland Raiders by a combined margin of forty-four points.

The 1969 AFL-NFL title game pitted the NFL's Baltimore Colts against the AFL's New York Jets, and there was little evidence to make anyone think that the Jets had much of a chance to reverse this early NFL dominance. The vaunted Colts team had steam-rolled through its regular season by going 13-1. After future Hall of Fame quarterback Johnny Unitas had gone down due to a preseason injury, all backup Earl Morrall did was step in to win the NFL Player of the Year award by throwing twenty-six touchdowns and record-ing a league-best passer rating of 93.2. On defense, meanwhile, the Colts had tallied five shutouts in 1968, including one in the NFL Championship game, when the Colts traveled to Cleveland and avenged their only loss of the year by drubbing the Browns, 34–0. Many commentators thought the 1968 Colts were the best team of all time.

The Jets had traveled a much less glorious path to the interleague showdown in Miami. They'd lost two of their first five games, famously squandered a late lead in the notorious "Heidi" game in November, and narrowly defeated Oakland (27–23) in the AFL Championship Game at Shea Stadium. And even though the team's popular and brash young quarterback, Joe Namath, won the league's MVP that year, in truth, he'd had an uneven season. In a loss to the Buffalo Bills, the AFL's worst team, he threw seven touchdowns— four to his own team, and three on interception returns to Bills defenders. Namath, in fact, had finished the regular season with more interceptions (seventeen) than touchdowns (fifteen) while completing just 49% of his attempts. But the charismatic star had gone on to lead his team on a valiant, game-winning drive in the championship game to send his team to Miami for the game that would be known as Super Bowl III.

To most observers, the Colts were odds-on favorites not just to win but to dominate the Jets. Added to the apparent disparity in tal-ent was the fact that two Jets starters, offensive lineman Winston Hill and safety Johnny Sample, had come to the Jets after being cut by the Colts. Hill, who said he had been dropped by the Colts because of how poorly he practiced against defensive end Ordell Braase, would be responsible for blocking Braase in the Orange Bowl on January 12.

Inside the Jets camp, however, players and coaches actually had to combat feelings of *overconfidence*. As the team watched film of the Baltimore Colts from the 1968 season, the Jets made a surprising discovery: the Colts' style played right into the Jets' hands. Wide receiver Pete Lammons remembered: "It seemed like every team they played was very predictable. They would never change a play at the line of scrimmage. With Joe, we always did that. And most of the teams they played didn't have very good passing quarterbacks like Joe. So I said out loud, 'Damn, coach, if we keep looking at these films we're going to get overconfident.'"[2] Matt Snell remembers that Lammons said, "'Don't show us any more. I guarantee we'll beat these guys if they play the same way.'"[3] Offensive lineman Randy Rasmussen recalled, "We were getting two stories. One from the outside telling us that we were going to get killed and the other from ourselves saying we thought we could beat them easier than the Raiders."[4]

So it was not a lone opinion that Namath famously expressed at the Miami Touchdown Club just days before the game, while receiving the Player of the Year award. The Jets quarterback responded to a heckler by boasting, "We're gonna win the game. I guarantee it." In Super Bowl lore, his statement would go down as The Guarantee. Jets coach Weeb Ewbank was furious with Namath for giving the Colts the quintessential bulletin-board quote. But Namath shrugged it off. He told Ewbank, "If they need newspaper clippings to fire them up, they're in trouble."[5] Dave Herman, an undersized guard whom Ewbank had just switched to tackle and was set to block 300-pound defensive end Bubba Smith, was also alarmed at what level of play Namath's bravado would bring out in the Colts, but Namath told him, "I'm not worried about you."[6] Privately, Namath confided to Sample: "If the Colts play the way they played in some of their games, we should win the game by thirty."[7]

Not so privately, Namath, a big fish in the small pond of the AFL, went on to question the skill level of quarterbacks in the NFL. He suggested that Baltimore's Earl Morrall, the NFL's Player of the Year, was not even as good as Babe Parilli, the Jets' thirty-eight-year-old backup quarterback. Namath also threw a challenge toward the Baltimore defense, saying, "I study quarterbacks, and I assure you, the Colts have never had to play against quarterbacks like we have in the AFL."[8]

They hadn't played against a team like the Jets, either. The Colts kicked off to the Jets to begin the game, and on the Jets' second play from scrimmage, halfback Matt Snell ran through a hole on the left and ran over Colts safety Rick Volk for a first down. Volk went off dizzily to the sidelines, and although he would return to the game, he would later require hospital treatment. Snell's hit announced that the AFL champs had come to play.

The Jets punted to the Colts moments later, and Baltimore, looking like the team that had gone 13-1, drove to New York's nineteen-yard line. But when Colts kicker Lou Michaels missed a chip shot at a field goal, the Jets had their first big break. "You could almost feel the steam go out of them," Snell recalled later.[9]

Near the end of the opening quarter, Namath completed a short pass to George Sauer, but Colts cornerback Lenny Lyles forced a fumble, and Baltimore took over on New York's twelve-yard line. Again, the Colts squandered a chance to score the game's first points. On third down, Morrall had wide receiver Tom Mitchell open in the end zone, but Jets linebacker Al Atkinson managed to nick the ball with his hand just enough to alter its path; it bounced off Mitchell's shoulder pad and into the waiting hands of Jets cornerback Randy Beverly for an interception.

This play touched off the biggest momentum change of the entire game. Beginning on their own twenty, the Jets marched to midfield on the strength of four consecutive carries by Matt Snell. Namath took over from there and connected for completions of fourteen and eleven yards to George Sauer, and a twelve-yarder to Snell. Two plays later, Snell scored on a four-yard run, and Jim Turner's extra point gave the Jets an early 7–0 lead.

Late in the second quarter, the NFL champions looked as if they might regain momentum when Tom Matte ran around the right end and went fifty-eight yards to the Jets' ten-yard line. But again, the Jets defense came up big. Sample intercepted a pass intended for Willie Richardson, and New York took over at the two-minute warning.

The Jets looked to run the clock out and punted back to Baltimore with just forty-three seconds remaining in the half. On the last play of the half, New York again got a huge break. The Colts ran a "flea-flicker"—a trick play in which Morrall handed off to Matte, who faked a run but then stopped and flipped it back to Morrall, who would then look for a receiver left open by a defense. The team had run it successfully earlier in the year, and here against the Jets, Colts receiver Jimmy Orr snuck deep behind the defense. Orr began waving his arms, signaling to Morrall that he was wide open. But unfortunately for Morrall, the quarterback never saw him; later, it was speculated that Orr's uniform had blended in with the background of the Florida A&M Band that was preparing to take the field for halftime. Rather than passing to the wide-open receiver for a likely game-tying touchdown, Morrall tried to force a pass to Jerry Hill. The Jets' Jim Hudson stepped in front of the pass and intercepted it, preserving his team's 7–0 into halftime.

Baltimore coach Don Shula tried to refocus his team in the locker room, and the Colts came out after the break looking to prove that the first half had been a fluke. But things quickly got worse for the NFL champions. Matte fumbled on the first play from scrimmage and Jets linebacker Ralph Baker recovered on the Baltimore thirty-three. Nine plays later, Turner kicked a thirty-two-yard field goal to increase the Jets' lead to 10–0. After the Colts failed to get a first down on their next possession and punted back to the Jets, Namath brought the Jets into field-goal range, and Turner converted another attempt, this time from thirty yards out. The kicker capped one last scoring drive for the Jets early in the fourth quarter with his third field goal of the game, stretching the Jets' lead to 16–0. Having been shut out through three-plus quarters, the Colts now needed to score at least three times to avoid the biggest upset in the history of the sport.

Perhaps the biggest shock of the game was the futility of the Colts' offense. Throughout the NFL season, Morrall and the Colts had stormed through the competition with ease. But the Jets had confused Morrall for three quarters with innovative defensive formations, and the NFL's MVP was unable to adjust. He completed just six of seventeen passes for only seventy-one yards and was intercepted three times in the Orange Bowl that day. Growing desperate, Coach Shula benched Morrall and turned to Unitas, the hobbled legend. Fans wondered if Unitas had a miracle in him as he led Baltimore to the Jets' twenty-five. But here, the old master overthrew Jimmy Orr, and Randy Beverly collected his second interception in the end zone.

Coach Ewbank then called upon the one-two punch of halfback Matt Snell and fullback Emerson Boozer. During the season, both running backs had missed games in order to fulfill commitments to the National Guard, a not-uncommon occurrence in professional sports at the time. Now, they joined together to mount a Jets ground attack that burned much of the remaining eleven minutes of the game. Unitas managed to march the Colts on their one and only scoring drive, culminating in a one-yard touchdown by Hill. But after Baltimore recovered an onside kick and drove again into Jets territory, the Colts stalled when a Unitas fourth-down pass fell incomplete.

Now, the Jets could begin to celebrate on the sidelines. Sticking to the run, the Jets offense used up all but the remaining eight seconds of the game. With the sounding of the final gun came the official proclamation to the football world: The upstart Jets from the inferior AFL had shocked the sports world by defeating—not just defeating, but dominating—the Baltimore Colts.

"Leaving the field, I saw the Colts were exhausted and in a state of shock," said Snell, who totaled a game-high 161 combined yards in rushing and receiving.[10] Namath, his pregame guarantee vindicated, ran off the field with his right hand raised and his index finger extended into the air to signal that his team was number one. He finished the game with seventeen completions on twenty-eight attempts (a percentage of 60.7) for 260 yards and no interceptions. For his efficient passing performance, his intelligent play, and perhaps for backing up his bravado, he was named the game's Most Valuable Player.

This might have been the biggest paradox of the Jets' win: Namath, the franchise's flamboyant, gunslinging quarterback, won by executing a controlled, conservative game plan—without throwing a touchdown, without attempting a single pass in the game's final quarter.

❁ ❁ ❁

On one level, the Jets' victory in Super Bowl III brought instant validation for not just the team but for the entire American Football League. But for some, the Jets' victory was a fluke written off by overconfidence on the part of the Colts. Some New Yorkers even felt the New York Giants of the NFL were still the best team in the city. Snell said, "I remember how a New York sportswriter came up to me and said that we wouldn't be considered real champions until we beat the Giants." Defensive end Gerry Philbin remembers: "I felt we had one more big game to play after the Super Bowl. We were always mentioned behind the Giants in New York. Even after we won the Super Bowl, people kept saying, 'You haven't beaten the Giants yet.' So playing them in the Yale Bowl that summer became a big thing for me. When we beat them it finally gave us credibility in New York City."[11]

But it was the Super Bowl that had given the AFL instant credibility and cemented plans for the merger of the two leagues, whose teams would face each other in regular-season contests for the first time in the fall of 1969. And thanks to a three-year, $18 million agreement that was struck between pro football and ABC television in May 1969, *Monday Night Football* would begin its thirty-six-year run the following year.

5. THE AMERICAN FAMILY

Of Kennedys, Corleones, and Portnoys

By the end of the sixties, the myth of a Camelot-on-the-Potomac had been reduced to mists on history's horizon. After President John F. Kennedy was slain by an assassin's—or, some argue, assassins'—bullets, his brother Robert had taken up the progressive torch for the family. An assassin's bullets had rung out again in April 1968 when James Earl Ray shot down Martin Luther King Jr. Bobby Kennedy reached out in Indianapolis that night to the African-American community, citing his own family's loss from bullets fired by a "white man," and—despite improbably quoting the Greek poet Aeschylus while talking to the inner-city crowd—his call for calm was effective in Indianapolis that night, if not throughout the rest of the nation. But then just two months and two days later, a grim trinity of events was completed when Bobby suffered the same fate as did his brother, struck down just minutes after winning the California Democratic primary.

In the bleakness of winter in 1969, the country watched as trials played out involving the assassinations of Bobby, Martin, and John. The murder trial for RFK's assassin, a Palestinian named Sirhan Sirhan, began at the Hall of Justice in Los Angeles on January 7. It had appeared during the preliminary arguments that there would be no trial, as the defense had sought a plea bargain: Sirhan pleading guilty in exchange for a life sentence to avoid execution.

The prosecution supported the plea-bargain proposal; not only would it save the time and expense of a trial, but, in addition, the prosecution's psychiatrist had examined Sirhan and diagnosed him as "psychotic," and thus not mentally responsible for the murder. But the presiding judge, Herbert Walker, disallowed the plea. Citing the fallout from the JFK assassination, the judge noted "a very much interested public continually point to the Oswald matter . . . and they just wonder what is going on, because the fellow wasn't tried."[1]

On his first day in court, the twenty-four-year-old Sirhan entered the courtroom wearing the blue-gray suit that his mother had bought him, along with a pale blue tie. He waved to his two brothers, Adel and Munir, in the back row of the courtroom. Prosecuting attorney David Fitts announced his intentions to seek capital punishment for Bobby's killer. Quizzing prospective jurors, Fitts asked, "Do you think after sitting here for three months with the defendant that you would have the courage to tell him face to face that for the murder of Senator Robert F. Kennedy he must die in the gas chamber?" Fitts needed to find out right away if any of the jurors could possibly turn squeamish at the thought of sending the accused to his death.

Fitts pointed out Sirhan's demeanor to the roomful of people as they began the process that would ultimately decide his fate on earth. Curiously, the accused wore a placid smile on his face. Would the jurors send a smiling man to his death? "You can see him now," Fitts said. "For all I know, he may smile at you all through the trial." Unphased, the defendant looked at the prosecutor and said, "I smile at you, too, Mr. Fitts."[2]

As the jury was accepted for the trial of Sirhan Sirhan, jury selection was under way in New Orleans for the trial of Clay Shaw, the fifty-five-year-old businessman whom New Orleans district attorney Jim Garrison had charged with conspiracy to murder President Kennedy. Garrison—a controversial figure whose book, *On the Trail of the Assassins*, would provide much of the fodder for the 1991

Oliver Stone film, *JFK*—would argue that Lee Harvey Oswald was merely a pawn in a conspiracy plot orchestrated by Shaw.

New Orleans attorney Dean Andrews had testified to the Warren Com-mission that a man named "Clay Bertrand" had called him the day after Kennedy's assassination and asked him to represent Oswald. Garrison argued that "Clay Bertrand" was an alias that Shaw used within the gay subculture of New Orleans. During the trial, an insurance salesman named Perry Russo identified Shaw as Bertrand, saying that he had seen Shaw/Bertrand at a party hosted by pilot David Ferrie at Ferrie's house, where the assassination of Kennedy had been planned. Aloysius Habighorst, the officer who fingerprinted Shaw upon his arrest, also testified that Shaw had confessed to him that "Clay Bertrand" was his alias.

In February, the court witnessed parts of the home movie taken by Dallas dress manufacturer Abraham Zapruder, which depicted the final seconds of president Kennedy's life. Zapruder testified: "I heard a shot and noticed the President leaning toward Jackie. Then I heard another shot which hit him in the head. It might have blown his whole head off." The Zapruder film would become the most famous amateur footage ever shot, capturing the grisly moment when some would say, America lost its innocence for good. On this day, Garrison displayed it to dispute notions of the "single bullet theory," arguing that the motion of the president's head upon the fatal impact—back, and to the left—implied that there was a second shooter stationed somewhere other than the book depository, where Oswald had been located.

As compelling as the Zapruder film was, however, Garrison's case began to unravel almost immediately. His chief investigator, Louis Ivon, appeared groggy and unconvincing in his testimony. Judge Edward Haggerty concluded that Officer Habighorst's testimony was not believable and threw it out. Perry Russo, whose story evolved as the investigation progressed, said on the witness stand, "I never said anything about any conspiracy. I didn't sit in on any conspiracies." Describing the party at Ferrie's house, he now said that both Shaw and Oswald were present, but added, "It was more like a bull session—or rather 'shooting the breeze.'"[3]

The jury did not even need one hour to acquit Shaw of the conspiracy charge. Garrison's attempt to prove the greatest murder conspiracy in the history of the nation went unfulfilled, though he would spend the rest of his life claiming that President Kennedy's assassination had been the result of a conspiracy.

That same month, an escaped con named James Earl Ray stood before a judge in Tennessee, where he had been extradited following his arrest in London's Heathrow Airport. On March 10, his forty-first birthday, Ray confessed to King's murder as part of a plea bargain to avoid the death penalty, on the advice of his attorney, Percy Foreman. Ray was sentenced to ninety-nine years and sent to the Brushy Mountain State Penitentiary in Petros, Tennessee. He later recanted his confession and suggested that King's death had also been the result of a conspiracy. Ray would die in prison, still maintaining his innocence.

Bobby Kennedy's killer would also stand trial for all the world to see. The defense began presenting its evidence on February 28, building a case that Sirhan was legally insane, due to his abusive childhood, engrained prejudices stemming from the Arab-Israeli conflict, and a head injury in 1966 that witnesses claimed had changed his personality. But at one point, Sirhan himself took offense to this argument and cried out, "I withdraw my original plea of not guilty and submit the plea of guilty as charged! I request that my counsel disassociate themselves from this case completely. Just execute me!"[4]

Sirhan took the stand in March. He initially claimed he could not remember anything about the night of the assassination, but he allowed that he might have experienced temporary insanity due to Kennedy's support of the Israeli air force. Among the rambling entries in his notebook, which had been confiscated shortly after the assassination, he had written, "my determination to eliminate R.F.K. is becoming more and more of an unshakable obsession. . . . R.F.K. must die. R.F.K. must be killed. Robert F. Kennedy must be assassinated."[5]

The trial ended on April 14 after fifteen weeks. After three days of deliberation, the jury returned with its verdict: Sirhan Sirhan was guilty of first-degree murder of Senator Kennedy, along with five counts of assault with a deadly weapon. On May 21, Judge Walker sentenced Sirhan to death in the gas chamber. Three years later, his sentence was commuted to life in prison when the state of California abolished the death penalty.

❋ ❋ ❋

A resonating theme of Arthurian legend is of King Arthur as the "once and future king"—the unifying leader prophesied to mystically return and set the wasteland in order once again. One Kennedy brother had been slain as a sitting president, and a second brother had died seeking the throne. In 1969, one didn't have to be a political observer to note the rise of a third brother, one who might potentially return the Kennedy mystique to the White House.

Ted Kennedy had decided over the final weekend of 1968 that he would challenge Russell Long for the position of assistant majority leader (the Majority Whip) in the Democratic Party. The fifty-year-old Long was a representative of the party's old-time, Southern faction; a senator since 1948, he was the son of Huey Long, the legendary Louisiana governor. Kennedy, meanwhile, had only served since 1962. But one thing that Joseph Kennedy had instilled in his children was the importance of timing, and the more Ted thought about it, the more he felt that 1969 was the year in which he would stake his claim to the next stage in his political career.

Many senators spent New Year's Day in front of their television sets watching the college bowl games. Depending upon the geographic location of their constituencies, the senators were either watching Penn State edge Kansas 15–14 in the Orange Bowl, Texas roll over Tennessee 36–13 in the Cotton Bowl, or the Rose Bowl in Pasadena, where 9-0-1 USC faced off against the 9-0 Ohio State. USC's O.J. Simpson, who won the Heisman Trophy with a combination of athleticism and grace on the field, ran for an eighty-yard touchdown that gave USC a 10–0 lead early in the second quarter. But Simpson also fumbled twice and threw an interception on a halfback pass—all part of five turnovers committed by the Trojans in the game. Behind an opportunistic defense, the running of fullback Jim Otis, and a sound game plan by quarterback Rex Kern, who completed just nine of fifteen passes but threw two touchdowns, the Buckeyes stormed back to win, 27–16.

Kennedy was in Sun Valley, Idaho, on New Year's Day for a ski trip, but he spent the day away from the slopes, calling his fellow senators to ask them for their support. Kennedy's efforts paid off, and in that Friday's Senate vote he unseated Long as the majority whip. As *Time* commented, "Long was simply outgunned by a more contemporary and compelling dynasty than his own."[6]

Kennedy declared, "The Democratic majority of the Senate has an obligation to the country to present the best possible programs in keeping with our historic role as the party of progress and change in the U. S."[7] His surprising victory had clear implications beyond the Senate. His national profile was on the rise. In the *Washington Post*, David Broder commented, "In a single bold stroke, the last of the Kennedy brothers leapfrogged" over his potential rivals for the Democratic presidential nomination. "The Massachusetts senator with the magic family name is, with his victory Friday, now a clear and present danger to Nixon's hopes for a second term."[8]

Indeed, in early March, a Gallup survey found that 94 percent of those polled could correctly identify Kennedy—a total usually attached to athletes, entertainers, and presidents and presidential candidates—and two out of every three Democrats would like him to be the nation's next president. Senate majority leader Mike Mansfield said, "It's preordained. With Ted, I'm afraid it's not a question of choice, it's a matter of destiny." As biographer Joe McGinniss would write, "It seemed clear that there would be no stopping Teddy—unless Teddy stopped himself."[9]

❊ ❊ ❊

The Kennedy family had had a complicated relationship with organized crime. Joseph, the patriarch, had made his fortune as a bootlegger, and stories of his wheeling and dealing with racketeers to help swing the 1960 election in favor of his son were more than just underworld legends. Frank Sinatra had purportedly used his mob ties to help JFK's presidential campaign, and the young president had had an affair with Judith Campbell Exner, a close friend of mobster Sam Giancana. But RFK had been a thorn in the side of organized crime while serving as U. S. Attorney General in his brother's administration. One popular conspiracy theory that still abounds holds that Mafia kingpins felt so betrayed by the Kennedys that they had a hand in one or both of the assassinations.

As Ted looked to assume the political mantle in his family, Americans were becoming fascinated with the world of the Mafia and organized crime. Playing in theaters that winter was Martin Ritt's *The Brotherhood*, a B-plus flick with Kirk Douglas miscast as Frank Gianetta, the son of a late Mafia don. (In an apparent attempt to make him look "more Italian," the filmmakers had the star sport a mustache, which served to make him look more like a well-dressed organ grinder than an underworld honcho.) Through an extended flashback, we learn that Frank avenged his father in a vendetta killing and then fled with his wife to a villa in rural Italy. His younger brother Alex is then ordered to track down Frank and kill him in retaliation for the unsanctioned vendetta slaying. Resigned to his fate, Frank sacrifices himself to save his brother.

The mysterious inner workings of Italian organized crime made the headlines in early 1969 with the publication of *The Valachi Papers: The First Inside Account of Life in the Cosa Nostra.* In 1963, Joseph Michael Valachi had been the first mafioso to publicly testify on the existence of the Italian crime organization, and as such had become a man whom *Life* said "may be the most important federal prisoner in U. S. history."[10] The stocky, graying Valachi had spent thirteen months during his incarceration in a federal prison writing some 300,000 words about his experiences, and the Justice Department (which had to waive a federal regulation preventing prisoners from publishing accounts of their criminal activities) picked journalist Peter Maas to edit Valachi's work.

When word of the project got out, however, Italian-American groups protested that Valachi's book would perpetuate ethnic stereotypes, and attorney general Nicholas Katzenbach canceled the arrangement, barring Maas from any further contact with Valachi. By then, Maas had already made a copy of Valachi's manuscript and had also acquired transcripts from the feds' interrogation of Valachi, and notes from a hundred hours of his own interviews with the aging mafioso. Maas compiled his work, and the book, told in the third person, was published by Putnam.

The Valachi Papers revealed the inner structure of the Cosa Nostra and its ruling body, a board of nine to twelve *capi* and operated through twenty-five to thirty "families," approximately 5,000 total members. Valachi, a soldier in the Vito Genovese crime family, had turned state's evidence and became the star witness for the McClelland Committee on organized crime in September 1963. His testimony revealed the previously unknown ways that the underworld was formally structured within a hierarchy governed by "honor" codes. As the Justice Department said, "He showed us the face of the enemy."[11]

At the time, it was rumored that his old crime boss, Vito Genovese, had put out a hit on Valachi for breaking the Mafia code of silence. Genovese, who was reputed to be one of the most vicious members of the American Mafia, was sent to prison in 1959 for selling heroin, but he had continued to reign over his crime family from behind bars, ordering murders and overseeing a multimillion-dollar empire. He died in prison in Springfield, Missouri, on Valentine's Day in 1969, forty years to the day of the infamous "St. Valentine's Day Massacre" in Chicago orchestrated by Al Capone.

The real-life empires of Genovese and Capone paled in comparison to the fictional one overseen by the crime boss in a new novel by Mario Puzo. Puzo, then forty-eight, was a first-generation American who had been born to a family of Neapolitan immigrants in the Hell's Kitchen area of lower New York City. A U. S. Air Force veteran, he worked in public relations and journalism, and he also published three novels, including a children's book, before setting his sights on commercial fiction. He began writing a novel based on stories he had heard on his journalistic beat about branches of the Cosa Nostra along the East Coast.

The Godfather, published in hardcover that March and in paperback later in the year, is the epic story of Vito Andolini, a child of Corleone, Sicily. Young Vito's father kills a local Mafia chief in a village feud, and soon afterward Vito's father is found dead. After his father's funeral, Mafia gunmen come looking for Vito, and the boy is hidden by relatives and sent off to America. Going by the name Vito Corleone, he starts out running a small-time racket among the tenements, but over the years, he builds an underworld network through a shrewd mixture of favors, intimidation, and brutality. Raised in a culture of vendetta, Corleone looks back on his life and remembers, "Strange men have come to kill me ever since I was twelve years old."

Puzo's novel spans the first decade of postwar America and runs parallel to history in the real-life mob migration from the East Coast to Las Vegas. As Don Vito faces his own mortality, he deliberates like King Lear on which of his three sons can best succeed him as head of the family. Michael, the youngest, is groomed as Don Vito's heir until he defies his father's wishes and volunteers for service in World

War II, choosing to fight for "strangers" rather than serving the Corleone family.

Like Vito Genovese, Michael must flee to Italy to evade a murder conviction. The long arm of a rival crime family in America reaches out to the Old Country, and a bomb meant for him inadvertently kills his young wife. Having now experienced firsthand the murderous forces of revenge that shaped his father's life, he sends a message home: "Tell my father I wish to be his son." Once back home and established as the new head of the family, Michael unleashes a campaign of violence that eliminates the heads of rival families and exposes traitors among the Corleone family ranks—including his brother-in-law, whom he also has murdered. In the triumphant and chilling scene near the end of the novel, Puzo describes Michael standing like a Roman emperor as he accepts the fealty of Clemenza, who christens the new family leader as "Don Michael." The transition of mafioso power to the first generation of Americans is complete.

The Godfather was a huge bestseller, providing material for Francis Ford Coppola's *The Godfather* (1972) and also for the flashback sequences of Coppola's *The Godfather Part II* (1974), both of which were enormously important in creating the archetype of the Mafia in the American imagination. But *The Godfather* was never the author's favorite among his own work. At times Puzo expressed regret that the book had negatively affected perceptions of Italian-Americans. Perhaps the most seductive element of Puzo's novel was not the mob crimes of which he wrote, but the notions of family, and, specifically, the code of honor that existed within these crime families. "Before *The Godfather*, who knew that criminals had families and believed in justice?" wrote Jules Siegel in 1999, after Puzo's death. "[Puzo] once told me that *The Godfather* wasn't about crime but about power and justice. He said that the Kennedys were an important influence in the characterization of the Corleones, and mentioned their compound at Hyannisport as an example of how he used elements of their lives in the novel."[12]

Another Mafia novel to spring out of the journalistic world in 1969 was Jimmy Breslin's *The Gang That Couldn't Shoot Straight*. The syndicated columnist with the gritty voice of New York City based his novel on true-life gang wars between "Crazy Joe" Gallo and Joseph Profaci, head of the Profaci crime family. In contrast to the well-oiled machine of the Corleone family, which wields unlimited power in influencing police, judges, unions, and even movie studio heads, Breslin presents a view of Mafia types more grounded in reality: small-time hoods who are often not that bright, wielding power among only the lower rungs of society. "When the protection-minded Mafia people came to America, they found the landowners had so many guards it was ludicrous," writes Breslin. "The National Guard shot down women and children during a strike against a Rockefeller mine in Ludlow, Colorado. The fiercest dons of them all threw up their hands in defeat and admiration. 'No can match,' the Kansas City outfit said."

In this seriocomic roman à clef peopled with such colorfully named characters as Tony the Indian, Joe the Sheik, Joe the Wop, Big Jelly Catalano, and Beppo the Dwarf, Gallo is transformed into Kid Sally Palumbo, a low-level muscle man who "couldn't run a gas station at a profit even if he stole the customer's cars," yet who dreams of becoming a big-shot crime boss himself.

The fictional portrayals of the Mafia popularized by Puzo and Breslin depicted Italian-American "families" as sources of strength within the immigrant experience and against the outside world. These groups consolidated and wielded power while biting off their own part of the American dream. According to the code: You mess with one of us, and you mess with *all* of us.

❋ ❋ ❋

Whereas Mafia families took care of their own, the 1969 offerings of Philip Roth and Woody Allen taught us that Jewish mothers fed on their own.

Philip Roth's commercial and critical achievement of the year, the novel *Portnoy's Complaint*, provides an enduring portrait of ethnic-American family life that is no less iconic than Puzo's *Godfather*. A professor of comparative literature at the University of Pennsylvania, Roth had won the National Book Award for his first book of fiction, *Goodbye, Columbus*, but *Portnoy*, his third novel, proved to be his breakthrough success. In a year in which one might say America's id was outmuscling its ego, Roth's protagonist, Alexander Portnoy, looked to "PUT THE ID BACK IN YID."

"She was so deeply imbedded in my consciousness that for the first year of school I seem to have believed that each of my teachers was my mother in disguise," the thirty-three-year-old Portnoy remembers in the novel's first sentence. *Portnoy's Complaint* is an extended monologue, with the title character recounting his life, and eventually breaking down, on his psychoanalyst's couch. Portnoy is modestly successful, the Assistant Commissioner of Human Opportunity in New York City, yet still single; his relationship failures all stem from a childhood and adolescence suffered under what *New York Times* reviewer Josh Greenfield called "that old sentimental favorite, the Jewish Mother, as not only a downright guilt-giver but also a deft castrater. . . . Standing by ever-silent is Alexander's father, the emasculated Jewish father." Portnoy tells his analyst, "These two are the outstanding producers and packagers of guilt in our time!"

Robbed of all privacy or dignity at home, Alexander is hounded in almost existential proportions by his mother. She berates him, loudly, at the sporting goods store for wanting an athletic supporter for his "little thing." ("Yes, Mother, imagine," he seethes, "for my little thing.") She yells at him through the bathroom door because she suspects he is constipated from eating French fries after school—the ultimate sin, perhaps even worse than what he's *really* doing behind closed doors—and insists he let her inspect the toilet bowl's contents. His compulsive masturbating comes across as an act that is less about gratification than it is about trying to assert control over his last frontier of privacy—and about confronting the "guilt-edged insecurity," a phenomenon that Greenfield noted "fuels the American-Jewish character in fiction."

"The very first distinction I learned," Alexander says, "was not night and day or hot and cold, but goyishe and Jewish . . . Jew Jew Jew Jew Jew Jew!" With his sexual conquests of WASP women, he doesn't seek assimilation into their social world as much as he acts out psychosexual aggression against their WASP parents, whose society kept his father held down under the wheels of capitalism. After having fetishized goy girls, he is, as he says, "torn by desires that are repugnant to my conscience, and a conscience repugnant to my desires." When he casts them aside and meets the proverbial nice Jewish girl in Israel—who, of course, resembles his mother—the compulsively sexual Portnoy suddenly becomes impotent, leading to his psychological breakdown.

As Roth's *Portnoy* flew off the shelves that February, *Play It Again, Sam: A Romantic Comedy in Three Acts*, the second play by a rising comic talent named Woody Allen, opened at Broadway's Broadhurst Theater. Allen himself starred in the role of Allan Felix, a nerdy film reviewer who has woman problems. Obsessed with the movie *Casablanca*, Felix seeks advice from Humphrey Bogart's character in the classic film, and a Bogartesque character (Jerry Lacy) appears and serves as Felix's mentor in the ways of love and seduction.

Felix's best friend and his best friend's wife attempt to set their friend up with women, but in a comically romantic series of events, Felix and his best friend's wife (played by Diane Keaton, then twenty-three and fresh from her appearance in the hit sensation *Hair*) fall in love. But at play's end, which mimics the much-quoted end of *Casablanca*, Felix convinces her that she must go back to her husband, and the heretofore pathetic Allan Felix ascends to the rank of heroic lover on par with Bogey's Rick.

Woody Allen and Diane Keaton hit it off over the course of the play's run. After one late rehearsal, the two went to a restaurant on Eighth Avenue and had their first significant conversation outside the world of the play. He reminisced later that he found her "completely hilarious. I just couldn't stop laughing." They began seeing each other outside of work and then lived together for a year. "Keaton was a major contribution to my life in an artistic way," Allen reflected two decades later. "She helped my taste develop a lot, and there is a lot of her influence in my taste."[13]

Allen relied on Keaton's insight while starring in his first movie, which he also directed, later in 1969. "When I first screened *Take the Money and Run* for her before it came out and she told me that it was good, that it was funny, that was all I needed to hear. I knew it would have its place if it was liked or not liked. And I've felt this down through the years. When she's liked things of mine, they're worthwhile."[14]

Take the Money and Run is a "mockumentary" following the trials and travails of Virgil Starkwell (Allen), a bumbling thief who makes Breslin's Sally Palumbo look like Vito Corleone. In the film's best-known scene, Virgil's attempted bank robbery is thwarted by a teller's inability to read his handwritten stickup note. The most noteworthy motif of the film, though, came from editor Ralph Rosenblum, who suggested that one of the film's slapstick scenes be scored with a Eubie Blake ragtime number. The use of up-tempo ragtime infused rhythm into the scene. "The whole thing came to life," Allen said. "I was suddenly just bouncing along. It made all the difference in the world. . . . Probably seventy-five percent of the movie that was released is from my first edit, but what Ralph did was the difference between living and dying."[15]

The sounds of ragtime would become a distinguishing feature of many Woody Allen films throughout his career, and the comic team of Allen and Keaton would become one of the most memorable in American film.

Like *Portnoy's Complaint*, Roth's novella "Goodbye, Columbus" also looks at Jewish sexual politics, but here both partners are from Jewish families and the obstacle is one of class. In Larry Peerce's 1969 film adaptation, Neil Klugman (Richard Benjamin), a Rutgers University graduate who works at a low-paying library job in Newark, falls for summer love, Brenda Patimkin (Ali MacGraw), a Radcliffe student from a wealthy suburban family. Neil and Brenda revel in their young love—or, at least, young lust. But the differences in their backgrounds continue to come up. Her parents disapprove of his lack of social standing, and he is turned off by the affectations of her parents and friends. In the film's bitter ending, Brenda and Neil meet at a hotel during a Jewish holiday break, but things begin to unravel for good when she informs him that her parents have found her diaphragm—evidence of her sexual activity with Neil—and that both wrote her separate letters expressing their disdain for the relationship. Neil suggests that Brenda subconsciously let them find it on purpose so that she could sabotage their relationship. It becomes clear to him that Brenda will never stand up to her parents and commit to him against their wishes, and they end their relationship.

The film *Goodbye, Columbus* was 1969's version of *The Graduate*, a story of rebellious young love in the face of family obstacles. But while Mike Nichols's 1967 film carries a counterculture message, exposing the hypocrisy and illicit sexuality just beneath the surface of suburban society, *Goodbye, Columbus* confronts a rigid social order more rooted in 1950s morality. (The film's tagline was "Every father's daughter is a virgin.") Neil and Brenda *don't* run away at film's end; instead, she's swallowed up by her family and their more-powerful desire to maintain their social status, thus protecting their place in mainstream American society. For those striving for acceptance and assimilation, the politics of youthful rebellion were a luxury they could not afford.

For well over a century, the desire to be accepted by the ethnic establishment had been a fundamental part of the immigrant experience in America. It was a battle waged by countless nineteenth-century Irish immigrants, including the Kennedy family. Thomas Maier writes:

> Since their arrival in this land, the Kennedys have been exemplars of the Irish Catholic immigrant experience in America . . . Their sense of being Irish, of being Catholic, and of being members of a family coming from an often oppressed immigrant minority—indeed, the very Irish notion of a Kennedy *clan*, as they often referred to themselves—carried through from one generation to the next. Most early histories and biographies of the Kennedys mirrored the storybook image that the family projected to achieve power. The popular notion of JFK as a Harvard-educated Anglophile, an almost perfect creation of America's melting pot, fit neatly with prevailing theories of assimilation.[16]

The election of President Kennedy was a powerful symbol for Irish-American Catholics, one that announced that their immigrant experience had come full circle by 1960. Now, at the end of the decade, as the most prominent Irish-American clan had become the nation's most famous family, the media's depiction of families, both real and imagined, spoke to the immigrant experience and the extent to which Italians and Jews had entered the popular culture—the first step toward assimilation in the United States of the late twentieth century.

ONEWALL RIOTS ALTAMONI
DE NAMATH ALTAMONI
JTCH CASSIDY AND THE SUNDANCE KID
UPATION OF ALCATRAZ ZIP TO ZAP THE NEW LEFT
ASY RIDER HARVARD STUDENT STRIK

II. REVOLUTION IN SPRINGTIME

We traditionally associate nakedness with judgments and eternity, and so on those beaches where we are mostly naked the scene seems apocalyptic.

—John Cheever, *Bullet Park*

H! CALCUTTA! THE WEATHER UNDERGROUND
EIL YOUNG & CRAZY HORSE TOMM\
5 DAYS OF RAGE APOLLO 11 BOEING 74\
HAMBURGER HILL
I CURIOUS (YELLOW) PORTNOY'S COMPLAINT CUYAHOGA RIVER FIRE
HES BREW LET IT BLEED CHARLES MANSON
I PHOTOS THE MORATORIUM WOODSTOCK
D ZEPPELIN
PLE'S PARK JIMI HENDRIX RICHARD NIXON HELLS ANGELS
E GODFATHER IGGY AND JEFFERSON
OODY ALLEN THE STOOGES AIRPLANE
DNIGHT COWBOY NUDITY THE MIRACL\
ZODIAC KILLER BOB & CAROL & TED & ALICE MET\
PERATION MENU CROSBY, STILLS & NAS\

6. America Undressed

Sex and nudity gain new exposure on the screen, stage, and printed page.

Was 1969 the first X-rated year? That great arbiter of public morals and mores, *Playboy*, reported:

> [W]ith the new wave of explicit erotica in the arts, movies are not only better but bawdier—and kinkier—than ever. . . . the inundation of sex on screen has exceeded even our permissive predictions. Erotica in films from the major studios now rivals that seen in grind-house sexploitation movies. . . . In 1969, the entire spectrum of human sexuality exploded on film with unprecedented frankness.[1]

For starters, United Artists released John Schlesinger's *Midnight Cowboy*, which would earn the distinction of being the first X-rated film to win the Oscar for Best Picture. The New York City premiere of United Artists's *Midnight Cowboy* in May was an immediate social sensation. The tagline announced, "Whatever you hear about *Midnight Cowboy* is true." Director Schlesinger's adaptation of the James Leo Herlihy novel gave us the unique character study of aspiring gigolo Jack Buck (Jon Voight) and "Ratso" Rizzo (Dustin Hoffman), a gimpy, tubercular street con. Jack leaves behind his small Texas town with dreams of hitting it big on the streets of New York City, but the city proves a little too big for him. His first trick, a society lady (Sylvia Miles), talks him into giving *her* money after sex. Even Rizzo takes him for cash by pretending to act as a pimp, but when Buck later spots him in a diner and confronts him, the two form an unexpected friendship out of their mutual loneliness. Buck moves into Rizzo's unheated apartment in a condemned building, and they form a symbiotic relationship with unspoken homosexual tones—a theme consciously developed by Schlesinger, a homosexual himself. The scene of Buck holding Rizzo's dead body in the back of a bus is one of the most memorable in Hollywood "buddy" films, and both Voight and Hoffman received Best Actor nominations.

The film's X-rated distinction is somewhat misleading, as in 1969 it merely denoted an adult-oriented film ("No one under 17 admitted"), not necessarily pornography; the film was later "downgraded" to an R rating. But its nude sex scenes (albeit brief and featuring no full frontal nudity), homosexual situations, and flashback montages of a group rape were shocking content for a mainstream film with A-list actors. The fact that a film about the relationship between an aspiring gigolo and a live-in male companion and pimp would gain such acceptance by the industry, and by the popular culture at large, showed just how much the underlying puritanical roots of American culture were being challenged at the end of the sixties.

Best-selling literature titillated as never before. "Penelope Ashe's scorching novel makes *Portnoy's Complaint* and *Valley of the Dolls* read like *Rebecca of Sunnybrook Farm*," exclaimed the *Long Island Press* of *Naked Came the Stranger*, the steamy 1969 bestseller. Bearing the cover photograph of a kneeling girl's bare behind, her long hair hanging wantonly down her shapely figure, the novel caused a scandal with its racy content. The attractive author appeared on talk shows in low-cut dresses to promote the book, the perfect embodiment of the sexual liberation that her novel offered its readers.

If the book's content caused a stir, it was nothing compared to that created by the "author's" appearance on *The David Frost Show* in England. When talk show host David Frost introduced "Penelope Ashe," a group of writers from New York's *Newsday* walked onto the set. The novel had been the joint effort of columnist Mike McGrady and twenty-four of his colleagues at *Newsday*. Convinced that sexual titillation, no matter how base, would make an otherwise poorly written book sell in America, McGrady commissioned his *Newsday* cohorts to write a formulaic sex novel that would possess no sustained plot, deep characterization, or social commentary—just sex. McGrady's sister-in-law played the role of Penelope Ashe for publicity appearances before the hoax became public.

Naked Came the Stranger is a revenge tale, of sorts. The "plot" of the novel centers on Gillian Blake, who cohosts a radio show with her husband Billy. When Gillian hires a private detective and discovers that her husband is having an affair with the show's newly hired production assistant, a twenty-two-year-old Vassar graduate, she resolves to get him back by sleeping with one man after another in their fictional New York suburb of King's Neck. Her plans for revenge provide the formulaic structure of the work: Each chapter describes her amorous adventures with a new man/stereotype, starting with the brutish neighbor, the neighborhood handyman, the man of God, the local hippie, the town's mafioso, and so on.

If McGrady's experiment was a cynical one, it was nevertheless successful. Sales of the book only increased—dramatically—after the hoax went public, and it soon made the *New York Times* bestseller list. Although the writing is not any worse than that of the scores of formulaic bodice rippers that have been published for decades, it nevertheless showed that, absent any sense of literary inspiration, sex alone *could* sell books. *Naked Came the Stranger* calls to mind a passage from Irving Wallace's *The Seven Minutes*, another bestseller from 1969: "It would be read, as other books would be read, for the wrong reasons. There were decent books, and there were indecent readers." At the heart of Wallace's plot is an obscenity trial surrounding the sale of a purportedly pornographic book that depicts the intimate thoughts of a woman during seven minutes of sex. The main character, Michael Barrett, turns down a lucrative job offer so that he can defend a California bookstore owner indicted for selling the novel. After winning the case, Barrett feels "the tiniest ping of concern. But then his concern evaporated. No one, in an open society, following the rules of that society, had the right to come between an idea and its audience."

Soaring to the top of the bestseller charts in 1969 was another book of mysterious authorship, *The Sensuous Woman*, a sexual "how-to" manual for women written by "J" (the one-letter pen name adopted by author Joan Theresa Garrity). Garrity presented a manifesto for the average woman looking to improve her sex appeal: "Some of the most interesting men in America have fallen in love with me," she boasts. "I have received marriage proposals from such diverse personalities as a concert pianist, a bestselling author, the producer of three of America's most popular television shows, a bomb expert for the CIA, a trial attorney, an apple grower, a TV and radio star, and a tax expert.

"Yet you'd never believe it if we came face to face on the street, for I'm not particularly pretty. I have heavy thighs, lumpy hips, protruding teeth, a ski jump nose, poor posture, flat feet and uneven ears. . . . Mothers, wives and girl friends think of me as the wholesome, apple pie, girl-next-door type."

Citing a vague epiphany that she'd experienced while fighting another shopper for a pair of silk shoes in the basement of Gimbel's department store, Garrity recounts reinventing herself from a frigid nobody into a "sexually responsive" woman achieving "real peaks of ecstasy." Using frank language, she advises her readers on issues of masturbation, sex for the single woman, lingerie, fellatio, and anal sex ("if you'll stop wailing like a banshee or playing Purity Raped for a moment, you will notice the beginning of a curious, warm and divinely demanding sensation and be secretly hoping he'll go on to the next step"). Speaking of using sex toys or other objects for masturbation, she unwittingly looks into the future and prophetically comments, "Next someone will figure out how to get orgasms from computers."

If "J" left any sexual questions unanswered, David Reuben sought to answer them in *Everything You Always Wanted to Know About Sex . . . But Were Afraid to Ask*. Dr. Reuben, a California psychiatrist, presented hypothetical reader questions and provided answers based, as the jacket copy boasted, on "the latest medical and psychiatric research material, as well as the sexual experiences of several thousand of his own private patients." The book covers, well, everything—from sexual physiology to aphrodisiacs, sexual dysfunction, masturbation, perversion, birth control, venereal disease, menopause, even "September sex."

In keeping with his "modern" mission, some of Reuben's revelations are indeed progressive. On frigidity: "The word frigidity is a misleading one and was probably coined by a man." On abortion: "In an era when man is transplanting organs, exploring distant planets, and manipulating living molecular structures, it is incredible that he is not allowed to control his own reproduction." Should girls wait until marriage to have sex? "That's fine, if she can get married at the age of fourteen. Otherwise it's asking a lot to expect a healthy, sexy young girl to wait seven long years to find out what it's all about." Is prostitution degrading? "Definitely. We make it that way. By looking down on those who sell sexual favors by making them criminals, by shutting them off from the rest of society, we succeed in alienating them completely. . . . In itself it is neither good nor bad."

In a book that was marketed as a source of social enlightenment, however, Reuben perpetuates many stereotypes seemingly out of mass-market novels. "No matter what they say, most strippers enjoy their work," he tells us. "They derive sexual satisfaction from displaying their breasts to large groups of men. They don't need much encouragement to display everything else." Prostitutes love their work, too, according to Reuben. He also dismisses the notion that homosexuals are "born gay" as "one of the many explanations homosexuals grope for in an attempt to understand their problem." He also adds, "Homosexuals thrive on danger. It almost seems part of their sexual ritual."

Though grounded in some questionable research and/or chauvinist social prejudices that still lingered in the late sixties, Reuben's book became a national sensation—selling more than a million copies in hardcover—for its focus on sexuality. And as Billy Blake's infidelity gave license to Gillian's subsequent adventures in neighborhood-hopping sex, Reuben's medical degree gave him license to peer "clinically" into the secret sex lives of Americans, such as that of the prostitute who bragged, "As long as the average woman thinks she has a golden vagina I'll be in good shape." Thanks to the pulp voyeurism of *Naked Came the Stranger, The Sensuous Woman*, and *Everything You Always Wanted to Know About Sex*, 1969 saw the sexual revolution move into the shopping aisles, reading groups, and night tables of mainstream America.

The transgressions and taboos of the flesh on the printed page were also established in a more literary context with books like Roth's *Portnoy's Complaint*. The novel became a cultural sensation as much for its scenes of graphic sexuality and masturbation as it did for its considerable literary merit. Soon after its publication, a *Time* article entitled "How to Deal with Four-Letter Words" considered how different newspapers throughout the nation handled the reportage of obscenities in books like *Portnoy*. (The *Chicago Sun-Times* stiffly referred to Roth's "generous use of the saltier nicknames for our reproductive organs and their congress with one another," while traditionally stodgy *New York Times* replicated passages from the novel that included the words, *penis, fellatio*, and *beating my meat*.)[2] Speaking to *Portnoy*'s sensation, in an episode of ABC's *Love*,

American Style, a black student radical expresses his surprise over the object of his affection having read the novel. "You read that?" he asks. She responds, "What do you think I am, Snow White?"

Nineteen sixty-nine saw the beginning of the rivalry between men's magazines *Playboy* and *Penthouse*—dubbed the "Pubic Wars." Nudity had slipped its way into the mainstream magazines through the advertising industry, which more and more featured nude models—and not just in fashion ads. One full-page corporate ad that appeared in *Time* used a nude model to make the point that "a conglomerate company was no more obscene than a naked girl." Another ad for women's underwear spoofed this cultural trend in copy that read, "It's time someone took a stand on nudity . . ." across the picture of a seductively posed nude woman, and on the facing page, a woman wearing panties with the words "We're against it" superimposed across her arms as they cover her chest.[3]

Sensing a change in the American moral climate, magazine publisher Bob Guccione brought *Penthouse*, which he'd published in the United Kingdom since 1965, to the other side of the Atlantic. *Penthouse* was known for the social taboo of showing female genitalia, and its debut U. S. issue featured cover model Evelyn Treacher and an interview with the recently acquitted Clay Shaw. Just one month earlier, *Playboy* had shown glimpses of pubic hair for the first time—just barely visible amid the light and shadows—in its spread of African-American actress and dancer Paula Kelly. In its December issue, the serendipitously named Gloria Root, sans pubic hair, would become the first *Playboy* model to appear in a full frontal nude centerfold.

As magazine publishers pushed the boundaries of "decency," the issue of art and censorship was at the forefront of legal debate in 1969. On the local and state levels, conservative attitudes still held sway. In

Boston, seventy-two-year-old judge Elijah Adlow ruled that the lesbian film *The Killing of Sister George* was a "lecherous, lustful picture" and sentenced the owner of the Cheri I movie theater to six months in jail plus a $1,000 fine.[4] The city of Cleveland declared the *Two Virgins* album cover obscene and instructed the Main Line record chain to remove it from its shelves. The sight of John Lennon's uncircumcised penis and Yoko Ono's pubic bush was equally offensive to New Jersey authorities, who seized thousands of copies of the record following a judge's ruling; the covers were subsequently destroyed.

To avoid similar legal issues, Atco Records opted to release the debut album from Blind Faith—the new "supergroup" consisting of Eric Clapton, Ginger Baker, Steve Winwood, and Rick Grech—with an alternate cover in the United States. *Blind Faith*, a laid-back album of blues rock, folk, and jazz improv, rose to the top of the Billboard album chart, and the Winwood-penned hit, "Can't Find My Way Home," was the perfect stoner anthem and ode to the mood of disorientation at the end of the decade: "I'm near the end and I just ain't got the time / And I'm wasted and I can't find my way home."

But the cover art, a Bob Seidemann photograph of a topless preteen girl holding a silver toy spaceship, was problematic. Seidemann recalls:

> I could not get my hands on the image until out of the mist a concept began to emerge. To symbolize the achievement of human creativity and its expression through technology a space ship was the material object. To carry this new spore into the universe, innocence would be the ideal bearer, a young girl, a girl as young as Shakespeare's Juliet. The space ship would be the fruit of the tree of knowledge and the girl, the fruit of the tree of life. . . . This was an image created out of ferment and storm, out of revolution and chaos.[5]

The alternate American cover simply showed a sepia-toned portrait of the band.

In April, the Supreme Court of the United States handed down a decision in *Stanley v. Georgia* that signaled a sea change in the State's ability to legislate obscenity. Police had searched the home of Georgia resident and bookmaker Robert Eli Stanley with a warrant to seize betting material. Although they hadn't found what they came for, they did find reels of pornographic films in his bedroom and charged with Stanley with possession of obscene materials. In a unanimous ruling, the court declared Georgia's anti-pornography law unconstitutional, holding that, "The State may not prohibit possession of obscene matter on the ground that it may lead to antisocial conduct."

With *Portnoy's Complaint* reigning as the fastest-selling hardcover in history, the Swedish film *I Am Curious (Yellow)* by director Vilgot Sjöman had the best first week of any "art film" ever shown in America.[6] Released in Sweden in 1967, Sjöman's film had become an unbelievable success in his home country (approximately 1.3 million of Sweden's 8 million citizens had seen the film). Barney Rosset, the owner of the Grove Press book publishing imprint, had paid $100,000 for American distribution rights, but in 1968, U. S. Customs officials had seized the film at the border and declared it an illegal, pornographic import. Rosset was no stranger to censorship battles, having been through the courts for the right to publish Henry Miller's *Tropic of Cancer*, William Burroughs's *Naked Lunch*, and D. H. Lawrence's *Lady Chatterley's Lover*. He successfully took his case to the U. S. Court of Appeals, and the film came to U. S. theaters in April 1969.

Curious arrived with much fanfare thanks to the publicity from the court case—and to early reviews, which only served to fan the fires of controversy. Norman Mailer declared it "one of the most important pictures I have ever seen in my life." Rex Reed declared it "vile and disgusting . . . a dirty movie . . . as good for you as drinking furniture polish," and called the director "a very sick Swede with an overwhelming ego and a fondness for photographing pubic hair." "Well," film writer Gary Giddins asks, "which do you think sold more tickets—Mailer's endorsement or the remark about pubic hair?"[7]

Audiences lined up in the more-permissive areas of the country to see *Yellow*, and the film broke all first-week records for so-called "art movies." New York's Cinema 57 Rendezvous drew just over $79,000 in the first week at $3 a ticket.[8] Reviewer John Nesbit remembers that when he was a college student in Champaign, Illinois, the local art house wouldn't show the film, so it played in the local porn theater.[9] As these viewers from "legitimate society" ventured into seedy movie houses for the first time, most were disappointed. Giddins reports, "When the crowds actually saw the picture, however, they felt cheated; pubic hair was in short supply, the sex was unerotic, and the running time mostly given over to a droll, Brechtian-Pirandellian, mock-vérité exploration of the chasm between the political and the personal."[10]

The film's plot revolves around Lena, an aspiring journalist and dabbling revolutionary who collects man-in-the-street interviews in Stockholm about class differences in society. As a mock documentary within a documentary, the film shows Lena Nyman as an actor being filmed by Sjöman himself, who plays the director-within-the-film. Sjöman uses stock footage of real-life figures such as Martin Luther King and Olof Palme, the leader of Sweden's Social Democrat movement, interspersed with questions from Lena to make it appear (sort of) as if she is interviewing them. She takes time out in between her interviews to lead pickets against the embassies of imperialists (the United States), fascists (Spain), and Communists (China), do topless yoga, and have sex on the balustrade of the royal palace.

Chief Judge J. Edward Lombard of the 2nd Court of Appeals declared, "Except for the sexual scenes in *I Am Curious (Yellow)*, the film was a continuous and unrelieved boredom."[11] Indeed, the scenes of sex and nudity are not especially sexy. (A young Roger Ebert would quip in his review, "They may not be sexy, but they are undeniably scenes."[12]) Even the full frontal shots of Lena while arguing with her lover serve more to expose her vulnerability than to satisfy any voyeuristic thrill. The scene that caused the most fuss was the one in which Lena kisses—or appears to kiss—the flaccid penis of her lover. (In arguing against its initial ban in America, the film's proponents pointed out that Lena's lips never actually make contact with the actor's genitalia.) Yet the legal and moral controversy surrounding the film was enough to make it one of the cinematic sensations of 1969.

Socially speaking, the film paved the way for a slew of censorbusting flicks. Giddins records that, "within a year or two, suburban theaters routinely programmed nudity-filled potboilers about nurses and stewardesses, soon to be followed by *Deep Throat*. Never again would audiences have to put up with socially redeeming values in the pursuit of pornography."[13]

❋ ❋ ❋

In John Cheever's 1969 novel *Bullet Park*, middle-class mother Nellie Nailles is shocked when she attends a play in Greenwich Village, and, in the course of the performance, one cast member turns his back to the audience and undresses. She fights the urge to walk out of the theater, telling herself that she "intended to be a modern woman and to come to terms with the world." The actor turns around and faces the audience, full frontal, and for Nellie this theatrical moment is "all true to life but some violent series of juxtapositions, concepts of propriety and her own natural excitability threw her into an emotional paroxysm that made her sweat. If these were merely the facts of life why should her eyes be riveted on his thick pubic brush from which hung, like a discouraged and unwatered flower, his principal member."

In a similar scene from Joseph McGrath's 1969 film, *The Magic Christian*, rich corporate executive Sir Guy Grand (Peter Sellers) and his adopted park vagrant (Ringo Starr) sit in the balcony at a performance of *Hamlet* as the actor in the title role, unexpectantly, begins to disrobe during his soliloquy. He shocks the upper-crust theatergoers in the front row by ending the scene in full frontal nudity—giving new meaning to the line about a "bare bodkin."

The arts had become a battleground on which conventional and conservative attitudes toward morality and decency clashed with increasingly liberal attitudes toward sex and nudity, and notions of "obscenity" were questioned like never before. For some, performative nudity signaled the end of American morality; for others, titillation became an act of artistic expression in and of itself. *Playboy* reported that Actors Equity had even found it necessary to establish a set of "rules and requirements regarding auditions and performances where nudity and acts of sexual nature are involved," including a stipulation that "actual sex acts during rehearsals or performances shall not be required of a performer."[14]

Even in its most explicit state, nudity on film was not "real." A naked body in a movie was not actually a naked body, of course, but a two-dimensional image—a representation—of a naked body that had once been naked in front of the camera, but which was now inaccessible in its corporal state to the viewer. On-stage nudity was quite another thing—a living, breathing, three-dimensional naked body before the eyes of a live audience. In March, *Newsweek* observed, "Only two seasons ago, in Robert Anderson's *You Know I Can't Hear You When the Water's Running*, the announced prospect of an actor's taking his clothes off drew gales of laughter. Today, nudity is an increasingly bare fact of theatrical life."[15] Even the otherwise progressive *Rolling Stone* joked in an issue late that summer, "Onstage nudity is getting out of hand."[16] It was the year of nudity onstage, and both on and off Broadway, live performances featuring nudity intrigued, titillated, and shocked audiences across the country.

Though not the first American play to feature nudity, *Hair* unquestionably did the most to initiate the stage-nudity craze, and it was the first production to include naked male and female actors together on a Broadway stage. After opening with a limited run at Joseph Papp's Public Theater in October 1967, *Hair: The American Tribal Love-Rock Musical* came to Broadway in a completely revised and recast version in the spring of 1968. In 1969, *Hair* grew into a national and international phenomenon, playing in theaters across the country, while the original Broadway cast recording topped the album charts and pop music groups scored hit records with covers of songs from the musical.

With lyrics by Gerome Ragni and James Rado, who also starred in the play, and music by Galt MacDermot, *Hair* was billed as the first "rock musical." Although a large part of its success was due to the fact that it was the first theatrical work to bring the sounds and rhythms of the younger generation to the stage, in retrospect, the music seems somewhat tame for something billed as a *rock* musical. Certainly none of the songs of *Hair* approached any of the heights of acid rock that had provided the unofficial soundtrack for the Summer of Love in 1967, let alone the increasingly varied genres—from jazz-rock fusion to proto-punk to heavy metal—that would identify 1969. Theater historian Barbara Lee Horn summarizes, "The score is not pure rock, but a confluence of jazz, blues, soul, country and western, raga and rock." Martin Gottfried called the blend, "middle-range rock," and Clive Barnes later wrote, "of course, *Hair* was not really a rock musical. It was intended for the tourists, for the parents."[17] In truth, the soundtrack has the sound and feel of how Madison Avenue might have scored its vision of the hippie generation. Nevertheless, with its pop melodies set to electric guitar, *Hair* was a far cry from the theater of *Oklahoma!, Kiss Me Kate*, and *Fiddler on the Roof.*

Even more so than the music, the story of *Hair* was founded in the morality of the new generation that Theodore Roszak named in his seminal 1969 study, *The Making of a Counter Culture.* Reflecting what Horn calls a "group-tribal activity searching for a new and meaningful way of life," the plot dealt with the younger generation's views on the Vietnam War, racial inequities, pollution, war, obscenity, psychedelic drugs, and sex. Set predominantly in the East Village, the action is centered around three characters—Claude, a draftee; Berger, a hippie and high school dropout; and Sheila, a college student and war protester—along with a supporting "tribe" consisting of a black hippie, an "ambisexual" hippie, a spiritual, pregnant chick, and a lost soul. On the other end of the cultural spectrum are Claude's parents; originated in Papp's theater as sympathetic characters who "attempted to bridge the generation gap," they evolved into more conservative authority figures and objects of ridicule—as stated in the song "I Got Life," figures stuck in an America two decades gone.[18]

The production's frenetic blocking and dance numbers were designed to break the fourth wall, literally introducing the audience into the world of the hippies. At the play's beginning, the cast appears scattered throughout the theater—in the balconies, in the orchestra, on the scaffolding. Before singing his ode to Donna, a sixteen-year-old virgin he'd lusted after and lost, the long-haired Berger finds a female audience member and sits in her lap, saying to her, "I know what you're thinking: Isn't he a cute one. What is it, a boy or a girl?"[19] At the conclusion of the final number, "The Flesh Failures / Let the Sun Shine In," audience members were pulled onstage to join the cast in a Bacchanalian dance.

The play's edgy themes sometimes resembled a checklist of incendiary shots from the cultural battlegrounds of the late sixties. In "Hashish," Berger leads the tribe in a song testifying to the merits of hash, cocaine, heroin, opium, and LSD. In the following number, "Sodomy," Woof warbles while rattling off the words *sodomy*, *fellatio*, *cunnilingus*, and *pederasty*, and then asks, "Father, why do these words sound so nasty?" before touting the joys of masturbation. As if enough taboos had not yet been broached, Hud, dressed like a medicine man, is carried to the stage by two white hippies and subverts racist slurs by proudly declaring for himself such labels as *colored, spade, black nigger, jungle bunny, jigaboo, coon, pickaninny, Mau Mau, Uncle Tom, Aunt Jemima, Little Black Sambo,* etc. The songs "Air," an indictment of pollution, and "Initials," in which LBJ takes the IRT and discovers the youth of the USA is on LSD, speaks to how the machines and discourse of the technological establishment are leading to social breakdown. "Walking in Space," a musical representation of psychedelic synesthesia, captures the mind-expanding euphoria of an acid trip and contrasts the beauty of the human mind and body with the ugliness of war that can bring an end to this beauty. Claude drops acid and the audience is treated to a hallucinated synopsis of American history.

It was just before intermission, at the end of "Be-In," when members of the cast disrobed entirely. They emerged from the scrim fully nude, covered by floral patterned lighting. In many ways, the nudity was the least-subversive element of the production. "People frequently took off their clothes at Be-Ins. It was part of the gesture of the times," said Tom O'Horgan, director of the Biltmore production. "This was a different kind of nudity [than was seen in] the nine million shows that followed and had to have a nude scene no matter what. The nudity was part of the freedom, part of the liberation."[20]

The combination of revolutionary (for Broadway) music, the hippie zeitgeist, and promised nudity made the show a hit at the Biltmore. "If we are in the midst of a generation revolution," wrote Irving Buchen in the fall 1969 issue of *The Journal of Popular Culture*, "then *Hair* may serve as one of those rare cultural midpoints for staking out an arc that seems to be pointing to new notions of morality, community and life-art styles."

If *Hair* was a somewhat watered-down, pop version of the hippie mythos, it also fed itself back into the popular culture. Numerous pop acts released renditions of songs from the musical, including four that placed records in the Top Five in 1969: the squeaky-clean Cowsills, who signed on as spokesgroup for the American Dairy Association in 1969 ("Hair"), Three Dog Night ("Easy to Be Hard"),

Oliver ("Good Morning Starshine"), and the Fifth Dimension, whose medley of "Aquarius / Let the Sun Shine In" went to number one. A one-year "birthday be-in" and concert for the musical was held at Wollman's Skating Rink in New York's Central Park on April 27, where producer Michael Butler received a gold record for sales of the Broadway cast album.

After he had obtained foreign rights to the play from Butler, executive producer Bertrand Castelli began to bring versions of the musical to countries throughout the world. In April 1969, the *New York Times* reported on the appearance of eighteen-year-old Princess Anne in the Shaftesbury Theatre audience in London. During the play's jubilant ending, the princess, dressed in a navy-blue pantsuit with a white blouse, joined cast and audience members onstage, flinging her arms and swinging her hips. Her spontaneous display raised the eyebrows of the royal family and showed just how far American youth culture had invaded the world zeitgeist that year. By October, productions of *Hair* were running in London, Paris, Copenhagen, Düsseldorf, Hamburg, Sydney, and even behind the Iron Curtain in Belgrade.

Back in the States, the third American company of *Hair* debuted at Chicago's Shubert Theater in October. The following month, an open call at Theater 80 at St. Mark's Place in New York drew more than 250 hopeful actors trying out for companies headed for Chicago, Toronto, Boston, and San Francisco. In December, *Playboy* published a photo essay on the "Girls of Hair," featuring (bare-breasted) actresses from productions of the musical being performed throughout the world.

Having returned to the New York production after taking the play to Los Angeles, Rado and Ragni were at the center of a mini-controversy when they were barred from the play in April by producer Michael Butler, who claimed that they had improvised too much without consulting him. Frank Gilroy, president of the drama guild, stepped in to help mediate the dispute. Rado, Ragni, and

Butler met at the Sheep Meadow in Central Park to settle their artistic differences, and the performers were allowed to rejoin the Biltmore production.

❊ ❊ ❊

At the opening of the second act of *Hair* (and just after the much-publicized nude scene), one of the characters mimics the imagined response of a hypothetical audience member: "We've seen the nude scene, Harry. Can we go home now?" Whereas the nude scene in *Hair* emerged as a spectacle that in some ways eclipsed the rest of the play, *Oh! Calcutta!*, the avant-garde theatrical revue that debuted at New York's Eden Theater in June, made no pretense of being about anything besides pushing the envelope of nudity. At the end of *Oh! Calcutta!*, as the cast members take turns voicing hypothetical responses from the audience, one apt response was, "This makes *Hair* look like *The Sound of Music.*"

The play was the brainchild of theater critic Kenneth Tynan, who enlisted the help of writers such as Samuel Beckett, Sam Shepard, Edna O'Brien, Jules Feiffer, and even John Lennon to write sketches for the revue. (Its name is taken from a painting by French artist Clovis Trouille, itself a pun on the phrase *O quel cul t'as!* ("What an ass you have!") Like *Hair*, *Oh! Calcutta!* grew from an off-Broadway spectacle into a cultural sensation thanks in large part to its use of full stage nudity. But while *Hair* featured a brief scene of skin-showing, *Oh! Calcutta!* featured rampant full-frontal nudity, and its sexual scenarios were much more explicit than anything *Hair* had ever approached.

Directed by Jacques Levy and producer Hillard Elkins, who described the play as a "kind of sexual Rorschach test,"[21] *Oh! Calcutta!* got right down to business with its burlesque opening, in which individual cast members improvised dance moves while discarding their robes. What followed was an uneven mix of skits united by the common theme of the sexual negotiations between men and women: A man and a woman leave a swingers' party and pretend to be Jack and Jill in a children's playroom, but the scene turns from corny innocence to absurdist violence when the frustrated "Jack" rapes "Jill," who then goes comatose. A lothario tries to loosen up his sexually prudish girlfriend. A plotting Casanova lures a coy woman into his lair and traps her in restraints, only to find out she's not as "pure" as she had seemed to be. Cast members sing anonymous letters to the editor in which the authors confess their sexual perversities. A sex study degenerates into a no-holds-barred farce. A son shocks his hayseed father into a heart attack with the details of his sexual peccadilloes. A newcomer is invited to sit in on a futuristic masturbation circle in which the individuals' fantasies are projected onto a screen, only to infect the rest of the group with fantasies of bestiality. In the most overtly sadomasochistic skit, a lecturer contrasts the behavior of a naked woman from a totalitarian state suspended against her will in a net with a woman from a democratic society bowing silently prostrate, willingly offering up her rear for punishment. Keeping the self-conscious sense of humor into the final song-and-dance number, the cast members recite imagined audience questions ("How come none of the guys have hard-ons?" "What do the women do when they get their periods?") and exclamations ("If they showed this in Washington, Agnew would shit!"). The production would remain at the Eden Theater for more than 700 performances, and then in 1971, the Belasco began a run of more than 600 performances.

Hair and *Oh! Calcutta!* were merely the most publicized examples of the theatrical trend for pushing the carnal envelope. Director Richard Schechner staged *Dionysus in '69*, his orgiastic adaptation of Euripides' *Bacchae*, in a Greenwich Village garage; the men in the cast were dressed in black jockstraps and the women were, as reported by *Time*, "braless beneath their shirts, and on some nights topless, if they are in the mood to improvise." The off-Broadway play

Geese included nude homosexual seduction scenes with both men and women—and played to packed houses. In a small East Village theater, the play *Che!* included simulated sex acts, some in the nude. One Saturday night in late March, actor Paul Georgiou, who portrayed the president of the United States in the play, arrived at the Free Store Theater in a Cadillac limousine and emerged nude. After the play's performance on its second night, police raided Free Store and arrested the cast, playwright, director, and even the production staff on charges of "consensual sodomy, public lewdness and obscenity."[22] In May, police returned and arrested cast members on the charge of public lewdness, and playwright Lennox Raphael was arrested for obstructing police.

❋ ❋ ❋

In conservative Miami, however, the citizens were not so ready to join the naked revolution. The Doors were booked for the Dinner Key Auditorium in Miami on March 1. Their increasingly erratic lead singer and mystical lyricist, Jim Morrison, arrived late from New Orleans and drunk off his ass. Bearded, he looked more like a late-sixties Jesus freak than the serpentine sex symbol of past years. "As we descended the stairs, it felt like entering a sauna—Dante's Inferno," drummer John Densmore later wrote. "Later I was to find out that there were over thirteen thousand people stuffed into [a] place meant to hold seven thousand."[23] The promoters had oversold the event, and to make matters worse, the stage was poorly constructed. The atmosphere was ripe for a meltdown.

The band slugged through its first few songs, then went into the theatrically charged number "Five to One." In the midst of the song, Morrison screeched and then began yelling at the crowd:

> You're all a bunch of fuckin' idiots. Lettin' people tell you what you're gonna do. Lettin' people push you around. How

long do you think it's gonna last? How long are you gonna let it go on? How long are you gonna let 'em push you around? How long? Maybe you like it. Maybe you love bein' pushed around. Maybe you love it. Maybe you love gettin' your face stuck in shit. Maybe you love gettin' pushed around. You love it, don't you? You love it. You're all a bunch of slaves. Bunch of slaves. You're all a bunch of slaves, letting everybody people push you around.

Then he yelled over and over, "What are you gonna do about it? What are you gonna do?"[24]

Morrison had been inspired by a performance he'd recently attended at the Living Theatre on the campus of the University of Southern California. The Living Theatre hosted a confrontational performance group that enacted the theories of the Theatre of Cruelty school. Performing nearly nude, the members would leave the stage and climb the aisles and over audience members, shouting revolutionary tracts. Their methods spoke to the loose-cannon lead singer from The Doors. Now liquored up in the conservative, southern city of Miami, Morrison was confronting his audience.

Hey, I'm not talkin' about no revolution. I'm not talkin' about no demonstration. I'm not talkin' about gettin' out [on] the street. I'm talkin' about having some fun. I'm talkin' about dancin'. I'm talkin' about love your neighbor 'til it hurts. I'm talkin' about grab your friend. I'm talkin' about love. I'm talkin' about some love. I'm talkin' about some love. I'm talkin' about some love. I'm talkin' about some love. Love, love, love, love, love, love, love. Grab your fuckin' friend and love him.[25]

The crowd grew rowdy. The band attempted to play through it all, but Densmore and guitarist Robby Krieger eventually gave up. As they started to leave, the left portion of the stage made a cracking noise and then sank several inches. Somebody jumped onstage and poured champagne on Morrison. He took off his shirt and called for the audience to get naked; many female audience members did, tossing blouses and skirts and bras and underwear to the floor. Morrison began to taunt the crowd: "You want to see my cock, don't you? That's what you came for, isn't it?"[26] He'd taken off his shirt and started to wave it in front of his pants like a bullfighter. More and more people began taking to the stage. Densmore and Krieger climbed the stairs up to the balcony as Morrison led the crowd in a snake dance.

Later, some would testify that he had indeed taken his penis out, though this was never conclusively proven. If any crimes were committed by Morrison that night, the cops who provided security for the evening seemed oblivious to it. Some even asked him for his autograph. Two days later, however, a review by Larry Mahoney in the *Miami Herald* declared, "The hypnotically erotic Morrison, flaunting the laws of obscenity, indecent exposure and incitement to riot, could only stir a minor mob scene toward the end of his Saturday night performance."[27] Fans came forward with bootleg recordings of the night, and a photo of Morrison kneeling in front of Krieger playing guitar surfaced. Densmore remembers, "They insisted that Jim was giving Robby head."[28] On March 5, the city of Miami issued a warrant for Morrison's arrest on a felony charge of lewd and lascivious behavior, as well as misdemeanor accounts of indecent exposure, public profanity, and public drunkenness. After returning from a band vacation in Jamaica, Morrison returned to Miami and surrendered to FBI agents, and was then freed on bail. "Six guys and girls are naked onstage every night in *Hair* and nobody calls the cops," he told the press.[29]

In the fallout from the arrest, concert promoters throughout the country canceled tour dates with the band, and radio stations stopped playing their songs. Two weeks after the Miami incident, thirty thousand people filled the Orange Bowl for a "Teens for Decency" rally, a Catholic-initiated demonstration against Morrison, the Doors, rock music, hippies, Communists, sexual permissiveness (including sex ed) . . . everything that was deemed godless and unpatriotic in 1969. Jackie Gleason, Kate Smith, and Anita Bryant attended, and Nixon sent a letter of support.

In November, the band would return to Miami for Morrison's trial. Prosecutor Terry McWilliams accused Morrison of starting a riot by calling for a revolution. Some local Jesus freaks testified that they'd seen Morrison's penis; other witnesses said he'd merely stuck his finger out the fly of his pants. The judge asked Doors keyboardist Ray Manzarek if he had seen Morrison's organ.

"No, I didn't, your honor, but I play the organ," Manzarek said, and laughter broke out in the courtroom.[30]

The trial would be completed in the fall of 1970. Morrison was found guilty of indecent exposure and obscene language, but not guilty of lewdness, lascivious behavior, or drunkenness. "The jury got the whole thing backwards," Densmore says. "Jim was drunk as a skunk, but he did not pull his dick out. So much for justice."[31] Manzarek agrees, and has said that people who claimed to see Morrison's penis had done so on the power of suggestion, or even mass hysteria. Judge Murray Goodman sentenced Morrison to six months and a $500 fine, but the singer was released pending an appeal.

The appeal was still pending when Morrison died in Paris on July 3, 1971.

7. A Whole New Ball Game

Major League Baseball avoids a strike and begins the first year of divisional play with four new franchises and a new commissioner; the Cubs jump out to first place while the Mets look to break from their losing tradition.

For the 1969 baseball season and thereafter, the home park of baseball's Washington Senators, formerly known as D.C. Stadium, was rechristened the Robert F. Kennedy Memorial Stadium. The team also had a new man at the helm. Ted Williams, the former Boston Red Sox slugger who'd earned his reputation as the best pure hitter in the history of the game, took over as manager for the struggling team at a reported annual salary of $65,000. The "Splendid Splinter" looked to improve the fortunes of the hapless Senators, who had finished in tenth place in 1968, thirty-one games under .500. "It's a whole new ball game in '69!" Williams declared to reporters.[1]

Washington's "Capital Punisher," leftfielder Frank Howard, would wage a powerful campaign that season. A giant among most baseball players of the era, the muscular, six-foot-seven All-Star slugger belted forty-eight home runs and knocked in 111 runs despite the cavernous dimensions of RFK Stadium. With the team pulling out a number of late-inning wins behind Dennis Higgins and Darold Knowles, who either won or saved a combined forty-eight games out of the bullpen, the franchise tallied its first winning season with a record of 86-76. Washington finished in fourth place, a distant twenty-three games out of first place, but its record represented a turnaround of forty-one games from the previous season, a feat for which Williams was named the American League's Manager of the Year.

As one legend returned to the stage, another was leaving it. Mickey Mantle announced his retirement in early March, calling an end to an eighteen-year career in which the Great Plains farm boy turned metropolitan sports hero won three MVPs and played in twelve World Series for the New York Yankees. Long plagued by injuries, Mantle had undergone surgery on five separate occasions to remove torn cartilage from his knees and bone chips from the shoulder of his throwing arm, and for eight seasons he'd bound his leg from ankle to thigh with seven-foot strips of foam-rubber bandages. The sight of Mantle rounding the bases after hitting his 500th home run two seasons earlier had been as painful to fans as it had been jubilant, and in 1968 he'd hit just .237 with 18 home runs in 144 games. "I can't hit when I need to. I can't steal when I want to. I can't score from second when I have to," Mantle said upon declaring his decision to hang up his spikes. "It was time to quit trying. I can no longer deliver what the fans expect of me."[2]

For millions of baseball fans in and outside of New York, the hard-hitting, hard-living Mantle had embodied the golden age of baseball. "Mantle is one of the last of a breed. The super-player is dying out," commented one writer. "Perhaps there can be no more superstars when players are more concerned with their pensions than they are with playing the game."[3]

The game faced a crossroads. As the decade neared its end, many sports fans felt that football, or even basketball, threatened to replace baseball as America's pastime. Whereas those sports offered the excitement of hard-hitting tackles, bombs, fast breaks, and back-and-forth shoot-outs, the average Major League Baseball game offered about as much scoring as your typical soccer match. By the late 1960s, as teams plated fewer and fewer runs, it became obvious that the caliber of Major League pitchers had far exceeded that of the league's hitters. In 1968, seven pitchers gave up an average of fewer than two runs per nine innings, led by Bob Gibson of the St. Louis Cardinals and his microscopic 1.12 earned run average. In July, eighteen Los Angeles Dodgers struck out in one game against Houston's Don Wilson, while Cleveland's Luis Tiant struck out nineteen Minnesota Twins in one ten-inning game. Don Drysdale of the Dodgers set a record by going fifty-eight and two-thirds consecutive innings without allowing a run, and Gibson set a World Series record by striking out seventeen Detroit Tigers in Game One. Meanwhile, only *three* hitters in the majors—future Hall of Famers Billy Williams, Hank Aaron, and Carl Yastrzemski—finished with batting averages above .300. In the 1968 All-Star Game held in the Houston Astrodome, baseball's best hitters had managed a total of just eight hits and produced just one run (when Willie Mays scored on a ground-ball double play in the first inning for the National League). In a culture where success is equated with scoring—either literally or figuratively—baseball seemed to have fallen behind the times.

Fearing the demise of the nation's pastime, Major League owners looked for a change. They forced William Eckert to retire from his post as baseball commissioner and walk away from the remaining three years on his contract. Eckert had earned public rebuke by not canceling games immediately following the assassination of Martin Luther King Jr. and Bobby Kennedy in 1968, but perhaps more crucially, owners were not confident that he would be able to handle a threatened players' strike. In his place, the owners hired Bowie Kuhn, a distant relative of frontier folklore hero Jim Bowie, who had served as legal counsel for the owners for nearly two decades. Although many owners wanted to see Kuhn stay on permanently, he was essentially hired on a trial basis with a one-year contract for a salary of $100,000.

Ironically, one of the first orders of business for the new commissioner—who would later say, "I believe in the Rip Van Winkle Theory: that a man from 1910 must be able to wake up after being asleep for sixty years, walk into a ballpark, and understand baseball perfectly"—was to appoint a committee to look into modernizing the game.[4] As *Time* opined, "The game itself must be streamlined to attract the action-mad modern fan."[5]

Baseball needed a facelift. It adopted a new logo designed by future comic book artist James Sherman to commemorate the 100th anniversary of the first professional touring team, the same logo (the abstract, white silhouette of a batter set against fields of blue and red) used by the game today. More important, the owners voted to tilt the playing field, metaphorically, more toward the offense. A new rule lowered the pitching mound at every stadium, officially from fifteen inches (though some stadiums were rumored to have mounds as high as twenty inches) to ten, thus limiting the downward leverage that a pitcher could generate.

The owners also voted to experiment with a new "designated pinch-hitter rule" in the spring's exhibition games. The rule allowed teams to slot a more proficient hitter specialist into the pitcher's spot in the lineup throughout the game. Not all managers embraced the change. "It takes the managership away from me. It ties my hands," said Leo Durocher, complaining about the loss of strategy involved in the selective pinch hitting that forces a pitcher to leave the game according to the traditional rules. "These rules are going in my wastebasket." Joe Cronin, president of the American League, said, "The battle of wits between managers, which I'm sure the spectators enjoy, would be virtually eliminated if these rules were permanently adopted."[6] (Ironically, the American League adopted the rule in

1973; today, National League teams also use designated hitters during interleague and World Series games played at American League stadiums.)

In addition, the league also expanded for the first time since 1962, when the New York Mets and Houston Astros had joined the National League. Owners approved the addition of four new squads to the majors in 1969: the Kansas City Royals and Seattle Pilots in the American League, and in the National League, the San Diego Padres and the Montreal Expos—the first "non-American" team in the majors. Now with twenty-four Major League teams in existence, both leagues were divided into two divisions, East and West. (Ignoring basic geography, the National League designated the St. Louis Cardinals and Chicago Cubs to the Eastern Division while placing the Cincinnati Reds and Atlanta Braves in the West.) Previously, a pennant race had been just that—a race for the pennant symbolic of a league championship. Now, teams would play 162 games merely for a division title and the chance to play in a five-game "pennant series," with the winners to meet in the World Series.

Normally, professional sports leagues add franchises when they reach new levels of popularity and marketability, but in this case, the 1969 expansion was enacted by Major League owners so that they could avoid entanglements from the federal government under the Sherman Antitrust Act, which prohibited monopolies. All would not be smooth sailing, however; for the first time in the sport's ninety-three-year history, the Major League Baseball Players Association boycotted the opening of spring training.

Despite Kuhn's Rip Van Winkle theory, the game of baseball was changing along with the rest of American society. St. Louis announcer Jack Buck later described a representative scene at O'Hare Airport in Chicago after the Cardinals arrived for a series with the Cubs during the 1969 season:

> The players were carrying music, wearing sandals and T-shirts. One of the players was wearing Levis without

undershorts and had a hole in the seat of his pants. I remember thinking, 'These are the Cardinals?' Almost all of them had long hair, some wore earrings. Other ballclubs were just as motley looking, depending on their leadership and the control the manager and owner had over the players. They were at the age to be rebellious, and they wanted to join in the activities going on around them. They wanted more freedom, and that's when Marvin Miller entered the picture with the players' union and started putting pressure on the owners.[7]

The realm of business, governmental regulations, and labor relations had crept into baseball. Marvin Miller, who had been elected executive director of the Major League Baseball Players Association in 1966, negotiated the first collective bargaining agreement in professional sports. But as spring training neared, Miller and the Players Association stood firm on sought-after points regarding the players' pension fund, among others; the players wanted $6.5 million and the owners were offering $5.3 million. "Anytime you can get a pension at 45, I'd like to be in on it," argued Minnesota Twins president Calvin Griffith, apparently forgetting the average length of the professional sports career. "I have to wait until I'm 65 before I can get a pension," he quipped.[8]

Late in February, the Players Association and baseball ownership agreed to a "seven-point plan" to preserve the beginning of the regular season. The terms included (1) players qualifying for retirement after four years of service instead of five; (2) for ten-year players, a $100 increase in monthly benefits at age fifty; (3) early retirement at age forty-five; (4) the establishment of a dental program; (5) an increase in life insurance to $50,000 for active players and $25,000 for presently inactive players; (6) improvements in disability, maternity, widows', and other health-care benefits; and (7) the payment of lump sums representing a portion of benefits to retired players.[9]

❀ ❀ ❀

Although Jerry Grote, the young New York Mets catcher who had started the 1968 All-Star Game, supported the players' boycott, he had reported to training camp anyway to honor his contract with the team. "If it had been any one of the 23 other teams," he said, "I wouldn't have signed. But this team has treated me well."[10]

The Mets, though, had not treated their fans very well during the first seven years of the team's existence. Baseball fans in the Big Apple had embraced the ironically dubbed "Amazin' Mets" as lovable losers. Lovable? Perhaps. Losers? They were the dictionary definition of a losing pro sports franchise in the 1960s. In the team's inaugural season, the Mets established a mark in futility by losing 120 games. They finished in the National League cellar in five of their first six seasons. In 1968, team chairman M. Donald Grant brought in former Brooklyn Dodgers star first baseman Gil Hodges and (more recently) Washington Senators manager to take over dugout duties for the team. In Hodges's first year at the helm, he guided the Mets to their best finish, with seventy-three wins— twelve games better than their previous high, but still sixteen games under .500.

Yet even this does not fully describe how bad the team was. Not only had the Mets never finished with a winning record, they had also never even been *two games* above .500 at any point during any of their first seven seasons. In fact, the team had never even enjoyed the distinction of being *one* game above .500 past the *first week* of any previous season.

Going into the 1969 season, there was little reason to believe the Mets would even make a run at .500, let alone challenge for the division title. Key positions in the team's lineup were unsure. The leading candidates for the corner infield positions at first and third and in the outfield—where players were usually expected to be productive hitters—impressed few fans. First basemen Ed Kranepool and

Art Shamsky had both hit under .240 in 1968, and the best options for third base, rookie Wayne Garrett, veteran Ed Charles, and utility infielder Kevin Collins, were so underwhelming that Gil Hodges wanted to convert rookie outfielder Amos Otis into a third baseman. (Otis resisted, and he was sent back to the minors early in the season.) Centerfielder Tommie Agee was coming off a miserable season in which he had hit a lowly .217, and rightfielder Ron Swoboda had yet to break twenty home runs or sixty RBIs in any of his first four seasons in the majors. Meanwhile, defensive-minded catcher Grote had little power, and the team's nominal second baseman, Al Weis, had hit an anemic .172 in 1968. The Mets offense was so weak that Bud Harrelson, a superior defensive shortstop who hit just .236 for his career, sometimes served as the team's leadoff hitter.

But the one thing that the team *did* have was pitching—good, young pitching, and lots of it—headed by Tom Seaver and Jerry Koosman. Seaver had won sixteen games to earn the National League Rookie of the Year Award in 1967, and he followed with sixteen more wins in 1968. That season, Koosman appeared on the scene with a sparkling nineteen-win debut season. Other young arms in camp in 1969 included rookie Gary Gentry, second-year starter Jim McAndrew, and two pitchers who could both start and relieve: quirky, left-handed screwball specialist Tug McGraw, and a young, right-handed fireballer from Texas named Lynn Nolan Ryan.

Grote, the man who caught them, ranked with the young Johnny Bench as the best in the game. Teammate Art Shamsky later told author Stanley Cohen: "Jerry Grote was the best catcher I've ever seen. I played a little with Johnny Bench, and he wasn't too far behind, but Grote was the best."[11] Grote was the best at gunning down runners on steal attempts, but more important, he was a master at coaching the Mets' staff. And at spring training in 1969, he liked what he saw in the team's stockpile of live, young arms. In fact, he was so enthusiastic that he told Long Island sportswriter Jack Lang that the Mets had a chance to win it all.[12]

The beginning of the Mets' 1969 season showed few signs of what was to come. They lost the season opener to the Expos—a team that had never played a game—and dropped seven of their first ten games. Aside from leftfielder Cleon Jones, who got off to a torrid start hitting over .400 in April, the Mets offense was punchless. After losing the first two games of a four-game weekend series in Chicago at the beginning of May, the Mets stood at 9-14, eight games behind the Cubs.

In the preseason, most commentators had looked to the Cubs as having the only realistic shot of dethroning the defending National League champion Cardinals in the National League East. Chicago's lineup featured a virtual All-Star infield, with veteran sluggers Ron Santo and Ernie Banks on the corners and young stars Glenn Beckert and Don Kessinger up the middle. Added to that were the sweet-swinging leftfielder and future Hall of Famer Billy Williams, a productive run producer behind the plate in catcher Randy Hundley, and an experienced pitching staff led by Ferguson Jenkins, Bill Hands, and Ken Holtzman. Fan favorite Banks declared giddily, "The Cubs are gonna shine in '69."[13]

Carrying high hopes, 41,000 fans had turned out to Wrigley Field on opening day—the team's largest crowd for a season opener in forty years.[14] The Cubbies won their first four games of the season. After Jenkins lost a game to Mudcat Grant and the Expos, Chicago rebounded the following day with a dramatic 7–6 win over Montreal with three runs in the ninth inning. When Banks knocked in the game winner with a bloop single to left field, a good portion of the 25,000-plus crowd that Sunday "stormed the field in a frenzy, similar to a World Series victory," writes Doug Feldmann. "It was a raucous display that Cub observers had not seen, it was believed, since Don Cardwell threw his no-hitter for the North Siders in 1960."[15]

The North Side of Chicago was a fun place to be in the spring of 1969. The Cubs won eleven of their first twelve games, and at the end of April stood two games up in first place. After the "getaway" game to end the series in Philadelphia, some members of the team left a note in the visitors' clubhouse for the defending World Series champion Detroit Tigers, who would be coming to Philly for an exhibition game on May 5: "See you in the World Series if you can make it."[16]

The series before that, the Cubs had taken three of four games on the Mets' home turf at Shea Stadium. The Mets paid a visit to Wrigley at the beginning of May and promptly lost the first two games of the four-game series. Chicago could have left New York for dead with a sweep or even just a split of the Sunday doubleheader on May 4, but here the Mets showed their first signs of life in the division. Starters Seaver and McGraw both went nine innings and won 3-2 decisions, with Ken Boswell recording a combined five hits on the day. Back in April, Seaver and Ryan had pitched back-to-back shutouts in Montreal, but that feat had been accomplished against an expansion lineup of castoffs and also-rans. The Seaver and McGraw victories came against a first-place team, and although the team left Wrigley still three games under .500, the doubleheader sweep served as a parting shot to a Cubs team that looked to be the team to beat in the division.

Encouraged, the Mets began to creep closer and closer to the .500 mark. On May 21, Seaver shut out National League West leading Atlanta, and the Mets lineup scored five runs off Braves staff ace Phil Niekro. With the win, New York's record improved to 18-18, marking the latest point in any season the franchise had not had a losing record. In the locker room after the game, many team members celebrated as if they had just pulled into first place. Seaver, emerging as the team leader, remained stoic, telling the reporters who had assembled to write about the miraculous achievement that ".500 is nothing to celebrate."[17]

Nor would it be easy to hold on to. Looking as if they were not able to handle even this modicum of success, the Mets lost their next five games, and dropped back into fourth place in the five-team division. When a young team—especially one with no record of success—falls into a rut like this, it often stays there. But in the spring of 1969, the Mets would not only show that they possessed the character to rebound, but also that they were on the verge of one of those special seasons that franchises only dream about. Beginning with a 1–0 shutout of the Padres on May 28 at Shea, the team rolled off the longest winning streak in team history. Seaver won his next three games, including the 5–2 victory over the Dodgers on June 3 that brought the Mets' record to 24-23—the franchise's first winning record past the month of April—and suddenly the Mets found themselves in second place in the East.

The following day, rookie Jack DiLauro got a surprise start and responded by delivering nine innings of shutout baseball against Los Angeles. But the Mets also were unable to score any runs off Dodgers starter Bill Singer, who struck out ten through nine innings. Neither team scored until the bottom of the fifteenth, when Wayne Garrett singled to center with Tommie Agee on first. As centerfielder Willie Davis charged the ball, it skipped through his legs and went all the way to the wall, and those of the 31,000 fans who had stayed into the late hours of the night cheered as Agee came all the way around to score the winning run.

New York went on to win the first games of its West Coast road trip, bringing their record to 29-23. But the Mets were still far behind the Cubs, who threatened to run away with the division. At the midpoint of the season in early July, Chicago had an eight-game lead in the division over the Mets, whom most commentators figured to fade in the second half of the season. The Cubs would send their entire infield—including Ron Santo, who had sixteen home runs and a league-leading seventy-three RBI at the halfway point—along with Ray Hundley to the All-Star Game at RFK Stadium that summer. Fergie Jenkins and Ken Holtzman were both on pace for twenty-win seasons, and Bill Hands, Dick Selma, and Phil Regan each had won nine games. Overjoyed Cubs fans read stories of what the players' wives would buy with their husbands' playoff bonuses. Chicago manager Leo Durocher said, "The way I see it, the only way we can lose is if we beat ourselves."[18]

8. Poison Ivy

The Harvard student strike and the armed standoff at Cornell rocked the Ivy League . . . and a small North Dakota town is nearly wiped off the face of the map during spring break.

When the calendar turned to spring, young men's fancies turned to revolution. The increasingly radical spirit of young people on college campuses was echoed by the American release of Lindsay Anderson's *If . . . .* The film stars Malcolm McDowell as Mick Travis, one of three British prep school students whose nonconformist manners cause them to be targeted by their betters within the school community, the senior "Whips." Allowed free rein over the school by an aloof headmaster, the Whips inflict such forms of abuse on the students as caning, forced cold showers, and the practice of "fagging"—senior students selecting effeminate underclassmen to act as their servants, with intimations of buggery never far behind. The prep school community is portrayed as a microcosm of the social establishment, with religious instruction and military training conflated as "God and country" indoctrination.

Travis the teen iconoclast hangs posters of Lenin and other revolutionaries in his room and spouts lines from anarchist tracts: "There's no such thing as a wrong war. Violence and revolution are the only pure acts. . . . One man can change the world with a bullet in the right place." He and his roommate Johnny (David Wood) sneak out of school, steal a motorcycle, and romance a local waitress

(Christine Noonan); their other roommate, Wallace (Richard Warwick), becomes attached to the underclassman whose pretty-boy looks have the Whips fighting over him.

The stodginess and rigidity of the academic setting render the film's end especially shocking. While performing work duty as punishment, the rebellious students discover an arsenal of weapons on campus. During the annual Speech Day "festivities," the students set a fire underneath the church that forces everyone outside into the central courtyard. From atop a building opposite the church, the three roommates and their two romantic partners fire guns and mortars into the courtyard. Much like the scene of McDowell's animalistic seduction of Noonan (or vice versa), the courtyard carnage is edited so as to imply the action takes place in a dreamlike state—an extreme fantasy of prep-school revenge and anarchy. The headmaster (Peter Jeffrey) steps forward and calls for the students to end the bloodbath, at which point Noonan—a sexy, cinematic Bernardine Dohrn—carefully draws a bead and shoots him squarely between the eyes.

❊ ❊ ❊

In 1969, campus violence would spread to all areas of the Academy. Just before dawn on April 9, five hundred Students for a Democratic Society (SDS) members and antiwar demonstrators marched to the home of Harvard University president Nathan Pusey on Quincy Street, a short distance from Harvard Yard. They chanted "Smash ROTC" and "ROTC must go," and then marched toward the Charles River. As they passed by Lowell House, some students on the third floor poured buckets of water on them and cursed them out.

In the hour after the noon church bells rang out across Harvard Yard, between 250 and 300 students and others entered University Hall yelling "Fight! Fight!" and took over the building. When English instructor Roger Rosenblatt exited Sever Hall after his class on

Wallace Stevens, he saw the red-and-black banner of the SDS hanging from the second-floor window of University. Students leaned out of the windows, and one yelled into a bullhorn, rallying the students in the courtyard. Across the yard, the sounds of The Beatles' "Revolution" blared out from the window of the freshman dorm.

The protesters—long-haired, dressed in jeans and T-shirts, mostly members of the SDS and the Progressive Labor group—had taken over the administration building to protest the Harvard administration's connection to the Vietnam War. A group had gone to the second floor and confronted college deans Franklin Ford and Fred Glimp, telling them to leave the building or else they would be forcibly removed.

Glimp told one of the protesters, "Get out of this building now."

The student responded, "You don't have the authority to tell me anything."

Downstairs, dean of students Robert Watson told the occupiers, "You have no right to be in this building. I am ordering you to leave or face discipline."

"We've taken the building; now get the fuck out of here," he was told.[1]

Some of the deans were roughed up as they were escorted out of the building. Burris Young saw a student man-handling a colleague who was in his sixties and had a bad back. "Don't bend him over, you son of a bitch!" Young yelled at the student. The dean did a double take and realized the young man was one of his former students. "What are you doing?" Young asked him.

"Burris, I have to," the student responded.

"Until then, we had never seen any rough stuff at Harvard," Young later reflected. "We were so *innocent*."[2]

But Harvard's innocence had not been lost overnight. In the fall 1966 semester, student demonstrations broke out in protest of a campus visit by secretary of defense Robert McNamara. In the fall of 1968, a Dow Chemical Company recruiter was held prisoner in a

Mallinckrodt Laboratory classroom by students protesting Dow Chemical's profiting off the sale of napalm to the U. S. government. That September, a marine who had gone AWOL sought sanctuary in the Divinity School Chapel, where Divinity students chained themselves to him in support. In October, Nobel Prize winner James Watson admitted that he had participated in a presidential panel that researched biological and chemical warfare.[3]

Things had heated up in the winter of 1969 just after the students returned to campus for the spring 1969 semester. In the first week of February, seven hundred people attended a faculty-sponsored meeting to discuss the role of the military in the university community. In March, a former Columbia University student named King Collins led a number of protesters as they took over a class on social relations. Days later, they entered Eliot House, stripped naked, and tossed their clothes in the laundry room washing machines, symbolically airing the school's dirty laundry.[4]

Following the takeover on April 9, Pusey—who had a reputation for being distant and patrician, even smug—issued a statement, asking, "Can anyone believe the Harvard SDS demands are made seriously?"[5]

But serious they were. Eventually, all members of the administration were expelled from University Hall by the demonstrators. The students sat down on folding chairs and enjoyed their revolutionary glow. (Ironically, the same students who employed rough tactics in physically removing the deans voted not to deface the walls of the building or to smoke pot; when someone crayoned FUCK AUTHORITY on the wall of Glimp's office, the others attempted to cover it with white spray paint.) Historian Michael Kazin, then with the SDS, remembered: "Mainly the atmosphere was fun. But it was more than an adolescent rebellion. We did not aim to simply desecrate the temple. We were fighting a war to stop a war."[6]

The occupiers issued a list of demands, including the abolishment of officer training programs, replacing ROTC scholarships with regular scholarships, and (in an effort to align themselves with the blue-collar community of Cambridge) the ceasing of tearing down university-owned slums, the rolling back of rent for Cambridge housing, and the formation of a Black Studies department. Later that week, an underground Boston paper called *Old Mole* published files that had been "liberated" by the occupiers and revealed ties between the Harvard faculty, the CIA, State Department, and the Defense Department. Under the headline READING THE MAIL OF THE RULING CLASS, the article announced, "The common style of corporate chieftains, warmakers and Harvard's elite is no accident: many prestigious Harvard professors and administrators are deacons of the church of American empire. Their hands are bloody. The work they do ends in the murder of millions and the looting of the resources of the world. Official Harvard is a dynamo of the imperialist machine."[7]

The student revolution had come to the nation's oldest and most prestigious university. It was a community of ivy and tweed, and as Roger Rosenblatt remembers in his memoir of the unrest, "As late as 1969, students in the Houses were still required to wear ties and jackets in the dining halls at lunch." He notes, however, that "Many of them complied with the rule. Others who did not were spoken to. And while it was generally recognized that this formality was antiquated, its symbolism remained intact. By the end of the sixties, there were students who did not bother to wear a shirt in the dining halls. One cannot overestimate the sense of social deterioration felt by many of the older faculty members when it became clear that fair Harvard would no longer dress at Brooks Brothers."[8]

A Harvard senior at the time, Al Gore walked by University Hall "feeling a swirl of emotions. I remember fringe statements on the left that held that violence was justified, but I don't know that many of us were swayed to the left. We had sympathy for the cause but not the tactics."[9] Martin Perez, an assistant professor and future editor in chief of *The New Republic*, said, "I went over to University Hall to gawk. And I remember having a thought about civility. I was thinking that it would be very hard for any teacher, ever again, to get automatic and reflexive respect—the sort of respect you and I gave teachers. I thought this was a bad thing. I also think that the sight of the takeover was the beginning of my turn politically, from left to right."[10]

For the first time in the university's 333-year history, the university called police onto the campus. Just before 5:00 A.M. on April 10, three buses of troops pulled into Harvard Square, and some four hundred local and state policemen emerged in riot gear. Resembling the showdown between police and protesters in Chicago during the 1968 Democratic Convention, police who hailed from working-class, Irish families faced off against the sons and daughters of the privileged elite. As Rosenblatt describes, the incident unleashed "at least two centuries of town-gown hatred." The descendants of immigrants who had faced "No Irish Need Apply" practices felt that they had "been treated like the servants they, in fact, were by generations of rich Harvard boys who lived on the Gold Coast."[11] The scene turned predictably ugly. The officers warned the students to vacate the building in five minutes, and, when the students failed to do so, the police charged the building with a battering ram and attacked the occupiers with clubs and mace. In the melee, a student in a wheelchair was beaten. (Future *Crossfire* commentator Michael Kinsley, a freshman that semester, later suggested the student was placed there in order to create anti-police sentiment.[12]) In all, 196 students, including 50 women from nearby sister school Radcliffe, were hauled off to jail.[13]

The SDS had not been universally supported by the student body. Members of the campus Right, and those who were simply put off by the radical tactics of the demonstrators, openly taunted them and called for the SDS to leave campus. Kirkpatrick Sale remembers, "Conservative groups at many schools felt free for the first time to form their own groups in explicit opposition to SDS without general disapprobation, and at a number of schools . . . open fights broke out between the two. Moderate students denounced SDS in a way that would have been unthinkable just two years earlier."[14]

But once again, police presence united a student body that had been divided over the revolutionary tactics. Rosenblatt wrote, "The actions of the police had swung opinions in favor of the occupiers, who in the folklore of the moment had become martyrs."[15] After the police raid, 6,000 Harvard undergrads joined 9,000 affiliated students for a rally outside Widener Library, and the student community staged a strike of university proceedings.[16]

Five days after the protest, approximately 10,000 students staged a four-hour mass rally in Harvard's Soldier Field and voted, narrowly, to continue the strike. The national press became fascinated with notions of the Cultural Revolution having come to fair Harvard. A *Life* magazine cover in late April touted the "Confrontation in Harvard Yard," and depicted a young boy looking inquisitively at a demonstrator. Poised defiantly in jeans and a T-shirt, with his back to the camera, the demonstrator modeled the unofficial logo of the Harvard occupation: the word STRIKE emblazoned in black letters across the abstract image of a red fist. The strikers' manifesto was:

> Strike for the eight demands. Strike because you hate cops. Strike because your roommate was clubbed. Strike to stop expansion. Strike to seize control of your life. Strike to become more human. Strike to return Paine Hall scholarships. Strike because there's no poetry in your lectures. Strike because classes are a bore. Strike for power. Strike to smash the Corporation. Strike to make yourself free. Strike to abolish ROTC. Strike because they are trying to squeeze the life out of you. Strike.[17]

That same month, in the picturesque lake country of upstate New York, a group of black students at Cornell University seized Willard

1969

Straight Hall in an armed takeover early Saturday morning during Parents Weekend. They maintained their occupation for thirty-six hours, and as they vacated the building, some of the occupiers brandished rifles for all the media to see. The subsequent pictures sent out on news wires throughout the nation provided dramatic images of just how much things had come to a head in the student revolt of 1969.

Unlike the building takeover and student strike at Harvard, the Cornell incident was completely rooted in racial tensions. Much as in the earlier incident at Swarthmore, Cornell had been comparatively progressive in black student affairs: It recruited black students from ghetto neighborhoods, established an Afro-American Center, a private dorm for black coeds, began plans for a Black Studies curriculum, and had even flown two students to New York City so that they could buy bongo drums for Malcolm X Day ceremonies in 1968. But with the increased enrollment of black students at Cornell came a growing black militancy in the campus community.

When university president James Perkins had rejected one of the most aggressive demands of the Black Student Union in late 1968—the establishment of a separate college to be administrated entirely by blacks—a group of students from the African-American Society (AAS) had staged a symbolic act in the Cornell administration building by waving toy guns and knocking over vending machines. The students were called to appear before a joint student-faculty disciplinary committee, but they refused to do so. White students on campus took issue with the show of black revolt. At the beginning of the winter semester in 1969, some were so scared that they began to carry knives with them as they made their way across campus.

Tensions only increased in the spring. A group of black students was charged with stealing cushions out of a girls' dorm. The charges were dropped on April 18, but three black students who had demonstrated against the charges were given what was described by *Newsweek* as "mild reprimands." Later that same day, someone threw a rock through the window of Wari House, a co-op residence for black female students. A burning cross was placed on the front steps. In the next few hours, sixteen false alarms were set off across campus, and campus authorities received two bomb threats.

A number of people maintained that these acts were all committed by black students in order to generate sympathy for the AAS and to provide justification for radical measures. Provost Dale Corson told author Donald Alexander Downs that he was "99.99 percent sure" that blacks had planted the cross, saying, "I've been told by black people involved and others on campus at the time. . . . It was part of a plot to stir up the students. Ruth Darling, a white student and AAS supporter, made inquiries following the incident and said, "It began to seem to me, even then, although I was ashamed of my feelings, that this was all part of a very sophisticated plan." English professor Dan McCall remembered, "I knew the guys who did it. And they were black." Even AAS treasurer Stephen Goodwin: "I knew it was a set-up. I knew of it. It was just to bring in more media and more attention to the whole thing."[18]

The university sought to maintain the appearance of normalcy. For Parents Weekend, President Perkins planned to deliver a speech entitled, "The Stability of the University." But just after 4:00 A.M. on Saturday, more than a hundred black students stormed into Willard Straight Hall, yelling, "Fire!" They pushed out forty employees as well as thirty visiting parents staying in the upper-floor hotel rooms. When one terrified woman tried to lock herself in her room, the protesters tore open her door with a crowbar.

A group of fifteen to twenty students from the white fraternity Delta Upsilon tried to fight their way into the hall and take it back. They climbed the stairs that led from the back of Straight to the main lobby. On the way they were spotted by female occupiers, who started screaming. Several male occupiers came running at the intruders with pool cues, chair legs, iron rods, hammers, baseball bats, and fire extinguishers; the frat brothers were repelled. Both groups shouted threats at each other as the white students retreated. A couple of DU students were heard vowing to return and burn the place down. The black students threatened to fill them "full of lead."[19]

Following the DU break-in, the occupiers smuggled in weaponry—rifles, shotguns, bandoliers, knives—on the advice of Cornell graduate student Harry Edwards, who had helped arrange the infamous "black power" salute at the 1968 Mexico City Olympics.[20] Edwards explained in a *Playboy* panel on student revolt, "I supported the decision of the black students at Cornell to arm themselves for self-defense because they had been attacked by white fraternity boys. Black people are *through* being attacked with impunity and without consequence."[21] Answering criticism of the sometimes extreme measure of student demonstrators, he argued, "I don't dig all this crap about the moderate majority. There isn't any middle of the road left in this country. You're either with the movement or against it, because if you're not willing to take the measures that are necessary to correct the problem—and they have to be radical measures today—then you automatically become part of the problem."[22]

The Cornell demonstrators chained the hall entrances closed, and one of the black students, Edward Whitfield, issued a statement announcing that the building had been seized in protest against the "racist attitudes" of the university. Another, Tom Jones, declared apocalyptically, "Cornell has one hour to live!" and added, "Now's the time when the pigs are going to die. James Perkins is going to be dealt with. The faculty is going to be dealt with."[23] Once again, white SDS members worked in concert with black student rebels and formed an extra line of defense outside the building. David Burak of the SDS said his group was "fighting and taking the lumps [blacks] have taken for 300 years."[24] Reaction to the takeover was mixed on campus. Some were "turned off" by the show of violence and described the takeover as an "ego trip" for black students trying to assert their masculinity. Others described the revolutionary act as "beautiful."[25]

Perkins suspended classes and declared a state of emergency. Meanwhile, his administration negotiated with the occupiers. To prevent the crisis from exploding into a potentially deadly one, the administration decided to waive any sanctions against the AAS and also agreed to the establishment of a center for the study of African-American culture. One faculty member provided perhaps the most practical assessment of the incident: "When it comes right down to it, guns work."[26]

With their key demands met, the AAS students left the building just past 4:00 P.M. on April 20. Associated Press photographer Steve Starr captured the chilling image of the black students leaving the building, touting their weapons and many rounds of ammunition. One senior remembered, "When they stepped out and I saw the ammunition on the belts and the rifles, my heart dropped to my toes."[27]

Perkins had avoided further violence, but he fell under attack by some members of the university community for giving in to the occupiers. He would term the whole incident, "A shattering experience." *Time* summarized, "Until recently, most Negro leaders preached racial integration . . . Today, new leaders preach black 'nationhood,' not integration per se."

The Cornell incident was a vivid illustration of this new age of black activism; rather than mere acceptance into mainstream American society, young blacks wanted the opportunities to help *shape* it. As graduate student Bill Osby said, "Having a black studies program on a white liberal campus may turn out to be almost impossible because the administration and the faculty are just not going to let the program get at the essentials. They will simply let us study black history and wear *daishikis* while we get ready to work for Xerox or IBM. I'm for a black studies program that helps to destroy white culture in the minds of black people."[28]

❊ ❊ ❊

Dissident demonstrations were so prevalent on college campuses that a satirical episode of *Love, American Style* imagined a university where protests were cataloged and run according to schedule. A black militant student named Harley Davis (Stu Gilliam) storms into the office of a university president (Barry Nelson), locks the door, and declares a "lock-in" while waving a beaker of what he claims is TNT. Davis announces his name, and the president picks up his folder and checks his records. "You're not, uh, with the Panthers, SDS, US, UJA, Neo-Afro-Nationalists?" Davis announces that he's an independent, to which the president says, "Oh, I'm sorry. I can't deal with any unregistered militants." Having a hard time deciphering just what Davis wants, the president tells him, "Mr. Davis, on this campus, there are 1,100 legitimate militants. I can't spend all my time talking to you." After the president arrives at a solution (the president's secretary agrees to go on a date with Davis), he suggests the two take their discussion to the science lab. Looking at his watch, he says, "Yes, the sit-in should be over by now."

The rash of radical demonstrations had a predictable backlash. An April editorial in *Time* argued, "When extremists halt classes, they kill the spirit of a university in somewhat the same way that the Nazis did in the 1930s."[29] In May, the magazine declared, "If there was one word that summarized the feelings of much of the U. S. toward the radicals last week, it was: 'Enough!'"[30]

Speaking to the U. S. Chamber of Commerce on May 1, Nixon labeled the student rebels as "ideological criminals" and "new barbarians." (He redubbed the traditional "May Day" as "Law Day" to reinforce his message.) Sounding very much like California governor and future right-wing president Ronald Reagan, Nixon said, "There can be no compromise with lawlessness and no surrender to force if free education is to survive in the U. S. It is time for faculties, boards of trustees and school administrators to have the backbone to stand up against this kind of situation."[31] The president stated that "We do not want [the federal government] interfering with our colleges and universities," a statement that affirmed a conservative stance while nevertheless invoking the threat of federal intervention—and noted that it was the role of these institutions "to provide an education in an independent, free way in the American tradition." Shrewdly—and fairly, in the mind of the country's mainstream mind-set—he cast the student radicals in the role of philosophical terrorists. "I think that young people, students, are correct in asking that they have a voice—a voice in determining what the courses should be, a voice in determining what the rules should be. But . . . under no circumstances should they be given control of colleges and universities."[32] Attorney general John Mitchell used similar rhetoric in calling for "an end to minority tyranny on the nation's campuses and for the immediate re-establishment of civil peace and the protection of individual rights."[33]

Nine days after Nixon and Mitchell called for an end to student-related disturbances, a throng of students from across the country made news when they descended on the small town of Zap, North Dakota. Chuck Stroup, North Dakota State University student body president in 1969, remembers that he went downstairs from his student government office to the offices of the NDSU student newspaper, the *Spectrum*, early that semester and suggested an idea for students who couldn't afford to make it to the traditional spring break destination of Florida. In March and April, he purchased classified ads in the *Spectrum* that comprised a series of cryptic and increasingly ambitious messages, such as "DRINK THE BARS (ALL TWO OF THEM) DRY IN ZAP. MAY 10"; "FREAK OUT 200 CITIZENS OF ZAP ON MAY 10"; AND "GLORIOUS FESTIVAL OF LIFE AND LOVE (TRANSLATION: BIG ORGY) WILL BE CELEBRATED MAY 10 IN ZAP!" *Spectrum* editor Kevin Carvell wrote a front-page story promoting the grassroots event that would turn Zap into the "Lauderdale of the North." The articles promised a "full program of orgies, brawls, freakouts and arrests," and asked readers, "Do you dare miss it?" Thus was born Zip to Zap: A Grand Festival of Life and Love.

Zap, a "city" of approximately one square mile located in the Knife River valley seventy miles north of Bismarck, could not have been prepared for how quickly the event snowballed. At the end of April, the *Bismarck Tribune* ran a front-page story that predicted, "Destiny is about to rear either its beautiful or tumultuous head, or both, May 10, to project this quiet Mercer County city of 300 into national fame in a coincidence of double exposure. Thousands of collegians plan to descend upon Zap in a zip-in, zap-out frenzy of welcoming spring, while shedding their winter blues." The story was accompanied by a photo of Norman Fuchs, the mayor of Zap, playing with a new toy called the "Zip-Zap" that the Wham-O Corporation (the maker of the Frisbee) was launching to coincide with the growing Zap happening. As Fuchs later said, his constituents saw the event as a chance to "put ourselves on the map here." In preparation, Zap's two bars stocked up with 10,000 cases of beer each, and the town's café came up with a promotion for "Zapburgers."[34]

Despite their apparent enthusiasm, Fuchs and his fellow residents began to fear that a monster had been created. In mid-April, the *Spectrum* reported that Zap citizens had become concerned about the threatened influx of young people and that Fuchs didn't want word of the festival to leak out. One resident, an attorney, tried to downplay the town's attractions: "I don't know what they would do here. We have a couple of bars. I'm not sure whether there is a restaurant now." A local history by Jerry Cooper and Glenn Smith summed up the prevailing cultural attitudes of North Dakotans:

> North Dakota's rural economy and homogenous white population had shielded it from the turbulent and violent racial upheavals that struck many cities during the 1960s. The state's acknowledged conservative social and political nature had also exempted it from the sometimes violent war protests

and college campus demonstrations. North Dakotans could look out at an apparently disorderly, riotous nation and take comfort that old values, including patriotism and respect for authority, still prevailed on the northern plains.

If Zip to Zap put its namesake town on the map, it also nearly wiped it off the map. After the Associated Press and ABC and CBS radio networks picked up the story of the planned festival and news spread across the nation, a reported 2,000 to 2,500 young people from as far away as Florida and Toronto, the vast majority of them male, descended upon the desolate hamlet on Friday night, the eve of the festival.[35] Having come from far and wide for the Great Plains version of a Bacchanalian orgy, the Zip-to-Zappers found themselves packed into a one-horse, two-bar town. As the temperature of the North Dakota night dropped below freezing, some people took wood from a demolished building nearby and started a bonfire on Main Street. "I just don't know about this darn fire," Fuchs was reported to have said, but things were out of his control by then.

Not long afterward, the riots started. Booths and tables were torn out of the two bars and fed into the bonfire, and the town's lone fire truck was taken apart. For the local residents, the signs of young out-of-towners fighting, sleeping, urinating, and vomiting in the streets was a nightmarish sign of just how out-of-hand things had become in the rest of the country.

Reports of the melee made it to the state capital, prompting governor William Gay to declare martial law and send in 500 National Guardsmen wielding five-foot clubs the following day. Zap's rowdy visitors were sent packing, leaving behind a torn and charred town littered with beer cans. Scanning the morning-after scene, Zap sheriff Ivan Stiefel said sadly, "They wrecked the whole town."[36]

Not even this cold and sleepy North Dakota frontier town had escaped the zeitgeist of 1969.

9. 1, 2, 3, What Are We Fighting For?

A U. S. Navy EC-121 reconnaissance plane is shot down off the coast of North Korea, and the Battle of Hamburger Hill is fought in Vietnam—and on the floor of Congress.

It was a honeymoon period for Nixon and the press. Three days after the covert commencement of Operation Breakfast, Nixon had told his cabinet that the war would be over by the following year. A day after Vietnam veterans marched in Central Park on April 5 to protest the war they themselves had fought in, the *New York Times* announced, NIXON HAS BEGUN PROGRAM TO END WAR IN VIETNAM. In early April, Nixon (via Kissinger) ordered Laird to prepare a time-table for what would come to be termed "Vietnamization": the "progressive transfer" of the war effort to the South Vietnamese military. His plan called for leaving American personnel to serve only in "support and advisory" roles for a finite period of time—an initiative that flew in the face of his preelection promises to Saigon.

The schizophrenic nature of Nixon's Vietnam policies would become apparent as Nixon's presidency progressed outside of its first hundred days. When senator Barry Goldwater had asked Nixon how long he would wait before bombing targets in the Communist nation, Nixon said he planned to give the peace talks at least six months. Goldwater later commented: "He didn't think the American public would stand for an all-out military assault on North Vietnam. He said he was in a no-win situation." Nixon added, though, that if the current strategy did not lead to progress at the negotiations in Paris, "he would then, perhaps, have to order a resumption of bombing."[1] This would prove to be his biggest challenge in Vietnam: depicting himself as a trigger-happy "madman" abroad while simultaneously playing the role of peacemaker at home.

Yet as Nixon deliberated on his Vietnam strategies, the incident that he would consider the first crisis of his administration occurred not in Southeast Asia but farther north. The thirty-one-man crew of a U. S. Navy EC-121 reconnaissance plane had been flying a spy mission forty-eight miles off the coast of North Korea on the night of April 14 when it was shot down by a North Korean MiG.

Relations between Washington and Pyongyang had been cool during the Cold War sixties, and the April 14 event called to mind the USS *Pueblo* incident from the previous year. In January 1968, the *Pueblo* had been performing an intelligence mission in international waters, a little more than fifteen miles east of the North Korean island of Ung Do, when Commander Lloyd Bucher found his ship surrounded by North Korean subchasers and torpedo boats. After a subchaser opened fire on the *Pueblo*, damaging the hull and wounding Bucher, the commander decided to go against navy regulations and surrender the ship without returning fire. In a February 1969 *Life* cover story on the ensuing naval investigation, the commander explained, "I decided that I would surrender the ship. Any further resistance on our part would result in the slaughter of the crew."[2]

Now, Nixon had to deal with his own Korean affair involving American personnel finding themselves in the wrong place at the wrong time. Desirous of maintaining an air of American might on the world stage, the president conferred with Kissinger, whose advice echoed Nixon's own "madman theory." "If we strike back," Kissinger told the president, "they will say, 'This guy is becoming irrational—and we'd better settle with him.'"[3]

When pressed by White House counsel John Ehrlichman on what a retaliatory strike against Korea might bring, Kissinger mused, "Then it could escalate."

"How far?" Ehrlichman asked.

"Well, it could be nuclear," Kissinger responded.[4]

Ehrlichman and others advised the president against retaliation. After deliberating for five days, Nixon chose not to retaliate but, in an act of executive transference, authorized the second stage of Menu—Operation Lunch. Later, Nixon would regret his failure to retaliate for the downing of the reconnaissance plane. He accused Ehrlichman of having "sold out to the doves," and Nixon placed his trust more and more in Kissinger.[5] The Korean incident in the spring of 1969 was a blip on the international radar that year, but it went a long way toward reinforcing Nixon's commitment to winning the Vietnam War, even as it appeared more and more unwinnable.

Nevertheless, he maintained the appearance of solidifying plans to end the war. Following a White House announcement in mid-April, that the first troop reductions would begin in the summer, Nixon optimistically revised his earlier prediction and said the war would be brought to an end within the next few months. On May 14, he gave his first televised speech about Vietnam and told the nation he supported a mutual withdrawal along with internationally super-vised democratic elections for the people of South Vietnam. That same month, speaking before a group of Quakers, Kissinger made a promise that now seems chillingly prophetic: "Give us six months, and if we haven't ended the war by then, you can come back and tear down the White House fence."[6]

Nixon announced plans in June for 25,000 troops to return home by August. Although this number represented a small percentage of the troops already in Southeast Asia, it helped support the notion of Nixon as peacemaker at the same time that he was deliberating on possible air strikes against North Vietnam.

* * *

As Nixon performed his diplomatic balancing act, a battle for a 3,000-foot mountain near the Laotian border provided one of the most contentious subplots of the Vietnam War in 1969.

In the folklore of the indigenous Montagnard tribespeople, Ap Bia was referred to as "the mountain of the crouching beast." Rising amid the vines, bamboo thickets, and waist-high elephant grass, it overlooked the A Shau Valley to the east. During the French-Indochinese Wars, Ho Chi Minh's commander in chief, General Vo Nguyen Giap, had declared, "To seize and control the highlands is to solve the whole problem of Vietnam." In 1966, the North Vietnamese had seized a Special Forces camp and established a permanent base there. Combined United States/South Vietnamese forces had made repeated attempts to drive the enemy from the area as recently as the failed Operation Dewey Canyon mission in February 1969. In May, commanding general Melvin Zais launched Operation Apache Snow, part of an aggressive assault campaign intended to destroy the enemy presence in the A Shau.

Three battalions from the 101st Airborne Division were flown by helicopter into the valley on May 10. U. S. intelligence had little information as to the size or location of enemy forces in the area, so the battalions would perform an intricate reconnaissance assault. If one unit encountered heavy resistance from the enemy, another one would be sent in to provide reinforcement; the initial battalion would then compel the enemy forces to dig in while the reinforcements would cut off its retreat and attempt to destroy it.

Late the following day, a U. S. battalion company ran into heavy fire within a kilometer of the summit. Helicopter gunships were ordered into the fray, but within the dense jungle, they mistook American soldiers for the enemy and rained down friendly fire, causing dozens of casualties. The next day, another company suffered losses on a steep ravine and could not get its wounded out of the area for two days. By then, it was determined that the enemy was present in greater numbers than expected, possibly bolstered by reinforcements from across the Laotian border. Captured documents indicated one of the enemy units in the A Shau was the 29th Regiment of the People's Army, veterans of the 1968 Tet Offensive that had earned the nickname "the Pride of Ho Chi Minh." Although recent experience had indicated that the North Vietnamese forces tended to retreat from costly battles, it now seemed that the forces in and around Ap Bia had dug in deep.

Over the next ten days, Allied and Communist forces squared off in a battle that proved to be a microcosm of the strategic hardships experienced by American forces in Vietnam. The jungle foliage combined with the mountainous terrain created nearly impossible conditions for the assault. U. S. forces had to maneuver through narrow trails that limited the effect of their frontal assault, and the geography prevented units from supporting each other. Brigade commander Colonel Joseph Conmy's Bravo Company seized the 916-meter southern peak of the mountain on May 15, but the dense vegetation prevented them from establishing an effective attack position until four days later. Meanwhile, enemy forces used the land effectively. They attacked from the rear and flanks, forcing American frontal assault units to defend a 360-degree radius. Given the close-range combat, the effectiveness of air support was severely limited, and even then, enemy bunkers were well entrenched and resisted air assault.

Inspired by a May 16 *Washington Post* story on the action on Ap Bia, Asso-ciated Press correspondent Jay Sharbutt flew to South Vietnam and interviewed Major General Zais, questioning the general on his decision to focus on ground infantry rather than using long-distance firepower. In a front-page *New York Times* article the following week, Sharbutt described soldiers questioning the wisdom of their commanders—something that would have been considered heresy in previous generations of war reporting. "Many cursed Lt.

Col. Weldon Honeycutt, who sent three companies Sunday to take this 3,000-foot mountain," Sharbutt recorded. "They failed and they suffered." He quoted one 101st Airborne member who condemned division commander Colonel Honeycutt by his radio codename, saying, "'That damn Blackjack won't stop until he kills every one of us.'"[7]

Facing public scrutiny, Zais considered abandoning the mission, but instead he ordered two fresh battalions, one American and one South Vietnamese, airlifted to the base of the mountain to provide support. Ultimately, after ten futile attempts to storm the peak in nine days, his men proved victorious. The enemy stronghold fell in the morning hours of May 20. The 3/187th reached the Ap Bia peak by noon and began clearing out enemy bunkers. Five hours later, it was secured. Allied forces proceeded to pursue the enemy eastward toward Laos.

The battle of Ap Bia would go down as one of the most heroic victories for U. S. forces in Vietnam. The reported 564 American casualties, including 84 deaths, were considerably less than the more than 600 enemy fatalities tallied by U. S. command.[8] But some within ranks questioned the ultimate importance of the lives lost there. As the Allied forces secured the mountain, one soldier took the surface of a rations box, nailed it to a tree, and wrote the words "Hamburger Hill" on it—a testament to the vicious fighting that had left a trail of men minced like meat. Soon afterward, another passing soldier added the commentary, "Was it worth it?" Much to the anger of military brass, the press popularized the name "Hamburger Hill" in referring to Ap Bia.

Military officers asserted that Operation Apache Snow had been a preemptive measure against an expected enemy offensive and not an arbitrary show of military might.[9] But Democrats ralled against the operation on the senate floor. On the same day that Ap Bia was secured, Ted Kennedy denounced the operation on the floor of the Senate, calling it "senseless and irresponsible . . . symptomatic of a mentality and a policy that requires immediate attention."[10] Later that week, George McGovern echoed Kennedy's sentiments, calling the mission a "truly senseless slaughter." Stephen Young from Ohio questioned Zais's military tactics. Recalling how Stonewall Jackson and Robert E. Lee had attacked Union forces at Chancellorsville from the rear and flanks simultaneously, Young said, "Our generals in Vietnam acted as if they had never studied Lee and Jackson's strategy. Instead, they flung our paratroopers piecemeal in frontal assaults. Instead of seeking to surround the enemy and seeking to assault the hill from the sides and the front simultaneously, there was just one frontal assault after another, killing our boys who went up Hamburger Hill."[11] (After Zais was made a lieutenant general and put in charge of XXIV Corps, Young would recall Ambrose Burnside's ill-fated frontal assault on Confederate forces: "President Lincoln fired Burnside. General Zais was promoted."[12])

Despite the relative military success of Operation Apache Snow, it had to be reevaluated when Zais's replacement, Major General John W. Wright, ordered the Allied forces to abandon their position on Ap Bia on June 5. To those paying close attention, the pullback did not come as a shock. On the same day that reports of the victory had run back home, the *New York Times* reported that unnamed sources "conceded privately" that American troops would soon leave the area and that "in three weeks the NVA will be right back in there."[13] Zais contended that capturing Ap Bia was a means to an end, not the end itself. "Its only tactical significance was the fact that the NVA were on it. The hill itself had no tactical significance," he told *New York Times* reporter Iver Petersen.[14]

Despite Zais's explanation, the wisdom of the operation must have seemed dubious when, in mid-June, more than 1,000 Vietnamese soldiers were reported to have entrenched themselves back on Ap Bia; U. S. planes drew fire when they flew near the mountain. For many folks back home, it seemed as if those who had died heroically in the jungle terrain of Ap Bia had died for nothing.

When asked about this turn of events, Wright said he was "prepared to commit everything that it takes . . . to do the job [again]." Senator Young called for the general to, "personally lead that assault and be in the forefront of those young GIs to take part in it," and suggested that Zais "be assigned to accompany him."[15]

Hamburger Hill became a rallying point for the antiwar movement as it spread from college campuses to the ranks of the military itself. *Life* estimated that at least twenty different "propaganda broadsides"—published not by student radicals but by GIs themselves—had appeared on the nation's army bases.[16] Kirkpatrick Sale records that there was a "GI resistance groundswell" in 1969, along with the establishment of sanctuaries on church properties and campuses for deserters, the incidence of which had increased by 25% from 1968.[17]

In late June, *Life* published photographs of 241 Americans who had been killed in Vietnam over the course of one week in mid-May. The article dramatically quoted the last line of a letter written by a soldier on Hamburger Hill to his family: "You may not be able to read this. I am writing in a hurry. I see death coming up the hill." Suddenly, the American public had faces to attach to the fatalities. In actuality, only five of the 241 had died as a result of the battle of Hamburger Hill, but as author Samuel Zaffiri remembers, "this quote confused many Americans who read the article, leading them to believe that most of those pictured had died storming Dong Ap Bia."[18]

Shortly after the article ran, President Nixon ordered General Creighton Abrams, commander of U. S. Forces in Vietnam, to avoid "such large-scale battles." The new policy was to be one of "protective reaction." Although hoping to score victories in Southeast Asia that would create an advantage at the Paris Peace Talks, Nixon found himself fighting an increasingly vocal enemy in the antiwar movement among his own population.

10. THE GREEN MIND

The Cuyahoga River fire and People's Park riots provide early impetus for the ecology movement.

The Cuyahoga River is an eighty-mile river that begins in the headwaters of Geauga County in northeast Ohio. Its name, an Iroquois word meaning "crooked river," describes the way in which the Cuyahoga works its way north-ward, curving snakelike through Cleveland and then emptying into Lake Erie. For decades, the river had been a dumping ground for pollutants from Cleveland and other cities along its banks, the accumulation of which had turned it into an oozing brown fluid that bubbled from gas beneath the surface. As the Federal Water Pollution Control Administration noted in 1969, "The Lower Cuyahoga has no visible life, not even low forms such as leeches and sludge worms that usually thrive on wastes." To make matters worse, during heavy rainstorms, the city's outdated storm system would flood the sewer mains and send untreated waste into the river, and then on into Lake Erie. A joke among the citizens of Cleveland went like this: Anyone who falls into the Cuyahoga does not drown—He decays.[1]

In 1968, the residents of Cleveland had passed a $100 million bond issue for cleaning up the river, and in early 1969 the city had formed a Clean Water Task Force to make periodic sweeps of oil and debris from the water. But on June 22, 1969, the stretch of the river that snaked through Cleveland became especially clogged with oil and debris in its bend. The mixture of debris and toxic chemicals proved combustible, and the river literally caught on fire. Water is a natural enemy to fire, and the sight of a body of water burning is a visual paradox, an absurdity that indicates the water has ceased to be water. Mayor Carl Stokes lamented, "What a terrible reflection on our city."[2]

The fire on the Cuyahoga burned brightly and briefly that day. Two railroad bridges that crossed the fire suffered damage, but the fire was out before photographers could capture images from the surreal scene. In reality, it wasn't even the first time that the river had caught on fire. The previous hundred years had witnessed as many as nine river fires on the Cuyahoga, including one most recently in 1952. The Cuyahoga River was also not the only river in America to have displayed a propensity for spontaneous combustion; Buffalo River in upstate New York, Rouge River in Michigan, and an outlet into the Baltimore harbor had all been sites of similar pollution-related fires. But news stories of the Cuyahoga fire helped fuel outrage from American conservationists over the state of the environment.

By the end of the decade, the nation's popular conscience had begun to focus on the effects of industrial waste on the natural world. A *Life* photo spread illustrated the pollution in urban and industrial areas throughout the nation. From the phosphate plants of Polk County, Florida, to the steelworks in East Chicago, Indiana, the images provided a sobering, hellish glimpse of the American landscape. In Missoula, Montana, the Hoerner Waldorf mill (nicknamed "Little Hiroshima" by citizens) was just one of six sawmills inside Missoula city limits pouring a steady stream of smoke into the air of Big Sky country—sometimes forcing drivers to turn on their headlights during daylight hours.

Photos of Los Angeles showed how the local smog developed its own weather patterns, carried northeast by prevailing winds into San Gabriel Valley and then creeping back over the city at night. A photographer pointed his camera down Pennsylvania Avenue in the nation's capital, using color film and leaving it exposed for a half-hour on a clear day. The resulting yellowish-brown tint of the image revealed the otherwise imperceptible smog. A Public Health Service study had determined that pollution was cutting down the amount of sunlight reaching the earth by 25% in New York City and by 40% in Chicago.[3]

An ecological disaster off the coast of California in late January underscored the urgency of the matter. A crack opened in the floor of the Santa Barbara Channel, sending subterranean streams of oil and natural gas spewing upward in the normally blue water just off the coast of California, creating a reddish-brown quagmire. For eleven days, at a rate of almost 1,000 gallons per hour, the gas and oil polluted an area of more than 400 square miles, and covered forty miles of beach with a "tarlike slime." One correspondent flying over the area reported that fumes from the slick rose 1,000 feet into the air.[4]

What made this catastrophe all the more unctuous was that it was the result of offshore drilling. For years, Santa Barbara officials had worried about the ecological effects of offshore drilling. In 1967, they had successfully lobbied the Interior Department to create a two-mile buffer zone extending beyond California's demarcation line. The shoreline was marred by slicks in 1968, and Santa Barbara had begged Stewart Udall, then Secretary of the Interior, to extend the buffer, but to no avail. County supervisor George Clyde remarked, "Always, Interior and oil officials led us to believe we had nothing to fear."[5] In turn, the Union Oil company had lobbied the U. S. Geological Survey—an arm of the Interior Department—to cut some corners in state and federal regulations, allowing them to drill five and a half miles offshore.

Union Oil drills burrowed 3,500 feet into the ocean floor off the Santa Barbara coast. During withdrawal, a substance called "drilling mud" was constantly pumped into the well to maintain equilibrium of pressure. On January 29, the drilling mud underneath

Platform A ran low and pressurized natural gas blew the well. Union Oil workers "capped" the hole in the ocean floor, but this merely increased the pressure from below. Boiling gas and oil came bursting out of the earth's core.[6]

Thousands of gallons of crude oil bubbled to the surface of the ocean waters, spreading across 800 square miles and along thirty-five miles of coastline. The slick's effect on the channel's ecosystem was staggering. Oil-soaked birds lay dead and dying along the beach. Cormorants and grebes were seen diving headlong into the oily waves looking for fish, usually never to return. The tide washed in the corpses of seals, as well as those of dolphins whose blowholes had been clogged by oil. Sea elephants, fur seals, and sea otters were also endangered by the expanding muck. For months afterward, gray whales were forced to avoid the Santa Barbara Channel as they migrated to their calving and breeding grounds in Baja California.[7]

Along the mucky beaches, hundreds of workers, along with inmates from state conservation camps, spread straw along the shore to soak up the oil and then shoveled straw and sand into trucks waiting nearby. "If there was any event that would mobilize the nascent environmental movement in 1969, that was it," wrote Ernest Zebrowski and Judith Howard. "Scruffy long-haired hippies scoured the beaches to rescue the mired feathered creatures, and millionaires used their luxury cars to transport tar-covered grebes to the emergency treatment centers at the Santa Barbara Zoo."[8]

Rough water prevented initial efforts to fix the hole in the earth, but eventually barges were able to tow 15,000 barrels of plasticlike sealant out to sea so that a crew could pump it into the oozing fissure. Planes dropped chemicals onto the water to help dissolve the slick, but this led to further fears among environmentalists and others. Before the slick was contained, 3 million gallons of oil had polluted the Santa Barbara coast.[9]

Fred Hartley, the president of Union Oil, traveled to Washington to appear before a subcommittee on air and water pollution to testify on the episode, which he put off as "Mother Earth letting the oil come out." Fed up with the outrage over the oil slick his company had created, Hartley commented, "I'm amazed at the publicity for the loss of a few birds."[10]

❀ ❀ ❀

Like most everything at the end of the sixties, issues of pollution and the environment became politicized and polarized. The New Left saw pollution as the residue of the military-industrial complex that President Dwight D. Eisenhower had warned the nation about upon leaving office. As Mark Hamilton Lytle argues in *America's Uncivil Wars*, "Marxists linked environmental destructiveness to corporate politics," while ecologists posited the Vietnam War—with the U. S. military's use of napalm and herbicides in the jungles of Southeast Asia—as an ecological crisis:

> By 1969 . . . Vietnam had become as much an environmental battle as a military one. Critics viewed it as one of the great ecological disasters of the modern age. Frustrated by the thick jungle canopy that afforded cover to the Vietcong, American generals decided to make war on the land as well as its people. They sprayed huge volumes of Agent Orange, which killed the vegetation and crops in an area roughly the size of Connecticut. Environmental destruction in Vietnam seemed to antiwar protesters an extension of the misguided effort to conquer nature. The terms "ecocide" and "ecotastrophe" described not only the assault on Vietnam's ecology, but a more general demonstration of the anthropocentric American way of life.[11]

During the Santa Barbara oil slick, the sight of chemicals being sprayed from above was grimly similar to the chemicals that American military forces were spraying on jungle foliage halfway around the world. "By 1969," Lytle concludes, "many in the New Left saw ecological politics as a way to revitalize protest."

In the spring of 1969, a small plot of land to the south of the University of California-Berkeley campus became an unlikely battleground between the New Left and the Establishment. The university had been buying up land with the plan to destroy abandoned houses and low-rent apartments that attracted hippies, druggies, and dropouts. One vacant lot along Telegraph Avenue had remained overrun with weeds and rubble since its purchase in 1967. Students and local citizens met in April 1969 to discuss what to do with the plot of land. Resident Michael Delacour presented the idea of reclaiming the area for the creation of a public park. Stew Albert, a veteran of the Berkeley Free Speech Movement of 1964 and co-founder of the "Yippies," was drafted to write an article for the underground paper, *The Berkeley Barb*.

Declaring himself "Robin Hood's Park Commissioner," Albert called for local citizens to take the lot away from the university and to turn it into a "People's Park." Two days later, a Sunday, hundreds of people showed up to clear the area and plant greenery. The day turned into a mini festival, with music and food provided free to the volunteers. Mario Savio, the most vocal leader of the Free Speech Movement, told a crowd, "Property is not a thing to keep men apart and at war, but rather a medium by which men can come together to play . . . a people's park."[12] Over the next few weeks, students and townies came together to beautify the area and create an urban oasis.

In a referendum, Berkeley students voted overwhelmingly in favor of keeping the impromptu People's Park. On May 6, university chancellor Roger Heyns promised that no sudden action would be taken, declaring his willingness to reach a compromise. But political activist Abbie Hoffman saw an opportunity to "suck Reagan into a fight."[13]

Professor John Searle said of the event: "I believe that [the] People's Park incident was extremely cynical on the part of the demonstrators. They wanted a confrontation. What mattered was getting people out in the streets demonstrating."[14] If so, they got what they wanted. Governor Reagan chose to make an example of the People's Park. "If there has to be a bloodbath," he infamously declared, "then let's get it over with." He overruled Heyns, and, in the early morning of May 15—"Bloody Thursday"—sent 250 California Highway Patrol officers and local police into the park. They cleared an eight-block area around the park, destroyed a large section of what the volunteers had planted, and installed a chain-link fence around the park to keep people out.

At noon, thousands of people gathered in protest in nearby Sproul Plaza, preempting original plans for an open discussion of the Arab-Israeli crisis. Student body president Dan Siegel took the mic and shouted, "Let's take back the park!" at which time police turned off the sound system. Unwilling to be silenced, the crowd moved down Telegraph Avenue toward the park, opening a fire hydrant and turning over cars while chanting, "We want the park!"

Police officers fired tear gas at the demonstrators, who hurled rocks, bottles, and pipes back at them. Reagan's chief of staff, Edwin Meese III, called in Alameda County sheriff's deputies, increasing the police total to nearly 800 men. "The Blue Meanies," nicknamed for their light-blue riot-gear helmets, fired buckshot at people sitting on the roof of the Berkeley Repertory Theatre. Student James Rector was fatally wounded and died four days later. Local carpenter Alan Blanchard was permanently blinded. The Blue Meanies chased retreating protesters down Telegraph Avenue and fired buckshot at their backs. At least 128 citizens were admitted to hospitals for serious injuries or trauma; 19 law enforcement personnel were treated for minor injuries. (Alameda County sheriff Frank Madigan would later admit, "things got out of hand."[15])

Reagan declared a state of emergency and sent in 2,700 National Guardsmen. Against the wishes of the city council, martial law was established in Berkeley: a curfew was put into effect, barbed-wire barricades were set up throughout the city, and Guardsmen fired tear gas on any large groups that assembled in public. Demonstrators taunted troops that remained stationed outside People's Park. Young women stripped naked to the waist and danced in front of them and gave them marijuana brownies and juice laced with LSD.

Ruth Rosen, a student at the time, remembers, "When the fence went up, the whole experience of People's Park changed. Governor Reagan brought in the National Guard. The city was occupied for a month. And what happened is the worst aspects of the movement emerged. People did things that were totally counterproductive. They tried to provoke the National Guard to fix their bayonets. They tried to cause skirmishes on the campus."[16]

City councilman John DeBonis maintained:

The park issue is not the issue. The issue is: "We must have a confrontation, a confrontation throughout the summer." They were out of confrontation issues, and as soon as you give them a park, they'll deal up another confrontation. We have been invaded by people outside of the state, outside of the city. We have been invaded by militants. This is, we're in a revolution. And the only thing, don't ever say we're going into a revolution. We're *in* a revolution. Now the thing is: Who's going to win it?[17]

Several thousand people gathered on May 21 in Sproul Plaza to memorialize James Rector. Guardsmen wearing gas masks trapped the crowd by pointing bayonets at them. "We realized the police were letting people into the plaza, but they were not letting people out," remembers Jentri Anders. "The police were beating people as they tried to get out." Then came the helicopters. (Rosen remembered hearing the choppers and thinking, "We're going to be shot at. We're the Vietcong.") They sprayed tear gas on the plaza. Demonstrators were seized by nausea and began throwing up. Some of the gas blew inside the nearby hospital and two elementary schools.[18]

Reagan met with university officials and berated them in a heated exchange about their handling of the People's Park fiasco. "Those people told you for days in advance that if the university sought to go ahead with that construction, on that property, that they were going to physically destroy that property." When told that many attempts had been made to negotiate with the demonstrators, the governor was astounded: "*Negotiate?* What is to negotiate? What is—don't you—wait a minute. On that issue, don't you simply explain to these students that the university has a piece of property that it bought for future construction of the campus and that it was now going ahead with the plan? What do you mean, 'negotiate'?"

"Governor Reagan, the time has passed when the university can just run roughshod over the desires of the majority of its student body," one administration member tried to explain. "The university's a public institution . . ."

But Reagan was not persuaded: "All of it began the first time some of you who know better, and are old enough to know better, let young people think that they had the right to choose the laws they would obey as long as they were doing it in the name of 'social protest,'" he said, and then walked out of the meeting.[19]

"We all felt very defeated," Rosen said. "It was a horrible experience to gas students at a peaceful rally. And it was one reason why people began to feel that we had to reassert what we really stood for. . . . And that led to the Memorial Day march."[20]

Two days after musical acts from the local music scene, including the Grateful Dead, Creedence Clearwater Revival, Santana, and Jefferson Airplane, put on an all-day benefit concert for the People's Park at San Francisco's Winterland on May 28, 30,000 citizens marched in Berkeley—this time with a city-issued permit—to protest the occupation of the city.[21] Demonstrators set out on foot and on bikes, flashing peace signs, and surrounding the park in a more peaceful show of protest. Girls stuck flowers into the barbed-wire fence and into the muzzles of Guardsmen's rifles. "For a brief moment in history in People's Park, the counterculture and political activists had a magical fusion. It was a way of looking at the future. It was utopian. It was a way of saying, 'If we had control of our lives, this is what it would look like.'"[22]

But eventually, the university's might won out—sort of. The administration paved over People's Park and turned it into a parking lot. But it was seldom used, perhaps because of the neighborhood's crime and vandalism, and eventually it became a weed-infested haven for dropouts and dealers once again.

❋ ❋ ❋

With such high-profile incidents as the Santa Barbara oil slick—described twenty years later by the *Los Angeles Times* as "The Oil Spill Heard 'Round the Country" and "the birth of the modern-day environmental movement"[23]—the Cuyahoga River fire, People's Park, and the increasing focus on industrial pollution throughout the country, the Ecology movement took off. Gladwin Hill would write in the *New York Times* later in the year that, "Rising concern about the environmental crisis is sweeping the nation's campuses with an intensity that may be on its way to eclipsing student discontent over the war in Vietnam."[24]

In September, Wisconsin senator Gaylord Nelson attended a conference in Seattle and proposed a nationwide demonstration, or "teach-in," focusing on the environment to be held the following spring. Separately, two months later at the National UNESCO Conference in San Francisco, faith-based activist and pacifist John McConnell suggested the idea for an "Earth Day" to be held on the spring solstice as a way of recognizing the need for peace and environmental balance. Both events took off the following year—McConnell's as a regional celebration on March 21 in San Francisco, Nelson's on campuses on April 22—and have become yearly rituals.

The coexistence of the two days has spawned a controversy over the years. Nelson's movement essentially co-opted the name "Earth Day," and although the United Nations recognizes "Earth Day" as occurring at the beginning of spring every March, the April 22 date remains the one most well-known as Earth Day in America. McConnell overstated the issue decades later, claiming "The most damaging lie about the environment is the statement that 'Earth Day is April 22.'"[25] Nelson, for his part, allows, "John McConnell may have used the phrase Earth Day before we did, [but] he knows our events were not similar. Ours was a political exercise. His was a peace exercise."[26]

McConnell designed an early version of the Earth Day flag, a field of blue with a picture of the planet Earth as photographed by *Apollo 10.* (The flag would later be updated with the so-called "Big Blue Marble" photo taken from *Apollo 17.*) In October, underground cartoonist Ron Cobb published his design for an Ecology sign to symbolize the need for environmental consciousness. Profiled in the September issue of *Playboy*, Cobb's bleak, nightmarish, abstract caricatures on issues such as pollution and racism ("visions of apocalypse") appeared in the *Los Angeles Free Press* and were syndicated in sixty college newspapers across the country. In 1969, he was working on his third book anthology, *Raw Sewage*, which would collect his work on pollution, along with plans for a guidebook on what was described as "points of interest in the post-nuclear rubble of Los Angeles." Said the artist, "I try to come up with things that don't exist yet."[27]

With grassroots environmental awareness having taken hold, the need for a new public policy became evident. This was highlighted by Supreme Court Justice William O. Douglas's damning article in July's *Playboy*, "The Public Be Damned," on the devastating toll that the

Army Corps of Engineers had taken on the environment throughout the agency's history. One first step in addressing this issue was the National Environmental Policy Act of 1969, signed into law by Nixon on the first day of the oncoming decade. As a result of the act, environmental impact statements would be required for all major federal government land development projects.

11. STAND!

The Stonewall riots inspire the Gay Rights movement, while the radical Weathermen faction takes over the SDS.

Around 1 A.M. on Saturday, June 28, in New York's Greenwich Village, police raided the Stonewall Inn.

The Stonewall, a two-story building on Christopher Street and Seventh Avenue, opened in 1967 and quickly became the leading gay establishment in the city. One patron described it as the "St. Peter's [Cathedral] in Rome" of the gay community.[1]

Author David Carter recalls that "as the decade approached its end—and especially in 1969—the subject of homosexuality was more and more in the air, whether in the context of the arts or politics or merely as a topic of conversation."[2] Changing definitions of morality, obscenity, and alternative lifestyles led to a sea change in American sexuality. As activist Earl Galvin told Carter, "gay men began to say to one another, 'Maybe this will be our year.'"[3]

The homosexual lifestyle remained a polarizing issue in America, and the debate over gay rights was becoming especially pointed in New York City. On June 17, incumbent mayor John Lindsay lost the Republican primary to Staten Island state senator John Marchi, who opposed gay rights reform. That same month, a vigilante gang in Queens was terrorizing gay men during their nighttime rendezvous in a Kew Gardens public park. The vigilantes even coordinated their harassment patrols via walkie-talkies while random youths assaulted gays who were found in the park. In the week following Lindsay's primary defeat, the vigilante gang went to the park with axes and saws and chopped down the trees—reportedly under the eyes of the police.

Meanwhile, in Greenwich Village, the area's gay bars had been targeted by the police. They raided five bars within three weeks' time in June, and three were closed for good.[4] According to Carter, a joint Interpol-NYPD investigation had unearthed an international Mafia bond theft ring operating in Greenwich Village, along with evidence of collusion among homosexuals who were being blackmailed by the Mafia. Circumstantial evidence indicated that the Stonewall, which was run by the Gambino crime family and tied to the Genovese family, was a site used by moneymen in the ring. "We weren't concerned about gays. We were concerned about the Mafia," deputy inspector Seymour Pine said many years later. Collaring homosexuals was merely a way for officers to pad their arrest records. "They were easy arrests," Pine explained. "They never gave you any trouble. Everybody behaved. . . . It was like, 'We're going down to grab the fags.'"[5] Whether the gay clientele simply provided an excuse for the NYPD to step up its actions against the Mafia ring, or vice versa, the police were out to close the Inn.

The Stonewall had been busted before, as recently as three nights earlier. Policewomen had been working the place posing as lesbians, and the feds had people staking out the place, too. Normally, the police gave warning before raids, and they usually came earlier in the evening, before peak activity, and tended to arrest cross-dressers and patrons without ID. On this night, however, they gave no notice and showed up when the place was hopping. Four plainclothes officers (two men and two women) showed up late that Friday night, June 27, while Pine and his partner, detective Charles Smythe, waited across the street in Christopher Park for their signal. No signal came, so Pine and Smythe decided to initiate the bust themselves.

This time, though, the clientele was not going to take things lying down. The spirit of defiance that permeated American society at the end of the sixties would now come front and center in New York's West Village, and—in a larger sense—in America's homosexual community. "They were acting differently," Pine said. "When we entered, they weren't going to go."[6]

As the police ushered patrons into paddy wagons, a crowd of gay and straight onlookers yelled angry insults at the policemen. Local residents—gays, street kids, even straights—joined the scene, and the spontaneous protest grew to about 2,000 strong. Some threw coins at them. Others took bottles from trash baskets and cobblestones from a nearby construction site and threw them at the police. The officers were forced to retreat back inside the club.

The crowd even removed a parking meter from the street and tried to use it to break the doors open. A Molotov cocktail was tossed inside the bar, but the police managed to put it out. Deputy inspector Seymour Pine later admitted, "I had been in combat situations, [but] there was never any time that I felt more scared than then."[7] Howard Smith, working then as a reporter for the *Village Voice*, recalled being "locked inside with the police . . . we could look through little peepholes in the plywood windows; we could see that the crowd . . . they were yelling, 'Kill the cops! Police brutality! Let's get 'em! We're not going to take this anymore! Let's get 'em!'"[8]

A female officer managed to escape through a vent in the back of the Inn and went to a nearby firehouse, where she called into the local precinct for backup. Pine remembers that it took the reinforcements from the Sixth Precinct a long time to show up. "We didn't tell them we were going to raid the bar, so I guess they showed us," he said.[9]

Two police wagons showed up and cleared the way for those trapped inside the Stonewall. A Tactical Patrol Force, trained to quell antiwar demonstrators, battled the crowd, and order was not restored until sometime around three in the morning. The following night, a crowd gathered outside the Stonewall and jubilantly chanted a slogan that had begun to appear as graffiti in the area that day: "Gay Power!" The mood was summed up by one Ronnie Di Brienza, who told Carter, "The establishment and their elite Gestapo, the pigs, have been running things too long. First you had the Negro riots a few years back, which woke up white cats like myself to the fact that, though I am white, I am just as much considered a nigger as the black man."[10]

Police showed up again to disperse the crowd and found themselves targeted by flying projectiles, and again the melee lasted into the wee hours of the morning. A rainstorm seemed to calm things down over the next few days. On Wednesday, the *Village Voice* ran two front-page articles on the riots, and that night the crowds were back again. When the police came, the crowds set trash cans on fire and yelled epithets at the police: *"Gestapo!" "Pig motherfuckers!" "Fag rapists!"*[11]

As Pine said, "things were completely changed . . . suddenly they were not submissive anymore." Gay poet Allen Ginsberg, who had happened by the Stonewall on Sunday night, said the riot was "beautiful—they've lost that wounded look that fags all had ten years ago."[12]

The riots in this little corner of the Village would spark a widescale movement in the homosexual community, and the name *Stonewall* would come to symbolize not just the riots but the beginning of a new era for gays and lesbians. Soon after Stonewall, the first Gay Liberation Front (GLF) group was founded in New York City in 1969. The GLF grew into a national organization with chapters expanding across the globe that attacked capitalist values and traditional definitions of gender and even expressed solidarity with the Black Panther Party and Third World nations. Perhaps the most controversial GLF policy would be its militant "outing" of suspected homosexuals, all part of an agenda to bring the gay lifestyle out of the closet and into the mainstream. In its mission statement, the GLF declared, "We are a revolutionary group of men and women formed with the realization that complete sexual liberation for all people cannot come about unless existing social institutions are abolished. We reject society's attempt to impose sexual roles and definitions of our nature."[13]

It was the end of the decade, and gays and lesbians had found their place on the revolutionary stage with the rest of America.

❊ ❊ ❊

Nearly one year after the "long hot summer" that had culminated in the ugly riots on the streets of Chicago during the Democratic National Convention, *Newsweek* observed that, "As the summer of '69 dawned, most riot experts, media pundits, and other students of the black mood were predicting that the pattern of civil disorders was about to enter a sinister new phase. The fire this time, ran the consensus, [would take the form of] carefully plotted, guerrilla-style uprisings aimed at people rather than property." In the basement of the Pentagon, the U. S. Army had personnel monitoring 150 "racially troubled cities" with twenty-four-hour teams. In New York City, Gotham's finest had bought a twenty-one-ton armored vehicle to be used in rescuing police or civilians from riot gunfire.[14]

In 1968 it had been New York and Chicago, but now the growing pattern of violence spread to smaller cities and suburbs, and even small towns such as Cairo on the remote southern tip of Illinois. As civil and racial unrest spread to Small Town, U. S.A., paranoia spread on both sides of the battle lines. Terry Ann Knopf with the Lemberg Center at Brandeis University noted, "Militants really believe the police are out to exterminate them all. So they stockpile arms. The police infiltrators learn of the stockpiles and begin surveillance. The spying makes the militants more convinced of the notion of extermination. The stage is set for battle."[15]

Indeed, the battle lines were being drawn. SDS delegates journeyed to the Chicago Coliseum for its national convention, which began on June 18. The proceedings had an air of defensiveness to them and quickly degenerated into a circus of contentiousness and infighting; one reporter described it as being "like a children's crusade gone mad."[16] Bernardine Dohrn announced that "no vultures" were allowed inside, and that the "regular bourgeois press" would be charged $25 for press badges. But when Mike Klonsky tried to have this policy ratified, Progressive Labor proponents shouted out that no members of the capitalist press should be allowed into the hall, and the SDS voted in favor of this ban.

This opening challenge between the PL and RYM set the tone for the rest of the proceedings. As things boiled over, a group of national leaders gathered in the back of the main stage in a heated discussion. Mark Rudd, one of the leaders during the student takeover of Columbia University in 1968, suggested the delegates take a recess. Kirkpatrick Sale describes what happened next: "Dohrn marched to the rostrum, hair flying, jaw set. 'We're going to have to decide,' she shouted into the microphone, 'whether we can continue to stay in the same organization with people who deny the right of self-determination to the oppressed—and anyone who wants to talk about that, follow me to the next room.'" With Klonsky and Rudd staring on, RYM supporters rose unsurely to their feet and gradually followed her out to the corridor. PL partisans chanted, "Sit down, Sit down . . . Stay and fight, Stay and fight . . . No split! No split!" Outside, the RYM forces shouted back, "Join us! Join us!"[17]

The following day, Dohrn took the microphone again, and this time she went off on another twenty-minute speech, "laying out every real or imagined sin of PL since its inception, quoting, citing, spinning, slashing, a performance so masterful that at least one person was convinced it must have been prepared days in advance. At last she paused. 'SDS can no longer live with people who are objectively racist, anticommunist, and reactionary. Progressive Labor

Party members, people in the Worker-Student Alliance, and all others who do not accept our principles . . . *are no longer members of SDS.*"[18]

By the end of the convention, the SDS had been split into two. In its radical fervor, the RYM assumed control of the national organization, led by a group that would come to be known as the "Weathermen." Prior to the convention, a committee of eleven RYM members (Karen Ashley, John Jacobs, Jeff Jones, Mark Rudd, and Steve Tappis from the New York area; Bernardine Dohrn, Gerry Long, and Howie Machtinger from Chicago; and Bill Ayers, Jim Mellen, and Terry Robbins from the Michigan-Ohio area) had drafted a manifesto under the title "You Don't Need a Weatherman to Know Which Way the Wind Blows" (a lyric from Bob Dylan's "Subterranean Homesick Blues"). The manifesto stated that "the main struggle going on in the world today is between U. S. imperialism and the national liberation struggles against it," asserted support for "black liberation struggles," and maintained the need for American youth to "escalate its protest at home, showing solidarity with the world-wide 'liberation forces' by opening another front in the anti-imperialist war, up to and including 'the need for armed struggle.'"[19]

Rudd was elected the new National Secretary, and the group that would be known as the Weathermen effectively took control of the SDS national body. Todd Gitlin, who had served as SDS president in 1964, later remembered: "They picked up the apparatus of the organization and the name of the organization, and they walked away with it. . . . it was organizational piracy . . . It was infuriating and depressing, and I sat in a state of horror watching the Weathermen running away with the student Left."[20]

Now under control of Rudd and company, the SDS was directed with a refocused radicalism. "This system is gonna be overthrown. It's gonna mean a fight," he declared. "And it's gonna mean a lot of white people risking a lot of things when they finally join on the side of the black people and the people of Vietnam and around the world who have already begun the fight."[21] In the radical philosophy of the Weatherman group, ghetto riots and the rise of the Black Panther Party in the United States were a manifestation of the larger worldwide tumult—from the Cultural Revolution in China to the student revolts in France and Mexico City, the urban guerrilla movement in Uruguay, Marxist rebellions in Angola, Mozambique, and other African nations, the Greek military junta that filmmaker Costa-Gavras indicted in 1969's *Z*—all signs that a global revolution was imminent. As Dohrn declared, "We must be on the side of the oppressed, or be on the side of the oppressor."[22]

The first initiative of the SDS Weathermen was to expand its radical consciousness beyond college campuses and into the cities. "The general idea was that working-class youth outside the colleges would be more revolutionary than the students at the colleges," Rudd remembered decades later. "So the summer of '69 was seen as a time when we would move off campuses, establish ourselves within working-class neighborhoods . . . organizing among working-class youth."[23]

That summer, devotees moved into the nation's urban areas— Chicago, Cleveland, Detroit, Milwaukee, San Francisco, Seattle, New York—into working-class neighborhoods. They sought out recruits for their ranks, raised consciousness about class war and revolutionary movements throughout the world, and trained them— literally—for the second American revolution yet to come by leading them in paramilitary exercises. Bill Ayers went to Detroit, where he was involved in several summer programs building collective housing: "And it was this kind of intense moment of trying to transform a group of relatively privileged students into fighters and steel ourselves for what we saw was the coming upheaval." David Gilbert described it as a constant "gut-check . . . [a] challenge [to] each other to be more violent . . . sometimes they'd just go all night."[24]

The extreme dogma of the Weathermen inspired a reactionary sentiment among moderates and conservatives who feared the radical directions in which the youth rebellion was headed. At the end of June, a student reactionary group of self-dubbed "squares" held a five-day National Student Conference on Revolution at Lake Forest College in Illinois. At the conclusion of the conference, they descended upon SDS headquarters in Chicago's West Side. Wearing shirts that read STRIKE BACK in parody of the STRIKE motto of the Harvard demonstration in the spring, they picketed the headquarters while chanting "SDS pigs!"

Undaunted, the Weathermen announced that in the fall, coinciding with the trial of the "Chicago 8" for their role in the riots at the 1968 Democratic National Convention, members from across the nation would flock in the tens of thousands to the Windy City. There, they would stage a "National Action"—a violent antiwar demonstration meant to incite a confrontation with the police and touch off the beginning of the modern-day American revolution.

ONEWALL RIOTS ALTAMONT
OE NAMATH
UTCH CASSIDY AND THE SUNDANCE KID
CUPATION OF ALCATRAZ ZIP TO ZAP THE NEW LEFT
ASY RIDER HARVARD STUDENT STRIK

III. THE SUMMER OF IMPOSSIBLE DREAMS

The strange, apocalyptic summer of 1969, the world seemed to be coming apart . . .

—James Howard Kunstler

H! CALCUTTA! THE WEATHER UNDERGROUN
EIL YOUNG & CRAZY HORSE TOMM
C5 DAYS OF RAGE APOLLO 11 BOEING 74
HAMBURGER HILL
M CURIOUS (YELLOW) PORTNOY'S COMPLAINT CUYAHOGA RIVER FIR
TCHES BREW LET IT BLEED CHARLES MANSON
AI PHOTOS THE MORATORIUM
ED ZEPPELIN WOODSTOCK
OPLE'S PARK JIMI HENDRIX RICHARD NIXON HELLS ANGELS
HE GODFATHER IGGY AND JEFFERSON
OODY ALLEN THE STOOGES AIRPLANE
IDNIGHT COWBOY NUDITY THE MIRACL
E ZODIAC KILLER BOB & CAROL & TED & ALICE MET
PERATION MENU CROSBY, STILLS & NASH

12. WALKING IN SPACE

Technological advances transform the entire world—and beyond.

At a joint session of Congress in May 1961, President John F. Kennedy had raised the stakes of the so-called "space race" with the Soviet Union by announcing, "I believe that this nation should commit itself to achieving the goal, before this decade is out, of landing a man on the moon and returning him safely to the Earth. . . . No single space project in this period will be more impressive to mankind, or more important for the long-range exploration of space; and none will be so difficult or expensive to accomplish."

In the waning days of December 1968, the astronauts of *Apollo 8* effectively saved the year by becoming the first manned mission to orbit the moon. With the end of the decade in sight, it would have been a critical setback to the entire NASA program if *Apollo 8*, only the second manned mission in the Apollo program, had failed. But the team of James Lovell, William Anders, and commander Frank Borman succeeded marvelously on their journey, venturing farther from Earth than any human had ever gone. *Apollo 8* circled the moon ten times, and the astronauts gathered information on possible landing sites for future Apollo missions.

With the safe return of the *Apollo 8* mission on December 27, the United States officially became prohibitive favorites in the space race—so much so that the Soviet Union issued a statement that its space program was going to concentrate on exploring other worlds with automated probes, rather than going for the silver medal in the moon race. On January 10, 1969, the Soviets launched their *Venera 6* probe toward Venus; it would land in mid-May after transmitting data on the Venutian atmosphere during fifty-one minutes of a parachute-aided descent.

The success of *Apollo 8* at the end of 1968 had thrust the United States ahead of the Soviet Union in the space race, but it had by no means made a moon landing inevitable. As momentous an achievement as that mission had been, the technological gap between *orbiting* the moon and *landing* on its surface—and then safely returning from it—was light years wide.

Apollo 9 launched on March 3, 1969, from the Kennedy Space Center in Brevard County, Florida. Astronauts James McDivitt, David Scott, and Rusty Schweickart performed a ten-day mission in the Earth's orbit. With NASA having achieved a lunar orbit just months earlier, the story of yet another manned orbit of Earth generated somewhat of a "ho-hum" response from America's civilian population. Yet *Apollo 9* was just as crucial of a mission in the Apollo program. It was the first manned test of the lunar excursion module (LEM) that would eventually land astronauts on the surface of the moon. According to Apollo historian Andrew Chaikin, "many [astronauts] saw *Apollo 8* as little more than a ride—no real flying involved. But *Apollo 9* was a test pilot's feast." McDivitt, in fact, had turned down a spot on the *Apollo 8* mission, choosing instead to remain on 9.[1]

During the ten-day mission, the astronauts of *Apollo 9* conducted a series of remote-controlled movements and dockings. The climax of the mission came on the fifth day. With Scott remaining behind in the CM, McDivitt and Schweickart climbed into the LEM, separated from the CM, and jetted out on their own for a six-hour minimission, journeying up to 111 miles from the mother craft. Performed in the sterile space of terrestrial orbit, these maneuvers seemed to merge space-age technology with the discourse of human sexuality: The docking probe of CM extended into a hole in the center of a conical protrusion on the LEM. Once the two modules were thusly "mated," three latches on the docking ring would create a "soft dock," at which point, twelve nitrogen-powered latches would fire, creating a "hard dock." Finally, silicon seals created an airtight fit between the two modules, allowing the astronauts to move freely from one chamber to the other.

Apollo historian Andrew Chaikin explains the docking procedure:

> Height and speed are inextricably linked. To slow down, the spacecraft must be kicked into a higher orbit (by adding energy with a burst of rocket). Conversely, speeding up requires dropping into a lower orbit (by using the rocket as a brake). A pair of astronauts who start out behind their target must lower their orbit until they catch up, but not for too long, or they will overtake it. If they start out ahead, they must raise their orbit, go slow for a while, and then descend in time to meet their target. Every burst of speed, every bit of braking, changes their height and therefore their speed. Catching the moving target—and staying there once they've arrived—becomes a feat of great complexity.[2]

The docking of the LEM with the CM became even more intricate when the sun blinded McDivitt upon their approach. "Dave, I just can't see it," he told Scott over the transmitter. "Let me get in a little closer," he said.

"Just keep coming easy like that," Scott advised him. "You ought to go forward and to the right a little . . . There you go . . . ," Scott said, guiding him in.

The two ships met in orbital intercourse. The command module probe nestled into the lunar module drogue, and the docking latches on both ships completed the seal. McDivitt breathed a sigh of relief. "I haven't heard a song like that in a long time!"[3]

The docking performed by *Apollo 9* was not without precedent. In mid-January, Soviet cosmonauts had successfully docked *Soyuz IV* and *Soyuz V* and then returned to earth. But more critically, *Apollo 9* was successful in two crucial tasks: first, Schweickart donned the new NASA spacesuit, the first self-contained suit (i.e., without the umbilical-like connection to the CM for life support), and proved that it could function outside the spacecraft—and allow an astronaut to function away from the immediate proximity of a NASA craft; second, in the climactic phase of the mission, Schweickart and McDivitt piloted the LM on a six-hour excursion, straying more than 100 miles from Scott and the CM before returning to dock safely.

After the successful orbital mission of *Apollo 9*, *Apollo 10* launched on May 18, beginning an eight-day round-trip mission that would take astronauts Thomas Stafford, John Young, and Gene Cernan closer to an alien surface than humankind had ever ventured. *Apollo 10* was part trial—testing the ability of the lunar module to descend from and return to the CM—and part scouting mission—as Young remained in the CM, Stafford and Cernan in the LEM were to scout the proposed landing area for *Apollo 11*, the *Mare Tranquillitatis* (Sea of Tranquility), one of the large, dark plains of basalt that ancient astronomers had mistaken for seas on the face of the moon.

For this mission, the CM was nicknamed *Charlie Brown* and the LEM *Snoopy*, in tribute to the *Peanuts* cartoon whose creator, Charles Schulz, had designed NASA stationery. Once *Apollo 10* made the lunar orbit, Stafford and Cernan climbed into *Snoopy* and began their descent toward the lunar surface. Hurtled horizontally at approximately 3,700 miles per hour—more than five times the speed of sound—above the moon, *Snoopy*'s altitude declined until the lunar horizon lost its curve. Tremendous mountains appeared in the distance, and as Stafford and Cernan got closer, they realized that these formations were not mountains but, in fact, the rims of gigantic craters, with cliffs four or five hundred feet high. Boulders fifty stories high were strewn across the area.[4] It was the most forbidding landscape humans had ever witnessed.

Suddenly, they came upon a sight experienced only by the astronauts of *Apollo 8*—an earthrise. Cernan cried out with glee: "Houston, this is *Snoopy*! We is 'Go' and we is down among 'em." They traveled along the Sea of Tranquility, identifying aloud craters and ridges that they had studied in simulations, getting as low as 14,500 meters above the surface.

During their return to *Charlie Brown*, as they jettisoned the descent stage, Cernan and Stafford experienced what would be classified later as a "combination of minor and easily correctable failures" that caused the module to suddenly spin out of control. "Son of a bitch. What the hell happened?"[5] Cernan cursed, in an understandable breach of protocol for the straight-laced NASA program. For eight seconds the moon's horizon spun wildly in their sight, but they were able to stabilize the craft and return to *Charlie Brown*. As *Snoopy* successfully docked with his master, television images were transmitted back to a tracking station in Goldstone, California, and then broadcast across the globe.

❉ ❉ ❉

As humankind made its first contact with an alien world, popular literature in America delighted in the imagination of exotic planets and alternate realms of existence.

Science fiction writer Ursula K. LeGuin won both the Hugo and Nebula Awards for her 1969 novel, *The Left Hand of Darkness*. This otherworldly novel takes the narrative form of a report delivered by Genly Ai, a representative from the galactic federation sent on a diplomatic mission to the planet Gethen, also called Winter, a world populated by a hermaphroditic species that is gender-neutral save for the *kemmer*—two days during the planet's lunar cycle when Gethenians can decide to take on either the male or female role in mating.

Even the great Russian émigré author Vladimir Nabokov imagined an alien world in his celebrated 1969 novel, *Ada, or Ardor: A Family Chronicle*. In many ways his most ambitious work, the many-layered novel is set (it seems) on an alternate Earth called Antiterra. The planet is a sort of alternate Earth with altered and almost amorphous geopolitics (North America and Russia are joined) and technology (electricity has been banned for some unstated reason; but there are modern planes, "dorophones," even magic carpets). Meanwhile, "Terra" (our Earth) is described as a planet that may just be the figment of a mass cultural hallucination. Nabokov's protagonist, Van, writes a novel called *Letters from Terra*, and receives letters from countless people who claim to be in contact with the people of Terra. But in this very Nabokovian novel, one can never be too sure of the reliability of narration. At novel's end, after the incestuous lovers Van and Ada Veen have been reunited for good, they die together—and die *into* the manuscript, swallowed by the reality of time and space it imagines.

While Nabokov's Van writes a lecture on the "Texture of Time," the protagonist of Kurt Vonnegut's *Slaughterhouse-Five, or The Children's Crusade: A Duty-Dance with Death* has become "unstuck in time." The narrator, perhaps Vonnegut himself, presents the life story of Billy Pilgrim, an American POW during World War II and survivor of the Allied firebombing of Dresden. After his mundane postwar life is jolted by a plane crash (from which he is the lone survivor) and his wife's accidental death, he goes on an all-night talk show and reveals that he had been kidnapped by a flying saucer and taken to the planet Tralfamadore. There, the Tralfamadorians—four-dimensional creatures who see time not linearly but all at once, spread out before them—kept him as an exhibit in an intergalactic zoo with another kidnapped Earthling, the pornographic actress Montana Wildhack.

Having learned the Tralfamadorian view of time—or perhaps simply suffering the effects of mental illness or brain damage—Pilgrim lives through bouts of being "unstuck" in time, constantly reliving key moments of his life and even foreseeing his own death. The end of the universe has been laid out before him by a Tralfamadorian: "'We know how the Universe ends,' said the guide, 'and Earth has nothing to do with it, except that it gets wiped out, too. . . . We blow it up, experimenting with new fuels for our flying saucers. A Tralfamadorian test pilot presses a starter button, and the whole Universe disappears.' So it goes."

The doomsday scenario offered in a 1969 novel written by a Harvard Medical School student named Michael Crichton was even more chilling, as it took place not on a wildly imagined planet but in pseudorealistic circumstances here on earth. Crichton, who had already written books under pseudonyms, established himself as the father of the techno-thriller with his use of scientific and technological details, imagined documents, and nonfictive voice of narration, a literary combination that had many readers writing the author to inquire if the events he described in the book had actually happened. In *The Andromeda Strain*, a U. S. military satellite returns to earth, near the isolated town of Piedmont, Arizona, carrying an extraterrestrial biological disease. The alien microorganism, named *Andromeda*, infects the residents of the town and kills them—either instantly, or indirectly by inducing suicidal insanity.

At a time when the threat of nuclear war seemed to be the nation's biggest fear, the story of an alien-borne biological crisis captured readers' imaginations. Indeed, as the world looked forward to a lunar landing, one concern was that the astronauts would bring back "outer-space germs" for which humankind had no cure. *The New Yorker* would spoof this fear with a cartoon in September, which showed a doctor assuring a bedridden boy, "I didn't say I ruled out the possibility of your having moon germs entirely. I merely said it was too early to tell whether you should be placed in quarantine."

❋ ❋ ❋

OFF TO THE MOON announced the *Life* cover story that profiled the astronauts slated for flight on *Apollo 11*. Astronauts who had been part of prior missions in the American space program had taken on celebrity status, but for *Apollo 11*, Neil Armstrong, Michael Collins, and Buzz Aldrin were the closest thing the social establishment had to rock stars. The three were photographed with their families: Armstrong fishing with his sons, making homemade pizza, playing piano with his wife; Collins trimming roses in his backyard; Aldrin and his kids on a visit to AstroWorld. All were essentially NASA-coordinated photo ops, as the three men were spending very little time with their families during the summer of 1969.

Armstrong, an Ohio-born test pilot, had been selected as an astronaut in 1962, and while on the *Gemini 8* mission—which featured the first successful docking of two spacecraft—became the first civilian ever to command an American mission into space. Collins, a West Point graduate, had been an astronaut since 1952, and was the pilot of *Gemini 10*. Aldrin, the best educated of the three, had a degree in mechanical engineering from West Point and a doctorate in astronautics from MIT. The pilot of *Gemini 12*, he was also a rendezvous technical junkie (nicknamed "Dr. Rendezvous" by his colleagues), and had been a pioneer in designing the NASA in-space docking procedure.

Aldrin had originally been tapped to be the first to walk on the moon, but in March, NASA officials changed their plans and decided Armstrong would be the one to take the most famous steps in the history of the world. A rivalry developed between Armstrong, with his civilian background, and Aldrin, the West Pointer with technological genius and, some said, a sizable ego. In late June, the two men ran a simulated descent to the lunar surface in the LEM. A thruster got stuck, and on a TV screen, the simulated moon surface came rushing up to them.

"Neil—hit ABORT," Aldrin told Armstrong. Then Mission Control echoed, "*Apollo 11*, we recommend you abort."

Armstrong didn't, and the simulation ended with the theoretical crash of the LEM. "Aldrin knew he and Armstrong were [theoretically] scattered across the moon in a thousand pieces," Chaikin writes. "He looked over at Armstrong, who was still absorbed in the problem."[6]

Armstrong, a Korean War veteran and an experienced test pilot, was not fazed by a *theoretical* crash—in May 1968, he had come within half a second of probable death during a Lunar Landing Training Vehicle test, ejecting just before the banking craft crashed in a fiery blaze. He also wanted to test Mission Control's ability to handle adversity on the landing. "In the simulations we challenged the procedures and exercised the procedures and put all the participants—in the control center and in the simulator—in [the] position of having to make fairly rapid and reasonable judgments in the situation that occurred," he later explained.[7]

But the incident caused tensions among the astronauts, as Aldrin was concerned that the incident reflected badly on the entire crew. The prospects for the unspeakably ambitious *Apollo 11* mission remained delicate—what Michael Collins would later describe as being a technological "daisy chain."[8] Chaikin relates that on the morning of the launch, although the unflappable Armstrong was confident that the mission would return home safely, he nevertheless felt that the odds of their successfully landing on the lunar surface were 50-50.[9]

Apollo 11 would take on an especially patriotic aura. The names of the CM and LEM, originally designated as *Snowcone* and *Haystack*, were redubbed *Columbia* and *Eagle*, respectively—the mythological female representation of America and the national bird of the United States. Yet while the combined technology that went into the construction of the *Saturn V* rocket, the CM, and the LEM were distinctly American, involving the service of thousands of U. S. companies and hundreds of thousands of laborers, the mission of Aldrin, Armstrong, and Collins carried the hopes of people across the entire globe.

At 8:32 on the morning of July 16, a throng of sunglasses-wearing spectators at the Kennedy Space Center on Merritt Island, Florida, watched, many snapping pictures on instamatic cameras, as America's newest power trio took off on their historic journey.

Seventy-six hours later, *Apollo 11* entered the lunar orbit. After a rest period—they had the most monumental of challenges ahead of them—Armstrong and Aldrin entered the *Eagle*. "You cats take it easy on the lunar surface. If I hear you huffing and puffing, I'm going to start bitching at you," Collins told them.

"See you later," Armstrong said calmly. Their exchange masked the seriousness of what lay ahead. The descent would require the utmost in concentration, precision, and accuracy. The target landing site on the Sea of Tranquility was an elliptical formation measuring eleven-and-a-half miles long by three miles wide—a minuscule area considering that the *Eagle* would begin its descent while hurtling at approximately one mile per second over the moon. Timing was a factor, as well; the mission had been calculated so that the sun would be approximately ten degrees above the moon's horizon, casting the geography of the Sea of Tranquility into sharp relief.[10]

On July 20, just after noon Houston time, the *Eagle* separated from the *Columbia*, and three hours later, after the requisite checks and preparations, Armstrong and Aldrin began their powered descent with the top of the *Eagle* pointed down at the moon. Armstrong looked down at their checkpoints on the surface and saw that they were running about two full seconds long. He began to calculate how this would affect the eventual landing.

At 46,000 feet, they turned the *Eagle* back over so that the landing gear would be pointed down toward the surface. Buzz Aldrin looked up from his computer and saw a familiar sight: "Got the Earth straight out our front window," he told millions back on his home planet. Just seconds later, the mood in *Eagle* suddenly changed. "Program alarm," Armstrong called out. A warning light on the console had turned bright amber, and Armstrong's computer was flashing an intermittent "1202" error . . . and neither he nor Aldrin knew what it meant.

What NASA would determine later was that a "1202" was essentially a signal of information overload. The mission checklist at this point had called for the rendezvous radar to be turned off, but as Aldrin explained nearly four decades later, "Being 'Dr. Rendezvous,' no matter what the checklist said, I was going to leave the rendezvous radar on and active so that if we had to abort, it was on and working and we could reacquire height as soon as possible in case we had to go back up."[11] But with the landing radar now beginning to receive data from the approaching lunar surface, the computer on *Eagle* was receiving more information than it could handle. "Evidently that combination was not anticipated by the guys at MIT; they're pretty narrow-minded," he joked.

Charlie Duke, the capsule commander ("CAPCOM") back at Mission Control—and as such, the only person allowed to communicate directly with the astronauts—quickly polled the control room and told the *Eagle*, "It's looking good to us. Over."

"What is it?" Armstrong asked Aldrin, then told Houston: "Give us a reading on the 1202 Program Alarm." They were at 33,500 feet now.

1969

Precious moments passed as details on the lunar surface became more and more clear to Armstrong and Aldrin. Finally, Steve Bales, the resident expert in LEM guidance systems at Mission Control, determined that the computer was experiencing a data "overflow" from the radar and that the computer was prioritizing data—and as long as this message was intermittent and not continuous, things were okay.

"*Eagle*, Houston," Duke said. "You're 'Go' for landing. Over."

"Roger," Aldrin answered. "Understand. Go for landing. Three thousand feet." Two seconds later, Aldrin called out a new alarm: "Program Alarm . . . 1201."

Armstrong: "1201 . . . Okay, two thousand . . ."

Duke: "Roger. 1201 alarm. . . . We're Go. Same type. We're Go."

Seven seconds later, Armstrong was concerned once again. Having been consumed with resolving the alarms within the cockpit, he had not focused on the landing site until they were below 2,000 feet. Now, he saw the West Crater of the Sea of Tranquility looming. By his reckoning, they were headed toward the outer northeast slope. If they attempted a landing there, the *Eagle* could tip over. If they weren't killed upon impact, the LM almost certainly would be incapacitated for ascent, forever stranding the two astronauts on the moon.

"Six hundred feet, down at nineteen [feet per second]," Aldrin said.

"I'm going to . . ." Armstrong muttered, and then switched to manual flight. He slowed the descent and flew the *Eagle* over the crater, tipped over (Armstrong would later describe) like a helicopter, flying to the west—over the crater and the surrounding boulder field—looking for a flat surface on which to land.

"Coming down nicely," Aldrin said at 102:44:23.

There was a smaller crater, just to west of the West Crater. "Gonna be right over that crater."

"One hundred feet down. . . . Five percent [fuel left]," Aldrin warned. "Quantity light."

The warning light initiated a critical ninety-four-second count-down, by the end of which the LM would need to be within seventy feet of the surface to ensure a safe touchdown on the landing gear. If the craft were any higher above the surface at that point, the dwindling fuel would leave Armstrong just twenty seconds to decide whether to continue or to abort and return to the command module.[12]

Armstrong remained focused on landing the craft. *Apollo 11* had come too far at that point, and—almost literally—the whole world was watching them. "Neil thinks things through thoroughly and does what he thinks is right, and usually it's the right thing to do," Aldrin later praised Armstrong. "I don't think anybody can come close to the skills that he had."[13]

But the landing would present its own challenges.

"Forty feet down," Aldrin said. "Picking up some dust." The descent thrusters were kicking dust in all directions, screening visibility. Due to the low gravity and lack of atmosphere, the dust particles fanned out, shooting out toward the horizon.

By the time the *Eagle* had descended beneath thirty feet, Armstrong had selected the landing site, but for some unknown reason, the craft began to drift backward and to the right. Flying manually, Armstrong ceased the backward motion, though the *Eagle* kept moving left.

As the abort limit approached, Aldrin called out, "Contact light"—signifying that at least one of the seven-foot probes attached to each of the LEM's three footpads had touched the surface. When this light came on, Armstrong was supposed to turn the engine off. But Armstrong couldn't see the light, nor could he hear Aldrin.

Three seconds later, Armstrong realized that they were *down*. Supported by the descent engines, the *Eagle* had settled almost imperceptibly on the lunar surface.

"Shutdown," Armstrong called.

"Okay. Engine stop," Aldrin said.

Armstrong looked outside. All was still, silent. It had been achieved—amazingly, improbably, and almost anticlimactically—102 hours, 45 minutes, and 40 seconds after takeoff, the *Eagle* had landed on the moon.

"We actually had the engine running until touchdown. Not that that was intended, necessarily. It was a very gentle touchdown. It was hard to tell when we were on," Armstrong later remembered.[14]

Aldrin and Armstrong spoke in technical chatter for a few moments, to complete shutdown. A good ten to fifteen seconds—a virtual eternity—after touchdown, Duke chimed in from Houston, clearing his throat: "We copy you down, *Eagle*."

"Engine arm is off," Armstrong said to Aldrin. Then he answered Earth, "Houston, Tranquility Base here. The *Eagle* has landed."

Tranquility Base? Duke paused. "Roger, Twan [sic]—Tranquility," he said excitedly. "We copy you on the ground. You got a bunch of guys about to turn blue. We're breathing again. Thanks a lot."

"Thank you," Aldrin said simply.

❈ ❈ ❈

Across America, Sunday-afternoon baseball games were halted by announcements over public address systems that inspired fans to burst out in spontaneous celebration. At Yankee Stadium, the crowd of 16,000 fans broke into a group rendition of "The Star Spangled Banner."

All gambling at the Riviera in Las Vegas stopped as the patrons and pit bosses watched Armstrong and Aldrin beat the longest of odds. At a summer stock performance in Detroit, Michigan, a performance of *Carnival* came to a halt as audience, cast, and crew watched on television sets that had been brought onto the stage. At a bungalow colony nestled among New York's Adirondack Mountains, 150 people huddled into a community building and watched on a television especially acquired for the event. Throughout the harbor in Marina Del Rey, California, the sound of air horns echoed in the air. Thousands of Boy Scouts gathered at their National Jamboree in Coeur d'Alene, Idaho, let out a cheer, many of them undoubtedly dreaming of when they would travel to the moon.

Taking a cue from cities in Australia, residents of the city of Cheyenne, Wyoming, decorated the roofs of their homes with Christmas lights so that they could help light the way home for *Apollo 11*. In Hagerstown, Maryland, lightning struck the steeple of a local church, and some of the more "pious" took it as a sign from God that man had ventured too far. In Manhattan's Central Park, tens of thousands of New Yorkers and summer tourists watched the landing on a triangle of large screens that had been set up by the three major networks, ABC, CBS, and NBC.

❀ ❀ ❀

Amazingly, NASA had scheduled for Aldrin and Armstrong to sleep after they landed. But the astronauts, having piloted the only craft in human history to land on an alien body, would have none of it. It took several hours for them to complete shutdown, enter data, do safety checks, and put on and secure their spacesuits. But at 9:28 P.M., they vented the oxygen from the module into the lunar vacuum. "The hatch is coming open," Armstrong reported, and he pulled a D-ring to lower a tray with a television transmitter on the side of the *Eagle* so that what happened next would be recorded for history.

Armstrong stepped outside. "The surface appears to be very, very fine grained as you get closer to it. It's almost like powder."

He made his way down the ladder.

"Okay, I'm going to step off the LM now."

He stepped off the ladder, placing his left foot onto the moon. It was 10:56 P.M. EDT back on Earth.

"That's one small step for man, one giant leap for mankind," he said. It was grand, eloquent—and nonsensical. He had intended to say "a man," and even after careful analysis of the transmission, it remains unclear whether the dropped *a* was the result of a glitch in the transmission or merely the most famous oral flub in human history. Regardless, Armstrong was the first human being to speak from an alien surface.

Aldrin came out next. He stepped down onto the surface and, before releasing his grip on ladder, tried a couple of practice hops to make sure the bottom rung was reachable by a hop from the surface.

"It has a stark beauty all its own," Armstrong said to Aldrin, lumbering over in his EVA suit.

"Beautiful view!" Aldrin said.

"Isn't it something? Magnificent sight out here."

This gave Aldrin a fittingly poetic way to describe the moonscape. "Magnificent desolation."

With some difficulty, Aldrin and Armstrong planted an American flag into the surface just yards away from the landing site. Back on earth, an estimated 600 million people—a fifth of the world's population—were watching their steps. People throughout the United States were holding "moonwalk" parties. When Armstrong came out of the LEM, the country held its collective breath and watched. In living rooms, bars, at public events, and outside storefront windows, Americans gathered to watch history.

THE EAGLE HAS LANDED—TWO MEN WALK ON THE MOON announced the *Washington Post* the following day. The *New York Times* broke from its policy against banner headlines and boldly printed MEN WALK ON THE MOON, and published a poem by Archibald MacLeish entitled "Voyage to the Moon."

> You were a wonder to us, unattainable . . .
> Now our hands have touched you in your depth of night.

Across the earth, people cheered the accomplishment of these NASA astronauts, claiming it as a victory for all humankind. The following day, in Lisbon, Portugal, the newspaper *Diario de Noticias* declared THE 21ST CENTURY STARTS TODAY.

Sitting in the *Columbia* command module, Michael Collins breathed a sigh of relief when the *Eagle* touched down safely on the moon. But he could not yet share in the feeling of triumph that gripped the citizens back on what Buckminster Fuller had termed "Spaceship Earth."

"I was a lot more worried, I guess, about getting them up off the moon than I was of getting them down onto the moon," Collins reflected many years later. "The motor on the lunar module was one motor, and if something went wrong with it, you know, they were dead men; there was no other way for them to leave."[15]

Just as humans had never landed on an alien body before *Apollo 11*, they had also never *taken off from* an alien body, and there remained the possibility that some crucial instrument might have been damaged during landing. If any malfunction had occurred, Aldrin and Armstrong would have been, at best, stranded on the lunar surface, doomed to deplete their life-support systems before any method of rescue could be hatched. In fact, this remained such a distinct possibility that a Nixon speechwriter had been told to prepare an address for the president to read in the event that such a disaster occurred. The contents of that speech, which Nixon prerecorded for television, have recently come to light:

> Good evening, my fellow Americans.
>
> Tonight I want to talk to you on a subject of deep concern to all Americans, and to many people in all parts of the world. Fate has intervened that the men who went to the moon to explore in peace will stay on the moon to rest in peace. These brave men, Neil Armstrong and Edward Aldrin,

know that there is no hope for their recovery, but they also know that there is hope for mankind through their sacrifice.[16]

Thankfully, there was never a need to broadcast such a speech—although a critical instrument inside the *Eagle* had been damaged just after Armstrong and Aldrin returned from their two-and-a-half-hour excursion on the lunar surface. During their pre-ascent checklist, they discovered that the knob for the main engine's circuit breaker had been broken off, most likely as they had moved around the cabin in their bulky suits. The crew of the *Eagle* was concerned at first, but they solved it in a manner that, given the precise design, planning, and execution required for a moon mission, was almost as preposterous as the problem—Aldrin used a felt-tipped pen to activate the switch.

Twenty-two hours after it had landed, the *Eagle* capsule successfully took off from the moon and began its journey back to the mother ship. The descent stage that remained on the moon bore a silver plaque with pictures of the western and eastern hemispheres, along with an inscription that was reminiscent of early science fiction films:

HERE MEN FROM THE PLANET EARTH
FIRST SET FOOT UPON THE MOON
JULY 1969, A.D.
WE CAME IN PEACE FOR ALL MANKIND

The plaque bore the facsimile signatures of the *Apollo 11* astronauts, along with that of Richard Nixon. *Eagle* also left behind a memorial bag with the contents of a gold olive branch pin, a patch from the original *Apollo 1* mission, and a silicon disk with statements of goodwill from America's "Space Age" presidents—Eisenhower, Kennedy, Johnson, and Nixon—and messages from the leaders of seventy-three countries around the world. (In his book, *Men from Earth*, Aldrin wrote that the bag also included medals commemorating Soviet cosmonauts Vladimir Komarov and Yuri Gagarin.)

"Oh my god, beautiful, a beautiful little thing. You see the LEM, a little golden bug down there among the craters, and it gets slowly bigger and bigger," Collins remembered. When the *Eagle* docked with *Columbia* and Aldrin climbed back into the CM, Collins grabbed him by both ears and almost kissed him on the forehead.

On July 24, the *Columbia* reentered Earth's atmosphere and successfully deployed its parachutes.[17] The astronauts splashed down in the Pacific Ocean near Johnston Atoll, west of Hawaii, and were retrieved by the USS *Hornet*. On board the ship, Armstrong, Aldrin, and Collins were placed in a quarantine trailer to check for the presence of any unknown pathogens they might have picked up from the moon. Still in quarantine, they were later transferred to a laboratory at the Johnson Space Center. As they watched footage of the media coverage of their mission, Aldrin turned to Armstrong and, perhaps unwittingly, made a joke that symbolized the importance of "media as message" in 1969. "Look," he said. "We missed the whole thing."[18]

❋ ❋ ❋

While Robert W. Taylor was serving as director of the Pentagon's Advanced Research Projects Agency (ARPA), Information Processing Techniques Office in 1968, he and another ARPA research director, J. C. R. Licklider, had written a paper on "The Computer as a Communications Device," a statement about the interactive potential of computers. Taylor, a former NASA employee, had financed Douglas Engelbart's now-legendary demonstrations at the 1968 Joint Fall Computer Conference in San Francisco, where he displayed early examples of the mouse, windows interfacing, hypertext, networking, and teleconferencing. Now, he would pioneer a mode of

1969

information technology that would have an immeasurable influence on the world as it approached the new millennium.

In Taylor's office at ARPA, he had three terminals: one to the Systems Development Corporation in Santa Monica, one to the Genie Project at UC Berkeley, and a third to MIT. Three decades later, Taylor remembered,

> For each of these three terminals, I had three different sets of user commands. So if I was talking online with someone at S.D.C. and I wanted to talk to someone I knew at Berkeley or M.I.T. about this, I had to get up from the S.D.C. terminal, go over and log into the other terminal and get in touch with them. I said, oh, man, it's obvious what to do: If you have these three terminals, there ought to be one terminal that goes anywhere you want to go where you have interactive computing. That idea is the ARPAnet.[19]

That's how Taylor came up with the idea for the ARPANET—a telecommunications network that could connect computers, even those at remote locations.

With Leonard Kleinrock overseeing a team of engineers, the first network connection was established at UCLA in September 1969. A second network node was established at the Stanford Research Institute the following month, and the first Internet message was sent from UCLA to Stanford on October 29. In 1969's version of Alexander Graham Bell telling Mr. Watson to "Come here," UCLA sent the first two letters of the word *login* to Stanford before the network crashed— which, one could say, was itself a sign of things to come. "As a result," remembered Kleinrock, "history now records how clever we were to send such a prophetic first message, namely 'lo.'"[20]

Technology was not just connecting man but also finding its way *into* man. One year after Philip K. Dick published his 1968 novel, *Do Androids Dream of Electric Sheep?*, which imagined a neo-noir, paranoid world in which android "replicants" were virtually indistinguishable from humans, Dr. Denton Cooley performed the first total artificial heart implant. Cooley implanted a pneumatic, double-ventricle pump designed by Dr. Domingo Liotta into the body of a dying, forty-seven-year-old-man who was suffering extreme heart failure. The patient remained alive for three days, at which point the artificial heart was replaced with a transplanted donor heart.

The extension of life was at the heart of author Norman Spinrad's paranoid sci-fi classic from 1969, *Bug Jack Barron*. Muckraking television host Jack Barron makes a startling discovery about the Foundation for Human Immortality, a cryogenics institute headed by a billionaire industrialist, which is buying children from poor families to use their youthful glands in a sinister medical transformation that unlocks the keys to immortality.

The onset of technology at the end of the decade was unprecedented, and pop artists pondered what this meant for the fate of humanity. That summer, the young British rock singer David Bowie quickly recorded a song called "Space Oddity," a psychedelic, five-minute sci-fi drama about an astronaut named Major Tom. With commentary on the instant fame of astronauts ("the papers want to know whose shirts you wear") and technology ("Here I am floating in my tin can"), the song ends enigmatically, with Major Tom transmitting a good-bye message to his wife and then disappearing into radio silence as his circuits go dead. Whether this is the result of mechanical failure or an intentional choice is unclear, and his seemingly peaceful journey into oblivion casts a strange light on the most remarkable technological achievement in human history.

"Space Oddity" wouldn't chart until its rerelease four years later. The number-one hit at the time of the moon landing was "In the Year 2525 (Exordium and Terminus)," from the one-hit-wonder duo of Zager and Evans. The song had been released by a small company two years earlier but became a widespread hit after an Odessa, Texas, radio station began playing it in 1969 and MCA Records picked it up.

1969

The song's grim prophecies of the fate of the human race over millennial intervals (thought-controlling drugs, atrophied limbs, reproduction through test tubes, a depleted earth) builds to the end of "man's reign," in what may be an eternal cycle of genesis and apocalypse in the universe. It was the perfect pop record for the year of god in the machine.

13. THE MISTS OF CAMELOT

The Chappaquiddick incident tarnishes the Kennedy image.

"**Y**ou know, this is quite a day on another front, too," President Nixon told William Safire. The same weekend that history was made on the surface of the moon, tragedy had struck the Kennedy family once again. In an observation that could just as easily have been applied to the Watergate scandal within his own administration a few years later, Nixon said, "It'll be hard to hush this one up; too many reporters want to win a Pulitzer Prize."[1]

The political future of Ted Kennedy had looked ever brighter in the first half of 1969. But as the months of 1969 ran on, those close to him felt he seemed lost at times. He was drinking more, behaving erratically. Some wondered if he was capable of playing the role of torchbearer for the nation's most famous political clan.

On July 18, Kennedy flew to Martha's Vineyard to participate in the Edgartown Yacht Club Regatta. Afterward, he would attend a party that his cousin and lifelong friend, lawyer Joe Gargan, had arranged in a rented two-bedroom cabin on nearby Chappaquiddick Island, an island five miles long and three miles wide and accessible only by ferry from Edgartown. The party was to be a reunion of sorts for the "Boiler Room girls"—six young women who had worked for Bobby's presidential campaign the previous year. Ted's wife, Joan, was in the midst of a difficult pregnancy and had stayed home to rest that weekend.

The Kennedy brothers had visited Chappaquiddick since their boyhood, and Kennedy had been a fixture at the annual Edgartown Regatta on Martha's Vineyard. Parties traditionally accompanied the regatta, and the ones in 1966 and 1967 had gone down as especially riotous ones, thanks in part to Ted's participation; stories of his behavior were still circulating around Martha's Vineyard.[2] Ted had missed the 1968 regatta in the wake of brother Bobby's death, but this weekend in 1969 saw him returning to Edgartown to race on board the *Victura*, a Wianno Senior boat that he had inherited from brother Jack.

After a disappointing finish in the regatta, Kennedy took the 150-yard ferry crossing to Chappaquiddick and drove to the rented cabin in his 1967 Oldsmobile Delmont 88. Unlike his room at the Shiretown Inn in Edgartown, the cabin had a bathtub, and Kennedy looked forward to soaking his aching back before the party.

Attending the party were Jack Crimmins, a legal aide and investigator serving as Kennedy's chauffeur; Charles Tretter, a Boston lawyer and occasional Kennedy aide; Joe Gargan; Paul Markham, a bank president and former U. S. attorney; Ray LaRosa, a civil defense official; and the six Boiler Room girls—Rosemary Keough, Mary Jo Kopechne, Susan Tannenbaum, Esther Newberg, and sisters Maryellen and Nance Lyons.[3]

Sometime later that night, Kennedy left the party with one of the Boiler Room girls, the attractive, twenty-eight-year-old Mary Jo Kopechne. Sylvia Malm, the twenty-one-year-old resident of Dyke House, which sat about a hundred yards from Dyke Bridge, later told her mother that she'd seen a black Oldsmobile speeding toward the narrow wooden bridge that spanned the freshwater Poucha Pond and led to the island's easternmost stretch of beach along the Atlantic Ocean, around 11:30 P.M.[4] Edgartown deputy sheriff Christopher "Huck" Look later reported that he saw a black car—either the Oldsmobile, or one that looked like it—headed toward Dyke Bridge around 1:00 in the morning. "It appeared to be a man and a woman, and maybe somebody else in the back seat."[5] He tried to speak to the driver as the car passed by, but the driver kept on his way toward the bridge.[6]

On Saturday morning, ferryman Richard Hewitt began service a half-hour early to accommodate Robert Samuel, a high school science teacher, and fifteen-year-old Joseph Cappavella, who were headed for a morning of fishing on Chappaquiddick. They spent an hour or so casting along East Beach and then came back to the dock. There, Samuel saw the sun hit a glint of metal just ten feet away from the south side of Dyke Bridge. Upon closer inspection, he realized it was the wheel of a car sticking out of the water.

Samuel and Cappavella went to the Malm house, and Mrs. Malm went to take a look. Remembering what her daughter had told her, she said, "You couldn't see what it was in the water, but I knew when they got it out it was going to be that black car."[7]

She called the Edgartown police, and chief Dominick Arena showed up on the scene. He changed into his bathing suit and braved the five-knot tide (which carried him north into the adjoining Cape Pogue Pond at first) to dive down and take a look at the submerged vehicle.[8] Unable to get a clear look at the vehicle, he called in the scuba team from the fire department. Meanwhile, he also called in the license plate number: L78 207. He would soon learn that the car was licensed to Edward M. Kennedy.

At about a quarter to nine, John Farrar, the thirty-three-year-old owner of the Turf and Tackle Shop in Edgartown, and also captain of the fire department's scuba search and rescue division, arrived with scuba gear that the volunteer fire department had just purchased.

(The town selectmen had been up in arms over such an exorbitant acquisition.) He went out to the submerged vehicle and, around the back of the car, saw two feet sticking up near the right side of the rear window.

The victim, a young woman, was found head up, with her head "cocked back and her face pressed into the foot well." Her hands clutched the top of the rear seat; her body was in a state of rigor mortis. As Farrar would later explain, the water would have "gushed through the two right windows" on impact, and, as the car turned over and settled into the water, a large pocket of air would have been trapped near the floorboards, where the victim's head had been positioned.[9]

Farrar tried pulling her out of the car, but the tide was so strong that he had to tie a chain around her body. The first attempt to pull her out failed when the chain came undone from around her torso, so Farrar retied it around her neck and this time was able to pull her lifeless body to shore.

He passed her body to Arena. The chief was struck by how "well groomed" she seemed—dressed in a white, long-sleeved blouse, dark sandals, wearing two bracelets and a ring. "If you'll forgive me," the chief later recollected, "if she hadn't been wringing wet, it was as if she were about to go to work or to a party because everything was in place." Later, it was discovered that underneath her clothes she was wearing a blue bra and no underwear.[10]

Farrar asked the chief if he recognized her.

"Thank God, no. I don't recognize her," he said, relieved that yet another Kennedy brother had not suffered a tragic fate. "It isn't one of the clan."[11]

❋ ❋ ❋

While the chief was sighing in relief because he didn't recognize the dead girl, Kennedy was in the main lobby of his hotel. He asked the clerk in the lobby for change so he could use the pay phone in the little shack outside the inn.

Local resident Tony Bettencourt saw Kennedy as he was placing the call. "Senator," Bettencourt said, "do you know there's been a girl found dead in your car?"

When Kennedy didn't respond, Bettencourt asked him if he needed a ride down to the bridge. Kennedy declined. He stayed in the phone shack and placed more calls.[12]

✳ ✳ ✳

Sometime very late Friday night or early Saturday morning, Ray LaRosa had been sitting on the front porch of the cottage when he'd seen a lone figure approaching in the dark. He heard Kennedy's voice telling him to get Markham and Gargan. LaRosa went in to fetch the two men, who went outside to meet Kennedy. "There's been a terrible accident," the senator told them. "The car's gone off the bridge down by the beach, and Mary Jo is in it."[13]

They got in a car and quickly drove out to Dyke Bridge. When they arrived, the headlights of their car shone on the underside of Kennedy's Delmont 88, which lay upside down in the saltwater currents of Poucha Pond, about ten feet to the right of the bridge.

Markham said, "Holy God."[14]

"I realized if Mary Jo was in that car, there was no hope," Gargan said later. "I said to myself, 'Oh shit, this is over! This is done. She's gone.'"[15]

The three men got out of the car. Gargan and Markham undressed and made their way out to the submerged car. They tried in vain to locate Kopechne in the dark waters. The current threatened to carry them away from the car, and at one point, Gargan says, he got trapped inside the car and almost drowned. He later remembered looking up and seeing Kennedy laying on the bridge on his back, his hands clasped behind his head, his knees drawn to him, saying aloud, "Oh, my God. What am I going to do?"[16]

Gargan and Markham gave up their search, and the three drove to the ferry landing. Gargan insisted that they needed to report the accident. Kennedy, he says, told him, "All right, all right, Joey! I'm tired of listening to you. I'll take care of it. You go back; don't upset the girls. Don't get them involved."[17] With that, Kennedy dove into the Sound and began swimming toward the mainland.

"I hope he drowns, the son of a bitch!" Gargan said.[18]

❊ ❊ ❊

Chief Arena went to the Malms' house to call the Shiretown Inn, where he knew Kennedy had been staying. Arena called in to the station and discovered that the senator was there waiting for him with Paul Markham. Kennedy was handed the phone.

"I'm afraid, Senator, I have some bad news," Arena said. "There's been another tragedy. Your car was in an accident over here. And the young lady is dead."

"I know," said Kennedy.

"Can you tell me, was there anybody else in the car?"

"Yes."

"Are they in the water?"

"No. Can I talk to you? Could I see you?" Kennedy asked.

"Do you want to come over here? Or do you want me to go over there?"

"I prefer for you to come over here."[19]

Arena agreed. Still dripping wet from his dive, he returned to his office to find Kennedy sitting at the chief's desk. "Our roles could have been reversed. The senator was in clean, dry clothes—poised, confident and in control, using my office and telephone. I'm standing in a puddle of water in a state of confusion," Arena said later.

Also in the room was Markham, whom Arena (a former state trooper) recognized from the Suffolk County Courthouse.

"Do you happen to know where Rosemary Keough is from so we can notify her next of kin?" Arena asked Kennedy. At that point, Arena thought the victim found in the car had been Rosemary Keough, as Keough's purse had been found in the car.

"It isn't Cricket," Kennedy said, using Keough's nickname. "It's Mary Jo Kopechne. I've already notified her parents."[20]

Arena asked Kennedy to give a statement. The senator asked if he could write his statement. Arena agreed. Kennedy said he needed privacy, and the chief agreed to this also. Kennedy went to a private office with Markham, to whom he dictated a statement.

A little while later, Arena returned to the private office. Kennedy was still dictating. "We're almost finished," Markham told Arena, an apparent sign for him to leave.[21] Again, Arena complied. Soon, the two delivered Kennedy's written statement. The senator had dictated as follows:

On July 18, 1969, at approximately 11:15 P.M. on Chappaquiddick, Martha's Vineyard, Mass., I was driving my car on Main Street, Chappaquiddick, on my way to get the ferry back to Edgartown. I was unfamiliar with the road and turned right onto Dyke Road, instead of bearing hard left on Main Street.

After proceeding for approximately one-half mile on Dyke Road, I descended a hill and came upon a narrow bridge. There was one passenger with me, Miss Mary _____ [unsure of how to spell her last name, they had left it blank], a former secretary of my brother, Robert Kennedy.

The car turned over and sank into the water and landed with the roof resting on the bottom. I attempted to open the door and the window of the car but have no recollection of how I got out of the car.

I came to the surface and then repeatedly dove down to the car in an attempt to see if the passenger was still in the car. I was unsuccessful in the attempt.

I was exhausted and in a state of shock. I recall walking back to where my friends were eating. There was a car parked in front of the cottage, and I climbed into the back seat. I then asked for someone to bring me back to Edgartown. I remember walking around for a period of time and then going back to my hotel room.

When I fully realized what had happened this morning, I immediately contacted the police.[22]

At the police station, Kennedy and Markham also placed calls to Rose Kennedy, warning her to stay out of the public eye so as to avoid questions from the press once the story broke, and to press aide Dick Drayne, instructing him to hold the press at bay. "I sat here all morning waiting for the roof to fall in," Drayne later said.[23] Meanwhile, they sent another attorney, William vanden Heuvel, to visit the Kopechne family, and they dispatched aide Dun Gifford, who had been vacationing on the island of Nantucket, to go see to it that Kopechne's corpse was taken off the island as fast as possible.[24]

Kennedy and Markham left the station, assuring Arena that they would return for further questioning. By noon that day, the press had gotten wind of the story. They camped outside the Edgartown Police Station, prodding Arena for information on the accident. Markham had told the chief not to release Kennedy's statement until they could get another Kennedy family attorney, Burke Marshall, to review it. Hours passed, and Arena finally released the statement to reporters.

Later, Markham called the station. "Chief, we haven't been able to get a hold of Burke Marshall. Could I ask you to hold up the statement a little bit longer?"

"I'm sorry. I've already released it."

"Oh, Jesus," Markham responded. He hung up before Arena could ask when Kennedy would return to the station.[25]

He never did. By Saturday night, Kennedy and every other person who had attended the party on Chappaquiddick Island had left Martha's Vineyard.

❀ ❀ ❀

On July 25, Kennedy appeared at the Edgartown District Court to stand charges in the case of the *Commonwealth v. Edward M Kennedy*. Thomas Teller, the court clerk, read the complaint against the senator: that he "did go away after knowingly causing injury to Mary Jo Kopechne without stopping and making known his name, residence and the number of his motor vehicle."

Kennedy said, "Guilty," and then repeated so that he could be heard: "Guilty."[26]

Kopechne's death was ruled accidental, and Kennedy was given a suspended sentence for leaving the scene of the accident. In the press, the story overtook the achievements of *Apollo 11* for front-page coverage, though in many quarters the sensationalism of the case was tempered by a collective sympathy for the Kennedy family. Although the *New York Post* charged that Kennedy "was the beneficiary of scandalous cover-up," it also put forth that nothing that had happened on Martha's Vineyard that weekend could "erase the record of gallantry" of the Kennedy family, that the "heroic past must temper any critical view of the present." The *Washington Post* said of the senator, "we suspect he will suffer enough in any case, this man who has already suffered the loss of an eldest brother shot down in a war, a sister killed in a plane crash, and two brothers murdered by assassins."[27]

Kennedy attended Kopechne's funeral on July 22 in Plymouth, Pennsylvania, wearing a brace around his neck. Doctors had reportedly said that he suffered a concussion, but many people looked upon the neck brace cynically, suspecting that he'd worn it to remind people that he, too, was a victim in this tragedy.

Although Kopechne's death was ruled an accidental drowning, Kennedy faced charges in the court held most dear by elected officials—the court of public opinion. The cover of *Life* said it all: THE FATEFUL TURN FOR TED KENNEDY: GRAVE QUESTIONS ABOUT HIS MIDNIGHT CAR ACCIDENT.[28]

The questions that were being asked collectively by the American press and public were: Had Kennedy been drunk when his car plunged off the bridge? With his beautiful wife Joan back home with their four kids, what was the senator doing out late at night, driving alone with a young woman? And why had he waited nine hours to report the accident?

In an attempt to answer these grave questions, Kennedy asked the three television networks to allow him to give a speech to the American public on the Friday following the accident. The speech would be likened to Nixon's "Checkers" speech from September 1952, in which Nixon—in one of the few instances in his career—had used the media to his benefit and saved his political career by effectively answering charges of accepting illegal campaign contributions. With practically every American with access to a television set having watched the moon landing at the beginning of the week, Kennedy's address capped perhaps the biggest week in the history of live news in the United States.

Beginning at 7:30 p.m. EDT, Kennedy addressed the nation from the library of his father's house, reading a prepared speech. In it, he explained that he'd left the party around 11:15 p.m., accompanied by Kopechne. He quickly denied the "suspicions of immoral conduct" between he and Kopechne, saying, "There has never been a private relationship between us of any kind. Nor was I driving under the influence of liquor." After recounting the overturning of his car into the pond, he said, "I remember thinking as the cold water rushed in around my head that I was for certain drowning. Then water entered my lungs and I actually felt the sensation of drowning. But somehow I struggled to the surface alive."

Kennedy said, "I made immediate and repeated efforts to save Mary Jo by diving into the strong and murky current, but succeeded only in increasing my state of utter exhaustion and alarm. My conduct and conversations during the next several hours, to the extent that I can remember them, make no sense to me at all." Although he noted that doctors had informed him that he had suffered a "cerebral concussion" in the accident, and that he was in a state of shock, he said, "I regard as indefensible the fact that I did not report the accident to the police immediately.

"Instead of looking directly for a telephone after lying exhausted in the grass for an undetermined time," he continued, "I walked back to the cottage where the party was being held and requested the help of two friends, my cousin, Joseph Gargan, and Phil Markham, and directed them to return immediately to the scene with me—this was sometime after midnight—in order to undertake a new effort to dive down and locate Miss Kopechne. Their strenuous efforts, undertaken at some risk to their own lives, also proved futile."

He recounted that when they had discovered the ferry was closed for the night, he "suddenly jumped into the water and impulsively swam across, nearly drowning once again in the effort, and returned to my hotel about 2:00 a.m. and collapsed in my room." The following morning, with his mind "somewhat more lucid," he first tried to contact Burke Marshall, and then "belatedly reported the accident" to the police.

Unlike the "Checkers" speech, Kennedy's formal explanation to the American public would not resonate as a convincing one. Although a subsequent Harris poll found that 68% of its respondents were predisposed toward an empathetic reaction—saying it was "unfair to be critical of the way Senator Kennedy reacted to the accident because the same thing could have happened to anyone"—55% felt he had not offered an "adequate explanation of what he was doing at the party or with the girl who was killed." A ratio of 44:36 felt he had not "told the truth," and only 38% believed his claim that he had not been driving under the influence.[29] Gargan would later condemn the speech: "It was made up, all of it, including thoughts and emotions."[30]

In the court of public opinion, Kennedy had all but convicted himself. As Brock Brower commented in *Life*, "the death of Mary Jo . . . might have ended 1972 as a matter of destiny, but the fact that he left the scene of the accident—'indefensible,' he himself said on TV—has perhaps ended 1972 even as a question of choice."[31]

After some reflection, Kennedy returned to his Senate seat, where he was welcomed with open arms by majority leader Mike Mansfield. But the memories of that ugly incident in Chappaquiddick would hang like a specter over his public image. Biographer Robert Sherrill wrote, "One can expand this nightmare to [Kopechne] hanging on for hours, slowly dying of terror and asphyxiation, while Kennedy tossed and turned on his bed in the Shiretown Inn and grumbled about the noises from the party next door, worrying about his own comfort and his political future."[32]

From the death of a young woman to the appearance of political might circumventing the justice system, to the feeding frenzy of those in the media who self-righteously stood in judgment of Kennedy without knowing how they themselves would have behaved in similar moments of terror, the incident was one of the ugliest of the decade. As Kennedy's presidential chances faded, Chappaquiddick would leave lasting memories of human nature at its worst.

14. SHAKING THE CAGE

Films of the New Hollywood school examine the counterculture idealism of commune life and free love.

For many young people on the fringes of society, the growing violence and paranoia across the American landscape was a sign that the nation was coming apart at the seams. There was a feeling that urban and suburban life had been marred by rampant consumerism and pollution, that white-collar life had threatened to remove humankind from its natural environment. The desire to escape the trappings of modern society and "recapture" a simpler, Edenic time from American's perceived past went hand in hand with an increasing ecological awareness and led to the back-to-the-land movement.

It was, as *Newsweek* dubbed it, the "Year of the Commune."[1] The collective societies that had sprouted up across the nation, especially in the West and Southwest—e.g. Morning Star Commune in Sebastopol, California, Lorien Commune in New Mexico, Red Rock in Colorado—followed the communal approach to sharing land as an antithesis to American material and consumer culture. Nancy Nesbit, a resident of the Modern Utopia commune, summed up the commune ethos: "Invest in some land in the country, build a log cabin, grow your own vegetables, forget that future vice-presidency at the local computer programming office."[2]

1969

The commune movement represented a rejection of urban America, which sociologist Desmond Morris analyzed in his 1969 book, *The Human Zoo*. Morris likened the modern city to a zoo for humans—a place where basic needs and services are attainable, but at the price of living in an unnatural environment. Some communes, most notably Drop City in Colorado, took a cue from the design theories popularized by Buckminster Fuller and created "organic" living spaces shaped like geodesic domes. "Living in a dome opens your fucking mind," said John Curl, a founder of Drop City. "No corners to hide in. Round like the sky."[3] The Pacific High free school in the Santa Cruz Mountains included several dome structures on its campus—including the "Bathtub Dome" where faculty and students shared group baths.[4] Dome-shaped dwelling spaces became so popular in the counterculture that the *Whole Earth Catalog* featured a number of such structures in its Fall 1969 issue. (Even a short-lived "bubble" movement popped up. Students at Antioch College designed an alternative "Nomadic/Pneumatic Campus" with an open-air classroom setting under a forty-foot-high translucent polyvinyl bubble. A "guerilla" performance troupe called Ant Farm traveled across the country giving shows using walk-in plastic bubble structures. Their goal was to show "a spatial expression of alternatives to the rigid architectural paths we were led down as children."[5])

In his classic 1969 treatise, *The Making of a Counter Culture*, Theodore Roszak theorized that modern society had arrived at an "era of social engineering" and had evolved into a "technocracy," a technical ruling class in which the totality of the human experience was placed within the context of the "industrial complex." As with the commune movement, Roszak argued, the rebellion against the technocracy as the dominant social order would be fought primarily by "the young [who] stand forth so prominently because they act against a background of neatly pathological passivity on the part of the adult generation" and their flowering "counter culture," a term Roszak coined with his work.[6]

With enclaves of young hippies spreading throughout the countryside, this social phenomenon captured the darker aspects of American imagination. Rumors of rampant drug use and sexual promiscuity occurring in these intentional communities shocked conservative Americans, while the whole notion of a *commune*—a word that shares its roots with *Communism*—was threatening to reactionaries. (One commune resident interviewed at the Woodstock festival joked that his parents thought he was living in a "Communist training camp."[7]) Some parents feared losing their children to these surrogate, counterculture "families."

To investigate the realities of commune life, *Life* sent reporter John Stickney and photographer John Olson to an unidentified commune for a July cover story. The title, "The Youth Communes: New Way of Living Confronts the U. S.," embodied the curious threat that such communes posed to some strands of so-called "straight" society. ("They almost invariably encounter hostility and even violence from local people," Stickney wrote.[8]) Most commune residents wanted nothing to do with the outside world. That was the whole point—to escape it. The residents were largely cognizant of society's attitudes toward them, and they often regarded the outside world with suspicion, including the "weekend hippies" who would stop by looking to freeload.

Shrewdly, the magazine had sent two of the youngest members of the staff: Stickney was twenty-three, Olson, twenty-two—both "well be-thatched [and] bell-bottomed."[9] To be allowed into the commune, the two had to meet with the commune residents for an hour to gain their trust, and they were given access only after vowing not to disclose the location of the commune site. Asked to be described as being "somewhere in the woods," this particular forty-one-member commune consisted of former teachers, actors, computer programmers, and welders, with the adult figures ranging in age from seventeen to thirty-two. The commune referred to itself generically as "the family"—not to be confused with the Manson Family, to be discussed later—and the eleven children were raised by the group as a whole. They grew their own food, made their own clothes, taught their own school lessons, made their own laws, and, often, followed their own religion—combining elements of Christianity, Buddhism, etc., into a unique blend of secular humanism.

During their time in the commune, in which they had to chip in with the chores, Stickney and Olson were accepted as "brothers" and invited to participate in the family gathering known as the "meeting of the spirit."[10] Their photo essay provided the rest of the nation with a rare glimpse inside one of the many communes where members had rejected the conventions of modern America and looked to themselves to reinvent it.

❉ ❉ ❉

After their work together on Roger Corman's 1967 movie, *The Trip*, a young Hollywood outsider named Dennis Hopper began talking to Peter Fonda about a new project—a motorcycle road-trip buddy picture set in the American Southwest. On the surface, their pet project (working title: *The Loners*) might have sounded like just another film in the tradition of Roger Corman's low-budget B movies, much like Corman's 1966 biker flick, *The Wild Angels*, in which Fonda had also starred. But both Hopper and Fonda were shooting for something more—the ultimate B movie that would bring the style and sensibility of new-wave European cinema to American movie screens. "I was interested in trying to make the first American art film, and also outside the studio system," Hopper explains in the documentary *Easy Riders, Raging Bulls*. Fonda wanted to challenge the model of the American capitalist system— to "shake the fucking cage," as he put it.[11]

Jack Nicholson, the actor who had written *The Trip*, convinced a bold young producer, Bert Schneider of Raybert Productions, to take a chance on the project, based on the premise that biker pictures made money. Schneider gave Hopper and Fonda money to film 16mm test shots of scenes involving the two lead characters (played by Fonda and Hopper) with prostitutes (Toni Basil and Karen Black) at the upcoming Mardi Gras in New Orleans. After seeing the footage, which the four improvised over four days of shooting, Schneider gave the go-ahead on production of the full script.

Directed by Hopper and cowritten by Fonda, Hopper, and novelist Terry Southern, the movie was renamed *Easy Rider*. Posters for the film didn't even show or make reference to a motorcycle. The tagline read, "A man went looking for America. And couldn't find it anywhere."

Fonda and Hopper play Wyatt and Billy—aka, Captain America and Buffalo Bill—two social outcasts who take the money from a drug sale and set out on their choppers from Los Angeles, bound for Florida, where they plan to ride out the metaphorical sunset. On the way, they pick up a hitchhiker (Luke Askew) and take him to his commune. Based on the New Buffalo Commune in Taos, New Mexico, the film's commune was constructed in the Malibu hills and peopled with hippies from the Topanga Canyon commune in the Santa Monica Mountains. Although greeted suspiciously by some members of the commune—one asks them, "Who sent you?"— Wyatt and Billy are welcomed into the group.

Life's Stickney had written, "Many of the settlers dropped out of teaching and other professions and are particularly ill-prepared to carve a living out of nature. The winters are harsh, the earth hard. Often they resort to shopping at the nearest stores."[12] True to life, the commune dwellers in *Easy Rider* are portrayed as "city kids planting food" who look apprehensively toward the winter. In one of the most poignant scenes of the movie, one of the communards (a bearded and stick-thin Robert Walker Jr.) leads the group in an intense and breathless secular prayer: "We have planted our seeds. We ask that our efforts be worthy to produce simple food for our simple tastes. We ask that our efforts be rewarded. We thank you for the food we eat from other hands, that we may share it with our fellow man and be even more generous when it is from our own. Thank you for a place to make a stand."

Wyatt approves of the commune and blesses them with a prediction of success: "They're gonna make it. Dig, man. They're gonna make it."

Wyatt and Billy ride eastward. When they join in a small-town procession, they're arrested and jailed for "parading without a permit." Behind bars they meet George Hanson, a drunken ACLU lawyer (Jack Nicholson) who helps them obtain their release. In return, they let Hanson accompany them, and that night around a campfire they introduce him to marijuana cigarettes—itself a revolutionary scene. "This is the first time that marijuana had ever been smoked in a movie that the people who smoked it didn't go out and kill a bunch of nurses or whatever," Hopper remembered.[13]

On the footsteps of the Deep South in eastern Louisiana, they're denied service at a local eatery because of their freakish looks. (To effectively convey the cultural tensions of the day, Hopper recruited local citizens to play rednecks in the restaurant, and he provided their inspiration by telling them that the bikers had raped and killed a girl on the outskirts of town.) That night around the campfire, Hanson explains the reactions of local citizens: "They're scared of what you represent to them. . . . What you represent to them is freedom. . . . I mean, it's real hard to be free when you are bought and sold in the marketplace. But don't ever tell anybody that they're not free 'cause then they gonna get real busy killin' and maimin' to prove to you that they are." His words prove prophetic when the locals attack the three in the middle of the night. They beat Wyatt and Billy and kill George with a machete; as a "straight" member of society, his transgression of associating with these freaks was worse than their being freaks.

Fleeing the scene of violence, Wyatt and Billy arrive in New Orleans and take up with two prostitutes (Toni Basil and Karen Black). During the trippy graveyard scene, Captain America asks a mausoleum statue that vaguely resembles the Statue of Liberty why she's left him. The scene recalls Hanson's earlier observation: "You know, this used to be a hell of a good country. I can't understand what's gone wrong with it." In a movie about the search for America, both were powerful statements. The band Steppenwolf echoed this sentiment in its nine-and-a-quarter-minute epic from 1969, "Monster/Suicide/America," which asked, "America, where are you now? / Don't you care about your sons and daughters?"

Having committed themselves to a quest that is spiritually devoid, Wyatt and Billy's fate seems somehow sealed. The next morning they are passed by two good ol' boys in a pickup truck who taunt them by aiming a shotgun at the bikers. Billy flips them the middle finger. The one with the rifle shoots Billy off his bike. Moments later, the men in the truck turn around to finish the job, and as Wyatt is passing by in search of help, the rifle-wielding redneck shoots his gas tank. Wyatt dies in a fiery explosion. In the final shot, the camera pans back into the sky to show the scene of fire and death beside the Mississippi River aqueduct—a symbol of division running through the middle of the nation itself.

Askew described the movie as "a metaphor for what happened in America after the Sixties. It became the kind of tag end, hungover sadness that happens right after a great age." And it was much more than that. Coming just two years after the cultural sensation of Arthur Penn's *Bonnie and Clyde*, Hopper and Fonda's project was important in establishing the American auteur movement, the "New Hollywood." In May, the same month that *Midnight Cowboy* premiered in New York, the duo—Fonda bedraggled in his long hair and beard, Hopper a modern-day prospector—were the toast of the Cannes Film Festival, where *Easy Rider* was given a special award for best first feature by a new director. Released in the United States in August, the film became the summer's drive-in sensation. The image of Fonda in his leather jacket and Captain America helmet and Hopper in his cowboy hat and fringed frontier jacket riding through Monument Valley to the sounds of Steppenwolf's "Born to Be Wild" became an iconic portrayal of freedom, counterculture rebels, and the American road.

❀ ❀ ❀

Moviegoers got another glimpse of commune life with the release of *Alice's Restaurant*, director Arthur Penn's follow-up to *Bonnie and Clyde*, a full-length film inspired by folksinger Arlo Guthrie's eighteen-minute signature song. Guthrie's song is a comical monologue based on his arrest for illegal garbage dumping following a Thanksgiving dinner in Great Barrington, Massachusetts, in 1965, and his subsequent experience in getting drafted for service in Vietnam. Guthrie's character is declared morally unfit to serve in the army and kill people because of his arrest for littering.

The second-generation Leftist makes dad Woody look downright conser-vative in comparison, with his hippie garb and long hair flowing out from under his Stetson hat. He visits friends Alice (Pat Quinn) and Ray (James Broderick), who move into a church that they purchased after its outgoing congregation hold a "deconsecration" ceremony. (Guthrie remembers that such a ceremony had actually been performed for the old Trinity Church on Van Deusenville Road in Great Barrington, Massachusetts. "They didn't want the hippies to meet Jesus," he commented.[14]) Ray and Alice hold a huge counterculture Thanksgiving in the church, and Ray leads his guests in a celebration of their communal gathering: "We're beautiful! We're doing it!"

After dinner, Arlo and his friends decide to help their hosts and cart their months' worth of garbage to the town dump. When they discover the dump closed in observance of Thanksgiving, they heap the bags onto a pile they see at the bottom of a cliff, using the perfectly folkie wisdom that "one big pile is better than two little piles, and rather than bring that one up we decided to throw ours down." Real-life Great Barrington police chief William Obanheim appears as himself, "Officer Obie," the one who arrests Arlo and his friends.

After a fictional series of soap-opera-like events, including the death of a junkie (Michael McClanathan) with whom Alice has had an affair, the movie builds to a wedding with Alice and Ray in the church. With everyone drunk and stoned afterward, Ray doesn't want the communal vibe to end and bids everybody to stay. He speaks of grand plans for building their own community and "the land that will feed us," but his desperation to hold on to the momentary spirit strikes everyone as sad. "Everybody could have his own house," he desperately tells Arlo. "We could all see each other when we wanted to, or not see each other. But be all there!" Later, he says, "I wish we had 'em back. We had a real place, we'd have all been together . . . not fuckin' each other. We'd all be some kind of family."

The movie ends on a down note, the church left with a mess, the residue of bacchanalia. Guthrie remembers, "They didn't believe it would succeed. And so they made a whole movie to show how valiant our attempt was to create a spirituality, to create a new life, the one the kids were talking about . . . but they didn't believe it, so the movie itself was a failure of our ability to do it."[15]

❊ ❊ ❊

In April, *Playboy* published Richard Warren Lewis's exposé, "The Swingers," on the "new breed of unabashed orgiasts and casual couples." Reporting on the swingers' scene that was "flourishing in the subcultural hothouse of southern California"—from a private party in the Hollywood Hills to a Sunset Strip penthouse, San Fernando Valley nightclub, "swingers only" nude swim parties in Palm Springs, swinger-friendly motels on U. S. 101 between San Francisco and Palo Alto—Lewis examined the proliferation of mate swapping and bisexual orgies. What had once been a "carefully guarded pastime indigenous to upper-income groups, especially the suburban nouveau riche, swinging has only lately been embraced by schoolteachers, mutual-fund salesmen, aerospace engineers and other members of the predominant middle-class."

Estimates on the number of Americans participating in swinger activities ranged anywhere from 500,000 to 14,000,000 as claimed by enthusiast Leo Gordon, the screenwriter of the 1969 movie *All the Loving Couples*, about three unsatisfied couples who combine forces for sexual stimulation—tagline: "It's all happening right in your neighborhood."

Indeed, the swinging craze was spreading to neighborhoods from coast to coast. Lewis described scenes from the Seattle suburbs to central Arizona, Cape Kennedy, Florida, Martha's Vineyard, New York City's East Side—even small New England towns such as Vergennes (pronounced *Ver-JENS*), Vermont. Dr. William Simon, a sociologist at the Illinois State Department of Mental Health (and formerly of the Institute for Sex Research at Indiana University) said, "Turning on to the swinging scene probably *has* saved a large number of marriages."[16]

But the institution of marriage would become increasingly fragile after California governor Ronald Reagan signed the Family Law Act on 1969. Effective January 1, 1970, the Act issued in the era of "no-fault divorce." The times were reflected in two television shows that premiered on ABC in September 1969. *The Brady Bunch* was the perfect prime-time sitcom for the era of the blended family. (The character of Carol, played by Florence Henderson, was conceived as a divorcée, although the network asked that no mention be made of her previous marriage.) Meanwhile, *Love, American Style*, an hour-long program that presented a collection of humorous vignettes on sex and romance, dealt frequently with "risque" topics such as divorce and swinging.

For his directorial debut, Paul Mazursky wrote a script that examined the mores of swinging and how the lifestyle would affect a young marriage. The veteran actor and screenwriter had found inspiration for his film in a magazine article on the Esalen Institute in northern California. Part school, part retreat, part spa, Esalen was established on the Big Sur coastline in 1962 as a center devoted to the advancement of holism and "human potential." Mazursky remembered seeing a picture of therapist Fritz Perls, sitting in a hot tub with a group of people, all of them naked. Perls, a German-born psychotherapist, had coined the term "Gestalt therapy" and was a leading figure at Esalen from the early 1960s until 1969, when he left the United States and started a commune based on Gestalt principles on Vancouver Island in Canada. "That's when I said to [my wife] Betsy, 'maybe there's a movie,' and we went to Esalen," Mazursky recalled.[17]

Esalen was merely the most popular of an estimated sixty to seventy encounter-group centers in the United States. The emerging trend in psychology was to focus on interpersonal interactions (or "transactions") rather than individual psychoanalysis, which was demonstrated by the Dr. Thomas A. Harris's #1 bestseller from 1969, *I'm OK—You're OK: A Practical Guide to Transactional Analysis.* Group therapy sessions created a social environment in which the dynamics of interpersonal communications could be examined. Ranging in size and duration (anywhere from a few hours to multi-day retreats), encounter groups focused on the immediate experience of the participants as they shed their inhibitions and defenses—and even, in some groups, their clothes—while seeking to more fully realize their "human potential," a new buzz-phrase in pop psychology. Facilitators loosely guided the discussions but avoided acting like "leaders," while encouraging the group to fill the leadership void through their own participation. "These groups are the most rapidly spreading social phenomenon in the country," said psychologist Carl Rogers.[18]

"We did a 24- or 48-hour marathon," Mazursky remembered. "We were the only couple there. The rest of the people didn't know each other, and they were picking on me—'you controlling bastard, you don't let that poor woman alone'—and she started to cry. Of course when we came out of it, we were very touched, but I thought it was funny."[19] Their experience provided the inspiration for one of the most provocative movies of the decade, *Bob & Carol & Ted & Alice*, which premiered at the New York Film Festival in late summer.

At the beginning of the film, thirty-something California couple Bob and Carol Sanders (Robert Culp and Natalie Wood) drive their Jaguar convertible to an Esalen-like center. There, much like the Mazurskys, they participate as the only couple in a group therapy session in which the facilitator leads them in a Gestalt-like session, combining touchy-feely platitudes with confrontational techniques. He tells the participants to take turns facing each other, bidding them, "See the other person there. Really, *really* look." A montage of scenes shows the couple riding a roller coaster of emotions (crying, arguing, confessions, group hugs) and experiencing personal epiphanies—the "gestalt" experience. "I do hide my feelings. I'm afraid of you," a weeping Carol tells Bob. Moments later, he tells her, "I love you," and the strength of their relationship seems reaffirmed.

Transformed, the couple is eager to share their experience with their friends, Ted and Alice Henderson (Elliot Gould and Dyan Cannon), who are mostly amused by their friends' sudden show of enlightenment, as well as their apparent attempts to fit in as members of the Love Generation: Culp's character has adopted a fashion— long hair, love beads, Nehru jacket—more suited to someone ten years younger, and both he and Carol spout lines like, "That's beautiful, man," and "The truth is always beautiful."

The idea that the truth is always beautiful is quickly tested when Bob returns home from a business trip to his wife and their son and confesses to Carol that he's had an affair. Putting her Esalen-like training to work, Carol digests this news and narrates her emotions as they happen, yet distantly, as if observing herself within a clinical atmosphere: "I'm not sure how I feel. Now let me see. I don't feel upset. I really don't. I don't feel surprised. I feel strange. I don't feel jealous."

After Bob and Carol shock friends Ted and Alice over dinner with news of the affair, Carol brings their enlightenment to phase two. "I had an affair," she announces to Bob, as if she's achieved a rite of passage herself—and her newfound lover is in their bedroom! Bob reacts jealously and threatens violence, but when she points out his hypocrisy, he says: "Lights are going on, baby, in my head. Lights are going on. Insight." Committed to showing how evolved he really is, Bob calls into their bedroom to the as-yet-unseen paramour: "Listen, I'm not going to hit. There isn't going to be any hitting. We don't do that in this house. It's a nonviolent household. We don't even allow any war toys in the house."

The logical conclusion of *Bob & Carol & Ted & Alice* (tagline: "Consider the possibilities") comes when the two couples spend a weekend together in Las Vegas. After Ted confesses that he, too, had committed an infidelity, Alice suggests that the four of them drop all pretenses of marital boundaries and do "what we came here to do . . . Orgy! Orgy! Orgy!" After much discussion, they all decide to go for it, but as they initiate foreplay—Ted with Carol, Bob with Alice—awkwardness sets in and they end their experiment. Roger Ebert argued, "*Bob & Carol & Ted & Alice* isn't really about wife swapping at all, but about the epidemic of moral earnestness that's sweeping our society right now. . . . Now this sort of honesty is all right for deep conversations over a cup of coffee in the student union, but it's dangerous when practiced by couples over thirty."[20]

Mazursky's film is as much about the Eisenhower generation trying to embrace the morality of the Love Generation as it is about infidelity, and with the ending of the two couples aborting their wife-swapping experiment before fully trying it, the notion of free love is rejected as a utopian goal of youth—a sexual Sugar Mountain. In all three films, the quest for a spiritual, utopian ideal of communal life and love comes up short. Ironically, these three offerings from the New Hollywood, here at the end of a decade of rebellion and change, ultimately served to reinforce the cultural status quo as it was in 1969.

15. WEST COAST KILLERS

The Manson Family and the Zodiac Killer terrorize California in the summer of '69.

While the idea of commune life seemed Edenic to some, the day-to-day realities were not always so. *Easy Rider*'s Luke Askew said communes were "pretty ugly scenes. They were run by usually two or three guys on a total power trip, total control over some poor chicks that they ran ragged, bunches of children around that weren't being taken care of."[1] As the communal lifestyle was celebrated on magazine covers and drive-in movie screens, one commune leader was formulating plans for an apocalyptic race and class war set amid the desolate dunes of Death Valley.

Born in 1934, Charles Manson had spent nearly half of his life in institutions. A convicted car thief and pimp, Manson had been sentenced to ten years' imprisonment in 1960 after violating probation by forging a Federal Treasury check. After being granted parole in early 1967, he moved to Berkeley and took up with a graduate student named Mary Brunner. Manson, a manic and curiously charismatic figure, convinced Brunner to let him invite other women to live with them; soon, he had accumulated a virtual harem. He dubbed his group "the Family."

Manson and his Family headed to the Haight-Ashbury district of San Francisco during the Summer of Love in 1967. In this wildly divergent culture, Manson was exposed to a number of different belief systems, ranging from the hippie Christianity of so-called "Jesus freaks," Scientology, and even the Church of Satan founded by Anton LaVey in San Francisco. Manson developed a seductive rap that combined elements of counterculture free love with a dark mysticism and paranoid, eschatological prophecies. As he attracted more and more followers—mostly young, vulnerable women—to live with him in this urban commune, the Family took on the characteristics of a full-fledged cult.

In 1968, the Family moved downstate to Los Angeles County. Dennis Wilson of the Beach Boys reportedly hooked up with two of Manson's female followers, and soon Manson and his Family had moved into Wilson's mansion, uninvited. While in prison, Manson had learned how to play guitar from Alvin Karpis—the Depression-era bank robber from Ma Barker's gang, whose capture had catapulted J. Edgar Hoover to prominence—and Manson had aspirations for a recording contract. Manson wrote a song called "Cease to Exist," which Dennis Wilson reworked for the Beach Boys. The group later recorded it under the title "Never Learn Not to Love" and released it in 1969.

Wilson eventually tired of the Family's freeloading and kicked Manson and his followers out of his house. In the summer of 1968, the Family moved to Spahn's Movie Ranch in the Santa Susana Mountains, once a location for shooting B-movie westerns. Owner George Spahn was in his eighties and nearly blind, and Manson was able to manipulate him through sexual favors administered by Family member Lynette "Squeaky" Fromme. (Fromme, it was said, earned her nickname from the noises she made when Spahn pinched her thighs.)

While learning how to play guitar in prison, Manson had also become obsessed with The Beatles. He saw the Fab Four not just as pop music pioneers but as messengers of a new, apocalyptic age. He explained to the Family that The Beatles' White Album contained coded messages that gave instructions for the forthcoming race war.

Manson had been predicting an uprising of urban blacks against white America, and he adopted the phrase "Helter Skelter"—the title of a proto-metal song on the White Album—as the name for his visions of the impending race war. He taught his disciples that another song on the album, the experimental tape-loop track "Revolution No. 9," was an allusion to Chapter 9 of the Book of Revelations, which spoke of a bottomless pit:

> And the fifth angel sounded, and I saw a star from heaven fallen unto the earth: and there was given to him the key of the pit of the abyss.
> And he opened the pit of the abyss; and there went up a smoke out of the pit, as the smoke of a great furnace; and the sun and the air were darkened by reason of the smoke of the pit.
> And out of the smoke came forth locusts upon the earth; and power was given them, as the scorpions of the earth have power.

Manson told his followers that *he* was the fifth angel, the one to whom would be given the key to the bottomless abyss. He also prophesied that the abyss was a secret underground city beneath the sands of Death Valley, where he and his followers would take refuge during the coming race war. Manson's group scouted out the geography of Death Valley, moving back and forth on dune buggies equipped with heavy weaponry, in preparation for these end times.[2]

❊ ❊ ❊

Upstate in Vallejo, on the evening of July 4, just after her husband Dean had gone to work at Caesar's Palace Italian Restaurant, twenty-two-year-old Darlene Ferrin made plans to go to the movies in nearby San Francisco with seventeen-year-old Michael Mageau. Ferrin called Mageau later in the evening and changed their plans, saying that she would either call or stop by his house later.

1969

She told her friends she planned to go buy fireworks, but Ferrin and Mageau ended up in the parking lot of the Blue Rock Springs Golf Course on the outskirts of town—a traditional lovers' lane spot. Mageau would later testify that a car had trailed them as they left his home in his Corvair, and that they had headed out of town in an attempt to lose it. Our knowledge of what happened next is dependent upon Mageau's testimony.

According to his statement, their car was the only one in the lot until another one pulled in behind them soon after; it might have been a '58 or '59 Falcon with California plates. It drove away, only to return minutes later. The driver pulled up just behind and to the left of the Corvair and turned off the headlights. A powerful light was directed at them from within the car. Mageau and Ferrin thought it was a policeman and began to look for their IDs. The driver got out of the car and walked up to the passenger side of the Corvair. He pointed the light into Mageau's face. There was a flash and a burst of smoke. The stranger had a gun, and he had begun to fire shots into the car. A bullet entered Mageau's right arm. Another one struck his neck. Nine bullets hit Ferrin—four in her arms and five in the right side of her back, piercing her lung and her left ventricle.

Mageau reached for the passenger-side door handle in desperation, only to discover that it was missing. The assailant started to walk away. Mageau cried out. The attacker came back to the car, and Mageau got a clear look at him for the first time. He was a white man, heavyset, approximately five-foot-eight. The man fired more shots—one into Mageau's knee, two more into Ferrin's body, which was slumped over the steering wheel. Then he got back into his car and drove away.

The Vallejo Police Department received a report of gunshots at the golf course, but they figured it was the sound of firecrackers being mistaken for gunfire. A short time later, though, three teenagers passing by the parking lot in search of a friend spotted Mageau crawling on the ground, crying out in agony. They called the police, who dispatched a car to the scene.

Darlene Ferrin was pronounced dead at the local hospital at approximately 12:38 A.M. Two minutes later, the Vallejo Police Department switchboard received a call that would later be traced to a gas station that sat right in front of the police department, and within site of the Ferrin household. A man spoke clearly and deliberately, as if reading from a script: "I want to report a double murder. If you will go one mile east on Columbus Parkway to the public park, you will find kids in a brown car. They were shot with a 9-millimeter Luger."

"I also killed those kids last year," he added. Then he added in a taunting voice, "Good-bye."[3]

Later that morning, around 1:30, the phone rang at Ferrin's house. Dean's boss, who stopped by for a party and stayed while Dean went to look for his wife, answered the phone. A few minutes later, Dean's parents received a similar crank call. Dean's brother got one next. In all three instances, they heard only the sound of heavy breathing on the other line.

❊ ❊ ❊

Gary Hinman was a thirty-two-year-old music teacher and doctoral student of sociology at UCLA living in Topanga Canyon. Hinman was a devout Nichiren Buddhist who actively sought converts. He also ran a small synthetic mescaline factory out of his house with the help of two partners, a married couple. Hinman routinely let people crash at his house on Old Topanga Canyon Road, including Manson and other Family members. Once, he had even helped Mary Brunner keep her baby—a little girl fathered by Manson and born in the spring of 1968 in a condemned house in Topanga Canyon—when Social Services had tried to take the baby away from Brunner.

Sometime in July 1969, Manson stopped by Hinman's place and got into a philosophical argument about their clashing worldviews: Manson wanted Hinman to sell all his possessions and come join the Family. "I'm sorry, Charlie," Hinman said. "I'm not going to sell all my things and come follow you." Manson threatened him with bad karma and then left. Sometime later, Manson called Hinman and asked him for either drugs or money, or both. Hinman refused once again.[4]

On July 24, Manson told one of his followers, a woman named Ella, to go over to Hinman's house, get money from him, and then kill him. Ella refused and then fled the Family compound with another member. The following day, Manson was out riding a dune buggy with Bobby Beausoleil. Thirteen years Manson's junior, Beausoleil was an actor and musician who had been nicknamed "Cupid" for his handsome looks and skills with women. He had acquired his own small harem of sorts before he met Manson at a house party in Laurel Canyon. Beausoleil said that he, too, was thinking of splitting. According to Beausoleil, Manson said to him, "Maybe I ought to slit your motherfuckin' throat."[5] Then, Manson changed the subject and asked him if he would go over to Hinman's and murder him.

Family member Bruce Davis drove Beausoleil, Brunner, and Susan Atkins over to Hinman's house that evening and dropped them off. Beausoleil and Hinman had a quarrel about money—possibly in regard to a bad mescaline purchase that Beausoleil had arranged for his friends in the Straight Satans motorcycle gang. Beausoleil pulled out a gun and began to pistol-whip Hinman.

Hinman still refused to cooperate. A call was placed to the ranch, and soon Davis returned to the house with Manson. Now the Family's maniacal leader was wielding a sword that he had gotten from the president of the Straight Satans. He yelled at Hinman and then lashed out and cut a deep gash into the side of Hinman's face, from his ear to his jawbone.

Manson and Davis left the other three Family members at the house, where they kept Hinman imprisoned over the next two days. They were able to get him to turn over the pink slips on his two cars, but they couldn't get any money from him. On July 27, either acting on orders from Manson or reacting to Hinman's screaming out the window—future testimony would be contradictory—Beausoleil stabbed Hinman to death. Hinman's body was placed under a bedspread in the corner of the living room. The words POLITICAL PIGGY were written in Hinman's blood on the wall just above his corpse.

❊ ❊ ❊

On July 31, the man who had claimed three victims—Michael Mageau had miraculously survived the July 4 attack—mailed three envelopes: one to the *San Francisco Chronicle*, one to the *San Francisco Examiner*, and one to the *Vallejo Times-Herald*. Each envelope contained a hand-printed letter, all of which conveyed the same message. The letter to the *Chronicle* read as follows:

Dear Editor

This is the murderer of the teenagers last Christmass [sic] at Lake Herman & the girl on the 4th of July near the golf course in Vallejo.
To prove I killed them I shall state some facts which only I & the police know.

Christmass [sic]
1 Brand name of ammo, Super X
2 10 shots were fired
3 the boy was on his back with his feet to the car
4 the girl was on her right side feet to the west
4 *July*
1 girl was wearing patterned slacks
2 The boy was also shot in the knee
3 Brand name of ammo was western
[Over]

Here is a part of a cipher the other 2 parts of this cipher are being mailed to the editors of the *Vallejo Times* and *SF Examiner.*

I want you to print this cipher on the front page of your paper. In this cipher is my identity.

If you do not print this cipher by the afternoon of Fry. [sic] 1 of Aug 69, I will go on a kill ram-Page [sic] Fry. Night. I will cruise around all weekend killing lone people in the night, then move on to kill again, untill [sic] I end up with a dozen people over the weekend[6]

Accompanying each of the three letters were coded messages, each consisting of eight rows of seventeen characters. After consulting with the Vallejo and San Francisco police departments, the *Chronicle* published its cryptogram on page four of its Saturday, August 2, edition. (In an adjacent article, Vallejo police chief Jack E. Stiltz was quoted as saying, "We're not satisfied that the letter was written by the murderer," and, in an attempt to bait the killer further, requested that the writer send a second letter with more facts to prove his identity.[7]) The combined *Examiner-Chronicle* edition published all three cryptograms on page nine of the Sunday edition. Meanwhile, the Vallejo Police Department sent the cyphers to Naval Intelligence at Mare Island Naval Shipyard. There, codebreakers from the National Security Agency and the Central Intelligence Agency took a crack at breaking the three-part message. But no one from these agencies could break the complex cyphers.

Meanwhile, tens of thousands of newspaper readers throughout northern California read the codes of the "cipher killer." One reader was Donald Harden, a high school teacher of economics and history in Salinas. Harden loved a good mystery, and with the help of a book on codes from their personal library, he began to try to unravel the enigma of the three-part code. After a couple of hours, his wife Betty joined him.

She suggested that the killer was an egomaniac and would thus start out his message with the word "I"; further, she guessed that he might start out with a phrase like "I like killing." According to their book on codes, the most common repeated consonant pair was the double "l," as in "kill."[8] This proved to be the key. By Monday evening, they had solved it. They informed the *Chronicle*, and Naval Intelligence verified their work; they had indeed broken the cipher killer's code.

On August 7, the *Examiner* received a letter in response to Chief Stiltz's earlier challenge. Printed in the same handwritten scrawl used in the first letter, it read:

Dear Editor:

This is the Zodiac speaking. In answer to your asking for more details about the good Times I have had in Vallejo, I shall be happy to supply even more material. By the way, are the police haveing [sic] a good Time with the code? If not, tell them to cheer up; when they do crack it they will have me.

On the 4th of July:

I did not open the car door. The window was rolled down all ready [sic]. The boy was originally sitting in the front seat when I began fireing [sic]. When I fired the first shot at his head, he leaped backwards at the same time, thus spoiling my aim. He ended up on the back seat then the floor in back thrashing out very violently with his legs; that's how I shot him in the knee. I did not leave the cene [sic] of the killing with squealing tires & raceing [sic] engine as described in the Vallejo papers.

I drove away slowly so as not to draw attention to my car. The man who told the police my car was brown was a negro about 40–45 rather shabbly [sic] dressed. I was in this phone booth having [sic] some fun with the Vallejo cop when he was walking by. When I hung the phone up the dam [sic] thing began to ring & that drew his attention to me & my car.

Last Christmass [sic]

In that epasode [sic] the police were wondering as to how I could shoot & hit my victims in the dark. They did not openly state this, but implied this by saying it was a well lit night & I could see silowets [sic] on the horizon. Bullshit; that area is srounded [sic] by high hills & trees. What I did was tape a small pencel [sic] flash light to the barrel of my gun. If you notice, in the center of the beam of light if you aim it at a wall or ceiling you will see a black or darck [sic] spot in the center of the circle of light about 3 to 6 in. across.

When taped to a gun barrel, the bullet will strike exactly in the center of the black dot in the light. All I had to do was spray them.[9]

On August 9, the *Chronicle* published the Hardens' solution to the code. As the letters had implied, the three coded messages were three sections of one long message. Taken together, they said:

I like killing people because it is so much fun. It is more fun than killing wild game in the forrest [sic] because man is the most dangerous animal of all. To kill something gives me the most thrilling experience. It is even better than getting your rocks off with a girl. The best part is that when I die I will be born in paradice and all the [sic] I have killed will become my slaves. I will not give you my name because you will try to slow down or stop my collecting of slaves for my afterlife. EBEORIETEMETHHPITI.

There was speculation that the mysterious "EBEORIETEMETHH-PITI" was an anagram for the killer's name, but if so, no one has ever discovered a plausible solution. But the killer now had a name, of sorts, one that he had given himself. Northern California had found itself haunted by someone known as The Zodiac. "By the late summer of 1969," author Michael Kelleher writes, "Zodiac must have believed himself to be nearly invincible."[10]

❋ ❋ ❋

On August 3, Manson headed north toward Big Sur with a guitar and a stolen credit card in search of more recruits for the Family. At about four in the morning of August 4, outside a gas station, he picked up a seventeen-year-old girl named Stephanie Schram, who was hitchhiking from San Francisco to San Diego. They camped out in a canyon that night, dropped LSD, and had sex. Manson spoke to her about his views on death, to the point that she became creeped out. But she continued on with him to Big Sur, where they spent time one night at the same Esalen Institute that had inspired *Bob & Carol & Ted & Alice*. Manson tried to share some of his music with his fellow enlightened beings, but they weren't impressed. In his eyes, the people at Esalen "were off on their little trips . . . the people wouldn't go on his trip."[11] Manson headed back to the Spahn Ranch in a foul mood, with Stephanie in tow.

Meanwhile, Beausoleil had left the Family compound. The increasingly paranoid atmosphere at the Spahn Ranch might have begun to get to him. After all, shortly before Manson had sent him to visit Hinman, he had threatened Beausoleil's own life. On August 5, Beausoleil left the ranch and headed to San Francisco, driving the Fiat that Hinman had owned. He stopped at a restaurant in Santa Barbara, where a policeman told him to remove the knife he had sheathed at his waist. Beausoleil stuck it in the tire well of the Fiat's trunk and drove on.

That night, the Fiat broke down as Beausoleil was driving on Highway 101 toward San Luis Obispo. He curled up in a sleeping bag in the backseat.

The next morning, he woke up to see a California Highway Patrol car parked behind him. The patrolmen had called in the car's license plate and learned it had been reported stolen. Hinman's body had been discovered on July 31, and police had put out an APB for his car. Beausoleil was arrested immediately and brought back to Los Angeles.

Manson, meanwhile, had taken Schram to her sister's in San Diego so that she could get her clothes and bring them back with her to the ranch. Stephanie's sister owned The Beatles' latest record, and Manson told her about its hidden messages that outlined "the whole scene" for what was to come. "People are going to be slaughtered," he told her. "They'll be lying on their lawns dead."[12] When they returned to the ranch, Manson met with the members of the Family and told them: "Now is the time for Helter Skelter."[13]

On the night of August 8, Manson sent four members of the Family—Susan Atkins, Tex Watson, Linda Kasabian, and Patricia Krenwinkel—to Benedict Canyon, to the bungalow at the dead end of a cul-de-sac on Cielo Drive. It was a secluded house, and as one of them would later describe, "you could almost hear the sound of ice rattling in cocktail shakers in the homes way down the canyon."[14]

Until recently, musician and record producer Terry Melcher had lived there with his then-girlfriend, Candice Bergen. Manson had met Melcher through Dennis Wilson and tried unsuccessfully to get Melcher to sign him to a recording contract. But by the summer of 1969, Melcher had moved to Malibu, and the house at 10500 Cielo Drive had been leased to film director Roman Polanski and his young wife, actress Sharon Tate.

Just past midnight and into Saturday morning on August 9, the emissaries from the Family staked out the place. Polanski was in England working on a film, but Tate, eight and a half months pregnant, was home. Also staying there was Jay Sebring, the famous hair stylist who had once been engaged to Tate, as well as Polanski's friend, Wojciech Frykowski, and his girlfriend, heiress Abigail

Folger. Sebring's Porsche and Folger's Firebird sat in the paved driveway next to Tate's rented Camaro.

First, Watson climbed the telephone pole near the entrance gate and cut the telephone wires. Around 12:30, as the girls lay hiding in the grass like snakes, Watson was spotted by eighteen-year-old Steven Parent, who stopped by briefly to see caretaker William Garretson in his cottage. As Parent asked what he was doing there, Watson ran up to the car, pointed a fifteen-inch revolver through the open driver's side window at Parent, and killed him with four shots—two to the chest, one to his head, one to his left arm.

With Parent's body slumped over in the bucket seat of his car, Kasabian kept watch by the gate as the others approached the house. Watson cut open the screen of an open window and climbed into the nursery on the north side of the house. He smelled the fresh coat of paint that had been applied just that afternoon. He walked south through the dining room and to the entrance hall so that he could let the others in.

They entered the living room, where a stereo was blaring and an American flag was draped upside down over the beige divan. Wojciech Frykowski was on the couch in front of the fireplace, reportedly sleeping off the effects of Tenamfetamine, a synthetic psychedelic drug.[15] Watson walked over to him, and standing on the zebra-skin rug in front of the fireplace, pointed his gun at Frykowski's head. Frykowski woke up and asked, "What time is it?"

Watson told him not to move, and Frykowski asked him who he was. Watson said, "I'm the devil and I'm here to do the Devil's business."[16]

Watson told Atkins to look for others in the house. Atkins found Abigail Folger in the guest room, lying in bed and reading a book. Folger, wearing glasses and a full-length white nightgown, and also stoned from the effects of Tenamfetamine, smiled at Atkins. Atkins smiled back and continued on to the next bedroom. There, Sharon Tate was lying on the bed in matching bra and panties and talking to her former boyfriend, who sat on the edge of the bed. Neither of them saw Atkins.

She went back and told Watson that there were three other people in the house. He instructed her to bring them into the living room. She led Folger at knifepoint into the room with the others, and then she did the same with Tate and Sebring. Watson told their four captives to lie facedown on pillows that had been arranged in front of the fireplace. When Sebring protested that Tate was pregnant, Watson pointed his gun at Sebring and shot him in the armpit. The bullet went through a rib, pierced a lung, and exited his back.

He fell to the floor, where he lay moaning.[17] Tate and Folger screamed.

Once again, Atkins led Folger at knifepoint back to the bedroom and had the heiress take the money out of her purse. They tied Frykowski's hands with a towel, and then they tied a nylon rope around Sebring's neck, and then Tate's and Folger's. Watson threw the end of the rope over a ceiling beam and pulled it tight so that the two women had to stand up. One of them asked Watson what they were going to do to them.

"You are all going to die," he told them.[18]

Watson ordered Atkins to kill Frykowski. Polanski's fellow countryman tried to make a break for it and ran for the front door. Atkins furiously swung her knife at him but lost it in the ruckus. As she clung onto their fleeing prisoner, Watson ran over and shot Frykowski twice. When the weapon misfired, he clubbed Frykowski with it.

As she knelt outside, Linda Kasabian turned to see Frykowski struggling outside. As she would later claim, she heard his desperate cries and then looked back at the lifeless body of Parent, and then, only then, did it occur to her that the occupants of the house were fated to die. "I saw Frykowski staggering out the door—drenched in blood—I looked in his eyes—he looked in mine—I saw the image of Christ in him; I cried and prayed with all my heart," she testified.[19]

Frykowski collapsed into a bush, only to stand again. His desperate cries for help echoed up and down the canyon. In the coming weeks, none of the neighbors would admit to hearing them.

In the commotion with Frykowski, Folger broke free of the nylon rope and ran toward the back bedroom of the house, where a door led outside to the swimming pool. Krenwinkel chased her. Watson spotted the wounded Sebring struggling to move on the floor and stabbed him multiple times and kicked his face. Then, Watson ran out to the front lawn where Folger and Krenwinkel were fighting. Folger said, "I give up. Take me."[20] Watson stabbed her over and over, tearing a gash in her stomach, and Folger fell to the ground. The heiress who had sought to work for society's underprivileged would be found later with twenty-eight stab wounds.[21]

Back in the house, Tate was sitting on the couch crying, with her ex-lover lying dead or dying nearby. Atkins would later tell a cellmate that Tate had said, "Please don't kill me, please don't kill me. I don't want to die. Please, I'm going to have a baby." Atkins bragged that she responded, "Look, bitch, I don't care about you. I don't care if you're going to have a baby. You had better be ready. You're going to die, and I don't feel anything about it."[22] As Atkins held Tate's arms, Watson stabbed Tate several times in her left breast through her bra. Then they all stabbed her, sixteen times in all.

Atkins tasted Tate's blood on her hands. "Wow, what a trip!" she later recounted for her cellmate, who asked Atkins if it had bothered her to kill an expectant mother. Atkins seemed puzzled. "Well, I thought you understood," she said. "I loved her, and in order for me to kill her I was killing part of myself when I killed her."[23]

Using a towel soaked with Tate's blood, Atkins wrote PIG on the front door of the house. Then the killers rode back to the ranch to give Manson a report on the first stage of Helter Skelter.

The housekeeper discovered the bodies the next morning and ran to a neighboring house to report the murders. The media swept in to cover the crime scene. The headline FIVE SLAIN IN BEL AIR went out on the AP newswire. As Ed Sanders wrote, "Fear swept the pool-sides of Los Angeles on the hot August morning as the news of the murders seeped through the network of phones."[24]

When Watson's crew gave their report to Manson, he was upset with how sloppy they had been in committing the murders. If Helter Skelter was to be launched, Manson told them, he would have to show them how to do it.

On the evening of August 9, Manson set out by car with Watson, Krenwinkel, Kasabian, Bruce Davis, and Leslie Van Houten. They drove down Sunset Boulevard, out to the Los Feliz district just south of Griffith Park. As they slowed down outside a house on Waverly Drive, Kasabian recognized a house where she and some other Family members had attended a party and taken acid the previous summer. "Charlie, I've been here before. You're not going to 'do' that house, are you?" she asked Manson.

"No," he said, "the house next door."[25]

In the house next door lived Leno and Rosemary LaBianca. Leno, forty-four, the chief stockholder in the State Wholesale Grocery Company, and Rosemary, thirty-eight, a shop owner and investor who was worth $2,600,000 on her own, had returned to their house at one in the morning. Rosemary was in the bedroom and Leno was in the living room.

Manson and Watson snuck in through an unlocked door in the back of the house and encountered Leno. "Be calm, sit down, and be quiet," Manson told him, waving a sword. Watson, armed with a bayonet, tied Leno's hands while Manson brought Rosemary into the bedroom, and then the couple was tied back to back with pillow-cases placed over their heads. Informing the couple that he was just robbing them, Manson took money out of Rosemary's purse, and then the two men left the house through the front door.

But outside, Manson gave Watson, Krenwinkel, and Van Houten instructions to kill the captives in the household. The women went inside, got a serrated knife and carving fork from the kitchen, and led Rosemary back into the bedroom. They placed her facedown on the bed, removed the pillowcase from her head, and tied the cord of a lamp around her neck. In the living room, Watson pushed Leno onto the couch, his hands still tied behind him. He raised the man's pajama top and then began stabbing him—in the throat and in the abdomen.

As Leno shrieked in pain, Rosemary began to struggle and screamed, "What are you doing to my husband?" She jerked away violently, the cord around her neck pulling the lamp onto the floor. Van Houten grabbed hold of her and Krenwinkel stabbed her, severing her spinal cord. Watson left Leno bleeding to death on the floor and joined the women in the bedroom. Rosemary's dress and nightgown were pulled up over her back and behind, and they stabbed her repeatedly.

Watson carved the word WAR into Leno's stomach. Krenwinkel stuck a fork into both bodies and then left it embedded in Leno's stomach, where she twanged it like a tuning fork. Using Leno's blood, the words DEATH TO PIGS and RISE were written on the walls of the living room. In the kitchen, Krenwinkel wrote HEALTER SKELTER, misspelling Manson's catchphrase.

The group raided the refrigerator—first feeding the family's dogs and then themselves. Afterward, Watson, Krenwinkel, and Van Houten hitchhiked back to Santa Susanna Pass, near the ranch.[26]

❀ ❀ ❀

Soon after the LAPD descended upon the scene at 10500 Cielo Drive, so did the press. News of the drugs found on the premises—psychedelics, cocaine—got out. One Hollywood insider grimly observed: "Toilets are flushing all over Beverly Hills; the entire Los Angeles sewer system is stoned."[27] Rumors circulated about Sebring's S&M leanings, and the press had a field day with tales of a sex-and-drugs party that had ended in ritualistic murder.

1969

Polanski learned of his wife's death from his business manager, William Tennant. Devastated, Polanski returned to the States, where he was questioned by the LAPD for several hours. When he showed up at the house, he said bitterly, "This must be the world-famous orgy house."[28]

As police looked for leads, a pall fell over the Hollywood Hills. Record executive Sally Stevens told journalist Michael Walker, "The paranoia started to come down. It was fairly frightening because no one really knew who was responsible for this. A lot of people left town because they thought they were gonna get it from whoever they imagined it was. Everyone thought at first it was a big dope dealer who was revenging himself on people."[29]

Among the members of the music community that had formed spontaneously in Laurel Canyon (home to the Mamas and the Papas, Crosby, Stills & Nash, John Mayall, and Joni Mitchell, to name a few), the mellow vibes turned somber. "A kind of lurking dread developed," remembered David Strick, a photographer from Los Angeles. Before the Manson killings, according to Strick, "when you had a party, there was no such thing as crashers. It was nonterritorial and completely open. That's why people could see hippies they've never seen before walking in and out of their wealthy houses and not think they were going to kill them. These were the same people you were passing a joint to."[30] Graham Nash said, "up until then everybody's door was open, nobody gave a shit—y'know, come on in, what the fuck—and then all of a sudden it was like: I gotta lock my car. I gotta lock my door. It was the beginning of the end . . ."[31]

16. An Amazin' Summer

Dominant pitching and timely hitting leads the Mets on a miraculous winning streak into first place.

While the nation seemed to be turned on its end in the summer of '69, the national pastime was about to be turned upside down in a rags-to-riches story that would be one for the ages. It had appeared to most fans that the story of the 1969 baseball season would be of the Chicago Cubs, who seemed poised to end two decades of frustration. Yet just beneath them within their own division, another team was building a Cinderella story of its own. After sweeping a three-game series in Pittsburgh the first weekend in July, the Mets were eleven games over .500 with a record of 45-34.

How the Mets were winning games was a mystery to many around the league. Sure, they had a pitching staff stocked with young guns, but their lineup lacked the punch one usually expects to see in a contending team. Cleon Jones was the only everyday player who hit .300—he would challenge for the batting title throughout the season and finish third behind Pete Rose (.348) and Roberto Clemente (.345) with a mark of .340—and in a year in which most teams had at least one player with 90 or 100 runs batted in (RBI), Tommie Agee and Jones were first and second on the Mets with 76 and 75 RBI, respectively. Only one other player, Ron Swoboda, had more than 50 RBI. Meanwhile, with his 26 home runs, Agee was the only Mets hitter to break the 15 home run mark. As a point of comparison, Harmon Killebrew of the Minnesota Twins led baseball with 49 home runs and 140 RBI.

As the Mets continued to climb in the standings, the Cubs' Ron Santo expressed his befuddlement at the Mets' winning ways. "I know the Dodgers won pennants with just pitching, but this Mets lineup is ridiculous," he ranted.[1] "It's a shame losing to an infield like that," he said of one game lineup that had featured Ed Kranepool, Wayne Garrett, Al Weis, and Bobby Pfeil—none of whom hit even .240 that year. "I wouldn't let that infield play in Tacoma," he said, comparing the Mets to the Chicago's triple-A affiliate.[2]

So how *was* Gil Hodges's team making a dent in Chicago's division lead? For one thing, his use of a platoon system produced favorable lefty-righty matchups that yielded deceivingly productive results. Swoboda's 52 RBI combined with 47 from Art Shamsky, who often spelled Swoboda against right-handed hitters, produced a two-headed output of 99 RBI from the rightfield position. The left-handed Kranepool and right-handed Donn Clendenon, a mid-season acquisition from the Expos, gave the Mets a power-hitting duo at first base, and skillfull hitter Ken Boswell and fluid glove man Al Weis complemented each other at second base. The team got little offensive production from catcher, shortstop, or third-base positions, but what the team *did* get was timely hitting. Grote recalled years later, "I only hit six home runs that year, but I think three of four of them won ballgames."[3]

Yet there was no doubt as to the secret of the team's newfound success. While the Mets' bats fell into periodic slumps, the team's pitching staff was consistently good and frequently great throughout the year. In the team's 162 regular-season games that year, Mets arms held their opponents to two runs or less an amazing *ninety-two* times. Leading the staff was twenty-four-year-old Tom Seaver, who in 1969 took that next step from being a promising young pitcher to "The Franchise." In perhaps the best season of his Hall of Fame career, he won twenty-five games while losing only seven and allowing 2.21 earned runs a game. The Mets' ace lived up to the role of a stopper—the guy who takes the mound and gets it done when his team needs it most. He won the game in May that brought the Mets to the .500 mark, and then he put them one win over .500 in June. The team seemed to build its winning streaks around Seaver wins, as he recorded three victories during the team's eleven-game streak in June and two during a seven-game streak early in the summer.

The team had taken five straight games and stood just five games behind first-place Chicago when the Cubs came to town for a three-game series at Shea Stadium, the first of two series between the two teams in July. "We need to take two-out-of-three each time," Hodges told the *New York Times*. "All our people couldn't be more ready."[4]

Nearly 55,000 fans showed up for the Tuesday afternoon opener on July 8, including 16,000 free passes that had been distributed to children. As the home team took the field, one sportswriter observed, "Their demonstrations of lung power even drowned out the blasts of low-flying jets from landing and taking off from nearby LaGuardia."[5]

The Cubs looked strong for eight innings and took a 3–1 lead into the bottom of the ninth. If one is to look for a point at which the miracle of the '69 "Miracle Mets" started, this may have been it. With no outs, centerfielder Don Young misjudged Ken Boswell's shallow fly to center, and Boswell pulled safely into second. Two batters later, Young tracked down a drive to the wall from Donn Clendenon, but the ball bounced out of the outfielder's glove, and the Mets ended up with men on second and third. Cleon Jones stepped to the plate and delivered a double down the leftfield line that scored both runners and tied the game. Three batters later, Ed Kranepool blooped a single just over the glove of shortstop Don Kessinger to score Jones and cap a game-winning, three-run rally.

"Yes, you can call it one of the most important victories in Mets' history. Of course, you've got to remember that I wasn't around for the whole eight years," Hodges said from behind his office desk in a postgame interview, a grin coming to his normally stoic face. "That's what we're all here for, to make believers out of all of you unbelievers." Amid a happy Mets locker room, Cleon Jones said, "Somebody said the Cubs aren't taking us seriously! Maybe they're taking us seriously now!"[6]

In the visitors' locker room, fingers were pointed at Young's two miscues in the final inning. Manager Leo "The Lip" Durocher growled within earshot of Young, "It's tough to win when your centerfielder can't catch a fucking flyball. [Fergie] Jenkins pitched his heart out. But when one man can't catch a flyball, it's a disgrace. . . . My son could have caught those balls! My fucking thirteen-year-old son could have caught those balls!"[7] Team leader Ron Santo added, "Don's a major leaguer because of his glove. When he hits, he's a dividend, but when he fails on defense he's lost—and today he took us down with him." The next day, the *Chicago Tribune* ran a headline, asking: portent of doom?[8]

The following night, Seaver took the mound feeling that he had come to the stadium that night with what pitchers call "his good stuff." "It was obvious even before the game," he would remember two decades later, thinking back on a game that would go down in Mets lore.[9]

While the Mets scored four runs that night, the Cubs were finding it hard enough to even reach base. Seaver retired the first three batters in the lineup, two on strikeouts, and then he struck out the side in the second. He sent them down 1-2-3 in the third, and then again in the fourth. And then again in the fifth and sixth, both times getting the third out on strikes. He had now gone through the entire Chicago lineup twice without letting one runner reach base. "I was aware from the fourth inning on that I had a perfect game, and I was going for it," he said.[10]

At that point in history, only eight times had a Major League pitcher tossed a complete game while retiring every batter he faced—allowing no batter to reach base by hit, walk, error, or getting hit by a pitch. But after retiring the top of the order for a third time in the seventh and striking out two more in the eighth, Seaver was just three outs from baseball immortality. He hadn't even thrown more than *two balls* out of the strike zone to any hitter during any one at-bat. As he came to bat in the bottom of the eighth, the game stopped for nearly two minutes as the Shea crowd gave Seaver a jubilant standing ovation for his efforts.

After Randy Hundley grounded out to Seaver to start the ninth, up stepped Jimmy Qualls, a rookie centerfielder whom Durocher had inserted into the lineup after Young's blowout the previous night. The light-hitting Qualls, who would compile an underwhelming .223 career batting average, swung at a Seaver offering and blooped a single into left field, not far from where Kranepool's game-winner had landed the night before. The game stopped again as the Shea crowd stood to recognize Seaver's brush with perfection, and two batters later he completed a one-hit, eleven-strikeout gem.

Recalling the game years later, Seaver ranked it as the best performance of his career. "That was the best game I ever pitched. It was better than my no-hitter with Cincinnati. I had great stuff that night, superb control, and a mastery of all my pitches."[11]

Chicago rallied for a win the following day, and just four days later the Mets were in Chicago for three more games, all daytime contests in the unlit park of Wrigley Field. Seaver lost a tough 1–0 decision in the opener, and Ron Santo celebrated the last out with his trademark move of jumping up and clicking his heels, to the delight of the Wrigley faithful. The Mets answered back the following day with a 5–4 victory, and Seaver answered Santo's gesture by jumping up and clicking his heels again and again. In the series finale, Cal Koonce and Ron Taylor pitched seven scoreless innings out of the bullpen as New York won, 9–5. Having achieved Hodges's goal of taking two out of three in both series with the division-leading Cubs, New York left town just three and a half games out of first place. Grote taunted the so-called "bleacher bums" of Wrigley Field, saying, "Notice where they all were in the ninth inning—they left, that's what. They're real great fans, aren't they?"[12] New York's lovable losers had announced that they were very much in a pennant race.

But not long after climbing into the division race, the Mets hit rock bottom. In a doubleheader on a rain-soaked field at Shea on July 30, the Astros scored a combined twenty-seven runs off Mets pitchers—including an eleven-run inning in the first game and a ten-run inning in the second. During that second-game outburst, Cleon Jones (who was nursing an injury) gingerly chased a double into the corner by catcher Johnny Edwards and tossed it lackadaisically back into the infield. After the play, Gil Hodges came out of the dugout, and instead of stopping at the mound for a pitching change, the six-foot-two former marine sergeant with a pastor's face continued past the mound, past the shortstop, and out to Jones in leftfield. The Shea crowd saw the two men exchange words, and then watched as Jones followed Hodges back to the Mets dugout. Hodges told George Vecsey of the *New York Times*, "I saw him favor his leg that inning. I didn't think he should play if he was hurting."[13] But more to the point, Hodges was sending the message to his team. Jones remembered, "It might have looked like he was trying to embarrass me, but he wasn't. Gil was just trying to make a point. We were getting our ass kicked and something had to be done, and that was his way of showing us that he wasn't satisfied with the way we were playing."[14]

As the season moved into the notorious "dog days" of summer, unbelievers said the "real" Mets had reappeared. By mid-August, New York was a distant nine and a half games behind the Cubs and had fallen behind the streaking Cardinals in the division standings. It had been said that man would land on the moon before the Mets would win a pennant, something that the crew of *Apollo 11* had made manifest a month before. Now, much like the command module at the end of that history-making journey, it looked as if the Amazin' Mets had come back to Earth.

But a ten-game home stand proved to be a perfect antidote for what ailed the team. The Mets swept back-to-back doubleheaders with the Padres behind strong performances from starters Seaver, McAndrew, Koosman, and Cardwell. The following Tuesday, Gary Gentry pitched ten innings of shutout ball, but the Giants' Juan Marichal matched him inning for inning and then some. The future Hall of Famer was still on the mound with one out in the bottom of the fourteenth when Agee—hitless in his first five at-bats—hit a home run over the bullpen fence in leftfield to win the game, 1–0.

New York took nine of ten on their home stand, and from August 16 until the end of the season, the Mets went on a historic run that saw them win 38 of 49 games, including 21 of 26 in the suddenly magical confines of Shea. They had come storming back in the pressure-cooked stages of the season, and now everyone was taking notice—not just of the team but also, the phenomenon of Mets fans, who now led the league in attendance. The *New York Post*'s James Wechsler wrote, "The Mets . . . embody the furtive hopes and desperate dreams of every underdog and lost soul in the universe, of every historian who maintains there are no iron laws of history, of every philosopher who sees man capable of rising above his seeming limitations, of every theologian who believes in the power of prayer, of every incorrigible long-shot better who refuses to be intimidated by the hardened experts."[15]

Even the national news media took note of the team, which now led the league in attendance. In September, both *Time* and *Life* devoted cover stories to the baseball's most surprising team. The *Life* cover captured All-Star lefty Jerry Koosman in mid-delivery under the headline METS IN THE STRETCH.[16] The orange and blue *Time* cover showed a cartoon kid in a Mets uniform and oversized batting helmet, looking to be the same age as the team itself, swinging for the fences. The magazine dubbed the Mets "Baseball's Wunderkinder" and "The Little Team That Can," and claimed, "If he had lived today, Job would undoubtedly be a fan of the New York Mets. . . . So is anyone with the slightest sympathy for the underdog, the smallest shred of a sense of futility, the least understanding of how it feels to lose, and lose, and lose."[17]

The Cubs, meanwhile, were feeling the pressure and beginning to look old and tired. In contrast to Hodges's platoon system and frequent substitution, Durocher went to the well again and again with his starting lineup, and by late summer, the Cubs were playing tired, and the bullpen was faltering. After their torrid 40-18 start to the season, the Cubs lost as many games as they won (52-52), and by the time the first-place Cubs came to visit Shea on September 8, their lead had shrunk down to just two and a half games.

Hodges had wisely shuffled his pitching rotation to send his two best starters, Koosman and Seaver, against the Cubs. In the Monday-night opener, the action touched off eventfully. Chicago pitcher Bill Hands tried to send a message by knocking down Agee with his first wild pitch, and then he did it again two pitches later. In the top of the second, Koosman responded by plunking Santo just below the elbow. In the third inning, Agee got back at Hands and hit a two-run homer. After the Cubs tied the game at 2–2 in the top of the sixth, Agee doubled and scored in the bottom of the inning. Koosman went the rest of the way and struck out thirteen, including three in the ninth, to give the Mets a 3–2 victory.

Superstitious fans will say the outcome of the following night's game was foretold in the fourth inning. With the Mets leading 4–0 as Billy Williams stepped up to bat with one out and a man on second for the Cubs, a black cat suddenly appeared on the field. It shot out to the batter's box, skittered to the on-deck circle and paused near Ron Santo, then walked over to the Chicago dugout and hissed at manager Leo Durocher before escaping underneath the stands. The Mets went on to victory behind Ken Boswell and Donn Clendenon, who each hit two-run homers, and Tom Seaver, who yielded just one run en route to his twenty-first win of the year. The Cubs left town that night with the slimmest of leads, just one half game in the standings.

Out went Chicago and in came Montreal for a doubleheader on September 10. In the opener, Jim McAndrew proved a lesson in endurance after allowing two first-inning runs by pitching ten shutout innings. With the game tied at 2–2 in the twelfth, Agee threw to Grote to nab the potential go-ahead run for the Expos at the plate. In the bottom of the inning, the Mets staged a two-out rally and Boswell singled in Jones to win the game. The Mets were now, for the moment, tied with the Cubs in the standings but in first place by percentage points, by virtue of an 83-57 record (.59285) to the Cubs' 84-58 (.59154).

During the second game, the Shea crowd took to watching the out-of-town scoreboard and following the score of the Cubs' game in Philadelphia. The Phillies pulled out to a lead, and when an electronic "F" was flashed to signal the final score of 6–2, the Mets had gone up half a game in the standings and were assured of going to bed in first place that night in the National League East. Fans began to dance in the aisles. The scoreboard operator flashed the message LOOK WHO'S NO. 1. To cap off the night, Nolan Ryan pitched the Mets to a 7–1 win, vaulting the Mets a full game on top of the division.

From that point in the season, the two teams went in opposite directions—the Mets kept rolling while the Cubs continued to implode. Two nights later in Philadelphia, Chicago's Dick Selma inexplicably threw a pickoff attempt to third base—which was empty—and the Phillies scored the tying run when the ball sailed over the head of a surprised Santo. Durocher almost literally blew his top, jumping up and hitting his head on the Shibe Park dugout roof. The Cubs dropped the game, 4–3, their eighth consecutive loss.

Meanwhile, the Mets could do no wrong. As they played a doubleheader with the Pirates at Forbes Field on September 12, with neither Cleon Jones, who was resting a nagging injury, nor Art Shamsky, at home observing Rosh Hashanah, the team found just enough to win—pitchers Koosman and Cardwell each tallied RBI singles in a pair of 1–0 Met wins.

When the Mets took the field on September 24 for its final regular-season home game, a Wednesday-night game with St. Louis, the team needed just one win to clinch the division. The often-timid Mets bats exploded for five runs in the first inning as they knocked Steve Carlton, the National League's starting pitcher from the 1969 All-Star Game, out of the box after just one-third of an inning. Anticipation built in the Shea stands as starter Gary Gentry carried a 6–0 lead into the ninth inning, and when Cardinals first baseman Joe Torre grounded into a game-ending double play, Mets announcer Lindsey Nelson officially proclaimed: "At 9:07 on September 24th, the Mets have won the championship of the Eastern Division of the National League!"

As the Mets players ran into the dugout and began spraying champagne inside the locker room, fans stormed the field to celebrate an event that had seemed unthinkable in the team's first seven years. In what the Associated Press called "one of the most incredible souvenir-snatching safaris in baseball history," the Shea crowd tore up as much as 1,500 square feet of sod. The AP quoted a police report the next day that summarized the festive damage: "They celebrated by breaking three wheels off the batting cage and stripping the netting off it. They celebrated by tearing up the all-weather matting in the coaches' boxes behind first and third base. They celebrated by taking pieces of the scoreboard. They celebrated by stealing home plate." Fans also sprayed graffiti across the wall in center field and stole the stadium's American flag from atop its outfield pole.[18]

❊ ❊ ❊

The Mets came to Chicago to end the season with an anticlimactic, two-game series. In the first, Hodges utilized twenty-one players in a 5–3 win, the team's 100th of the season. Fans in Chicago's North

Side seethed with this final indignity in a season that had begun so promisingly. During the season finale on October 2, one member of the Bleacher Bums tossed a smoke bomb onto the field near Cleon Jones that sent a stream of red smoke wafting into the air. Later, a procession of Bums left their seats, made their way past the Wrigley Field ushers, and found their way down to the top of the home and visitor dugouts, where they tried to take over the show. They eventually returned to the leftfield stands, and after the last out of a meaningless 6–5 Cubs win, they climbed over the ivy-covered outfield wall and jumped onto the field. Some ran around the infield and slid into bases, urged on by civilian base coaches. In the ugliness, one girl severely hurt her back and was taken to the hospital, and another girl suffered an ankle injury. Amid the commotion, the park's organist mockingly played "Happy Days Are Here Again." The season had come to a bitter conclusion. As one player had said before the final game, "This is just like the last day of school. I can hardly wait for it to end."[19]

For the young guns from the borough of Queens, however, the season had just begun.

17. Heaven in a Disaster Area

Woodstock highlights the year of the outdoor music festival.

It was the year of the outdoor music festival. On June 20–22, 1969, the summer festival season kicked off with the Newport Pop Festival at San Fernando Valley State on Devonshire Downs in Northridge, California. A crowd of 150,000, the largest recorded gathering for an outdoor music festival to that date, witnessed a show featuring such acts as The Jimi Hendrix Experience, The Byrds, The Rascals, the Chamber Bros., Three Dog Night, and Booker T. & the MGs. After what was described as a subpar performance on Friday night, Hendrix returned on Sunday afternoon and jammed with an all-star band that included Eric Burdon and Buddy Miles. A week later, he headlined the bill of the Denver Pop Festival at Mile High Stadium, which also included Johnny Winter, Joe Cocker, Creedence Clearwater Revival, Poco, Frank Zappa & the Mothers of Invention, Iron Butterfly, Three Dog Night, Tim Buckley, and Big Mama Thornton.

Both three-day festivals were marred by riots as police battled thousands of gate-crashers, and the attendees went a little wild themselves. At Newport Pop, fans dangled from the front of the stage as they tried to climb up during Hendrix's Sunday jam. At Denver Pop, police fired tear gas at the crowd during the Experience's set. The trio was rushed offstage and into an equipment truck. Fans climbed onto the truck and almost caused the roof to cave in while the band was trapped inside. It would be the last gig played by the Experience. Disillusioned by the whole scene and by the new directions that Hendrix wanted to take, bassist Noel Redding left the group immediately afterward and returned to London.

In the first weekend of July, a record 85,000 people attended the 1969 Newport Jazz Festival in Rhode Island, an event that was perhaps even more controversial than the Newport Folk Festival in 1965 when Bob Dylan had famously "plugged in" for his electric-rock performance, shocking purists. At the Newport Jazz '69, avant-garde jazz acts such as Sun Ra, Rahsaan Roland Kirk, and Miles Davis shared the bill with jazz-pop group Blood, Sweat & Tears and the funk-rock group Sly and the Family Stone, along with straight-out rock acts such as Jethro Tull, Johnny Winter, and Led Zeppelin.

The heavy guitar rock of these acts attracted a younger audience than the Festival had been used to. Unable to afford the price of a hotel room in the city of Newport, many kids attempted to sleep on the beach but came up against a city ordinance preventing public vagrancy. Unruliness and gate-crashing shocked the more "cultured" fans who had come to see Buddy Rich or Bill Evans. George Wein, founder of the festival, called it "four of the worst days of my life."[1]

At the beginning of August, the Atlantic City Race Track was host to a three-day festival, with artists including Johnny Winter, Crosby, Stills, Nash & Young, Joni Mitchell, the Mothers of Invention, Santana, Jefferson Airplane, Canned Heat, Joe Cocker, Chicago, Little Richard, Dr. John, Tim Buckley, The Moody Blues, The Doors, The Buddy Miles Express, and Hugh Masekela. The Atlantic City festival attracted a total of 110,000 music fans, and the facilities quickly proved inadequate. Organizers were forced to bring in water trucks that became makeshift outdoor showers. Those who were desperate enough or simply didn't care put up with the lack of privacy and stood in line for the chance to take showers as others looked on.

And all this was merely prelude to the three-day happening that occurred in upstate New York later that month.

❊ ❊ ❊

The rural town of Woodstock, New York, had become the home of a number of leading musicians. Located in the Catskill Mountains, Woodstock had flourished as an artists' colony in the nineteenth and early twentieth century, and members of both the Hudson River School of painters and the Arts and Crafts Movement had taken up residence there. In the 1960s, leading members of the rock and folk movements flocked to the town, drawn by its rural environment, artistic history, and counterculture vibe. Such musicians as Ed Sanders of The Fugs, Paul Butterfield, Bob Dylan, and The Band counted themselves among the residents of Woodstock. Van Morrison moved to Woodstock in February 1969, and Hendrix moved not far away, to Shokan, New York, where he planned to establish a musical commune based on his new vision of a jam band utopia, which he began to call Gypsy Sun and the Rainbows.

A twenty-three-year-old former Miami head shop owner turned band manager named Michael Lang and a twenty-six-year-old Capitol Records executive named Artie Kornfeld hatched plans to build a recording studio in this artistic community. They soon joined forces with venture capitalists Joel Rosenman, a Princeton- and Yale-educated lawyer, and John Roberts, a Wall Street investor, who had placed an ad in the *New York Times* dubbing themselves, "Young men with unlimited capital looking for interesting and legitimate business enterprises." As a way of raising funds for the planned studio, the group came up with the idea of holding a music festival in Woodstock.

Lang himself had produced the Miami Pop Festival in January 1968, which had drawn 80,000 people. Roberts suggested the festival be stretched over the course of two or three consecutive days, and thus was born Woodstock Ventures, Incorporated.[2]

They zeroed in on a possible site in Woodstock owned by a man named Alexander Tapooz. But with visions of the 50,000 concert-goers who were projected to attend, and with the images of recent rock music festivals fresh in their minds, Woodstock residents protested and forced Woodstock Ventures to look for an alternate site.

They arranged to lease Howard Mills's 300-acre industrial park in the Town of Wallkill, in Orange County, New York. Lawyers for Woodstock Ventures made the case that the cleverly titled "Music and Arts Fair" would focus on arts and crafts, accompanied by some music, primarily folk and jazz. The Wallkill Zoning Board granted initial approval, and plans moved forward—until a memo against smoking marijuana that was circulating among the construction crew became public and touched off the fears of local residents; the Music and Arts Fair was, in fact, a hippie rock festival!

To the older and more conservative members of the establishment, rock festivals meant an onslaught of undesirables: hippies and freaks reveling in sex, violence, and—especially—drugs, the element that was corrupting the youth of America even in its most "straight" families. One of Vice President Agnew's daughters was suspended from the National Cathedral School in Washington on suspicion that she had used pot, while senators George McGovern and Alan Cranston and California assemblyman Jesse Unruh all had children arrested on marijuana charges.[3] Intrinsic to recreational and mind-expanding experiences of the alternative culture of hippies, marijuana had become so popular that it had grown scarce, reportedly due to clamp-downs by authorities in Mexico. (One urban legend had it that a Mexican marijuana guild had hired a Vietcong colonel to serve as an adviser to growers beleaguered by police planes that sprayed napalm and defoliants.)

Enterprising weed growers in America were scrambling to fill the void left by the scarcity of the choicer Mexican variety; in

Nebraska alone, an estimated 115,000 acres were growing pot plants to be harvested come the fall.[4] One report said that pot had "disappeared from the streets—even in southern California. New Jersey grass, the world's vilest, is fetching twice the price normally commanded by Mexican ordinaire."[5] Smokers and tokers could still get their hands on homegrown "Tennessee blue" and "Bethesda gold" (like the would-be swingers in *Bob & Carol & Ted & Alice*, who have to settle for "beautiful, downtown Burbank brown" instead of "Acapulco gold"). But authorities said the shortage of kind bud from south of the border was driving users toward harder drugs, such as acid, hash, speed, barbiturates, and especially heroin.[6]

Mills received death threats when news of the rock festival hit. A town board meeting drew a packed house of people, where someone wondered if Wallkill would become the scene of another Chicago convention. A group called the Wallkill Concerned Citizens Committee circulated a petition against the festival. Confronted by public outcry, the Wallkill zoning board bowed to pressure and obtained a court injunction against Woodstock Ventures.

"More than anything else, I really feel they were deliberately misleading the town," town supervisor Jack Schlosser later said of the Woodstock organizers. Schlosser maintained that it hadn't been a bias against rock festivals but simply the sheer number of people that the rock festival would attract that scared town officials. In July, The Town of Wallkill passed a new resolution against gatherings of more than 5,000 people in one place. Al Romm, editor of the *Times Herald-Record*, wrote, "The law they passed excluded one thing and one thing only—Woodstock."[7]

It was four weeks before the festival, approximately 50,000 tickets had already been sold, and Woodstock Ventures was back at the drawing board. "Wallkill died hard," Michael Lang remembered two decades later. "'It was a drag, but it was not a shock. And it was, 'O.K., let's go find another one.'"[8]

Lang took a motorcycle trip along the bucolic roads of Sullivan

County and came across a 600-acre farm owned by dairy farmer Max Yasgur near White Lake, in the town of Bethel. At the intersection of Hurd and West Shore roads, the land formed a natural amphitheater in a thirty-seven-acre alfalfa field. "It was made in heaven. It was a bowl with a rise for a stage. What more could you want?"[9]

Just the year before, Yasgur had leased a segment of his land to the Boy Scouts of America for its National Jamboree. He'd heard about the legal obstacles that Woodstock Ventures had encountered, so when Lang approached Yasgur about using his land as a concert site, Max and his wife Miriam were receptive to the idea. Not only did they come to an agreement in principle, but the Yasgurs also had enough respect within the conservative and predominantly Jewish community that he was able to help convince unsure members in the community that the concert would be a good thing for Bethel. Thus, the eventual site for Woodstock was found—nearly seventy miles away from the original town that had inspired it.

ROCK RUMBLE IN RIP VAN WINKLE COUNTY read the headline in the local Saratoga Springs newspaper.[10] The Woodstock Music and Arts Fair, with its slogan of "Three Days of Peace and Music . . . An Aquarian Exposition"—a nod to the beginning of the astrological Age of Aquarius that was believed to coincide with the approaching new millennium—was scheduled for Friday, August 15, through Sunday, August 17. It was fast becoming not just a music festival but also a cultural event. The directions spread across the nation: Head north on the New York State Thruway, get off on Exit 16, take the Quickway west, and look for the signs to the show. For better or worse, the festival was on, and thousands upon thousands of kids across the country made plans to meet in the rolling hills of the Hudson River Valley for the third weekend in August.

Woodstock Ventures threw a mini concert for the Bethel site workers on August 7 that featured a roster of local rock bands, along with a performance from an acting troupe called Earthlight Theater. The eighteen-member group staged a musical comedy titled *Sex*.

Y'all Come, during which they stripped naked. It was exactly the kind of thing the locals were worried about. About 800 town residents signed a petition to prevent the Woodstock festival, and even discussed forming a human barricade across the Route 17B "Quickway" that led into town, but people had already started flooding in as early as the Tuesday before the festival officially began.[11]

In they came—young people from New York City and New Jersey, from Boston, from as far away as Colorado and California, by cars and pickup trucks and station wagons and buses and motorcycles and moon buggies and hearses. Townspeople stood on the curbs in the surrounding villages and watched the music fans roll in . . . a veritable army of hippies and freaks. Monterey Pop had been about colorful clothing and California girls and good vibrations. Woodstock was about backpacks and beards and bandanas and bonfires and tents and tepees. The former had been a be-in; this was a pilgrimage.

The inflow of vehicles proved to be more than the sleepy Sullivan County roads could handle. By Friday, traffic had literally backed up for as many as fifteen miles, creating the worst jam in the history of upstate New York.[12] Hundreds upon hundreds of cars were temporarily abandoned, and many thousands of fans with tickets were unable to make it to the festival. "Automotive casualties looked like the skeletons of horses that died on the Oregon Trail," wrote *Rolling Stone's* Greil Marcus. "Fat, bulbous vacationers (for this was Jewishland, the Catskills, laden with chopped liver and bad comedians) stared at the cars and the freaks and the nice kids, their stomachs sticking out into the road. It was a combination of Weekend and Goodbye, Columbus. Here we were, trying to get to the land of Hendrix and the Grateful Dead, all the while under the beady eyes of Mantovani fans."[13]

As the weekend began, eyes across the nation looked toward upstate New York with curiosity, wondering—in some cases, hoping—that the festival would turn into disaster. Lang and Kornfeld knew it, but it was their early decision that helped avoid disaster. Given the ad hoc arrangements that had to be made for setting up the Sullivan County site—along with Yasgur's cows, which needed to graze freely or else they would grow upset and not give milk—the hurricane fencing that was to be constructed around the festival site was not completed on time, and masses were able to gain entrance to the festival without paying. Rather than calling in the police— perhaps an infeasible option given the traffic bottleneck—the organizers made the decision to go with the flow and allow free admission to the grounds. It was a decision that ensured that Woodstock Ventures would dip well into the red. A camera crew caught one advisor despondently telling Lang and Kornfeld, "You are now giving the world's greatest three-day freebie."[14]

Meanwhile, the question of how to keep the growing crowd entertained—and not rioting—had to be confronted when the scheduled opening act, Sweetwater, was still stuck in traffic at their 3:00 stage time. A helicopter was sent to search for them. (Helicopters would end up transporting many of the performers onto the festival grounds after the highways came to a standstill.) The crowd grew restless, and, as an added threat, a contingent of the notorious Hells Angels motorcycle gang arrived about an hour later. "I said, 'Oh, no, here it comes.' Something had to crack, you know. And I saw them get sort of swallowed up in it, in just the whole spirit of the thing. They went off and found their little area and did their thing," recalled Lang. "And I suddenly realized how strong this was. And that it was going to work."[15]

With Sweetwater still nowhere in sight and a gathering of approaching storm clouds casting a dark hue over the Catskill horizons, Lang convinced folksinger Richie Havens, who was originally scheduled to play later in the evening, to take the stage and officially kick off the festival just after 5:00. Havens responded with a hypnotic nine-song set that energized the masses while framing the weekend with an awareness of, as he told the crowd, "the people that are going to read about you tomorrow." The singer strummed his acoustic guitar fervently while belting out songs like the antiwar tale "Handsome Johnny," and an improvised number to close his set, "Freedom"—with lines from the traditional Negro spiritual "Sometimes I Feel like a Motherless Child," a song that Sweetwater had covered for its biggest hit, thrown in for good measure. With his African tribal gown drenched in sweat, the echoes of his *Freedom-ah* still reverberating in the air, he exited the stage to the handclap beat of the crowd. Woodstock was on.

Schedules were reshuffled, and since acoustic acts required less setup, folk acts ruled the first evening. Havens was followed by Sweetwater, Bert Sommer, and Tim Hardin. After a three-raga interlude by Ravi Shankar, who had to cut his set short due to rain, folksingers Melanie, Arlo Guthrie, and Joan Baez closed the evening. "The New York State Thruway's closed, man!" Guthrie told the crowd. The star of *Alice's Restaurant* looked out over the crowd, and, speaking as one of them, exclaimed, "A lot of freaks!" The young fans who had flocked into Sullivan County were indeed conscious of the fact that locals viewed them as freaks—only now, they had emerged from the fringes of society and, for one weekend, were front and center. Guthrie sang three songs, including "Coming into Los Angeles," his whimsical ode to a drug smuggler dreading the customs man.

Joan Baez came out under a sprinkling rain to close the first day. With mist rising from her mouth as she spoke in the cold night air, she dedicated her first song, "Joe Hill," to her husband David Harris, who was serving time in prison for evading the draft. Earlier in the year, she had released her eleventh record, *David's Album*, as a tribute to him. After Baez closed with the folk standards, "Swing Low, Sweet Chariot" and "We Shall Overcome," the crowd bedded down in their tents and tepees, or simply on the bare ground, and settled in for the night. It would be a wet one, as thunderclouds dropped five inches of rain within three hours.[16]

FETE ON FRIDAY: FREEDOM, POT, SKINNY-DIPPING, read the local *Times Herald-Record* newspaper as the sun rose on Saturday.[17] The festival was a scene unto itself, with an American Indian art exhibit, a "Movement City" pavilion where political groups distributed radical literature, a children's playground, a food service tent provided by the California commune known as the Hog Farm. There was a free stage area for bands, jugglers, and other amateur performers—Baez had been performing there before being told it was time for her performance on the main stage—and several areas in the woods where dealers sold marijuana, mescaline, acid, and hash. At one point during the weekend, stage announcer Chip Monck uttered the famous PSA: "The warning that I've received, you may take it with however many grains of salt you wish, that the brown acid that they're circulating around us is not specifically too good. It's suggested that you do stay away from that. But it's your own trip, so be my guest. But please be advised that there is a warning on that."[18] There were ad hoc head shops set up in the woods, and volunteers established "trip tents" where people on bad acid trips could go for assistance.

And there were the skinny-dippers. The sense of the normal rules having been suspended was established early on by the thousands upon thousands who had gotten onto the festival site without paying. Now, many attendees—those who lived outside of straight society, and those who were just leaving it behind for the weekend—reveled in the festival's alternative decorum by disrobing entirely and swimming naked in the lake-sized Filippini's Pond that ran northward along Hurd Road, or in one of the other two nearby bodies of water. Men and women swam together, baring breasts and behinds and pubic hair as if going *au natural* in public was, well, the most natural thing in the world. Woodstock town historian Bert Feldman became the unofficial censor, reminding the nude swimmers to cover up when they were in front of television cameras.[19] As storms turned the festival site into a virtual mud bath, some of the

Woodstock crowd even shed their clothes on land and walked around naked in the cleansing rain.

✻ ✻ ✻

While storm clouds appeared off and on in the skies above Bethel that weekend, a much larger storm formation was brewing above the waters of the Gulf of Mexico. The tropical storm that would be known as Hurricane Camille was born west of Grand Cayman Island on Thursday, August 14. Traveling north, it passed through the extreme western tip of Cuba on Friday night, with sustained winds of up to 115 miles per hour and continued on its way toward the Gulf Coast.

At the National Hurricane Center (NHC) in Miami, director Robert Simpson knew that Camille was bound for the Gulf Coast. Exactly where she would make landfall . . . he could only make an educated guess. At 11:00 P.M. CDT on Saturday, a hurricane warning was issued for the northwestern coast of Florida, from Fort Walton to St. Marks, with a hurricane watch put into effect for the coast as far west as Biloxi, Mississippi.[20]

Simpson was in contact with the National Weather Service in Washington, but what they were telling him contradicted his own instincts. "The people in Washington who were analyzing the satellite images were sure the storm was losing intensity. I was sure the storm was getting stronger. I was convinced it was becoming close to a record storm just from the way the eye structure was changing."[21]

✻ ✻ ✻

Saturday at Woodstock touched off just after noon with a percussion-heavy set from the little-known New England band, Quill. During yet another delay Saturday morning, Country Joe McDonald stepped in one day earlier than his scheduled performance with his group, The Fish, to entertain the morning crowd solo. He led the crowd in his "Fish Cheer," with its now-famous call of "Gimme an F . . . a U . . . a C . . . a K . . . What's that spell?"—leading into his "I Feel like I'm Fixing to Die Rag," a sardonic antiwar sing-along. "Listen people, I don't know how you expect to ever stop the war if you can't sing any better than that. There's about three hundred thousand of you fuckers out there. I want you to start singing," he told the crowd, rousing them to their feet. Michael Doyle writes, "The call-and-response ended with what had to be the loudest uttering of an obscenity ever."

The deep-voiced Chip Monck, who designed the stage lighting for Woodstock and also served as the festival's unofficial emcee, made an announcement for someone to go backstage: "I understand your wife is having a baby." Pop star John Sebastian came out wearing a tie-dyed suit and carrying his acoustic guitar, flying high and feeling no pain. "Oh boy, this is really a mind-fucker of all times, man. I've never seen anything like this, man," he said. "Just love everyone around you and pick up a little garbage on your way out and everything's gonna be all right." He spoke movingly, if incoherently, but the smile never left his face and a mood of mellowness descended upon the festivities. "You know, like, the press can only, uh, can only say bad things unless there ain't no fuck-ups, and it's looking like there ain't gonna be no fuck-ups. This is gonna work."

Sebastian had been the leader of the successful pop group, The Lovin' Spoonful, before leaving in 1968 and spending some time in a commune. His presence and performance at Woodstock lent a sense of pop music legitimacy to the festival, and as he closed with the song "Younger Generation"—during which he had to stop and ask the crowd to help him remember the words—he left the hundreds of thousands of listeners with good vibes. Robert Spitz wrote, "Something magical transformed the stage when John Sebastian ambled out, waving at his fans, and it was at that moment that [John]

Morris [of Woodstock Ventures] thought that the Woodstock Music and Art Fair truly became a festival."[22]

The afternoon and evening consisted of an impressive roster, with Santana, the Incredible String Band, Canned Heat, the Grateful Dead, Creedence Clearwater Revival, Janis Joplin, Sly & the Family Stone, and The Who. Santana, a San Francisco-based group founded by the slickly smooth jazz-fusion guitarist Carlos Santana, played a unique blend of rock infused with jazz and Latin rhythms. The band had developed a West Coast following off of its explosive live sets at venues such as the Winterland and Fillmore West, but they had yet to even release their debut album and were scared to death about playing at the summer's biggest gig. When they were rushed onstage at Woodstock, Carlos was still floating high on mescaline, and he found himself looking out at "an ocean of flesh, hair, teeth, and hands."[23] They delivered a steaming set highlighted by the frenetic jam, "Soul Sacrifice," which would be featured in Michael Wadleigh's documentary film, *Woodstock: 3 Days of Peace and Music*, and helped launch the band's career.

Canned Heat's falsetto hit "Going up the Country" became the unofficial anthem for the festival, and the band kept the mood going strong with its version of muscular blues-rock and boogie. As Bob Hite, the group's heavy, bearded singer, belted out "A Change Is Gonna Come," a young bead-wearing fan made his way onstage and hugged him. Hite waved off security, spoke to the fan during Alan Wilson's guitar solo, and even lit a cigarette for the kid, who waved triumphantly as the crowd cheered his moment of glory.

The Grateful Dead was one of the most anticipated acts, their legend as a live band starting to build. In June, the Dead had released their third album, *Aoxomoxoa*, known just as much for its psychedelic-inspired, sun-and-skull cover design as it is for its transition from the group's quasi-blues origins to acoustic-leaning jams, as evidenced in classic tracks like "St. Stephen," "China Cat

Sunflower," and "Cosmic Charlie." Surveying the scene in Max Yasgur's pasture, Jerry Garcia said in awe, "It's really amazing. It looks like some sort of biblical, epochal, unbelievable scene."[24] But the band's four-jam performance of "St. Stephen," "Mama Tried," "Dark Star / High Time," and "Turn on Your Lovelight" would be remembered as a lackluster one—too loose and free-form, years before the tribe of Deadheads would come to expect that of the band.

The main stage had been designed as a rotating platform to allow for the following act to set up on the rear half behind a screen while the current act was performing, but the Dead's equipment was so heavy that the turntable sagged and stopped turning. The rain was pouring and the wind was so strong against the light-show screen that was fixed to the stage that stagehands feared it would lift the stage up off its foundations. Workers took knives to the screen and cut wind holes. Just as the band went into "St. Stephen," percussionist Mickey Hart looked over at Garcia and saw how scared he looked, and thought, "Oh, man, we're in trouble."

Behind them, workers were warning that the stage was in the process of collapsing. Plus, the band was pretty tripped on LSD: "speckled tablets from Czechoslovakia," remembers Phil Lesh. Plus, faulty grounding produced shocks when band members approached their mics. "Our sound man at the time decided he was gonna change the ground in the middle of the whole thing," Weir recalled. "It was not done right or something. Every time I touched my instrument, I got a horrible shock and [Garcia] was getting the same thing."[25] As the band left the stage, Garcia said to someone, "It's nice to know that you can blow the most important gig of your career and it doesn't really matter."[26]

Following the Dead, Creedence Clearwater Revival stepped onstage as perhaps the hottest band in the land. With three Top Ten albums released in 1969, *Bayou Country* (in January), *Green River* (August), and *Willie and the Poor Boys* (November), Creedence signing on to do the festival had added credibility to Woodstock

Ventures as they looked to add acts to the roster of talent. The fact that CCR played Woodstock has been forgotten by many people, most likely due to the band's absence from the documentary film and the initial soundtrack release. But the band's "down home" rock made perfect sense in the festival's bucolic setting, and they churned out a smoking set chock full of hits including "Born on the Bayou," "Green River," "Bad Moon Rising," "Proud Mary," "I Put a Spell on You," "Night Time Is the Right Time," and "Suzy Q." Fogerty, though, would remember it with bitterness. The band was forced to go on way past midnight after a longish set by the Dead, and much of the crowd was—for one reason or another—unconscious. "We were ready to rock out and we waited and waited and finally it was our turn. My reaction was, 'Wow, we get to follow the band that put half a million people to sleep. . . . These people were out. No matter what I did, they were gone. It was sort of like a painting of a Dante scene, just bodies from hell, all intertwined and asleep, covered with mud."[27]

Janis Joplin performed next as one of the festival's headliners. She had hooked up with a new backing group, the Kozmic Blues Band, in a move away from acid rock toward the tradition of the great Stax-Volt R&B records. Insecure since adolescence, Joplin had taken to a life of dope and sex. At Woodstock, she arrived with girlfriend Peggy Caserta in tow. "I can't fix in the tent," Joplin told Caserta during the several hours' wait for her time to go onstage. "There's too many people coming and going. There's no privacy. Come on, let's go find a place to fix." According to Caserta, they shot up in one of the stench-ridden portable toilets on the site. When she came on to play, she was clearly on something—booze, dope, maybe both—and people called out to her, asking her if she was high.

Because of her incoherence, it's gone down that her Woodstock performance was a poor one. But while it might have been an uneven one, footage of her set shows that it was, at the very least, heartfelt. Photographer Henry Diltz said, "She really screamed in agony in those songs. She really meant it. You could see that in the way she contorted her face and her body and everything."[28] Her renditions of "Work Me, Lord" and "Ball and Chain" show that she had progressed from 1967's acid-rock leading lady to queen of down-and-out blues and boogie. By the end of the night she was waving her hands in the air, pumping her fists, and rolling her hips with the music like the female lead of a soul revue.

It was well into the early-morning hours, and out came Sylvester Stewart, aka, Sly Stone, the high priest of rock and funk in 1969. Sly and the Family Stone's album *Stand!*, released in May, became the soundtrack for the summer of '69 in the nation's steamy urban areas. "Stand!," "Dance to the Music," and "Everyday People" were catchy pop songs that seethed with underlying urban unrest. Just two weeks earlier, the group had incited a near riot at the Atlantic City festival, and at Woodstock, in an eight-song joint ("M'Lady," "Sing a Simple Song," "You Can Make It If You Try," "Stand!," "Love City," "Dance to the Music," "Music Lover," and the euphoric climax of "I Want to Take You Higher") Sly had the concertgoers yelling "Higher" with as much soul as was ever found in the Catskill woods. Miles Marshall Lewis writes, "Sly provided one of the undeniable highlights of the star-studded show; the band is historically credited for waking up the massive, lagging crowd."[29] On a bill that had already featured Canned Heat, CCR, Janis, and the Dead, *Rolling Stone* said that, "Sly and the Family Stone, apart in their grandeur, won the battle, carrying to their own majestically freaked-out stratosphere."[30]

And then came The Who. In a year of musical firsts, 1969 had seen the release of The Who's *Tommy*, the first "rock opera"—not an *opera*, really, but more simply a concept album intended for live performance in its entirety. The story of *Tommy* is, depending on one's perspective, inventive and genre-expanding or pretentious and silly, or all of these. Tommy is a boy rendered deaf, dumb, and blind after witnessing his long-lost father murder his wife's lover. Tommy achieves fame as a pinball player, becomes the head of a religious cult, is abandoned by his disciples, but ultimately achieves enlightenment. The recorded version—released as double album—begins with an "Overture" with rock drums and guitar mixed with French horns and other classic instrumentation, and includes hits like "Pinball Wizard," "I'm Free," and "See Me, Feel Me."

Tommy had been a pet project of Pete Townshend's for years, an extended concept that followed in the footsteps of the band's nine-minute suite, "A Quick One While He's Away," from the band's 1966 record. The Who released the album in May and gave its debut American performance at Detroit's Grande Ballroom that month. A month before Woodstock, *Rolling Stone's* Rick Sanders and David Dalton rushed to find significance in *Tommy*: "And now we have a double album set that's probably the most important milestone in pop since Beatlemania. For the first time, a rock group has come up with a full-length cohesive work that could be compared to the classics."

Summed up Townshend: "It's about life."[31]

Performed live at Woodstock, *Tommy* was pure spectacle. After opening with "Heaven and Hell" and "I Can't Explain," the band performed *Tommy* in its entirety, culminating in the final climax of "We're Not Gonna Take It (See Me, Feel Me)." With Roger Daltrey in a fringed leather jacket and pre-*Godspell* curly locks belting out vocals, Pete Townshend jumping about in a white jumpsuit and displaying his windmill guitar assault, Keith Moon delivering his proto-heavy metal attack on drums, and John Entwhistle calmly laying down a powerful bass line, The Who showed itself to be cohering like never before, moving from mid-sixties mod-pop to late-sixties progressive rock. At Monterey in 1967, Pete Townshend and Jimi Hendrix had feuded over which band was going to follow which, and history would say Hendrix had won the battle of pyrotechnics that day. But at Woodstock it was The Who that delivered perhaps the most entertaining performance of the festival.

It was also marred by momentary controversy when Yippie leader Abbie Hoffman attempted to go on stage just after the band played "Pinball Wizard." He grabbed the mic and began to yell, "I think this is a pile of shit! While John Sinclair rots in prison—" Already annoyed with the presence of Michael Wadleigh's camera crew on stage, Pete Townshend cut Hoffman off: "Fuck off . . . fuck off my stage!" Accounts vary as to whether Townshend hit Hoffman with his guitar or merely bumped into him; regardless, he quickly ended Hoffman's attempt at a revolutionary statement to the Woodstock Nation. Townshend said, "I can dig it," but moments later added, "The next fucking person that walks across this stage is gonna get fucking killed!"[32]

Jefferson Airplane, joined by legendary session keyboardist Nicky Hopkins, took the stage as the sun rose early Sunday morning. Dressed all in white, her normally straight black hair puffed out in a perm, Grace Slick addressed the sleepy crowd. "All right, friends," she said. "You have seen the heavy groups, now you will see morning maniac music, believe me. Yeah. It's a new dawn." The Airplane debuted two songs from their new album: the environmentally themed "Eskimo Blue Day" and the revolutionary call of "Volunteers." Commenting on Woodstock, Slick told author Jeff Tamarkin, "It was unique in that there were a half-million people not stabbing each other to death. And it was a statement of, look at us, we're 25 and we're all together and things ought to change."[33]

✳ ✳ ✳

Saturday afternoon and evening, Hurricane Camille came to a virtual stop in the Gulf of Mexico. There it sat, raging with winds now up to 150 miles per hour, and most analysts predicted that when it did resume moving northward, it would follow the Coriolis effect and veer away from the Mississippi Delta region and toward the Florida panhandle. At midnight, the NHC observed that Camille was 310 miles due south of Pensacola, Florida, and was now moving northward again while drifting toward the west, seemingly aimed straight at New Orleans. But conventional wisdom had it that Camille would ultimately steer eastward. Simpson predicted it touching land somewhere on the Florida panhandle early Sunday night.[34]

The NHC went about trying to determine the intensity of the storm surge that would hit the coastline. As fierce as they are, the wind and driving rains of a landfall hurricane are merely secondary to the storm surge that results from winds driving the ocean's surface. As the waves rush upon the rising ocean floor near the coastline, the water pushes itself up and over itself, forming giant tides as it hits land.

At 5:00 A.M. CDT on Sunday, the NHC extended its hurricane warning 140 miles westward to Biloxi. The projected landfall as of daybreak was Mobile, Alabama.

❁ ❁ ❁

Meanwhile, up north, the headline in the New York *Sunday News* announced: HIPPIES MIRED IN A SEA OF MUD. Thousands had left, driven home by the rain, mud, hunger, exhaustion, or all of the above. Hugh Romney of the Hog Farm took the stage and announced, "What we have in mind is breakfast in bed for 400,000 Now . . . it's gonna be good food, and we're gonna get it to ya. It's not just the Hog Farm either . . . it's everybody. We're all feedin' each other. We must be in heaven, man! There's always a little bit of heaven in a disaster area." The menu in heaven consisted mostly of rolled oats and bulgur wheat served with stir-fry vegetables.[35]

In the afternoon, Joe Cocker and the Grease Band touched off the third day's schedule of performances. Singing soulfully and on the edge of pain, he seemed to embody the lost soul of Janis at Monterey. In his silver-starred boots and long-sleeved tie-dyed shirt, Cocker flailed wildly in a St. Vitus dance of his trademark spastic gestures, a convulsion of sweat and mutton chops and air-guitar as the Grease Band sang high-pitched and out of tune behind him. They put on a five-song set, including covers of the classic Ray Charles hit "Let's Get Stoned" and The Beatles' "With a Little Help from My Friends."

After Cocker's set, the rain clouds came again, this time bringing the heaviest downfall of the weekend, along with winds that sent the stage crews scrambling to cover the wires and amps. Country Joe and the Fish were due on next, and guitarist Barry Melton, swept up in back-to-the-land mysticism, grabbed the mic and led the crowd in an anti-rain dance chant: "No rain! No rain!" It kept raining. People huddled under plastic tarps and umbrellas. Others set up an impromptu slip-and-slide in the mud. Those given to paranoia spread rumors of a government conspiracy. "I want to know how come the fascist pigs have been seeding the clouds," one man said to a cameraman from Wadleigh's film crew. "There's been airplanes going over twice with all the smoke coming out of them seeding the clouds, and I want to know what that stuff is going down and why the media doesn't report that stuff to the people." One group of festivalgoers formed an impromptu percussion jam with sticks and tin cans and glass bottles, joining in a primal chorus and chanting "Peace! Peace! Peace! Peace!"[36]

After the worst of the rain had passed, there were more guitars with Leslie West's hard rock band, Mountain, and Ten Years After with Alvin Lee. Lee and company played a blistering, ten-minute version of "I'm Goin' Home." In the middle of the song, the crowd joined on top of the rhythm section with a handclap beat as Lee jammed on his big red Gibson guitar while moving through a medley of the white man's blues ("Babe, Please Don't Go" / "Blue Suede Shoes" / "Whole Lotta Shakin' Goin' On"), and then they watched transfixed as the band crossed the musical bridge to the song's frenetic finale. With a big grin on his face, Lee took a watermelon that had been tossed onstage and carried it off the stage like a trophy.

Captured on both the film and the soundtrack, the performance would catapult the band into stardom.

One of the original inspirations for the Woodstock concert, The Band followed with a set primarily taken from *Music from Big Pink*, including "Chest Fever," "Tears of Rage," "Long Black Veil," "Wheels on Fire," and "The Weight." (The group's self-titled second album, which would include classics like "Across the Great Divide," "Up on Cripple Creek," and "The Night They Drove Old Dixie Down," would be released the following month.) "It was funny. You kind of felt you were going to war," Levon Helm would write. "I think we drove down to Stewart Airport [in Newburgh], and they helicoptered us into the landing zone. . . . It was the final day of the festival, and they'd run out of fresh food and water. There weren't any dressing rooms because they'd been turned into emergency clinics. . . . The crowd was real tired and a little unhealthy."[37]

Texas bluesman Johnny Winter came on in the midnight hour to play his brand of electric blues-rock on songs. The albinistic guitarist jammed on such standards as "Johnny B. Goode" and "Rock Me Baby" as well as his own "Mean Town Blues." The white man's blues gave way to the jazz, pop, and blue-eyed soul of Blood, Sweat & Tears. While they might have been one of the least counterculture of acts to play the festival, BS&T was one of the most successful recording acts of the year. With their horn-rich sound and the brassy voice of its new lead singer, David Clayton-Thomas, the band had already reached number two on the Billboard Hot 100 twice that year with "You've Made Me So Very Happy" and "Spinning Wheel." In the fall, their cover of Laura Nyro's "And When I Die" would become the third song from their number-one album *Blood, Sweat & Tears* to reach number two on the singles chart.

The mellow early hours would provide the perfect setting for Crosby, Stills & Nash. Woodstock was only the second time the recently formed supergroup had played live, and as Stills famously declared, they were "scared shitless." As they had waited at LaGuardia Airport for a charter plane to take them upstate, the band wondered what they'd gotten themselves into. "At the airport, we kept hearing all of these news reports that it had gotten completely out of hand, that there were a million people, that it was very tense, that they didn't know whether to call the National Guard or drop flowers."[38] (The former was debated by Governor Nelson Rockefeller, but the latter occurred during emergency food drops.)

The trio had originated out of Laurel Canyon jam sessions with Byrds founder David Crosby, Stephen Stills from Buffalo Springfield, and Graham Nash from the Hollies. As soon as they had begun singing together on their own, the three musicians could tell they were on to something special—a hypnotic, harmonic sound tinged with psychedelic textures. Their debut album, *Crosby, Stills & Nash*, released in the spring, provided many of the songs for the set: the classic "Guinnevere," "Marrakesh Express," and the haunting "Suite: Judy Blue Eyes." Joining them for part of the set was Neil Young, who was about to add his unique vocals and guitar work as an official fourth member. On Crosby, Stills, Nash & Young's 1970 album *Déjà Vu*, they would release their version of Joni Mitchell's "Woodstock," her ode to the festival.

❀ ❀ ❀

As Simpson worked overtime to not only track the fury of Camille, but also to disseminate warnings to the communities that would encounter her wrath, he grew concerned about the area's rural residents. His reports to the National Weather Service in Washington would have been teletyped and radioed to New Orleans, the area's military bases, and offshore oil platforms. But the NHC had no direct contract with civil defense officials, the local Red Cross, or even the Salvation Army. To his growing alarm, he realized he had no control over the information that could be delivered to people in low-lying areas or on the islands scattered throughout the Delta region.

Sunday afternoon, about eight hours before landfall, the navigator of a C-130 plane that ventured into Camille's path computed steady wind speeds of 190 miles per hour. After the plane made a treacherous exit and returned to base, copilot Robert Lee Clark reported: "Just as we were entering the wall cloud, we suddenly broke into a clear area and could see the sea surface below. What a sight! No one had seen the wind whip the sea like that before. Instead of the green and white splotches normally found in a storm, the sea surface was in deep furrows running along the wind directions. The velocity was far beyond the descriptions used in our training." [39]

Camille was not only moving again but also picking up speed, moving at fifteen miles per hour toward the coast, and not veering eastward as predicted. The winds at the outlying areas of the cyclone formation were now playing havoc as far west as the mouth of the Mississippi River, and the latest trajectory implied that Camille would now hit land at or near Gulfport, Mississippi.

After a hurricane advisory was issued for the Gulf Coast from Gulfport, Mississippi, to Pensacola, Florida, residents began an exodus in search of safer locales inland. Around the same time as the warning, an eighteen-wheeler capsized on Route 49 in Gulfport, blocking one of the three main roadways inland. Instead of stopping traffic altogether to allow for the removal of the wreckage, authorities decided it more prudent to leave the vehicle where it was and allow motorists to drive around it. Traffic jammed up even worse as residents and workers lined up to evacuate the region. [40]

The Gulf waters were growing ever more turbulent. From its source at Lake Itasca in Minnesota, the Mississippi River cuts the country in two as it journeys southward to its mouth in Plaquemines Parish, the "birdfoot"-shaped delta at the very southeastern tip of Louisiana. Under normal conditions, the Mississippi River dumps two billion cubic feet of water per hour into the Gulf of Mexico. But on the night of August 17, the waters of the Mississippi met a greater force in the Camille storm surge. As the waters from the Gulf of Mexico rose sixteen feet higher than the Mississippi, huge whirlpools formed at the mouth of the delta, and then the unthinkable happened—the waters of America's "Big River" began to run backward. As far as 120 river miles—from the mouth of the Mississippi to Carrollton, Louisiana—the currents were running northward.[41]

Things happen during natural disasters that seem to defy the natural laws of physics. The crew of the *Rum Runner* schooner had pulled into Lake Borgne, a lagoon due east of New Orleans, and dropped anchor, seeking haven from the raging Gulf while (as they thought would happen) Camille passed by and headed eastward. But Camille had passed over Plaquemines Parish on its way toward the Mississippi coastline. The resulting surge plowed into the lagoon. The *Rum Runner* began taking on water, more than the crew could bail, and so they climbed on deck and took shelter under tarps, holding on for their lives. One final maelstrom of wind and water tipped the ship over 90 degrees, propelling the men overboard—and they found themselves deposited onto a dry lakebed. With the ferocity of the surge and the inversion of the low pressure storm, the waters of the 240-square mile lagoon had been blown away by Camille's winds and sucked into the right front quadrant of the hurricane. Now, it was being transported with full force toward the Mississippi coastline, where Camille would make landfall twenty-five miles *west* of Biloxi.[42]

❈ ❈ ❈

Things rolled past schedule into Monday morning, and somewhat fittingly, the first two acts were throwbacks of sorts: The Paul Butterfield Band, a couple years past its prime, and the newly formed retro-doo-wop group Sha Na Na, a doo-wop revival group that was anachronistic in its choreographed moves, greased hair, leather vests, gold-sequined jackets (five years too early for the *American Graffiti*–inspired retro phenomenon) and uncool beyond words.

By the time Jimi Hendrix, the final performer and the festival's true headline act, took the stage Monday morning, all but roughly 50,000 of the festival crowd had departed, driven away by filth, hunger, and exhaustion. "Having waited up all night, the audience understandably seemed as groggy as we were, and it was horrible to see people packing up and leaving as we came on," Mitch Mitchell said. "Monday morning was back to the grind for a lot of people who'd come, and it couldn't be helped."[43]

Hendrix almost hadn't made it. He and his band had arrived on the festival grounds around 8:00 the night before. While they waited in a farm shack, said one witness, Hendrix was "ill, dosed . . . by drinking the water backstage. He seemed really sick, or really high, and was sweating bullets. I was feeding him vitamin C, fruit, and having him suck on lemon slices. As we sat there, he seemed nervous and didn't think he could pull it off." Hendrix had gone into the medical tent and crashed on a stretcher. "We didn't know who he was. Just a black man laying on the stretcher," a nurse remembered. "Then everybody started saying, 'Hey, isn't that Jimi Hendrix?' There was a big stir about it. He lay on the stretcher for about thirty minutes before roadies hauled him out."[44]

Monck incorrectly introduced the group—with Mitchell on drums but Billy Cox on bass, Larry Lee on backing guitar, Jumma Sultan and Jerry Velez adding percussion—under the old name of the Jimi Hendrix Experience. Hendrix came out dressed in his fringed Native American tribal shirt and jeans and moccasins and a red bandana. "I see that we meet again, hmmm . . . ," he said to the crowd, and reintroduced his new group as Gypsy, Sun and Rainbow.

They glided into a set beginning with "Message to Love" followed by "Get My Heart Back Together" (later, "Hear My Train A-Comin'"), "Spanish Castle Magic," "Red House," "Mastermind" (a Lee original, with himself on vocals), "Here Comes Your Lover

Man," and "Foxy Lady." With the new lineup, sleepy crowd, and hangers-on surrounding them onstage, Hendrix's gypsy band struggled through some numbers. They played out of tune at times, and Sultan and Velez were almost inaudible. Sound engineer Eddie Kramer describes, "After the band bludgeoned their way through 'Foxey Lady,' [sic] Hendrix sensed his audience's confusion. 'I know it's not together,' he remarked from the stage, continuing in a mocking tone, 'You're tuning up between every song! This isn't together! That isn't together!' Well, you all ain't in uniform!"[45]

After "Jam Back at the House (Beginning)," "Izabella," Curtis Mayfield's "Gypsy Woman" (Lee on vocals again), and "Fire," they launched into an epic, thirteen-minute version of the demonic blues number, "Voodoo Chile (Slight Return)," which Hendrix introduced as his "new American anthem until we get another one."[46] His fingers sliding up and down the bridge of his cream-colored, left-handed Fender Stratocaster, he played the song's last few demonic wah-wahs, and then the band touched off a sonic avalanche leading into an electric version of the country's "old" anthem, "The Star-Spangled Banner." The Woodstock set showed how Hendrix had moved away from his Monterey psychedelic theatrics toward a serious exploration of electric rock and blues.

For his instrumental interpretation of Francis Scott Key's patriotic tune, Hendrix pulled out all the stops, bending and torturing the tune's melody to create an anthem for the land of free love and the home of a brave new world. In his pyrotechnic sound effects, one heard machine guns and falling bombs, the sounds of chaos straight out of the Southeast Asian jungles. David Fricke writes: "If the Experience tried to play power-jazz at the speed of light, Hendrix at Woodstock was a rough prototype for a new black-rock futurism, the missing link between Sly Stone's taut, rainbow-party R&B and George Clinton's blown-mind, ghetto-army funk: 'Dance to the Music' plus 'Message to Love' equals 'Cosmic Slop.'"[47] "It was the most electrifying moment of Woodstock, and it was probably

1969

the single greatest moment of the sixties," wrote Al Aronowitz of the *New York Post*. You finally heard what that song was about, that you can love your country, but hate the government."[48]

Hendrix would later reflect:

> They made me sing it in school, so it was a flashback. We're all Americans, aren't we? When it was written then, it was played in what they call a very, very beautiful state, nice and inspiring, your heart throbs and you say, 'Great, I'm American!' But nowadays when we play it, we don't play to take away all this greatness that America's supposed to have. We play it the way the air is in America today. The air is slightly static, isn't it? You know what I mean?[49]

The last notes of "The Star-Spangled Banner" led right into the early Hendrix hit, "Purple Haze," a four-minute jam followed by "Villanova Junction," and then "Hey Joe" to close the two-hour set. He said "Thank you" and unplugged, bringing an official end to Woodstock.

❀ ❀ ❀

Camille passed over the eastern tip of Plaquemines Parish, where some 20,000 residents were all but trapped—connected to New Orleans by just one two-lane highway. Then, at approximately 11:30 P.M., Hurricane Camille made landfall at Bay St. Louis in Hancock County, Mississippi.[50] She hit the mainland with the highest storm surge ever recorded on U. S. coastland. Anecdotal reports from the stately Richelieu Manor Apartments complex in Pass Christian, where the water rose to within a foot of the third floor, indicated that the surge had risen to twenty-eight feet above sea level.[51]

Meteorologists concluded that just before landfall, Camille's winds had reached a record speed of 201 miles per hour.[52] Boats were washed inland and collided with houses. The areas of Clermont Harbor, Lakeshore, Waveland, Bay St. Louis, Pass Christian, Long

Beach, Gulfport Beach, and Biloxi were decimated. Ship's Island off the coast of Mississippi was literally torn in two by the surge, dividing the body of land into East and West Ship Islands that are separated today by a stretch of water known as Camille's Cut. Twenty-six counties (all or parts of) in Mississippi, two in Alabama, and nine parishes in Louisiana were declared disaster areas. In Mississippi and Alabama, 3,868 homes were destroyed and 42,092 were damaged.[53]

Camille headed north to Tennessee, moved into Kentucky, and then curved eastward across the southern tip of West Virginia and through Virginia. As Camille headed on its way out to the Atlantic, where it eventually spent itself over the Atlantic Ocean, 256 people lay dead in the receding waters (143 along the Gulf Coast, and 113 as a result of the floods in Virginia). The total damage was more than $1.4 billion.[54]

In the aftermath, residents were left to deal with widespread waste, as well as a human element: looters. Video footage of the affected areas showed homeowners guarding the remnants of their homes with shotguns. Others put up signs warning potential looters that they would be shot on sight. And then there were the snakes and fire ants that had been unearthed by the floodwaters and plagued survivors and rescue workers. To combat the fire ants, authorities called in crop dusters that spread toxic pesticides across hundreds of acres of already-polluted land.

※ ※ ※

The crowding, conditions, and ad hoc planning at the Woodstock festival had created its own microcosmic disaster area. "I can always tell who was really there," Barry Melton said later. "When they tell me it was great, I know they saw the movie and they weren't at the gig." A sullen Joplin said soon after her performance, "I can't relate to a quarter of a million people." Garcia recalled, "As a personal experience, Woodstock was a bummer. It was terrible to play at . . ." He would later say, "Playing for four hundred thousand people is really peculiar. . . . We didn't enjoy it, playing there . . ."[55] Pete Townshend said simply, "Woodstock was horrible."[56]

Although admitting that the "great bulk of freakish-looking intruders behaved astonishingly well," a *New York Times* editorial sensationally declared the whole thing A NIGHTMARE IN THE CATSKILLS. The editorial went on to ask, "What kind of culture can produce so colossal a mess?"

As the festival attendees left Yasgur's farm, leaving behind garbage strewn across the rustic landscape, it was up to the media and the rest of the country to deliberate on the cultural significance of the festival.

In one sense, Woodstock had been a success for what *didn't* happen—more than 400,000 young people had congregated and it did *not* lead to mass rioting or destruction. The world did *not* end. The biggest success of the festival was proving that it could be done at all. As one festivalgoer said: "It was like balling for the first time. Once you've done it, you want to do it again and again, because it's so great." *Rolling Stone* commented: "And they will do it again, the threads of youthful dissidence in Paris and Prague and Fort Lauderdale and Berkeley and Chicago and London criss-crossing ever more closely until the map of the world we live in is viable for and visible to all of those that are part of it and all of those buried under it."[57]

Many Sullivan County residents even praised the young crowd for acting politely and peacefully. One farmer complained it had been "a shitty mess." Another man bemoaned that fifteen-year-old girls had slept outside in the fields.

Three people had died at Woodstock: One person overdosed on heroin, another was run over by a tractor, and another died of a ruptured appendix. Hundreds had died in Hurricane Camille. Many thousands more American soldiers were dying in Vietnam. But to many members of the older generation, the fact that a mass gathering of kids could have a Saturnalian weekend in the woods was more threatening than the lack of emergency preparedness for a storm or the drafting of young men to die in a war on the other side of the globe.

❊ ❊ ❊

The subculture that Abbie Hoffman would dub "Woodstock Nation" in his 1969 book of the same name would die almost as soon as it was born. Ironically, while the crowding and traffic jams created by Woodstock had ruined many a vacation for tourists with poor timing that third weekend in August, Woodstock Nation spawned tourists of its own who flocked to its namesake town as if making a pilgrimage to the counterculture mecca. In *Chronicles*, Bob Dylan remembers: "At one time the place had been a quiet refuge, but now, no more. Roadmaps to our homestead must have been posted in all fifty states for gangs of dropouts and druggies. Moochers showed up from as far away as California on pilgrimages. Goons were breaking into our place all hours of the night. . . . I wanted to set fire to these people. These gate-crashers, spooks, trespassers, demagogues . . ."[58]

Van Morrison later told Richard Williams for *Melody Maker* magazine, "When I first went, people were moving there to get away from the scene. Then Woodstock itself started being the scene."[59] In the weeks following Woodstock, Morrison was working on his follow-up to the timeless *Astral Weeks*. *Moondance* would become an instant classic, the embodiment of his mystical version of "Caledonia soul," with songs like "And It Stoned Me," "Caravan," "Into the Mystic," and the title track. Soon afterward, Morrison and his wife Janet Planet would pack up and move to California, leaving the Woodstock "scene" behind.

Meanwhile, Madison Avenue observed the whole Woodstock "thing" as an emerging trend and sought to co-opt it. One ad for the

Shortline bus line in New York State quoted drivers "rap[ping] about the kids they took to the Woodstock Festival." One driver said, "I don't understand why they wear long hair but now I don't care. It's a free country. And they're the most no-griping, no-complaining, patient and generous, respectful bunch of kids I ever met. Come on, kids, and ride with me. It's a pleasure driving with you."[60] The headline of a United Van Lines ad depicting four shaggy young vagabonds played with cultural fears under the clever headline, SOME PEOPLE (EVEN) UNITED CAN'T HELP, but then explained in smaller copy: "If you can pack your possessions on the back of a bike, you won't have much use for our services." A new store called The Gap—named after the "generation gap"—opened on a San Francisco street corner in 1969 as a retail store aimed at the counterculture, selling records and blue jeans. The Woodstock Generation was on its way toward becoming the Pepsi Generation.

Yet the legacy of the Woodstock Music and Art Festival would remain. As Michael Lang told NBC's Gabe Pressman during the three-day happening:

> You have this culture and this generation, away from the old culture and the older generation. You see how they function on their own, without cops, without guns, without clubs, without hassles, everybody pulls together and everybody helps each other, and it works. It's been working since we got here, and it's going to continue working. No matter what happens when they go back to the cities, this thing is happening and it proves it can happen.[61]

ONEWALL RIOTS ALTAMONT
OE NAMATH
JTCH CASSIDY AND THE SUNDANCE KID
UPATION OF ALCATRAZ ZIP TO ZAP THE NEW LEFT
ASY RIDER HARVARD STUDENT STRIKI

IV. AUTUMN APOCALYPSE

To hear this summery music on one of the last clement days of the year was like some operatic reprise where the heroine, condemned to death, hears in her dark cell . . . .

—John Cheever, *Bullet Park*

H! CALCUTTA! THE WEATHER UNDERGROUND
EIL YOUNG & CRAZY HORSE TOMMY
C5 DAYS OF RAGE APOLLO 11 BOEING 747
HAMBURGER HILL
1 CURIOUS (YELLOW) PORTNOY'S COMPLAINT CUYAHOGA RIVER FIRE
CHES BREW LET IT BLEED CHARLES MANSON
I PHOTOS THE MORATORIUM WOODSTOCK
D ZEPPELIN
OPLE'S PARK JIMI HENDRIX RICHARD NIXON HELLS ANGELS
IE GODFATHER IGGY AND JEFFERSON
OODY ALLEN THE STOOGES AIRPLANE
IDNIGHT COWBOY NUDITY THE MIRACLE
ZODIAC KILLER BOB & CAROL & TED & ALICE METS
PERATION MENU CROSBY, STILLS & NASH

18. "There Are No Words"

The Miracle Mets complete a dream season.

After winning the National League Eastern Division with a regular season record of 100-62, the Mets headed to Atlanta for Game One of the first-ever National League "pennant series" with the Braves. Atlanta had won a close race in the West by three games over second-place San Francisco and four games over third-place Cincinnati.

In the best-of-five series, New York's starters would uncharacteristically struggle against a Braves team that boasted two future Hall of Fame power hitters in Hank Aaron and Orlando Cepeda. The Braves' championship series program depicted an Atlanta player stepping off *Apollo 11* onto a lunar home plate; but surprisingly it was the Mets lineup—which had been no-hit by Pittsburgh's Bob Moose at Shea in late September—that took off in the series.

In Game One, Jerry Grote got things started with an RBI single off Phil Niekro in the second inning as Art Shamsky recorded the franchise's first-ever postseason run, and Boswell scored moments later on a passed ball. Staff ace Seaver allowed eleven Braves to reach base through seven innings and left the game with his team trailing, 5–4. But in the top of the eighth, Wayne Garrett's leadoff double touched off a five-run rally that was aided by two Atlanta errors, and Ron Taylor pitched the final two innings to preserve a 9–5 win.

The following afternoon, the Mets lineup came out hot from the start. Tommie Agee singled off starter Ron Reed, and Garrett walked to begin the game. Gil Hodges, wanting to keep the pressure on the Braves, called a double steal that moved both men into scoring position, and Ed Kranepool's two-out single scored the first run. In the second, Agee homered after Reed had walked Mets pitcher Jerry Koosman, and Shamsky added an RBI single. Bud Harrelson's double and Garrett's single plated two more in the third, and Ken Boswell added a two-run homer in the fourth. Steady all year, Koosman took the mound with a 9–1 lead in the bottom of the fifth, but he nearly imploded. Eight batters later, the score was 9–6, and he was pulled with two outs and two runners on base. Ron Taylor came on and was the recipient of some good luck when catcher Bob Didier lined one right at Boswell for the third out, and from then on he and bullpen mate Tug McGraw held Atlanta scoreless. In the seventh, Cleon Jones's two-run shot padded New York's lead. Although the Braves lineup knocked out three home runs, they also committed three errors in the field, and the Mets won the slugfest, 11–6.

The two teams flew north for Game Three on October 6, the Mets' first postseason home game in team history. This time Atlanta struck first with Hank Aaron's two-run blast over the fence off Gary Gentry in the first inning—the future home run king's third round-tripper in three games. When Aaron doubled to put two men on for Atlanta with no outs in the third, Hodges decided he'd seen enough and came out to signal for a new pitcher. As a dejected Gentry left the mound, in came Nolan Ryan, the young fireballer who'd gone 6-3 for the Mets in ten starts and fifteen relief appearances for the team that season, to get out of the jam. Homers from Agee and Boswell over the next two innings gave New York a 3–2 lead, and after Ryan temporarily surrendered the lead on a two-run shot to Cepeda in the top of the fifth, Garrett's two-run homer and Boswell's RBI single in the bottom of the inning grabbed the lead back for good.

Ryan saved the day by pitching the last seven innings out of the bullpen, giving up only two runs and striking out seven, and when Garrett grabbed a ground ball from Tony Gonzalez and threw to Kranepool for the final out of the game, the Mets won the game 7–4 and claimed the National League championship. Ecstatic fans ran onto the Shea Stadium field to celebrate. To avoid the melee, the Mets players ran off the field and into the locker room, where bottles of champagne waited, ready for spraying. Once baseball's lovable losers, the Mets were going to the World Series.

In the Fall Classic, the upstart Mets would face a team that some were calling the best ever. The Baltimore Orioles had won 109 games in the regular season under fiery manager Earl Weaver. Like Atlanta, Baltimore brought a lineup with two future Hall of Famers, right-fielder Frank Robinson and third baseman Brooks Robinson, along with a powerful All-Star slugger in first baseman Boog Powell. But unlike the Braves, against whom the Mets had hit .325 as a team in the series, the Orioles also had a stellar starting rotation that boasted not one but two twenty-game winners, Mike Cuellar and Dave McNally. The team's number-three starter was only Jim Palmer, himself a future enshrinee in Cooperstown. To top it off, while Atlanta had helped the Mets by committing six errors in three games, Weaver could point to players at three key positions who would win the Gold Glove in 1969: Brooks Robinson, shortstop Mark Belanger, and centerfielder Paul Blair. To this day, Robinson is regarded as the best defensive third baseman in baseball history, while Blair's name is still mentioned when discussing the greatest to ever roam centerfield.

In the American League Championship Series against the Minnesota Twins, Baltimore had swept three straight games and showed that it could win all kinds of ways. In Game One, Blair's bunt single brought home a run in the bottom of the twelfth inning and won the game 4–3. Game Two also went into extra innings, and in a performance that would be unheard of today with the modern game's reliance on relief pitching, McNally pitched an eleven-inning, complete-game shutout, striking out eleven along the way. Curt Motton's pinch-hit, game-winning single in the bottom of the eleventh made a hard-luck loser out of Minnesota's Dave Boswell, who merely pitched ten and two-thirds innings and was pulled with the eventual winning run on second base. In Game Three, the Orioles closed out the series with a bang, triumphing 11–2 on the strength of five hits and five RBI from Blair, four hits from left fielder Don Buford, and three RBI from catcher Elrod Hendricks.

Needless to say, the oddsmakers selected the Orioles as the favorite in the sixty-sixth annual World Series. But still the Mets were confident. Rookie outfielder Rod Gaspar, primarily a bench player who hit all of .228 in the regular season, tried to play Joe Namath and publicly predicted that the Mets would win in four games straight. The Orioles laughed him off. When told of the bold prediction, Frank Robinson said, "Bring on Ron Gaspar."

"Not Ron. That's Rod, stupid," teammate Merv Rettenmund corrected him.

"Okay," Robinson said, "bring on Rod Stupid."[1]

The best-of-seven series began in Baltimore's Memorial Stadium on the afternoon of Saturday, October 11—postseason games were played in the day back then—and nonbelievers in the Miracle Mets felt vindicated when the first batter to face Game One starter Seaver, Don Buford, hit the second pitch out of the park for a home run. In his second poor postseason performance, Seaver gave up four runs in just five innings, and Cuellar pitched the Orioles to a 4–1 win. The real Mets had *finally* surfaced, said the cynics.

But in Game Two, the Mets returned to the form they had displayed throughout the latter stages of the 1969 season. With neither team having managed a run through the first three innings, Donn

Clendenon ended Dave McNally's string of twenty-three consecutive scoreless innings with an opposite-field solo home run in the fourth. In contrast to his first postseason outing against the Braves, Koosman came out sharp against the Orioles and carried a no-hitter into the seventh inning. But then Blair singled, stole second, and scored on a Brooks Robinson single. With the scored tied 1–1 in the top of the ninth, Ed Charles singled with two outs, and Grote executed a perfect run-and-hit to send him to third. Due up next was Al Weis, who had hit just .215 that year. Rather than pinch-hitting for Weis, Hodges left him in to face McNally, and Weis rewarded his manager by lining a single into leftfield to score the go-ahead run.

Koosman got the first two outs of the ninth, but then he lost his control and walked both Frank Robinson and Powell, putting the potential tying and winning runs on base. Hodges called Taylor out of the bullpen to face Brooks Robinson. Robinson pulled a hard grounder at Charles, and the man known as "the Glider" snagged it and moved to step on third base for a force out; but in a split second he decided he wouldn't get to the base before Robinson, so Charles threw to Clendenon at first, who picked the ball out of the dirt and preserved the Mets' first World Series win.

After a travel day, the series resumed in New York on October 14. Game Three brought out many local celebrities to see the first World Series game to be played at Shea, including Jacqueline Onassis, Broadway star Pearl Bailey, and Mayor John Lindsay. It had been a trying year for Lindsay. After enduring strikes by the city's transportation workers, sanitation workers, and teachers earlier in his term, he took another public relations hit after a Sunday blizzard dumped fifteen inches of snow on the city on February 9, 1969. City officials discovered that nearly half of its snow-removal equipment had become inoperable because of poor upkeep. Come Monday, schools, streets, trains, and retail shops were shut down. Thousands of New Yorkers were unable to make it to work, and thousands more were stranded at Kennedy Airport. Hundreds of accidents occurred on metropolitan-area highways; forty-two people were killed and 288 were injured.[2] The situation was most grim in the borough of Queens, where half of the fatalities had occurred. As the mayor and his advisors toured Queens that Tuesday, local residents booed their leader. One woman yelled, "Just try to get elected again!"[3] Indeed, Lindsay lost the Republican mayoral primary to state senator John J. Marchi, and he would take his chances in the November general election while running as an Independent against Marchi and Democratic nominee, Mario Procaccino. With the Mets having captured the city's imagination among both fans and non-fans alike, Lindsay hoped that he would catch a little of that Mets magic.

The third game pitted Palmer, who won the clincher in the American League series, against Gentry, who looked to redeem himself after his last outing. But it was Palmer who was touched early for runs. Agee led off the game with a home run to center, and one inning later, Gentry helped his own cause with a double that drove in two runs to give the Mets a 3–0 lead.

The Orioles put runners on first and third with two outs in the fourth. Hendricks came to bat and sent a drive deep into left-center. ("I haven't hit a ball that hard to left field in years," Hendricks said after the game.[4]) Agee turned and sprinted back in pursuit of the sinking drive, reached across his body, and snared it with a backhanded catch just in front of the 396-foot sign on the outfield wall. The white of the ball stuck out of the web of his glove like a scoop of ice cream as Agee caromed into the fence, but he hung onto it to end the Baltimore threat.

Grote doubled in a run in the sixth to increase New York's lead to 4–0. But in the top of the seventh, the Mets catcher known for showing tough love to his pitchers when needed got frustrated with Gentry when he issued three two-out walks to load the bases. Up stepped Paul Blair, representing the potential tying run for the Orioles. Hodges once again went to Ryan to help pick up Gentry, but this time it was Agee who came to the rescue one more time. Ryan quickly got two strikes on Blair, but the Orioles' outfielder drove Ryan's third pitch deep into right-center. Agee ran to his left with thoughts of catching the ball on the run, but then he realized the wind was pushing it down. Agee pounded his glove, dove just in front of the warning track with his arm extended, and cushioned the ball safely into his glove.

The Shea crowd exploded. Grote stood at the top of the Mets dugout with a huge grin on his face and welcomed Agee with his hand extended. For the rest of the game and into the next, fans would be buzzing about the two remarkable plays on which Agee had most probably saved five runs. Commentators would compare his fielding displays to Willie Mays's famous over-the-shoulder catch in the Polo Grounds during the 1954 World Series. It was here, perhaps, that the Orioles began to wonder if they were fighting against fate. When Ryan caught Blair looking at strike three for the last out of the game, the Mets walked away with a 5–0 win and an improbable 2–1 lead in the series.

The following day was National Moratorium Day, a combined protest against the war and memorial for the 38,000 Americans killed to date in Vietnam. Outside the stadium, young protesters carried signs and handed out literature. Mayor Lindsay had ordered the flags at all buildings owned by the city, including Shea Stadium, to be flown at half mast, but baseball commissioner Bowie Kuhn ordered that the Shea flag be flown at full mast. Billy Graham, a supporter of the Vietnam War, was scheduled to throw out the ceremonial first pitch, but he was replaced by Casey Stengel, the team's original manager, who had popularized the phrase "Amazin' Mets" back when they were anything but amazing.

Cuellar and Seaver were the starters for Game Four. Seaver had been recently quoted as saying, "If the Mets can win the pennant, why can't we end the war?" The Moratorium committee had latched onto Seaver's words as an endorsement of their cause, but just before the game Seaver clarified, "I'm a ballplayer, not a politician.

I did not give them permission to use me. I have certain feelings about Vietnam, and I will express them as a U. S. citizen after the Series is over."[5]

In the midst of this controversy, Seaver proceeded to go out and throw the best postseason game of his career. He strung together one scoreless inning after another, and as the game entered the ninth inning, the only run scored by either side came courtesy of a Donn Clendenon home run. But in the top of the ninth, consecutive singles by Frank Robinson and Boog Powell put Orioles runners on first and third. This is when another Mets outfielder rose to the occasion to make the third of three outstanding catches for which the series would be remembered.

Brooks Robinson swung at a Seaver offering and blistered it into the right-center-field gap. Rightfielder Ron Swoboda—who early in his career had earned the nickname "Rocky" for his defensive struggles—stepped into the gap, dove out with his body perfectly parallel to the ground, reaching as far as he could with his glove hand for the ball. If not for perfect timing, the ball would have skipped past Swoboda's glove and likely gone all the way to the wall. Perhaps in some parallel universe, it did just that: Both runners scored as Robinson pulled into third with a triple, and Baltimore scored a come-from-behind win in Game Four to regain momentum in the Series. Perhaps in this alternate reality, the Orioles went on to win the Series, while the '69 Mets had to settle for being an intriguing footnote in baseball's long, storied history.

But Swoboda's timing *was* perfect, and he caught the ball just inches above the outfield grass. Frank Robinson tagged up and scored from third to tie the game, but the Shea crowd didn't seem to care. The fans of this miracle team had witnessed yet another miraculous catch, and one batter later, Swoboda made another fine (though not nearly as difficult) catch on a line drive to halt the Orioles rally.

Seaver pitched the Mets into the bottom of the tenth inning with the game still tied 1–1. Grote led off by blooping a double into shallow left field, and with Rod Gaspar pinch-running for him, J. C. Martin went up to bat for Seaver with the plan to bunt the potential winning run over to third. He laid down a good one, and when Baltimore reliever Pete Richert fielded it and threw to first, the ball hit Martin and bounced away. Gaspar scampered around with the winning run, and suddenly the Mets had a 3–1 advantage in the series. A replay indicated that Martin might have been running outside the base path on his way to first when he was struck by the ball. But the umpires did not call interference, and once again the upstart Mets seemed to be destiny's darlings. They were now just one game away from winning baseball's greatest prize.

On the other side, the Orioles simply hoped to eek out a win in Game Five and bring the Series back home, where the Mets had scored just three runs in two games. And the chances of a return trip to Baltimore looked good when Koosman surrendered two home runs in the third inning—one to opposing pitcher McNally and another to Frank Robinson—to give the O's a 3–0 lead. But Koosman calmed down, and the score stayed that way until the sixth inning, when controversy struck.

In the top of the inning, Koosman appeared to hit Frank Robinson with a pitch, but plate umpire Lou DiMuro ruled that the ball had hit Robinson's bat first, and did not award Robinson first base. Weaver jumped out of the visitors' dugout to argue along with a furious Robinson, but to no avail. Robinson disappeared for a minute into the dugout, and when he reappeared he was booed lustily by the Shea crowd. To add insult, Koosman struck him out. The Orioles would not score again in 1969.

In the bottom of the inning, a dramatic counterpoint to the Robinson incident occured when a McNally pitch hit Cleon Jones on the foot and ricocheted into the Mets dugout. Jones started down to first, but again DiMuro called him back and ruled that the ball had hit the ground, not his foot. As Jones argued his case, Hodges walked onto the field with a ball marked by the black smudge of shoe polish.

Koosman told author Peter Golenbock, "After the ball bounced, it came into our dugout. The ball came to me, and Gil told me to brush it against my shoe, and I did, and he came over and got the ball from me and took it out there and showed the umpire, 'There is shoe polish on the ball.'"[6]

DiMuro inspected the ball and awarded Jones first base. Incensed, Weaver hopped out of the dugout to argue again, and this time DiMuro ejected him from the game.

The Mets would take advantage of the "shoe polish" play. The very next batter, Donn Clendenon, hit a high drive over the leftfield fence to cut into the Orioles lead. An inning later, mighty mite Weis ripped into a McNally pitch and sent it over the wall in left-center to tie the game. The Weis family had driven to the park that day with Jerry Grote's wife; Weis's son, Dan, who was celebrating his birthday that day, told her, "My dad's gonna hit a home run for me for my birthday today."[7] For Weis, the career .219 hitter who batted .455 in the World Series, it was the first home run he'd ever hit at Shea Stadium.

In the eighth, Cleon Jones doubled off the outfield wall in left-center. Swoboda followed with a looping double that landed just in front of Don Buford in leftfield, and the Mets faithful screamed as Jones raced home with the go-ahead run. Moments later, the Mets added an insurance run when Powell failed to handle a liner from Grote, and reliever Eddie Watt lost hold of Powell's throw while covering first, allowing Swoboda to come around and score.

Protecting a 5–3 lead, Koosman walked Frank Robinson but then retired both Powell and Brooks Robinson. Second baseman Davey Johnson hit a deep fly ball to left that might have made many a fan hold their breath, but when Jones stopped moving backward and calmly settled under the ball just shy of the warning track, it was all over.

He collected the ball and brought his hands down as he practically knelt to the Shea grass in a solemn gesture. Veteran baseball writer George Vecsey wrote, "Shea Stadium was caught quivering as Jones sighted the ball, and the whole city erupted as he caught it, and the fans poured onto the field, and the New York Mets were the champions of baseball. There were a million exciting things happening and it was hard to focus on any one incident. But out in left field, if you had been looking there, you would have seen Cleon Jones, with fans racing over to pummel him, stop for a moment, drop quickly to one knee. Later, he explained his brief genuflection. 'Someone was good to us.'"[8]

The Mets, the laughingstock of baseball in their first seven years of existence, were now the best team in all of the land. All jubilant hell broke loose. Fans ran onto the field in celebration. Some collected dirt from the infield; others dug out home plate as a souvenir. It was just before 3:30 on that Thursday afternoon, October 16, and throughout the city, New Yorkers began their celebration. White-collar confetti danced downward upon spontaneous revelers. (The City Sanitation Department would record that a thousand tons of paper had fallen upon the city's streets that afternoon—more than that from the ticker-tape parade for the *Apollo 11* astronauts.[9]) Strangers danced in the streets, young with old, black with white— one of the few moments of harmony during a year that had seen the nation divided by age and race.

Champagne had flowed in the Mets clubhouse before in 1969, but never as sweetly as this. Mayor Lindsay made his way down to join in the fun, and the *New York Daily News* captured a grinning Lindsay enjoying the celebration. The picture of Grote and Gaspar pouring bubbly onto the mayor's well-coiffed hair proved to be a priceless photo opportunity. "We spent the whole campaign trying to cut Lindsay down to size, humble him," said campaign manager Richard Aurelio of the mayor, who sometimes appeared too aristocratic to relate to the city's populace. "We never could have planned anything that effective."[10]

Even Lindsay's critics would have to admit he threw a good party.

The following Monday, the city honored the Mets with an official ticker-tape parade from Battery Park to Gracie Mansion, two months after the astronauts of *Apollo 11* had been so honored. Speaking at the annual Al Smith Dinner, Lindsay introduced himself as "John 'Mets' Lindsay. Now New York needs just one more miracle."[11]

On Election Day in November, he got his miracle, winning reelection without the endorsement of his own party. The mayor who'd been dared to try and get reelected during the infamous February blizzard pulled in 41% of the vote, with Procaccino getting 39% and Marchi, 22%[12] His comeback win was one for the political annals of big-city politics.

Yet it paled in comparison to the story of the '69 Mets, the most improbable champions of the century.

19. NIXON'S WAR

The Moratorium and Mobilization unite the antiwar movement, while the story of the My Lai massacre rocks the American conscience.

Nixon had entered the White House concerned that if he did not end the war quickly, it would cease to be Lyndon Johnson's war and become Nixon's war. It turned out to be a self-fulfilling prophecy. In his *Washington Post* article, "Breaking the President," columnist David Broder wrote that, "the men and the movement that broke Lyndon Johnson's authority in 1968 are out to break Richard M. Nixon in 1969. The likelihood is that they will succeed again, for breaking a President is, like most feats, easier to accomplish the second time around." William Safire concurred: "In October 1969, after a long-enough interval to make Vietnam Nixon's War, 'they' set their sights on Richard Nixon."[1]

The first big blow against Nixon came on October 15, the day of a nationwide demonstration calling for a moratorium on the war. The idea of a national day of protest was the brainchild of Jerome Grossman, a fifty-two-year-old envelope manufacturer from Massachusetts who had worked for antiwar candidate Eugene McCarthy. He discussed his idea for having a general labor strike with fellow McCarthy campaign worker and Harvard Divinity School student, twenty-six-year-old Sam Brown. Brown convinced Grossman that organizing a nationwide strike was too unrealistic and persuaded him that a day of nonviolent discussion and debate would be more feasible. The two formed a Vietnam Moratorium Committee late in the spring of 1969, but they held off on putting it into effect when Nixon's first announcement of troop withdrawals cooled the antiwar movement. They set a date for September, but then Brown put it off until mid-October so that college students, who comprised a large part of the peace movement, would be back and settled on campus, and also to let the Moratorium gain momentum from increasing discontent with the ineffectuality of Nixon's handling of the war.[2]

Senators Mike Mansfield and George McGovern led the peace movement in Congress. Democrats were not the only ones to attack Nixon's war policies. In late September, New York senator Charles Goodell, a Republican who had been appointed to fill the seat vacated by Robert Kennedy's assassination, introduced a foreign-service bill amendment that would suspend funds for the war on December 1, 1970. Nixon responded immediately with a political sleight of hand, arguing that such an amendment would give the impression that "the United States is going to be stuck in Vietnam till the end of 1970, that there's no hope of ending the war before then."[3]

Looking to steal the thunder of the antiwar movement, Nixon announced on September 16 that the United States would withdraw 60,000 more troops from Southeast Asia within the following three months. Three days later, he added that draft calls for November and December would be canceled.[4] But despite these announcements, he was losing the American people. In September, 52% of Americans polled now disapproved of Nixon's handling of the war, up from 26% in April.[5]

Against Nixon's will, M-day was a major success as a mass demonstration. Half a million people assembled outside the White House. In New York City, a quarter of a million people demonstrated. George McGovern, who in the week leading up to the Moratorium called for all American forces to be withdrawn from

Southeast Asia, spoke to the demonstrators in the nation's capital, then flew north, speaking before a crowd of 100,000 in Boston Commons, and then jetted on to an assembly in Bangor, Maine. "The president has described Vietnam as our finest hour," he told the demonstrators. "It is not. It is our worst hour."[6]

Not everyone who participated in the Moratorium supported an unconditional withdrawal from Southeast Asia. Many people were simply fatigued with the war and frustrated with the molasses-like movement toward its end. The Moratorium represented a movement away from the radical exclusivity of the Far Left toward a more inclusive dynamic. As one Columbia University student said before the M-day events, "It will be nice to go to a demonstration without having to swear allegiance to Chairman Mao."[7]

In a show of what he would describe as "cool contempt," Nixon put out the word that while protesters marched around the White House on October 15, he had been watching a football game on television.[8] (It was a Wednesday.) Vice president Spiro Agnew, playing the role of Nixon's hatchet man, called the Moratorium "absurd."[9]

In reality, the president was very concerned about the Moratorium demonstrations. Much like Nixon's military tactics of troop withdrawals concurrent with expansion of the war's scope, his reaction to public criticism of his handling of Vietnam seemed inherently conflicted. On the one hand, he sought to convey the message of a leader unaffected by the antiwar protest, even as he argued that the demonstrations "destroyed whatever small possibility may still have existed of ending the war in 1969."

If Nixon was committed to a strategy of scoring military victories in order to create a favorable situation at the Paris peace talks, historian Robert Mann writes that the president could only blame himself for "allowing his government's policy to be set in the streets." Nixon and his advisors had been planning for Operation Duck Hook, a massive bombing operation aimed at Hanoi, Haiphong, and other key industrial areas of North Vietnam, and which also called for the mining of harbors and rivers, the bombing of dikes, and even tactical nuclear strikes on the Ho Chi Minh Trail. But in the wake of the Moratorium, he canceled Duck Hook, and, in his own words, "began to think more in terms of stepping up Vietnamization while continuing the fighting at its present level rather than trying to increase it."[10] Nevertheless, he remained suspicious of the war protesters and viewed their attacks as personal. "Seeing himself in any case the target of a liberal conspiracy to destroy him," Mann wrote, "he could never bring himself to regard the upheaval caused by the Vietnam War as anything other than a continuation of the long-lived assault on his political existence."[11]

Nixon remained committed to the idea that the majority of the nation supported his handling of the war. On November 3, he reclaimed his earlier momentum with a nationally televised speech in which he appealed to the "silent majority": "I know it may not be fashionable to speak of patriotism or national destiny these days . . . Let historians not record that when America was the most powerful nation in the world we passed on the other side of the road and allowed the last hopes for peace and freedom of millions of people to be suffocated by the forces of totalitarianism. . . . And so tonight—to you, the great silent majority of my fellow Americans—I ask for your support."[12]

Nixon posited himself as a leader willing to make the tough decisions, committed to not taking the easy way out. He outlined the choices before him: "I can order an immediate, precipitate withdrawal of all Americans from Vietnam without regard to the effects of that action . . . Or we can persist in our search for a just peace, through a negotiated settlement, if possible, or through continued implementation of our plan for Vietnamization if necessary . . . I have chosen this second course. It is not the easy way. It is the right way."[13]

As William Safire remembers, Vice President Agnew had used the "silent majority" phrase several times in a speech back in May, saying "it is time for America's silent majority to stand up for its rights," but it "had never taken hold" in the popular culture.[14] Nixon's "silent majority" address of November 3, however, proved shrewdly effective in providing a rallying point for every American who still felt "My country, right or wrong," who still believed in the Domino Theory and feared the worldwide spread of Communism, or who simply felt that war protesters were drugged-out, long-haired freaks. Safire wrote, "If the job of a leader is to lead, Nixon did his job on November 3, 1969."[15]

But if the antiwar movement represented the minority, they continued to be a vocal minority. On November 15, an estimated 300,000 demonstrators, the largest political gathering in American history, marched along the ten blocks from the Capitol to the Washington Monument in a Mobilization Rally.[16] On the way, the marchers stopped in front of the White House and held up coffins while shouting out the names of American soldiers killed in Vietnam.

Folk singer Pete Seeger remembered the sea of humanity that gathered in the National Mall that day. A few days earlier, he had heard a young woman in Poughkeepsie singing "Give Peace a Chance," the song that John Lennon and Yoko Ono had recorded along with visiting celebrities and media members during their "Bed-In" in Toronto that spring. He led the Mobilization gathering in a group rendition of the song. "After about five minutes, the whole hundreds of thousands were singing, and it was like a gigantic ballet." In between one verse, he shouted to the White House, "Are you listening, Nixon?"[17]

Senator McGovern, an emerging leader in the peace movement, told the crowd:

> We love America enough to call her to a high standard. We love America enough to call her away from the folly of war to the blessings of peace. . . . We are here as American patriots, young and old, to build a country, to build a world, that seeks the ways of peace—that teaches war no more. We meet today to reaffirm those ageless values that gave us

birth—'life, liberty and the pursuit of happiness.' We meet to declare peace—to put an end to war, not in some vanishing future, but to end it *now*.[18]

❁ ❁ ❁

Reports of the "Incident in Song Chang Valley" had been circulating in newspapers throughout the world, courtesy of AP photographer Horst Faas and reporter Peter Arnett. On August 12, North Vietnamese forces attacked a U. S. post in a dense jungle region in the Song Chang river valley about thirty miles south of Danang. They shot down a helicopter, killing eight people, including Lieutenant Colonel Eli Howard and AP photographer Oliver Noonan. Alpha Company from the 196th Light Infantry Brigade's 3rd Battalion, which had been under Howard's command, set out to the crash site. After being pinned down by enemy fire for five days in stagnant, 100-degree air, the company's "mud-caked survivors were exhausted, thirsty, hungry—and scared."

Howard's replacement as battalion commander, Lt. Col. Robert Bacon, radioed Alpha Company to recover the bodies of the men who had died at the foot of Nui Lon hill. Lt. Eugene Shurtz Jr., a twenty-six-year-old ROTC graduate who had been in command for just three weeks, radioed back, saying, "I am sorry, sir, but my men refused to go . . . We cannot move out."

"Repeat that, please," Bacon responded. "Have you told them what it means to disobey orders under fire?"

"I think they understand, but some of them [have] simply had enough—they are broken. These are boys here who have only 90 days left in Viet Nam. They want to go home in one piece. The situation is psychic [sic] here."

When Shurtz had ordered his men to advance, they refused and demanded to be flown by helicopter to speak to the Inspector

General. "Everybody was afraid," one of the GIs later explained. "We felt we should wait for more support." When Bacon asked how many men would not go, Shurtz told him, "they all stick together."

The army denied that the incident was an act of mutiny, or even that it was unusual. Lt. Col. Bacon shrugged it off, saying, "I've seen similar things happen before," and no action was taken against any of the soldiers, although Shurtz was transferred to a desk job at battalion headquarters and replaced with a battle-experienced captain.

But the story had people back home questioning the nation's battle commanders. A published letter home from one soldier in another company in the Song Chang area expressed concern with his inexperienced officer: "If I think my life will be in danger by doing some of his crazy things, I'll just tell him I'm not going anywhere."[19]

❊ ❊ ❊

While the battles of Hamburger Hill and Song Chang struck a sympathetic chord for the trials of the American servicemen in Southeast Asia, the breaking of yet another story from Vietnam in November did immeasurable harm to how the mission—and the morality—of American soldiers were perceived by the public back home.

In late October, journalist Seymour Hersh got a phone tip about the Calley trials in Fort Benning. "The Army's trying to court-martial some guy in secret at Fort Benning for killing seventy-five [sic] Vietnamese civilians," he was told. In November, Hersh flew to Fort Benning and happened to find Calley in the officers' quarters. He interviewed Calley, who, Hersh remembers, "told me . . . a little bit about the operation; he also told me how many people he had been accused of killing." Hersh later recalled feeling that Calley "was as much a victim as those infants he and his men murdered at My Lai 4."[20]

Hersh went back home to Washington and wrote an article that began: "Lieutenant William L. Calley, Jr., twenty-six, is a mild-mannered, boyish-looking Vietnam combat veteran with the nickname of 'Rusty.' The Army says he deliberately murdered at least 109 Vietnamese civilians during a search-and-destroy mission in March, 1968, in a Viet Cong stronghold known as 'Pinkville.'"

❀ ❀ ❀

In early 1969, a Popsicle maker in Phoenix named Ron Ridenhour began composing a letter, thirty copies of which would be sent to the White House and members of Congress. "It was late in April, 1968," he began, "that I first heard of 'Pinkville' and what happened there . . ."

Twelve months earlier, Ridenhour had been a helicopter gunner serving in Vietnam. In March 1968, he flew over a hamlet that had been designated My Lai 4, codename: Pinkville, in the village of Song My. As he looked down from the cockpit of the chopper, he could see no signs of life—no men, no women, no children, nothing. As he kept looking, he spotted something in a nearby rice paddy. It was the corpse of a woman. The body had been placed in a spread-eagle position. A patch of the U. S. Army's 11th Brigade had been placed between her legs, "as if it were some type of display," he would remember, "some badge of honor."[21]

Ridenhour could not make sense of what he'd seen. But soon afterward, working now for a reconnaissance unit in Duc Pho, he heard stories from five people who had been in My Lai 4 on March 16, 1968. They told him of the nightmarish events that had transpired that day.

In the winter of 1968, North Vietnamese and insurgent Vietcong forces launched a combined offensive against American and South Vietnamese during the Tet holiday. During the *CBS Evening News* coverage of the campaign that would change the tide of the Vietnam

War, millions of Americans heard correspondent Walter Cronkite unscripted remark: "What the hell is going on? I thought we were winning this war."[22]

By March 1968, U. S. intelligence determined that the Vietcong's 48th battalion, a key participant in the Tet attacks, had taken refuge in the village of Song My. Charlie Company of the 1st Battalion, 20th Infantry Regiment, 11th Brigade was sent to purge the insurgents from the area. The soldiers in Charlie Company were physically and mentally fatigued, strangers in a strange land where the difference between insurgents and civilians was sometimes impossible to decipher—where death could come just as easily from a female villager concealing a grenade as it could from a uniformed enemy soldier with an assault rifle. One saying among GIs held that "Anything that's dead and isn't white is VC."[23] Another grim plan circulating among marines proposed: Put all the "loyal" Vietnamese on a raft at sea; kill everybody else and turn the nation into a parking lot; then sink the raft.[24]

Testimonies would later conflict each other as to the orders the men of Charlie Company were given. Some said their mission was to find and neutralize Vietcong soldiers. Others said that their orders were to destroy the hamlet and everyone they encountered. Regardless, on the morning of March 16, Charlie Company moved into the village, encountering no resistance from Vietcong forces. Although the exact reason for the events that transpired would become a never-ending controversy, what is known is that the hamlet became a shameless scene of mass carnage. By the end of the day, a platoon under the command of Lt. William Calley killed more than 500 villagers—men, women, and children. Bodies of the Vietnamese were dumped into mass graves. Some of the women had been raped by U. S. soldiers before they were killed.

Ridenhour drove to headquarters in Chu Lai and confirmed that Charlie Company had attacked My Lai 4 on that day. He started to ask around for more information. Some personnel told him to give up his line of inquiry, but others added to the horrible stories he'd heard.

In March 1969, these stories were still burning within him. He talked to his former writing teacher from high school, Arthur Orman. Ridenhour wanted to be a writer, and he discussed with Orman the possibility of his writing a magazine article about the My Lai incident. But Orman convinced Ridenhour to keep his mission pure. "I thought it would cheapen what he was doing if he tried to sell the story," Orman said later.[25] Ridenhour agreed.

So he dictated a letter to Orman's secretary recounting the things he had seen and heard. Orman had worked for the Army Adjutant General's Corps, where he'd learned at least two things: (1) The best way to beat bureaucracy is through repeated effort; and (2) The Army responds to Congress. So they made thirty copies of the letter and sent them all to Washington: nine to the president, the others to members of the House and Senate. Two representatives, Morris Udall from Arizona and L. Mendell Rivers from South Carolina, had staff members who were impressed enough to pass the letters on to their bosses. At the beginning of April, Udall wrote to Secretary of Defense Melvin Laird. Soon afterward, Rivers forwarded his letter to the Armed Services Committee. The investigation that would ultimately uncover the My Lai 4 tragedy was under way.

The army began to interrogate members of Charlie Company, and on September 5, Lt. Calley was charged with killing or causing other soldiers to kill 109 civilians. Twenty-five other soldiers were charged with related crimes. The commanding officer, Captain Ernest Medina, was not charged.[26]

That same day, the public information office at Fort Benning announced that Calley had been charged with murdering civilians. The Associated Press picked up the story, which was published in the *New York Times* on September 8, albeit buried on page thirty-eight. The *Miami Herald* ran a piece about Calley soon thereafter, as did the *Columbus Enquirer*. But the full magnitude of the story had yet to break, and Ridenhour feared that the incident would go away and Calley would be sent up as a scapegoat.

Hersh tried to sell the story to both *Life* and *Look* magazines, but they and other newspapers resisted. "By that time I had been Eugene McCarthy's press secretary and speechwriter in 1968, and in September 1969 I had the lead article in the *New York Times Magazine*," he commented in his book. "I had worked for the AP. As press secretary for a guy running for president, I knew every reporter, and I was taken seriously. I still couldn't get a newspaper to run a story."[27]

He finally found a taker in the Dispatch News Service. The small Washington news agency wired the story to fifty newspapers across the nation on November 12, and thirty chose to run it the next day. Three days later, a *New York Times* correspondent stationed in Saigon, Henry Kamm, went with representatives from *Newsweek* magazine to interview My Lai survivors at the hamlet to which they had been relocated. Kamm's piece said that 567 villagers had been killed in the massacre, though the *Washington Post* suggested that the number had been exaggerated.

Then, on November 18, a *Cleveland Plain Dealer* reporter and future Hollywood screenwriter named Joseph Eszterhas received a phone call from a former schoolmate, Ron Haeberle, an ex-GI who had taken pictures documenting the brutality at My Lai 4. On November 20, the paper published an interview with Haeberle, along with several photographs, including some of women and children that had been slaughtered in the attack. In one of the most disturbing images, the dead bodies of women and babies are shown strewn in a ditch, their corpses scattered in grotesquely random angles.

Haeberle's photos provided visual proof for those Americans who had chosen to believe that reports of the atrocities had either been exaggerated or fabricated. They also opened the door for the television interview of Paul Meadlo, a member of Charlie Company whom Hersh tracked down in Indiana. With the help of David Obst of the Dispatch News Service, Hersh landed Meadlo on the *CBS Evening News*, on November 24, when he was interviewed by Mike Wallace. As the *Washington Post* described, many viewers "sat in sheltered living rooms, perhaps starting in on a dinner martini,"[28] and listened to Meadlo recount his killing villagers that day:

Wallace: How many people did you round up?

Meadlo: Well, there was about 40–45 people that we gathered in the center of the village. And we placed them in there, and it was like a little island, right there in the center of the village, I'd say. And—

Wallace: What kind of people—men, women, children?

Meadlo: Men, women, children.

Wallace: Babies?

Meadlo: Babies. And we all huddled them up. We made them squat down, and Lieutenant Calley came over and said, "You know what to do with them, don't you?" I said, "Yes." So I took it for granted that he just wanted us to watch them. And he left, and came back about ten or fifteen minutes later, and said, "How come you ain't killed them yet?" And I told him that, "I didn't think you wanted us to kill them, that you just wanted us to guard them." He said, "No, I want them dead. So—"

Wallace: He [Lt. Calley] told this to all of you, or to you particularly?

Meadlo: Well, I was facing him. So, but the other three, four guys heard it and so he stepped back about ten, fifteen feet, and he started shooting them. And he told me to start shooting. So I started shooting, I poured about four clips into the group.

Wallace: You fired four clips from your. . .

Meadlo: M-16.

Wallace: And that's about—how many clips—I mean how many—

Meadlo: I carried seventeen rounds to each clip.

Wallace: And you killed how many? At that time?

Meadlo: Well, I fired them automatic, so you can't—You just spray the area on them and so you can't know how many you killed 'cause they were going fast. So I might have killed ten or fifteen of them.

Wallace: Men, women, and children?

Meadlo: Men, women, and children.

Wallace: And babies?

Meadlo: And babies. . . .

Wallace: Now, you're rounding up more?

Meadlo: We're rounding up more, and we had about seven or eight people. And we was going to throw them in the hootch, and well, we put them in the hootch and then we dropped a hand grenade down there with them. And somebody holed up in the ravine, and told us to bring them over to the ravine. . . . they had about seventy, seventy-five people all gathered up. So we threw ours in with them and Lieutenant

Calley told me, he said, "Soldier, we got another job to do." And so he walked over to the people, and he started pushing them off and started shooting. . . . And so we started pushing them off, and we started shooting them, so all together we just pushed them all off, and just started using automatics on them. . . .

Meadlo, who had lost a foot to a landmine in Vietnam, candidly described the feeling of catharsis that he felt during the time of the massacre. "I was getting . . . *my buddies getting killed or wounded or—we weren't getting no satisfaction from it, so what it really was, it was just mostly revenge.*"[29]

The *Washington Post* devoted three pages to the Meadlo interview in its Sunday edition. Pretty soon, it was *the* story of the war. Not only had American atrocities been uncovered for the national media, but stories emerged to indicate that although My Lai 4 might have been the most horrific episode of the war, it was not an isolated incident. Speaking later at a conference on My Lai, Hersh remembered:

> Correspondents who had been in Vietnam in 1965 and 1966 went back to their files. One of these guys was an AP reporter who was with the first group of Marines to go ashore in 1965. Johnson didn't tell anybody they were doing offensive operations. He just said that they were going ashore in defensive positions. This correspondent was attached to this first unit, and he described the murder of a bunch of civilians. On the second day of the war, there were a bunch of Vietnamese civilians in a cave, and he describes somebody shooting in the cave and throwing in a hand grenade—in a Sunday piece! He had been there and seen this four years earlier![30]

In the end, Calley was delivered up as a scapegoat. Although reports seem to agree that more than 500 unresisting Vietnamese were killed in the My Lai incident, Calley was the only one convicted of murder; he served three and a half years under house arrest at Fort Benning. "It knocked me out that Calley was the one that they came down on," Hersh told a conference audience later.[31] Medina was acquitted of any wrongdoing in the ensuing Army investigation.

For many outraged Americans, the incident had uncomfortable similarities to the Nuremberg war crime trials following World War II, only this time, it was an American lieutenant—and by extension, the rest of Charlie Company—who sought to defend their actions by saying they were "following orders." And it made Americans realize, perhaps for the first time in the history of the country, that it did not have a monopoly on morality.

❊ ❊ ❊

On December 15, Nixon announced an additional 50,000 soldiers would return home in the next four months. In that first year, Nixon announced withdrawals totaling more than 100,000 troops, leading commentator Walter Lippman to remark, "This must be just about the first time in the history of warfare that a nation has thought it could prevail by withdrawing combat troops and reducing its military presence."[32] Even with those troop withdrawals, 434,000 U. S. troops would remain in Vietnam.[33]

On December 2, the House overwhelmingly approved a resolution commending Nixon's efforts to achieve "peace with justice" in Vietnam. It seemed that he had weathered the storm during his first year in the White House. As the year came to an end, the "Silent Majority was with him despite the press," Safire reflected.[34] Nixon, as Mann wrote, "concluded that now was the time to hold steady and resist the urge to tailor his policy to suit his congressional detractors and the louder critics in the increasingly radical antiwar movement."[35]

20. DAYS OF RAGE

The streets of Chicago are once again the scene of violence as the Weathermen take to the streets, and an early-morning police raid results in the death of Black Panther chairman Fred Hampton.

With the violence of the Democratic National Convention still fresh in the minds of the country and the militant SDS Weathermen planning further disruptions in the Windy City to coincide with the trial of the "Chicago 8," Haskell Wexler's *Medium Cool* used the 1968 Democratic Convention as the real-life backdrop for a fictional narrative that examined the role of the media in late-sixties America.

Wexler's narrative follows a hard-edged television cameraman named John Cassellis (Robert Forster). As the film opens, Cassellis and Gus, his soundman (Peter Bonerz) are filming the wreckage of an auto accident, with the injured and probably dying victims still inside. In a scene that frames the rest of the movie within the theme of journalistic distance, only after getting adequate footage do they call an ambulance. Reviewing the film, Vincent Canby noted how television "certifies the reality of events and, at the same time, removes them by equating their meaning to that of the commercials—the cheerful haiku—that frame them."[1]

An Oscar-winning cinematographer making his directorial debut with *Medium Cool*, Wexler set the film in Chicago in the spring and summer of 1968 and created a form of *cinéma vérité* reminiscent of both Italian neorealism and French New Wave filmmaking by working in footage that he himself shot of the DNC inside the International Amphitheater, of the Illinois National Guard during training drills that prepared them for dealing with demonstrators, and even the actual riots outside the convention. These Chicago street scenes are worked into the action of the story: When Cassellis's love interest, a displaced West Virginia widow named Eileen (Verna Bloom), can't find her son, she walks through Lincoln Park in her bright yellow shirtwaist dress looking for Cassellis so that he can help. (In one scene, we can hear a crew member off screen shout, "Look out, Haskell, it's real!" as the rioters are teargassed.[2]) Wexler also enlisted the services of real-life newsmen to play Cassellis's colleagues, as well as that of thirteen-year-old Harold Blankenship, a real-life slum child from the Appalachian Country, who plays Bloom's son.

Before his redemptive relationship with Eileen, Cassellis is a womanizer who seems to care for little besides his work. "Jesus, I love to shoot film," he says while watching a documentary of Martin Luther King. Even this professional devotion seems to be one of craft rather than community. He has an awakening when he and Gus go into the ghetto to shoot footage of a crime scene. They find themselves confronted by the militant blacks in the apartment building, who accuse the journalists of coming to the ghetto only to "take" what they need (footage) without trying to engage the people.

Intrigued, Cassellis interviews one of the men to document the realities of ghetto life, thus legitimizing the black experience within the dominant medium-is-the-message society. But he quits his job when he finds out that his network has been providing footage of public demonstrations to the FBI, a violation of the work that is sacred to him. He takes to the chaotic streets of Chicago as a freelancer to film the riots, and Eileen eventually finds him there, with Gus's help. As her son returns home, unbeknownst to them, they ride off to random death in a car accident. Recalling the film's opening scene, a film crew drives by and dispassionately documents their death for the evening news. Canby called it "a film of tremendous visual impact, a kind of cinematic 'Guernica,' a picture of America in the process of exploding into fragmented bits of hostility, suspicion, fear and violence."[3]

❈ ❈ ❈

The trial of the Chicago 8 began on September 24 with Judge Julius Hoffman presiding. The defendants were an odd mix: Yippie leader Abbie Hoffman; Black Panther Party cofounder Bobby Seale; former SDS president Tom Hayden; left-wing activist Jerry Rubin; SDS officer Rennie Davis; 54-year-old pacifist David Dellinger; John Froines, a chemist with a PhD from Yale; and Northwestern University assistant Lee Weiner. All stood accused of violating Title 18 of the 1968 Civil Rights Act, which made crossing state lines with the intent to incite a riot a federal offense—a provision added by Congress as a deterrent to "outside agitators," as they were called in those days.

The pool of 300 potential jurors was comprised almost entirely of white, middle-aged, middle-class members. Journalist J. Anthony Lukas would remark that they reminded him of "the Rolling Meadows Bowling League lost on their way to the lanes." Defense attorneys William Kunstler and Leonard Weinglass, both from the Center for Constitutional Rights, sought to screen jurors for cultural biases with a list of fifty-four proposed questions that they submitted to the Judge Hoffman. These included such questions as "Would you let your son or daughter marry a Yippie?"; "Do you know who Janis Joplin and Jimi Hendrix are?"; "If your children are female, do they wear brassieres all the time?" But the seventy-four-year-old Hoffman disallowed all but one fairly obvious question: "Are you—or do you have any close friends or relatives who are—employed by any law enforcement agencies?" The voir dire lasted three hours and yielded a jury of ten women (eight white, two black) and two men (both white).[4]

With the trial under way, the Weathermen were distributing militant posters in hopes of inspiring urban activists throughout the nation to join forces and make this political pilgrimage to Chicago for what they were now calling the "Days of Rage," set to run from October 8-11. The words and images captured how extreme the New Left radicalism had become by the end of the sixties: the slogan BRING THE WAR HOME; the song title "Light My Fire," transformed into a literal call for conflagration; the dark pun "Piece Now" accompanied by pictures of guns and bombs.

An advance contingent of Weathermen arrived in the Windy City on October 6. They came ready to battle riot squads, equipped with motorcycle helmets, boots, clubs, and iron bars. Bill Ayres and a group of others touched off the week's chaos by blowing up a statue in Haymarket Square. Ayers later characterized the Days of Rage as "an attempt to break from the norms of a kind of acceptable theater, of 'Here are the antiwar people—containable, marginal, predictable—and here's the little path where they're gonna march down, and here's where they can make their little statement.' We wanted to say, 'No, what we're gonna do is whatever we have to do to stop the violence in Vietnam.'"

But if the Weathermen were expecting the DNC Part II, or perhaps the Woodstock of revolutionary politics, it turned out to be neither. Mark Rudd remembers, "We were told that hundreds of thousands of people were coming," but instead, just a few hundred showed. "And I thought, 'We are really in trouble. How are we gonna get out of this?'" Ayers said, "I remember kind of a secret feeling that somebody would come along and rescue us from what we were about to do."[5]

On the night of October 8, a few hundred demonstrators congregated in Lincoln Park, ostensibly for a rock festival dubbed "Wargasm." But when no musicians showed up, the crowd built a small bonfire and held a three-hour rally. Then a signal was given, and they headed down Clark Street in a rampage with sticks, bats, clubs, chains, iron bars, and rocks, smashing storefront and residential windows and vandalizing cars in the affluent Gold Coast neighborhood in Chicago's North Side. There, the rioters ran smack dab into the police squads that were waiting for them in a barricade at the intersection of State and Division, where a terrible fight ensued. Dozens of people were injured, and one out of every ten Weathermen members was arrested.[6]

Speaking to the extreme measures of the Weathermen, Naomi Jaffe would recall, "Violence can mean a lot of different things. We felt that doing nothing in a period of repressive violence is itself a form of violence. That's really the part that I think is the hardest for people to understand—that if you sit in your house, and live your white life, and go to your white job and allow the country that you live in to murder people and to commit genocide and you sit there and you don't do anything about it, that's violence."[7]

The Weathermen who got away slept in a local United Methodist church at the invitation of its ministers. The following day, one demonstrator announced, "Last night was a beginning for us. The ruling class and their Gold Coast decadence will walk the streets a little less secure tonight. If they hadn't dug it before, they better dig it now: They are the enemy."[8] In the black-and-white rhetoric of radicalism, you were either part of the solution, or part of the problem.

Midday Saturday in Haymarket Square, one Weathermen leader declared, "We are going to take the lessons we have learned here in Chicago home with us as we go back. We are going to bring the war home!"[9] But within the bravado of these words was the call for a retreat. They had not started the second American Revolution that grim week in Chicago. Meanwhile, the National Guard was called in to keep protestors outside the federal courthouse, and the trial of the Chicago Eight proceeded.

The judicial proceedings were a study in cultural extremes. While district attorney Thomas Foran's team were all business suits and index cards, the defendants were a picture of blue jeans and beads and headbands. They often sat with their feet up on chairs or the table, snacked on jelly beans, made faces, cracked jokes, read newspapers, and sometimes slept. While Hayden and some of the others favored a rigorous deconstruction of the State's case, Rubin and Hoffman played to the press in mocking the seriousness of the trial, appearing in court dressed in judicial robes, blowing kisses to the jury, and even displaying the flag of the National Liberation Front of South Vietnam on the defense table. Hoffman became a rock star of sorts among the counterculture for his role in the trial. When court was in recess, he spoke to supporters at mass rallies, called into Bob Fass's radio show on WBAI FM in New York to give nightly updates on the court proceedings, and performed a comic monologue at Chicago's Second City improvisational theatre.

A month into the proceedings, the mood of the trial went from farcical to grotesque. Seale demanded that he be allowed to represent himself or else or have a continuation of trial until his attorney of choice, Charles Garry, had recovered from gall bladder surgery. Judge Hoffman denied Seale on both requests. The defendant maintained his protests of the proceedings and attempted to question witnesses as his own representation.

Hoffman grew impatient with Seale's disruptions. "I am warning you that the court has the right to gag you. I don't want to do that. Under the law you may be gagged and chained to your chair."[10]

When the chief prosecutor objected to Seale's conduct, Seale began to shout epithets at him. Marshals converged on Seale and brought him to the floor as they struggled to control him. Hoffman grew so incensed with Seale that he ordered Seale bound and gagged. Court officers fastened his wrists and ankles to a wooden chair and sealed his mouth with adhesive tape. Even this did not silence Seale. He managed to wriggle one hand free and ripped the tape from his mouth. "You Fascist dog! You Fascist pig!" he yelled at the judge.[11]

Peter Doggett writes, "What followed was a tableau from the dark ages. Seale was locked onto a metal chair, with handcuffs, leg irons and choking gag forced around his head and into his mouth." As Seale uttered garbled words into his gag and struggled for breath, Abbie Hoffman cried out, "This isn't a court, this is a neon oven."[12]

On November 5, the judge severed Seale's case from the rest of the group's, charged him with sixteen counts of contempt, totaling four years in prison sentences, and had him carted off to jail.[13]

❊ ❊ ❊

Throughout the year, militant black organizations had clashed with the police in cities across the nation. On March 30, Detroit police engaged in a gun battle with the New Republic of Africa group. On April 2, New York City police arrested twenty-one Black Panthers on charges of conspiring to blow up several targets over Easter weekend, including police stations, railroads, department stores, and even the Bronx Botanical Garden. Over the next three months, police raided Black Panther Party (BPP) offices in Los Angeles, Des Moines, New Haven, Detroit, Chicago, Denver, San Diego, and Indianapolis. It seemed as if the government had declared war on the Panthers.

And, in fact, they had. Covertly, the FBI had been monitoring the BPP through a nationwide counterintelligence program (COINTELPRO), including massive surveillance campaigns that used wiretaps, bugging, mail tampering, live tailing, and burglaries. The FBI planned to make their campaign even more aggressive, in an attempt to bring down the group through violence within the ranks of fellow militant black activists.

The COINTELPRO activity against the Panthers involved the use of government informants paid to infiltrate the Party. It would later come out that the FBI had six informants in the BPP New York office, none of the six knowing about the other.[14] COINTELPRO also initiated a disinformation campaign consisting of fabricating correspondence and other documents, including derisive cartoons, designed to foster splits between BPP officials, as well as within the larger community of black activists. The technique had been successful in causing a rift between leaders Huey Newton and Eldridge Cleaver, and it also fanned the flames of tension between the BPP and the rival Black Nationalist group, the US Organization, which had been formed by Ron Karenga, a Cal State-Long Beach professor and the founder of the Kwanza holiday. The Bureau distributed a round of fraudulent cartoons on the streets designed to look like they had been done by the BPP and US as attacks upon each other.

On January 17, 1969, US gunmen murdered Los Angeles Panther leaders John Huggins and Alprentice "Bunchy" Carter on the UCLA campus. The gunmen would later claim to be on the FBI payroll.[15] Following the incident, the San Diego field office sent a memo to headquarters in February in which it claimed some credit for inspiring the gun battle and recommended the distribution of cartoons to "indicate to the BPP that the US organization feels they are ineffectual, inadequate, and riddled with graft and corruption." Later that summer, US members wounded two Panthers in an ambush in San Diego and then killed another member, Sylvester Bell, the following day. Afterward, the San Diego office circulated a memo on the "efforts being made to determine how this situation can be capitalized upon for the benefit of the Counterintelligence Program."[16]

❉ ❉ ❉

On May 21, fisherman John Mroczka drove his Triumph motorcycle out to his favorite trout spot, beneath a small bridge that overlooked the Coginchaug River in Middlefield, Connecticut. After parking his motorcycle, he spotted what appeared to be a mannequin partially submerged in the river. But as he got closer, he realized it was the corpse of an African-American male. His hands were bound with clothesline, and a makeshift noose made out of a clothes hanger was wrapped around his neck.

The body was of nineteen-year-old Alex Rackley, a member of the New York chapter of the Black Panther Party. For three days leading up to his murder, Rackley had been held prisoner in the home of Warren Kimbro at the Ethan Gardens in New Haven, which also served as the headquarters for the local Panthers. George Sams and Landon Williams had flown in to "whip East Coast chapters into shape." According to coauthors of *Murder in the Model City*, Paul Bass and Douglas Rae, Sams and Williams "evoked the paranoia that dogged the Panthers throughout their history: anyone, at any moment, could find himself accused of collaboration with the FBI or local police. Such collaboration was a capital offense."[17] Sams was especially given to shows of paranoia, constantly waving a pistol to underscore his commands.

The local Panthers were preparing for the speech that Bobby Seale was to make at Yale on May 21. Rackley volunteered to help Kimbro roll up posters for the event. But the Panthers became convinced that Rackley was an FBI informant, and on May 17, Rackley was told to leave the premises—he was being kicked out of the Party. He left but then returned, at which point the Panthers began to beat and torture him. He was tied to a chair and had boiling water poured on him until he confessed his guilt. He was then tied to a bed for three days as his wounds festered and he lay in his own waste.

Why had the Panthers become convinced that Rackley was an informant? Bass and Rae hypothesize that they had confused his identity with that of Alex McKiever, the former president of the Afro-American History Club at Benjamin Franklin High School in New York, who had recently gone underground to flee an indictment in a bombing conspiracy charge. McKiever's disappearance convinced Party members that he was a police informant.

There was indeed an informant among the ranks of the New Haven Panthers, but it hadn't been Rackley—it was Kelly Moye, a thirtyish delivery man for a local package store who liked to show up for Party meetings. Nick Pastore, who headed up the intelligence division for the New Haven police, had paid Moye to spy on the Panthers. On the evening of May 20, it was Moye's car that the Panthers commandeered to transport Rackley north to Middlefield. They wrapped a Nehru jacket around Rackley to conceal him, put him in the backseat of the car, and drove off.

The New Haven Police Department would later claim they had information that the Panthers had kidnapped a member of the New York chapter and were holding him in Kimbro's Ethan Gardens apartment. "We did not have enough information to make arrests, but we had the apartment under surveillance," Jim Ahern wrote in *Police in Trouble*. Pastore would say his men knew an interrogation was taking place, but they didn't know it involved torture.[18] The officers would also claim that they tried tailing Moye's car but lost it somewhere along the way.

Kimbro had them drive north to a deserted stretch on Route 157 in Middlefield. Rackley was ordered out of the car, and the group walked into the marsh near the bridge. Then, Kimbro would testify, Sams told him, "Ice him. Orders from National." Kimbro shot Rackley in the back of the head. Rackley fell to the mucky ground. Sams took the gun and handed it to Lonnie McLucas, who fired a bullet into Rackley's chest. Then they drove off, leaving him for dead. Later, in the ensuing court trial, expert medical testimony suggested that Rackley may have held on for up to four hours before dying in the marsh that night.[19]

The night after his body was found, shortly after midnight, police raided Kimbro's apartment. Sergeant Vincent DeRosa knocked down the door and found women sleeping on the living room floor, some holding babies. Kimbro lay on the floor next to a rifle. Detective Billy White grabbed the rifle and then recognized Kimbro;

they had worked together in a city program to fight poverty, and Kimbro had once coached White's younger brother in football. A black policeman charged up the stairs and pointed his gun at Kimbro's wife, who had emerged partially dressed from the shower. The police officer turned his head away, ashamed. Not only was the woman half naked, but he recognized her; she was his son's godmother.[20]

Sams and Williams had fled the city by then, and in the ensuing weeks, the FBI would use the Rackley murder as justification for a nationwide campaign against the Panthers. Raids on Panther headquarters followed in Chicago, Detroit, Indianapolis, San Diego, Philadelphia, and Los Angeles. Bass and Rae recount that "whenever the pretext involved a trip about George Sams's whereabouts, Sams managed to escape just before the G-men busted down the door, upturned the furniture, and made off with weapons or documents."[21] In the first week of June, the FBI tracked down two Panther suspects, Landon Williams and Rory Hithe, in Denver, and then Lonnie McLucas was nabbed in Salt Lake City. On June 15, J. Edgar Hoover would release a report in which he declared, "the Black Panther Party, without question, represents the greatest threat to the internal security of the country."[22]

Police finally caught George Sams in Toronto in August. In an attempt to cut a deal, Sams testified that Bobby Seale had ordered Rackley's murder. The feds now had license to go after the nation's top Panthers. "We had no solid evidence to link him to Rackley's death or torture," Chief Ahern wrote later. "Despite my personal feelings about the case, it was a fact that there was no sufficient hard evidence against Seale, and the New Haven Police Department never requested an indictment against him."[23]

That month, Bobby Seale was arrested and charged with Alex Rackley's murder. The following day he was released on bail but then immediately rearrested and secretly moved by police so that he could stand trial with the Chicago 8.

❀ ❀ ❀

Federal agents and local police departments continued their nation-wide siege on Panther headquarters well into the fall. On September 8, police raided the Panther Breakfast Program in Watts, California, while police in San Francisco raided the BPP headquarters there after attempting to arrest two Panthers for illegal use of sound-truck equipment. The FBI and police raided the BPP office in Philadelphia on September 23. Police raided the Chicago and Los Angeles offices in October and the San Diego offices in November.

The Chicago headquarters drew the most interest from the FBI, as this was where a young, charismatic Panther was emerging within Party ranks. Twenty-one-year-old Fred Hampton, raised in the Chicago suburb of Maywood, had become a leading voice in the NAACP while studying pre-law at Triton Junior College. In 1968, he had become enamored with the principles of black self-determinism and the Maoist politics of the Black Panthers, and he had moved to downtown Chicago where he became deputy chairman of the Party's Illinois chapter. Hampton was a natural organizer with a gift for persuasive public speaking. In 1969 he had forged a truce between rival Southside gangs Blackstone Rangers and the Black Disciples. He also was on the verge of striking an alliance between the Panthers and the Blackstone Rangers, which boasted several thousand members. As Ward Churchill and Jim Vander Wall document in their book, *Agents of Repression*, if Hampton had been successful in bringing the Rangers into the Party, the merger would have doubled the Party's *national* membership.[24] At the same time, the Chicago office was also attempting to form an alliance between the Panthers, the SDS, a white, working-class group called the Young Patriots, and a Puerto Rican group known as the Young Lords. (The Young Lords were part of a growing "Brown Power" movement throughout the nation, including the Brown Berets and Mission Rebels in San Francisco, Los Lobos in San Jose, and the Mexican American Youth Organization in southern Texas.) Hampton no doubt struck fear into the hearts of the FBI when he declared, "Now we are all one army."[25]

COINTELPRO operations against Hampton and the Chicago BPP headquarters combined the use of an inside informant along with its successful disinformation campaign. Special Agent Roy Mitchell, an assignee to the Racial Matters Squad in the FBI's Chicago Field Office, recruited a black man named William O'Neal, who had been arrested for car theft and impersonating a federal officer, to act as an FBI informant in exchange for the dropping of his charges and a monthly stipend. O'Neal had been accepted by both Hampton and minister of defense Bobby Rush to the point that he became director of Chapter Security and Hampton's own bodyguard. According to Mitchell, by February 1969, O'Neal was functioning as the "number three man" in the Chicago BPP office.

"We tried to develop negative information to discredit him, just like we did everybody else," O'Neal later said. "We, me and the FBI, tried to come up with signs of him doing drugs or something. And we never could; he was clean, he was dedicated. I've had private conversations with him. We got along pretty well."[26]

Hoover approved an anonymous letter mailed to Jeff Fort, the head of the Rangers, which warned him, "The brothers that run the Panthers blame you for blocking their thing and there's supposed to be a hit out on you."[27] In March, a letter to Hampton warned him, "A Stone friend tells me [name deleted] wants the Panthers and is looking for somebody to get you out of the way. Brother Jeff [Fort] is supposed to be interested . . ."

The relationship between the Panthers and the Rangers cooled. In March, the FBI office worked with O'Neal to "create a rift" between the Panthers and the SDS, whose office was also on West Madison. One method for achieving this was the distribution of a fraudulent cartoon under the BPP name expressing anti-white racist sentiments. In April, the COINTELPRO was expanded to impede the BPP's efforts at forming a "rainbow coalition" in Chicago, and then in May and June, special agent Marlin Johnson was instructed to destroy the Panther's Free Breakfast for Children Program in Chicago. On July 16, the police and Party members engaged in gunfire; Panther member Larry Robeson was mortally wounded and six other Panthers were arrested. The police raided the headquarters on July 31, destroyed food and supplies for the Breakfast Program, broke typewriters, set fires, and arrested several more Panthers. They would return for another raid on October 31.

Back in May, Hampton had been prosecuted by State's Attorney Edward V. Hanrahan for stealing $71 worth of ice cream in Maywood in 1967—for which he received a sentence of two to five years in Menard prison. But he obtained an appeal bond and was released in August. The FBI followed his actions and determined that his release from prison "had led to a resurgent Chicago BPP chapter becoming one of the strongest in the country, with one of the most successful Serve the People programs."[28] In early November, Hampton spoke before the UCLA Law Students Association and then met with national leaders of the BPP, who informed him that he was to be appointed to the Party's Central Committee.

After O'Neal updated Mitchell, the two met downtown on November 19, at which time O'Neal drew a detailed floor plan of Hampton's apartment, right down to the placement of furniture, the windows to Hampton's bedroom, and the bed where he slept with his pregnant fiancée, Deborah Johnson. "Mitchell became more specific during that time," O'Neal said. "He wanted to know the locations of weapons caches. He wanted to know if we had explosives. He needed to know who was staying at what locations, who spent the night where. His information didn't change so much as he requested more detail. And I knew why; the shoot-out on the south side had pretty much laid the foundation within the party, within the Black Panthers; we knew that the police would react some type of way."[29]

Around 4:45 on the morning of December 4, fourteen members of the Chicago police department—nine white and five black officers—led by Sergeant Daniel Grove raided Hampton's West Monroe apartment. Hampton and fellow Party leader Mark Clark were killed in the action. Four of the seven other occupants of the apartment were wounded by gunfire. All seven were charged with assault and attempted murder and led off the property.

Hanrahan told the press, "The immediate, violent criminal reaction of the occupants in shooting at announced police officers emphasizes the extreme viciousness of the Black Panther Party. So does their refusal to cease firing at the police officers when urged to do so several times." In a re-creation that the police taped for the media, the officers involved in the incident indicated that they had knocked on the door and identified themselves; a voice inside said "Just a minute." After waiting, they entered and were fired upon from within the two bedrooms. Sgt. Grove said, "We enter, a shot rings out . . . there's a woman [Brenda Harris] lying on the bed with a shotgun, calmly pumping it, pointing in my direction, and fires." The Chicago police department claimed that they had engaged in a fifteen-minute gun battle with the occupants of the apartment.

But the Panthers' version of the incident was drastically different. They claimed that the police had entered the apartment without warning and begun firing. In the days following the raid, they opened the apartment to the public to show Hampton's blood-stained bed as evidence that he had been shot, defenseless, in his sleep. "Don't touch nothing, don't move nothing," visitors were told. "We want to keep everything just the way it is."

"The next thing I knew," Harris said, "they had busted into the door and came in shooting. They shot me, they shot Mark Clark." Deborah Johnson, Hampton's fiancée, who was eight and a half months pregnant, recounted the event:

> [Hampton] never said a word, he never got up off the bed. A person who was in the room, they kept hollering out, "Stop shooting, stop shooting, we got a pregnant woman [or] a

pregnant sister in here." . . . They pushed me and the other brothers by the kitchen door and told us to face the wall. Heard a pig say "He's barely alive, he'll barely make it." I assumed they were talking about Chairman Fred. So then they started shooting, the pigs they started shootin' again. I heard a sister scream. They stopped shooting. Pig said, "He's good and dead now." The pigs went around laughing, they were really happy, you know, talking about Chairman Fred's dead.[30]

William O'Neal remembered:

Bobby Rush came to the office, he had just come from over there, maybe the coroner's office. In any case, we walked back over there and we both were speechless. We just walked through the house and saw where—what had taken place and where he'd died, and it was shocking. And then I was, you know, I just began to realize that the information that I had supplied leading up to that moment had facilitated that raid. I knew that indirectly, I had contributed and I felt it, and I felt bad about it. And then I got mad. You know, I had— And then I had to conceal those feelings, which made it worse. I couldn't say anything, I just had to continue to play the role.[31]

Hanrahan released an official, "exclusive" version of the raid to the *Chicago Tribune*, later citing that paper's "very balanced, fair report of the events that occurred." In the article, photographs showed clearly isolated marks on the back door that, according to the article, were bullet holes from weapons fired from the Panthers inside at the police on the outside of the apartment. When asked about the article, Hanrahan said, "I stand wholeheartedly behind it as absolutely accurate." But when a reporter pointed out to him that the marks on the door were, in fact, nail heads, Hanrahan backtracked: "I do not intend to quibble about that account. . . . I have said that we released the pictures. We have not characterized or described the conditions that they portray other than to say that that is an accurate portrayal of that particular object."[32] In other words, the objects shown in the photograph were the objects shown in the photograph.

At the funeral for Fred Hampton, Bobby Rush told those gathered, "We can mourn today, but if we understood Fred, if we are dedicated that his life wasn't given in vain, then there won't be no more mournings tomorrow. Then all our sorrow will be turned into action." It was reported that Rush's apartment had been broken into on the night of December 4, as well, and speculation that he also would have been killed if he'd been home at the time. "Yes, I would have been murdered," he told one reporter. "I still think there is a great possibility of people trying to murder me. All the moves in the past initially have been on the part of the police. They murdered Fred Hampton, they're out to murder me, just like they'll murder anybody that's black in this country."

But Rush, who called Hanrahan a "madman," voiced a message of moderation. "There won't be any retaliation by the Panthers. I think that the time will come when the people themselves will take the power that belongs to them, into their hands, and move to guarantee life, liberty, and the pursuit of happiness. . . . We won't be forced underground until the people, we really feel satisfied that we've done our duty, performed our duty to educate the masses of the people to the injustices that the power structure inflicts upon poor people in this country."

Hampton's attorney was Francis "Skip" Andrews, a white man who wore a goatee and spoke with a Southern accent. Andrews rallied with the Panthers in the aftermath of the attack. "What they don't understand," Andrews told Hampton's supporters, "is that you can't kill Chairman Fred. What they didn't understand is that anyone who would try to kill him is and shall ever be an enemy of the people, and that whoever would do that can only be appropriately called not a person, but a pig."[33]

Four days after the raid in Chicago, a forty-member SWAT team equipped with an armored personnel carrier, AR-15 automatic rifles, helicopters, tear gas, and dynamite, along with more than one hundred policeman, raided the Panther headquarters in Los Angeles at 5:30 in the morning. The Panthers staged an armed standoff for four hours, refusing to come out until the press had arrived on the scene. Although six Panthers were wounded and thirteen were arrested, none were killed. The raid had been organized after Panthers George Young and Paul Redd had allegedly thrown a police officer out of their headquarters at gunpoint on November 28; later that day, it was alleged that another Panther, Geronimo Pratt, had aimed a machine gun at a police car as it passed by.

The SWAT team had arrived with a search warrant issued by municipal court judge Antonio Chavez. Sergeant Raymond Callahan had told Chavez that the reason for the search would be to look for weapons—six machine guns and thirty M14 rifles—that had been stolen from the Camp Pendleton marine base when George Young had been stationed there. (Young later went AWOL.) What Callahan had neglected to tell Chavez was that Young had been in the stockade at the time the weapons were stolen.[34]

With Seale now separated from the case, the trial of the "Chicago 7" reached a new phase of its circus-like atmosphere on December 11, 1969, when the defense begant to call its witnesses. The roster included several celebrities from the counterculture, including Timothy Leary, Allen Ginsberg, Phil Ochs, Arlo Guthrie, Pete Seeger, Judy Collins, and Counrty Joe McDonald. Ochs and Collins both sang songs from the bench. Ginsberg was prompted to recite passages from his erotic poems by the prosecution in their attempt to color his testimony. During a heated exchange between attorneys and the judge, the poet chanted "Om" in an attempt to instill a Zenlike peace to the proceedings.

When the Chicago 7 trial ended in the winter of 1970, the remaining seven defendants were acquitted of conspiracy charges but found Hoffman, Rubin, Dellinger, Hayden and Davis guilty of crossing state lines to incite a riot. They were each sentenced to five years in prison, in addition to sentences for 159 counts of contempt of court doled out to all defendants along with Kuntsler and Weinglass. The Seventh Circuit Court of Appeals would later reverse all convictions on the basis that Hoffman had not allowed sufficient screening of jurors by the defense, and because he had shown a "deprecatory and often antagonistic attitude toward the defense." The court also reversed all contempt charges against the eight defendants, ruling that contempt charges exceeding sentences of six months required trial by jury. During the appeals process, it was also determined that the FBI, with the knowledge of the prosecution and Judge Hoffman, had bugged the defense attornies' offices during the trial.[35]

Meanwhile, as more details of the Hampton case emerged, the Chicago police came under increased scrutiny. Lawrence Kennon of the Cook County Bar Association said, "Based on available evidence, namely the physical condition of the home and its contents, the physical condition of the remains of Fred Hampton, the search warrant was merely a subterfuge, and the mission of the police was to murder and maim." Maywood councilman Tom Streeter, a white man, said, "This blatant act of legitimatized [sic] murder strips all credibility from law enforcement. In the context of other acts against militant blacks in recent months, it suggests an official policy of systematic oppression."[36]

All charges against the Panthers who had been in the apartment that night were dropped, and public pressure led to an investigation of the officers' actions. A federal grand jury determined that Sgt. Grove had briefed his thirteen officers prior to the raid that Panthers were inside the apartment, which contradicted at least one officer who had denied knowledge that any Panthers were there: "All we knew was that guns were in there." According to the grand jury report: "The great variance between the physical evidence and the testimony of the officers raises the question as to whether the officers are falsifying their accounts."

Ballistics experts found that all but one of the ninety shots fired on the premises that night had been fired by the police; the remaining one seems to have been fired by Clark as a reflex after he had been shot while holding a gun. In the end, the findings were critical of the police but did not hold them criminally liable for the attack: "Unquestionably, the raid was not professionally planned or properly executed, and the result of the raid is 2 deaths, 4 injuries and 7 improper criminal charges . . . the physical evidence and the discrepancies in the officers' accounts are insufficient evidence to establish probable cause to charge the officers with the willful violation of the occupants' civil rights."[37]

The families of Hampton, Clark, and the survivors from that night sued the government for violating their civil rights. More than a decade later, the case was settled out of court.

21. COWBOYS AND INDIANS

Postmodern Westerns speak to the end of American mythology, while the rise of American Indian culture goes hand in hand with the counterculture movement, and the seizure of Alcatraz Island begins the "Red Power" movement.

Butch Cassidy and the Sundance Kid hit screens nationwide in October, offering a sixties-style subversive antihero tale sanitized for Hollywood and couched within a big-budget buddy film. Director George Roy Hill's movie for Twentieth Century Fox was loosely based on the real life of Butch Cassidy and Harry Longabaugh, members of the "Wild Bunch" outlaw gang that operated out of the "Hole in the Wall" hideout in the Big Horn Mountains of Wyoming in the late 1800s.

Together, Paul Newman and Robert Redford made handsome, congenial bank robbers that are liked even by the local sheriff and the bank representative who has been repeatedly robbed by them. Later, it's revealed that Butch had never killed a man until, ironically, their attempt to go straight. The two well-mannered bandits have a chemistry built around ruses and one-liners, along with a mutual affection for Etta Place (played by Katharine Ross, who had won overnight fame as Elaine Robinson in *The Graduate*). The forty-four-year-old Newman had already been nominated for Oscars for his performances in *Cat on a Hot Tin Roof*, *The Hustler*, *Hud*, and *Cool Hand Luke*. Redford, thirty-three, had starred in some smaller pictures, but *Butch and Sundance* would skyrocket him into the upper echelon of leading men.

It was the original year of the postmodern Western, with such classic films as *Butch and Sundance, The Wild Bunch, Once Upon a Time in the West,* and even *Midnight Cowboy* deconstructing frontier mythology and dealing with the death of the Old West. In the first scene of *Butch and Sundance,* the opening card-game ruse is filmed in sepia tone and the characters in their rascally prime are bathed in an antique light. As they leave the bar, the sepia gives way as color gradually bleeds in, visually transporting the gunfighters into the future. The scene in which Butch and Etta go for a ride on the recently invented bicycle (accompanied by the soundtrack of B. J. Thomas singing, "Raindrops Keep Falling on My Head") links the film to the onset of wheeled transportation, car culture, and the end of frontier life.

The demise of the Wild West represents an end to their world, and much of the film sees the legendary Butch and Sundance suddenly facing their own mortality. When their second train robbery goes awry—Butch uses too much dynamite and obliterates the safe and everything around it, prompting Redford's ad-lib, "Think ya used enough dynamite there, Butch?"—a specially commissioned posse on horseback jumps out of a freight car, forcing the pair to flee. They head into the mountains and double up on a single horse in an attempt to split up their pursuers, who are following their tracks. But as they watch from their perch atop a mountain, they see the posse in the distance as it examines where the horse tracks split. The posse chooses the right tracks to follow, leading Butch and Sundance to utter the film's recurring line: "Who are those guys?"

The outlaws discover that the bounty hunters include the famous American Indian tracker, Lord Baltimore, and a fierce lawman named Joe Lefors, and as they chase Butch and Sundance—besting the outlaws' evasive tactics, turn for turn—the robbers gradually realize they've met their match. They seek amnesty from a friendly sheriff (Jeff Corey), but he yells at them prophetically, "Don't you understand? It's over!" Back at Etta's place, a newspaper story reveals that the posse has been hired by the railroad to kill them, and the words "Who are those guys?" become a mantra for the unstoppable force of time, come to send them into the past.

They flee again with Etta in tow, this time to Bolivia, where they are forced to overcome their comical language barrier before achieving success as bank robbers in a foreign country. Fearing capture, they decide to go straight, and Butch and Sundance take jobs as payroll guards for a mine; but after they kill a pack of Bolivian *banditos* on their first day, the two decide they'd rather rob for themselves than kill for others. The famous robbers are both wounded during a final standoff with the local police, and they give up their cover and make one desperate, last-ditch counteroffensive charge—not realizing that one hundred Bolivian cavalrymen have surrounded the place with rifles ready. In the classic final scene, the image of Butch and Sundance with guns ablazing is frozen and turns back into a sepia frame as the sound of gunfire greets them, forever capturing these western outlaws in the dusty annals of history.

The Wild Bunch, released by Warner Brothers, also played off the theme of an outlaw "wild bunch," though of a much more graphic nature. Soon after word of Twentieth Century Fox's production of the William Goldman screenplay for *Butch and Sundance* reached director Sam Peckinpah, he fell in love with another, suspiciously similar script penned by Walon Green and Roy Sickner, about an outlaw gang working on the Texas-Mexico border in 1913 during the time of the Mexican Revolution. The film's tagline reflected the same themes found in *Butch and Sundance*—the end of an era and the characters of the Old West being left behind: "Unchanged men in a changing land . . . Out of step, out of place, and desperately out of time." An alternate one announced, "Suddenly a new West has emerged. Suddenly it was sundown for nine men. Suddenly their day was over. Suddenly the sky was bathed in blood."

There are several similarities between the two films: a gang of outlaws given to infighting; a posse ambush hired by the railroad, with posse members emerging on horseback from a freight car; a journey south of the border; wheeled technology (in *The Wild Bunch*, an automobile) as a symbol of an impending future age; and the antihero protagonists meeting their death by greater numbers in a final shoot-out. But that's where the similarities end. *Butch and Sundance*, after all, was 1969's date-movie Western, a three-way love story with pretty actors playing lovable criminals who don't kill anybody until they leave the country. Peckinpah's film is an opera of violence starring grizzled actors portraying murderous villains in a brutal world.

Pike Bishop (William Holden) is the leader of the gang, and Dutch Engstrom (Ernest Borgnine) the most loyal member. Both actors were in their fifties at the time, and Holden was at least a decade removed from his "golden boy" period. (Lee Marvin was originally slated to play the role of Pike, but the actor opted to accept a role in another 1969 Western—Paramount's hopelessly corny adaptation of the Lerner and Lowe stage musical, *Paint Your Wagon*, for which both Marvin and Clint Eastwood infamously did their own singing.) Disguised as U. S. Cavalry troops, the bunch rides into San Rafael, Texas, to rob a railroad office.

As they ride into town, they pass a group of children playing in the dirt, and their seemingly innocent smiles and laughter are transformed when the camera reveals the source of their amusement: They are torturing a scorpion by placing it atop a hill of fire ants. As the ants devour the scorpion, the children set the hill on fire. While foreshadowing a sense of disaster, the scene also establishes the notion of ever-present violence and cruelty, something that exists even from childhood. A later scene showing a child being breastfed by a woman wearing a bandolier implies that violence is inbred in humanity. "The whole underside of our society has always been violence and still is," Peckinpah later said. "Churches, laws—everybody seems to think that man is a noble savage. But he's only an animal, a meat-eating, talking animal."[1]

The Wild Bunch was one of the most violent wide-scale releases to come out of Hollywood that anyone could remember. Warner Brothers announced that the weapons and ammo used in the shooting of the film—239 rifles, shotguns, revolvers, and automatic weapons firing more than 90,000 rounds—was "More than was used in the entire Mexican revolution!"[2] It wasn't just the sheer volume of shoot-outs in the film but also the nature of the armed confrontations. Rather than romanticizing violence, Peckinpah confronts his audience with the brutality of blood, dirt, sweat, pain, and anguish. The montages of death presented in the movie wash over the viewer in waves of red, and slow-motion death scenes borrowed from the cinema of Akira Kurosawa intensify the violence. Author David Weddle describes, "The effect was not realistic, as some critics would mistakenly assert, but decidedly surrealistic. Gothic in its horror, poetic in its beauty."[3]

Peckinpah explained, "The point of the film is to take this façade of movie violence and open it up, get people involved in it so that they are starting to go in the Hollywood television predictable reaction syndrome, and then twist it so that it's not fun anymore." During the days of the first "living-room war," the scenes from Peckinpah's blood opera resembled the images from Vietnam that Americans saw on the nightly news. The film was deemed so violent by the Motion Picture Association of America that they required significant editing before "downgrading" it from an X rating to R, a testament to Peckinpah's vision of an American mythology founded on frontier violence. "It's ugly, brutalizing, and bloody fucking awful. It's not fun and games and cowboys and Indians. It's a terrible, ugly thing. And yet there's a certain response that you get from it, an excitement because we're all violent people."[4]

The surviving members of the bunch escape, leaving behind a street scene strewn with the bodies of both sides. Deke (Robert

Ryan), a former gang member now working as a bounty hunter for the railroad, leads a posse in pursuit of Pike's men as they ride across the border into a poor yet strangely Edenic village that is home to gang member Angel (Jaime Sánchez). Angel discovers his village ravaged by the forces of the corrupt General Mapache, his father killed, and his lover, Teresa, gone off willingly with Mapache's men. The bunch seeks out the general to trade horses, and Angel sees Teresa acting as a whore for Mapache's men. Initially ashamed at his seeing her, she defiantly laughs in his face and flaunts her betrayal by falling wantonly into the general's arms. Overcome with rage, he draws his pistol and shoots her dead. The rest of the bunch steps in to avoid a full-blown conflict, and they agree to work for Mapache in robbing a U. S. Army train of its weapons.

Angel agrees to take part only if he can keep a case of weapons and give them to his Agua Verde countrymen. (This subplot is similar to the storyline of 1969's *100 Rifles*, in which Burt Reynolds plays a Yaqui Indian who robs a bank to buy guns for his people so that they may fight repression by a corrupt Mexican government.) But when they deliver the guns to Mapache in installments, in exchange for gold, Angel learns that his stolen portion was reported to the general by Teresa's mother in revenge for her death. Dutch, whose life was saved by Angel during the robbery when he pulled Dutch back onto the train, leaves Angel behind, telling Mapache, "He's a thief. You take care of him."

Pike leads the group back into town to plead for Angel's life, only to find him being dragged from the back of a car by Mapache and his men as children whip him and villagers ride on his back like a horse. The climactic scene begins when Pike and his three remaining men strap on their guns and march back into town to demand Angel's release. Mapache slits Angel's throat, and Pike shoots the general in a blind rage. When the other three draw their guns, they realize that they've caught Mapache's men off guard. Peckinpah called this scene "a strange, existentialist little number . . . everybody has got their hands up and [Pike's bunch] can get up, and they know it, and they look at each other and they start to laugh because they know this is the end and they want it all." Pike fires point-blank at Mapache's German military advisor and kills him, signaling that, as Weddle writes, ". . . the apocalyptic battle was to begin."[5]

The final gun battle fully embodies Peckinpah cinema, as the ensuing orgy of violence spares neither men, women, nor children. One of Pike's men uses a Mapache prostitute as a human shield and then discards her body when it's been shot up. Pike takes shelter in one of the women's rooms, and when his back is turned, she picks up a gun and shoots him in the shoulder. He yells "Bitch!" in anger, spins, and shoots her dead. Later, a child delivers the killing shot to Pike, recalling the movie's opening scorpion scene. When Deke's posse arrives in town the next day, the carnage on the streets has turned the place into a picnic for vultures. He stays behind as the rest of his posse leaves, only to be killed by Agua Verde villagers and an older member of the bunch, Sykes, whom Deke had wounded earlier in the film. In the final moments, Deke and Sykes join forces to fight in Pancho Villa's revolution, the only option left for men of their dying breed.

Harmonica, Charles Bronson's character in *Once Upon a Time in the West*, describes the mythic men of the Old West as members of "an ancient race." Directed by "Spaghetti Western" pioneer Sergio Leone and released in the United States in 1969, the film is an epic revenge narrative with inverted typecasting—the gritty Bronson plays the "good guy," while Henry Fonda, an American institution as a leading man, plays Frank, a cold-blooded killer for hire. The story literally takes place at the end of an era, as the two gunmen stage a very personal battle in a remote Arizona outpost just as the transcontinental railroad arrives there for the first time, marking the death of the Wild West and the advent of the modern world.

Harmonica haunts Frank throughout the film for reasons unknown. When asked his name, Harmonica instead gives the names of people Frank has killed in the past. Frank finally confronts him near the film's end, and the two arrive at a mutual recognition that their fates are intertwined. "I know that now you'll tell me what you're after," Frank says.

"Only at the point of death," Harmonica responds, signaling the beginning of the end that comes with a trademark Leone gun duel. Staring at each other, the two characters walk as if choreographed into a dusty clearing, their eyes glued to each other, Ennio Morricone's music rising as if from the dust as the two men engage in a *pas de deux* of death. Only then is their history revealed in a flashback sequence: Many years earlier, Frank had hung Harmonica's older brother from a wooden overhang while he stood on Harmonica's shoulders. As an act of cruel humor, Frank had stuffed a harmonica in the younger brother's mouth, saying, "Keep your lovin' brother happy," forcing the crying kid to play until he collapsed to the ground and his brother dropped to his death. After reliving this memory, Harmonica draws and shoots Frank. As the villain lies on the ground dying, the victor reveals his identity by taking the same harmonica from a string around his neck and stuffing it in Frank's mouth.

Once Upon a Time in the West ends with the last of the gunfighters squaring off in a final battle at the end of the Old West. The completion of the Union Station welcomes the transcontinental railroad, a symbol of the approaching modern world that would swallow up the open range, and in his cinematic elegy to the mythical Wild West, Leone includes several allusions to classic Hollywood Westerns. Christopher Frayling counts references to *High Noon*, *3:10 to Yuma*, *Shane*, *The Searchers*, *The Magnificent Seven*, *The Man Who Shot Liberty Valance*, and *My Darling Clementine*, to name just a few. Perhaps the most obvious allusion comes from the flashback hanging scene, which was filmed in Monument Valley in Utah.

Although Leone's film was an Italian production filmed in Italy and Spain, his choice of Monument Valley recalled the work of legendary American film director John Ford, who used the picturesque, butte-studded region as a setting for a number of his films, beginning with the classic *Stagecoach* (1939), featuring John Wayne in his break-through role.

John Wayne would receive his first and only Best Actor Oscar for his performance in the 1969 film, *True Grit*. This adaptation of the Charles Portis novel was one of the more traditional Westerns released that year: an "eye for an eye" revenge plot in which an aging, drunken, potbellied, eye-patch-wearing U. S. marshal named Rooster Cogburn (Wayne) is hired by a determined young woman named Mattie Ross (Kim Darby) to track down the man who killed her father. Joined by Mattie and a Texas Ranger named La Boeuf (Glen Campbell), Cogburn chases the villain (Jeff Corey) into Indian terri-tory, where he's taken up with the outlaw Lucky Ned Pepper (Robert Duvall).

Over three decades as a leading man, Wayne had forged his own stock type: a fighting man of the outdoors, unyielding in his princi-ples and his adherence to a code. In the year of postmodern weap-ons, veteran Wayne's performance stood almost as an anachronism. "In any acting, I have to identify with something in the character," he told *Life*. "There are some parts I won't play—anybody dishonest or cruel or mean for no reason. I've killed men on the screen, but it was always because they didn't follow the code."[6] Describing Rooster Cogburn, Wayne said, "He feels the same way that I do. He doesn't believe in pampering wrongdoers, which certainly fits into the category of my thinking. He doesn't believe in accommodation. Neither do I."[7] An outspoken conservative and a proponent of the Vietnam War, the actor admitted that his political beliefs differed from the "prevailing attitude" of those in the movie industry. He even sounded like fellow ex-actor Ronald Reagan in comment-ing on the rash of campus demonstrations across the nation: "The disorders in schools are caused by immature professors who have encouraged activists."[8]

John Dominis, who spent time photographing Wayne and rising star Dustin Hoffman for an article contrasting the two actors, said, "The two men are the best examples I know of the way America seems to be polarizing." In contrast to Wayne, the jingoistic icon and latter-day American myth maker, Hoffman was "urban America: young, liberal, intellectual and basically pessimistic about the future."[9]

Just two years after his landmark performance as Benjamin Braddock in *The Graduate*, Hoffman scored one of the most acclaimed performances of his career as street con Ratso Rizzo in *Midnight Cowboy*. John Schlesinger's film is not a "Western" in the conventional sense, but the story nevertheless plays with images of Western movies and western mythology. Jon Voight's Joe Buck, a naive, wannabe gigolo, leaves behind his small Texas hometown, where the marquee of the local cinema invokes the name of John Wayne in *The Alamo*. But with the film having left town and the letters just beginning to fall off (J HN AYNE THE A AMO), Schlesinger signals an inversion of the cowboy icon.

Reversing the traditional pattern of East-to-West frontier movement, Buck heads east to New York City in search of opportunity and personal reinvention, much like the original frontiersmen had done by going west. He carries plans to brand himself as an "urban cowboy," an export from the frontier donning a fringed jacket and cowboy hat; in his 42nd Street hotel room, he hangs a "beefcake" poster of Paul Newman starring as a modern-day cowboy in Martin Ritt's *Hud* (1963). In her essay on *Hud* and *Midnight Cowboy*, Ann Barrow argues that the "new cowboy" of American cinema "stands juxtaposed beside the traditional hero, setting the stage for the demythologizing of the basic structure of the Western plot where the cowboys or gunmen arise out of the landscape in order to pave the way for a civil society. . . . In both *Hud* and *Midnight Cowboy*, the literal landscape of capitalistic America meets the myth of the open frontier, or autonomous individuals, and of equal opportunity."[10] Once in New York, the city nearly spits him out as Joe proves a failure as a hustler. The film depicts an intrinsic American icon returning east, only to find the new frontier and a new America.

In their own search for America, Wyatt and Billy in *Easy Rider* travel throughout the American Southwest as modern-day cowboys on metallic horses. "I thought of this as a Western . . . just two guys, rather than being on horses, out by the side of the road, you know, making their campfire and camping outside of town, so a classic kind of Western," Dennis Hopper said. "Two loners, two gunfighters, two outlaws: Billy the Kid and Wyatt Earp." (Similarly, the climactic chase scene in Lee Madden's *Hell's Angels '69*, in which outlaw bikers chase Tom Stern, Jeremy Slate, and Conny Van Dyke across the desert on bikes, comes across like a modern-day re-creation of Indians on the warpath chasing two cowboys and their woman on horseback.) In *Easy Rider*, Billy dreams of living the life of his frontier forefathers, being "Out here in the wilderness, fighting Indians and cowboys on every side," and their trip even takes them through John Ford country in Monument Valley—with the sound of The Band's "The Weight" substituted for a cattle-trail ballad.

❀ ❀ ❀

American Indians seemed to be much on the minds of counterculture members at the end of the decade. In his short story, "Because My Father Always Said He Was the Only Indian Who Saw Jimi Hendrix Play 'The Star-Spangled Banner' at Woodstock," Sherman Alexie writes, "During the Sixties, my father was the perfect hippie, since all the hippies were trying to be Indians."[11]

As part of their back-to-the-land yearnings, many hippies took to Native American fashions as a gesture to the peoples who had originally had the land to themselves, before the onset of industrialization brought by European whites. Even Hendrix, himself part

Cherokee, performed his famous Woodstock set in a fringed tribal jacket and moccasins. Historian Philip Deloria said that such hippies were merely "playing Indian": "'Indians could be both civilized and indigenous. They could critique modernity and yet reap its benefits. They could revel in the creative pleasure of liberated meanings while still grasping for something fundamentally American. . . . Not only in the communes but in politics, environmentalism, spirituality, and other pursuits, Indianness allowed counterculturists to have their cake and to eat it."[12]

During the People's Park incident, a poster designed by activist Frank Bardacke linked the movement with the struggles of the American Indian. The poster bore a picture of Geronimo brandishing a rifle, and the copy grandiosely positioned the fight over People's Park as an act of righting a historical wrong by reclaiming land in the name of its original inhabitants: "A long time ago the Costanoan Indians lived in the area now called Berkeley. They had no concept of land ownership. They believed that the land was under the care and guardianship of the people who used it and lived on it."

But 1969 was not just about co-opting the history of Native Americans by "playing Indian." Landmark works such as the Pulitzer Prize–winning novel *House Made of Dawn*, the stage play *Indians*, and the American Indian manifesto, *Custer Died for Your Sins* helped to increase awareness of Native American culture and history. And as the days grew shorter in late 1969, a radical group of indigenous tribal members launched a takeover of an infamous American institution—and found lots of non-Indian Americans rooting for them.

The Pulitzer Prize for Fiction in 1969 went to *House Made of Dawn*, a novel by N. Scott Momaday, a Kiowa Indian who grew up on Navajo, Apache, and Pueblo reservations. Abel, the protagonist, was a composite character based on some boys the author had known on the Jemez Pueblo in New Mexico. Abel returns from World War II in 1945 to his home in Walatowa, New Mexico, to live with his grandfather Francisco. After participating in native ceremonies, Abel goes out drinking and ends up stabbing an albino horseman to death. He's sent away to prison for seven years and then released into an Indian relocation program in Los Angeles, where he rooms with Ben Benally, a Native American who has successfully assimilated into urban America. Unable to similarly assimilate, Abel is beaten badly in an encounter on the beach and decides to return to Walatowa, where he cares for his ailing grandfather on his deathbed. In the early-morning hours after Francisco passes away, Abel goes out to the field where the ceremonial "Race of the Dead" takes place, and the novel circles back on itself, returning us to the opening scene with Abel running along with the apparitions of this latter-day vision quest.

Most notably, Momaday's novel was an achievement in its description of native rituals, and their importance in a culture that was threatened by modern American society. "My father was a great storyteller and he knew many stories from the Kiowa oral tradition," said the author. "He told me many of these stories over and over because I loved them. But it was only after I became an adult that I understood how fragile they are, because they exist only by word of mouth, always just one generation away from extinction. That's when I began to write down the tales my father and others had told me."[13]

In May 1969, Arthur Kopit's stage play *Indians* debuted in the United States at the Arena Stage in Washington, D.C., and then opened at New York's Brooks Atkinson Theatre in October. The experimental production, which received a Tony nomination for Best Play, is peopled by many of the legendary characters of the Old West, from Buffalo Bill, Wild Bill Hickok, Annie Oakley, and Jesse James to Sitting Bull, Geronimo, Chief Joseph, Red Cloud, and Crazy Horse. Buffalo Bill (Stacy Keach in the New York production) confronts the legacy of his own role in the White Man's ruination of Indian culture, including his mass slaughter of buffalo and his exploitative "Wild West" show, which starred real-life Indians like Sitting Bull reenacting scenes from the history of the American Indian wars for the amusement of spectators.

The play opens with three glass cases on the stage—one displaying an effigy of Buffalo Bill, one with an effigy of Sitting Bull, and the third with a buffalo skull, bloody Indian shirt, and a rifle. Buffalo Bill rides onto the stage to announce the beginning of his famous "Wild West" show, but then he gets lost in a defense of his life while he is rattled by an off-screen voice that urges him to begin the show.

In the course of thirteen disjointed scenes, the play reinterprets key events from the Indian wars of the late nineteenth century—the breaking of treaties and other government deceptions, the slaughter of the buffalo, the banning of the Ghost Dance, the murder of Sitting Bull. Kopit was inspired to write the play as a response to a statement of "regret" that General William Westmoreland made in 1966 after the killing of Vietnamese civilians. In the final scene, Colonel James Forsyth is reminiscent of Westmoreland as he surveys the carnage of the Wounded Knee Massacre at the Pine Ridge Agency in December 1890. Shrugging off the slaughter of Lakota Sioux men, women, and children, the colonel says, "One can always find someone who'll call an overwhelming victory a massacre."

As Buffalo Bill stages one final desperate apology for the White Father, he is interrupted by the death of Sitting Bull, followed, one after another, by the rest of the Indians in the play. The music of the Wild West show blares obscenely over them, as if to wipe out their memory, and then the light shines on the three glass cases, reminding the audience of a culture now rendered into museum pieces.

Vine Deloria Jr., a theologian and former executive director of the National Congress of American Indians, gave long-overdue voice to Native Americans in their struggles against legal discrimination and cultural prejudice with his surprise 1969 best-seller, *Custer Died for Your Sins: An Indian Manifesto*. Deloria's book is a rare achievement—amusing in its sardonic voice, yet deadly in its logical attacks on common perceptions of the American Indian and on the U. S. government's indefensible mistreatment of America's indigenous people.

Deloria begins by deconstructing the white stereotype of the noble savage Indian tied primitively to the land: "The more we try to be ourselves, the more we are forced to defend what we have never been. The American public feels most comfortable with the mythical Indians of stereotype-land who were always THERE. These Indians are fierce, they wear feathers and grunt. Most of us don't fit this idealized figure since we grunt only when overeating, which is seldom." And then there is the stock type of the "friendly Indian companion" as handed down by popular culture and literary chronicles, from Squanto and Pocahontas to Tonto. "Squanto, who had welcomed the Pilgrims and helped them destroy the tribes in Connecticut and Long Island, was reworked as a 'friendly' Indian as opposed to Massasoit, the father of King Philip the Wampanoag chief, who had suspicions about the Pilgrims from the very start."

Deloria also turned his eye toward modern-day "Indians" who sought to co-opt the cultural heritage of Native Americans:

> During my three years as Executive Director of the National Congress of American Indians, it was a rare day when some white didn't visit my office and proudly proclaim that he or she was of Indian descent. Cherokee was the most popular tribe of their choice, and many people placed the Cherokees anywhere from Maine to Washington State. Mohwak, Sioux, and Chippewa were next in popularity. Occasionally I would be told about some mythical tribe from lower Pennsylvania, Virginia, or Massachusetts which had spawned the white before me.

Deloria laces his damnation of White America with disarming wit. "Indians have been cursed above all other people in history. Indians have anthropologists." His wry observations include a cataloging of jokes that Natives Americans use to comment on their state. One Indian joke goes thusly: When Columbus landed, one Indian turned to another and said, "Well, there goes the neighborhood."

In another version, the Indian says, "Maybe if we leave them alone they will go away."

This line, related to the war in Southeast Asia, held particular insight at the time: "The current joke is that a survey was taken and only 15% of the Indians thought that the United States should get out of Vietnam. Eighty-five percent thought they should get out of America!"

But Deloria is entirely serious in his literary assault on the federal government. Commenting on the Cold War and the common perception that Commies couldn't be trusted, he reminds the reader, "America has yet to keep one Indian treaty or agreement, despite the fact that the United States government signed over four hundred such treaties and agreements with Indian tribes. It would take Russia another century to break as many treaties as the United States has already violated."

His biggest target is the policy of "termination," the series of acts beginning with a resolution sponsored by Representative William H. Harrison (the great-great-grandson of President William Henry Harrison, the famed Indian fighter from the 1811 Battle of Tippecanoe) in 1953, and continuing until 1964. These acts sought to end federal trusteeship of tribal territories. Ostensibly intended to help Indians assimilate into mainstream American culture, the laws in actuality removed protected status from nearly 1.4 million acres of reservation lands and officially stripped tribal affiliation from more than 100 tribes. Deloria equates this bureaucratic form of genocide with the practice of settlers giving blankets infected with smallpox to the Indians. "People often feel guilty about their ancestors killing all those Indians years ago. But they shouldn't feel guilty about the distant past. Just the last two decades have seen a more devious but hardly less successful war waged against Indian communities," he concludes.

"The United States operates on incredibly stupid premises," Deloria writes. "It always fails to understand the nature of the world and so does not develop policies that can hold the allegiance of people. It then alienates everyone who does not automatically love it." In an era of increasing radicalism, Deloria examines the often-complicated relationship of American Indians to the larger Civil Rights movement, concluding: "Until we can once again produce people like Crazy Horse, all the money and help in the world will not save us. It is up to us to write the final chapter of the American Indian upon this continent."

❊ ❊ ❊

According to the oral histories of local Indians, Alcatraz Island, located in the middle of San Francisco Bay, has been used as a place of banishment for ostracized tribal members. Native Americans also used the island as a refuge when trying to flee the missions established by Spanish Franciscans in California during the late eighteenth and early nineteenth centuries. In 1850, the U. S. Army built a fortress on the island. It was used for detaining Confederate prisoners during the Civil War, and several Native Americans were imprisoned on the island during the height of the Indian Wars in the late nineteenth century and into the early 1900s.

The Department of Justice converted Alcatraz into a maximum-security penitentiary during the Great Depression. Over the next three decades, it housed more than 1,500 of the nation's most notorious public enemies, including Al Capone, George "Machine Gun" Kelly, Clarence Carnes (aka, the Choctaw Kid), and Robert Stroud, the famous "Birdman of Alcatraz."

Due to its decaying infrastructure and its increasing cost of upkeep, the prison was closed by order of U. S. Attorney General

Robert Kennedy in March 1963. Since then, it had remained vacant, an abandoned facility described by *Newsweek* as a "decaying white elephant." Suggestions for what to do with the island varied, from turning it into a nudist colony or a bird sanctuary to making it the site of a huge, plastic "Statue of Liberty West."

In the spring of 1969, businessmen Lamar Hunt—founder of the newly legitimized American Football League—outlined a plan for turning "The Rock" into a museum park celebrating the U. S. space program, along with an 1890s-style shopping center. San Francisco's Board of Supervisors approved the plan, but then San Francisco dress designer Alvin Duskin launched a protest campaign. Fearing that Hunt, the son of a Texas oil millionaire, wanted to turn the island into a deepwater dock for oil tankers, Duskin published a full-page newspaper ad that called Hunt's proposal "As Big a Steal as Manhattan Island." With the Santa Barbara oil slick fresh in their minds, 8,000 readers clipped out "coupons" from the ad and mailed them to the city's supervisors to show their opposition to the plan. Facing election season, the board voted in October to table the proposal for six months.[14]

Then, in November 1969, a group of Native Americans led by Richard Oakes, a twenty-seven-year-old Mohawk activist, seized Alcatraz in a peaceful "invasion." San Francisco's American Indian Center, which had been used for social programs for 30,000 Indians, had burned to the ground in October, and Oakes's group sought to claim the island as the new location for its center. The island had been declared federal surplus land in 1964, and under a long-forgotten treaty dating back to 1868, American Indians were entitled to claim possession of surplus land from the U. S. federal government. A group of Sioux Indians led by Richard McKenzie had claimed the island in 1964 and "occupied" it for just four hours.[15]

Oakes, a handsome, charismatic leader and natural organizer, had developed one of the nation's first American Indian Studies departments at San Francisco State University and had also worked with students at UCLA. In 1969, he devised a plan for roughly seventy-five students and activists from the pan-Native American movement Indians of All Tribes (IAT) to sail out to the island and claim it. But on the planned day of November 9, none of the boats that had been arranged for transportation to the island showed up. Oakes entertained the press that had assembled while a Red Lake Chippewa named Adam Fortunate Eagle found the owner of a three-masted ship and convinced him to circle the island. When they got within 250 feet, Oakes jumped off and swam to shore, and four others followed. They reached the island safely and "claimed" it, but then the local Coast Guard brought them back to the mainland.

That night, however, twenty members of the party boarded a fishing boat and sailed out to the island. Fourteen of the group ("Eleven braves and three squaws," *Newsweek* quipped) stayed overnight and announced an offer to buy the island for "$24 in glass beads and cloth"—the purported price that Peter Minuit had paid for the island of Manhattan in 1626. Rather than turning it into a nudist colony, space park, or shopping mall, Oakes's occupiers said Alcatraz should be turned into an institute of Native American studies, along with a museum, cultural center, and a health facility for Indians.[16]

The group left the next day aboard Coast Guard vessels, but in the early-morning hours of November 20, Oakes and a contingent of approximately eighty IAT activists set out from nearby Sausalito on three boats and returned to the island. When they landed, the caretaker on duty, Glenn Dodson, cried in mock alarm, "Mayday! Mayday! The Indians have landed." Then he winked at Oakes. "I'm one-eighth Indian myself," Dodson told him.[17]

"This time, we have come to stay," Oakes said. The Native Americans settled into Alcatraz. Coast Guardsmen made what was described as a "half-hearted effort" to form a blockade around the island in their cutters, to prevent sympathetic activists and volunteers from bringing necessary supplies onto the island, but there were too many ships running food, clothing, and money to the island. One delivery included, symbolically, two Thanksgiving turkeys.

Government officials gave IAT members twenty-four hours to leave, but they refused to vacate the premises. Oakes phoned in a message to the office of the San Francisco Department of the Interior, saying:

> We invite the United States to acknowledge the justice of our claim. The choice now lies with the leaders of the American government—to use violence upon us as before to remove us from our Great Spirit's land, or to institute a real change in its dealing with the American Indian. We do not fear your threat to charge us with crimes on our land. We and all other oppressed peoples would welcome spectacle of proof before the world of your title by genocide. Nevertheless, we seek peace.[18]

The Indian group forged a truce with the authorities, and food shipments to the island were permitted. The Army Corps of Engineers also provided the services of a water barge, as there was no running water on the island.

Once installed on the island, IAT issued a statement entitled, "The Alcatraz Proclamation to the Great White Father and His People," in which they declared the island was a "suitable" location for an Indian reservation because of the following:

1) It was isolated from modern facilities, and without adequate means of transportation.

2) It had no fresh running water.

3) It had inadequate sanitation facilities.

4) There were no oil or mineral rights.

5) There was no industry, and so unemployment was very great.

6) There were no health-care facilities.

7) The soil was rocky and nonproductive, and the land did not support game.

8) There were no educational facilities.

9) The population had always exceeded the land base.

10) The population had always been held as prisoners and kept dependent upon others.

The proclamation further stated that "it would be fitting and symbolic that ships from all over the world, entering the Golden Gate, would first see Indian land, and thus be reminded of the true history of this nation. This tiny island would be a symbol of the great lands once ruled by free and noble Indians."[19]

On Thanksgiving Day, more than a hundred Native Americans sailed out to the island to join the IAT occupiers in their show of "Red Power." IAT was indeed there to stay. Oakes established a rule of government—a true democracy, with everybody on the island voting on all major decisions. Each person was assigned a task, ranging from cooking to laundry to sentry detail to the teaching of Native arts and crafts. Someone scrawled graffiti across a metal panel that declared YOU ARE ON INDIAN LAND.

In a year of many things, 1969 was also the year of the underdog, and the Alcatraz Occupation garnered a good deal of public support. Businesses and private citizens donated money, food, and supplies. A local longshoreman and Blackfoot Indian named Joseph Morris rented pier space and set up a ferry for transporting both supplies and people to the island. The occupation also became a cause célèbre. In December, radio stations KPFA in Berkeley and KPFK in Los Angeles began broadcasting a daily show with occupier John Trudell. The daughter of sports legend Jim Thorpe, a Sac and Fox Indian, took part in the occupation for several months and liaisoned with celebrities such as Marlon Brando, Dick Gregory, Jonathan Winters, and Jane Fonda, who each visited Alcatraz in a show of support. Creedence Clearwater Revival donated $15,000 to the IAT takeover.

Sensing the public support and wanting to avoid yet another episode of violence in what had been a violent year, the federal government visited the island several times to negotiate with the occupiers. Unfortunately, conditions on the island soon began to deteriorate. The water main and fuel line began to leak. The government shut down the electricity and phone lines. Meanwhile, a number of non–Native Americans from the San Francisco underground drug culture had moved onto the island. Many of the students left the island to return to school, and Oakes and his family left the island after his thirteen-year-old stepdaughter fell to her death. But a core group remained until June 11, 1971, when a contingent of federal marshals, General Service Administration (GSA) and FBI agents, and Coast Guard members removed the final fifteen occupiers from Alcatraz—nineteen months after the IAT had taken the island.

Although the occupation ultimately proved unsuccessful in its goal of claiming the island, it was a defining moment for "Red Power" and the recently formed American Indian Movement (AIM). AIM leader Russell Means said, "Before AIM, Indians were dispirited, defeated and culturally dissolving. People were ashamed to be Indian. . . . Then there was that spark at Alcatraz, and we took off. . . . We put Indians and Indian rights smack dab in the middle of the public consciousness."[20]

Alcatraz did for AIM what Stonewall did for the Gay Rights movement. In the years following Alcatraz, Indian activists staged seventy-four occupations of federal facilities, several of which involved people from the Alcatraz occupation. Both AIM and the Alcatraz-Red Power Movement (ARPM) grew into an active, nation-wide organizations.

Lost in the more-famous memories of 1969 are how the myths of the American West began to vanish. With "updated" Westerns pondering the death of an old order and new activist voices bringing increased attention to the indigenous American experience, the country could never again view its past in the same way.

22. The Hippie Apocalypse

Stones, Angels, and death at the Altamont Speedway free concert

All things dark and Satanic seemed to converge in northern California at the end of 1969.

On Saturday, September 27, Bryan Hartnell and Cecelia Shepard rode out to the Lake Berryessa reservoir in California's idyllic Napa Valley. The two students had met at Pacific Union College in nearby Angwin, but Shepard was transferring to Cal-Riverside, and Hartnell had spent the day helping Shepard pack up her things for the move. Around 4:00 P.M., they headed out in Hartnell's white Karmann Ghia to spend some time alone together at the lake on her last day in town.

Sometime after 6:00 in the early fall evening, as they lay on a blanket on the narrow peninsula that extended into the lake, Shepard spotted a man in the distance, a muscular and stocky man with dark hair. Just as she saw him, the man seemed to disappear behind a group of trees about 250 feet away.[1]

Some moments later, the dark figure appeared from behind a tree about twenty feet away from the couple. "My god, he's got a gun," Shepard said to Hartnell, who looked up and saw the man wearing a large, square-shaped black hood—like an executioner would wear—and a breastplate that had a circle-cross emblazoned on it. He had a bayonet-length knife sheathed to the left side of his belt, along with a loop of rope. A gun holster hung from the right of his belt, and he held a blue-steel semiautomatic pistol in his hand.

His pants were bloused into his military style boots. The man told the shocked couple that he wanted their car to drive to Mexico.

Hartnell, a sociology student, tried to keep the man calm by talking to him. But the man told him, "Time's running short. I'm an escaped convict from Deer Lodge, Montana. I've killed a prison guard there. I have a stolen car and nothing to lose. I'm flat broke."[2]

He instructed Hartnell to turn over and lie down on his stomach. He had Shepard throw Hartnell's wallet to him and then ordered the girl to hog-tie her friend. When she was done, the man hog-tied her on the ground in the same position and then retied Hartnell's binds more tightly. Hartnell asked the man if the gun was indeed loaded. The man silently popped open the gun and showed him the cartridge.

Moments later, the dark figure told them, "I'm going to have to stab you people." Hartnell later claimed that he asked the man to stab him first. He was told, "I'll do just that."[3]

Shepard screamed as she watched her friend getting stabbed repeatedly in the back. Then the man turned to her and began sticking her with his long knife, again and again—in her chest, in each breast, in her stomach and groin. Hartnell, helpless but still alive, lay silent and motionless until the man had satisfied his bloodlust and walked away, leaving the bloody couple for dead.

The executioner strode off to Hartnell's car, where he wrote the symbol of his circle-cross on the car door with a black felt-tipped pen. Beneath it he wrote:

VALLEJO
12-20-68
7-4-69
SEPT 27-69-6:30
BY KNIFE[4]

A little after 7:30, the Zodiac Killer placed a call to the Napa County Sheriff's office to alert them of the murder. "I want to report a murder . . . no, a double murder. They are two miles north of Park Headquarters. They were in a white Karmann Ghia. . . . I'm the one who did it."[5]

The Zodiac's information was incorrect; while Shepard would die of her grisly wounds two days later, Hartnell would survive and provide another eyewitness account of the mysterious killer that continued to terrorize northern California.

❀ ❀ ❀

Earlier in the year, park rangers at the Death Valley National Monument had clashed with hippies who had been recruited by director Michelangelo Antonioni for an outdoor love-in scene in his forthcoming film, *Zabriskie Point*. The film would follow two beautiful, young radicals (played by Daria Halprin, a UC Berkeley freshman and member of an avant-garde nude dance troupe, and Mark Frechette, a carpenter who had been living in an urban commune in Boston) who meet anonymously, perform revolutionary acts, and then part after a naked romp in the desert—a perfect representation of the mood at the decade's end. But the visions that Charles Manson had for launching his Death Valley apocalypse would capture the imagination of Americans more than any big-screen story.

The LAPD had announced on August 12 that they had ruled out any connection between the Tate and LaBianca murders. Four days later, the Spahn Ranch was raided, and Manson and twenty-five members of the Family had been arrested as suspects in an auto-theft ring, only to be released soon thereafter on a warrant technicality.

California Highway Patrolmen raided Spahn Ranch again on October 12, looking for stolen dune buggies and other contraband. "There are indications that Manson was about to undertake his wildest scheme of all: a series of assassinations of prominent Los Angeles citizens against whom he held grudges. The dune-buggy locusts would raid from The Hole, destroy, then return," Ed Sanders tells us.[6] The CHPs found Manson hiding in a bathroom cupboard and arrested him.

As Manson sat in jail in November, Susan Atkins, who had been implicated in the murder of Gary Hinman, began to spin a sinister tale of goings-on in the desert wastelands. She told two fellow inmates at the Sybil Brand Institute for Women in Los Angeles about the Tate and LaBianca murders. One of the women alerted the prison authorities, and Atkins was offered a plea bargain to avoid the death penalty in exchange for her testimony about the events of August 8 and 9.

The LAPD issued warrants for the arrests of Watson, Krenwinkel, and Kasabian. (Van Houten's connection would be established later.) On Decem-ber 1, police chief Edward Davis held a press conference in the auditorium at the LAPD headquarters announcing that the homicides of Tate, Sebring, Folger, Frykowski, Parent, and the LaBiancas had been solved. In the coming weeks, the entire nation would hear tales of the dark hippie messiah and the cult he had grown within the counterculture of California.

Paul Body, an area musician and doorman at the Troubadour Club, told author Michael Walker, "Once people found out that hippies were killing people, it was a whole different thing." Famed supergroupie Pamela Des Barres remembered, "The Manson murders changed the idea that hippies were safe, that hippies were harmless, that hippies could inflict no harm on anybody."

Gail Zappa said, "If you were surprised by the Manson murders, you weren't connected to what was going on in the canyon."[7]

❋ ❋ ❋

The Zodiac Killer struck again on October 11, this time under the Saturday-night lights of San Francisco. Just past 9:30 P.M., driver Paul Stine's cab was stuck in traffic in San Francisco's theater section when he was approached by a husky man wearing a dark jacket. Stine, a married English PhD student at San Francisco State University who drove a Yellow Cab at night to pick up extra money, was no doubt happy to pick up the fare. The man got in the backseat and told Stine to take him to a destination in the Presidio Heights section of the city.

When they arrived at the corner of Washington and Cherry streets, his fare leaned forward, pointed a gun into the right side of Stine's head, and pulled the trigger.

With Stine lying dead in the driver's seat, the man got out of the car and got back in on the front passenger side. As he sat in the front seat going through Stine's clothing, a group of teenagers saw the scene from a second-story window across the street. They called the San Francisco Police Department just before 10:00 P.M. and described a husky, white man wearing a dark jacket. The SFPD then sent out a bulletin to patrol units, but erroneously described the perpetrator as a "Negro male adult."[8]

Two officers in a patrol car in the area stopped a husky-looking man in dark clothes walking away from the scene and toward the Presidio army base just a block away. He was a white man. The officers asked him if he'd seen anything unusual, and the man pointed up the block and said he'd seen a man waving a gun and walking in the other direction. The officers headed off in search of the figure described but didn't find him.[9]

Three days later, the *San Francisco Chronicle* received another Zodiac letter. The envelope contained a piece of Stine's bloody shirt-tail, along with a handwritten letter that read:

> This is the Zodiac speaking. I am the murderer of the taxi driver over by Washington St + Maple St last night, to prove this here is a blood stained piece of his shirt. I am the same man who did in the people in the north bay area.

The S.F. Police could have caught me last night if they had searched the park properly instead of holding road races with their motorcicles [sic] seeing who could make the most noise. The car drivers should have just parked their cars and sat there quietly waiting for me to come out of cover.

School children make nice targets. I think I shall wipe out a school bus some morning. Just shoot out the front tire + then pick off the kiddies as they come bouncing out.[10]

The *Chronicle* waited until the police allowed it to be published, which they did on Friday, October 17. An emergency bulletin was sent out to the superintendents of area schools, and children were accompanied by armed police escorts, highway patrol cars, and even Cessna aircraft on their way to and from school.

Then, around 2:00 in the morning on October 22, the operator at the Oakland Police Department received a call from a man claiming to be the Zodiac Killer. He demanded that one of the nation's two most famous lawyers, F. Lee Bailey and Melvin Belli, appear on the Channel Seven morning talk show so that he could call in and talk to him. Bailey was unavailable, but Belli was reached at his opulent penthouse on Telegraph Hill, and arrangements were made for him to appear on the show. For the event, the show started a half-hour earlier than its usual 7:00 A.M. time slot. With host Jim Dunbar urging viewers to keep the lines open, a man placed several calls and spoke with Belli at intervals of no longer than nine minutes before hanging up. Belli asked if the caller could give him a less-ominous name to use, and the caller offered "Sam."

"I don't want to go to the gas chamber. I have headaches. If I kill I don't get them," the caller said.

"I wouldn't think that they'd ask for capital punishment. We should ask the district attorney. You want me to do that, Sam? You want me to talk to the district attorney?"

There was a small scream on the phone.

"What was that?" Belli asked.

"I did not say anything. That was my headache," said Sam.[11]

In a call that took place off the air, Belli agreed to meet Sam at a location in Daly City. Belli showed up—followed by police, television and radio crews, reporters, and photographers. They waited for forty-five minutes, but Sam never showed up. Subsequent calls to Belli from Sam were traced to the Napa State Hospital, where it was learned they had been placed not by the Zodiac but by a mental patient there.

On November 8 and 9, the real Zodiac mailed separate letters to the *Chronicle*, both of which included swatches of Stine's shirt. In the first, written on a humorous greeting card, he wrote, "I thought you would need a good laugh before you hear the bad news, and you won't get the bad news for a while yet." He boasted of having killed again:

> Des [sic] July Aug
> Sept Oct = 7[12]

Police would never definitively establish who the "7" included. The letter also included a cryptogram, but this one would never be solved.

In the second letter, seven pages long, he recounted his being stopped by the two policemen after the Stine murder. He railed against the police and warned of his future activities: "I have grown rather angry with the police for their telling lies about me. So I shall change the way the collecting of slaves [sic]. I shall no longer announce to anyone when I committ [sic] my murders; they shall look like routine robberies, killings of anger, & a few fake accidents, etc."[13]

The Zodiac (or Zodiac copycats) would continue to send letters to newspaper editors in the ensuing years, claiming as many as thirty-seven total victims, though no additional murder would be conclusively attributed to the mysterious murderer. The identity of the Zodiac Killer remains a mystery to this day.

1969

❊ ❊ ❊

While police were trying to unravel the Zodiac mystery, music fans were looking for clues in Beatles song lyrics and album covers to decipher whether Paul McCartney was dead. According to an urban legend that circulated throughout the American pop media that fall, McCartney had died in a car crash in 1966 and had been replaced secretly in the group by the winner of a Paul McCartney lookalike contest. Rumors of McCartney's demise had sprouted earlier in the UK but were first printed in an article in the Drake University student newspaper on September 17, 1969. On October 12, an Eastern Michigan University student called Detroit disc jockey Russ Gibb to declare McCartney was dead; as proof, he had the DJ play "Revolution No. 9" from the White Album backward to produce the backward-masked words "Turn me on, dead man."

Michigan University student Fred LaBour then wrote an article for the college paper outlining the "Paul Is Dead" theory. The article was reprinted in campus papers nationwide, and fans searched with morbid fascination for clues that would lead them to uncover the answer of McCartney's supposed death. Some listeners said they heard the phrase "I buried Paul" at the end of "Strawberry Fields."

The cover of *Abbey Road* further fueled the rumors. The image of the four crossing the street was interpreted as a symbolic funeral: Lennon, dressed all in white, is the cleric leading the procession; behind him is Starr, dressed in an undertaker's suit; McCartney, walking barefoot and walking out of step with the other three (he's shown leading with his right foot while the others lead with their left) is the departed; and Harrison, bringing up the rear in a denim shirt and jeans, is the gravedigger. The license plate on the Volkswagen parked on the curb contains the letters *28IF*— supposedly the age he would have been if he had not died. This last "clue" illustrated how eager people were to believe in this fantastic tale; in reality, he was twenty-seven in the fall of 1969.

The rumors were so prevalent that the mainstream media picked up the story. Esteemed NBC news anchor John Chancellor discussed the legend and said, "All we can report with certainty is that Paul McCartney is either dead or alive." *Life* eventually sent a team of journalists to Scotland to track down the Beatle during a vacation. He appeared—living and breathing—with wife Linda and their two children on the cover of the November 7 issue, under the headline PAUL IS STILL WITH US.[14]

Meanwhile, as McCartney returned to the ranks of the living, Mick Jagger had taken to playing the role of Satan. The cover of the group's *Their Satanic Majesties Request* album had depicted Jagger as a mystical wizard in a dark robe and conical hat. On the epic "Sympathy for the Devil" from *Beggars Banquet*, a first-person narrative written by Jagger, he sang in the first-person voice of Lucifer while bragging about his legacy of destruction throughout history. Even the Greek letter emblazoned on the black shirt he wore on the band's 1969 U. S. tour spoke to something sinister—Omega, the symbol of the last, the end. The *Get Yer Ya-Ya's Out* live album from the tour would famously record a fan shouting a request to Jagger: "'Paint It Black,' you devil!"

The year 1969 represented a creative peak for the Rolling Stones. With the *Beggars Banquet* album climbing well into the Top Ten, the band spent most of the year recording tracks for the classic *Let It Bleed* (the band's third consecutive December release). Then, just before the release of that album, they headed down to the Muscle Shoals Sound Studio in Alabama to begin sessions for what would become the classic *Sticky Fingers* (released in 1971).

But it was also the most controversial year in the band's history. Brian Jones had become increasingly disinterested and undependable, and he was making less and less of a contribution to the group in the studio. In June, after Jones was refused a visa for the band's U. S. tour, he was kicked out of the band. On July 3, Jones's body was discovered at the bottom of his swimming pool at his home in East

Sussex, England, the first in a series of tragic rock 'n' roll deaths over the next two years.

The Stones went on with their plans to give a free concert to be held on July 5 at London's Hyde Park, where the group Blind Faith had given its debut performance just one month prior. The group debuted their new lineup, featuring Jones's replacement, the twenty-year-old former John Mayall & the Bluesbreakers guitarist Mick Taylor. The Stones dedicated the concert to Jones and played before a crowd ranging in estimates from 250,000 to 500,000 people.

Experimental filmmaker Kenneth Anger was on hand to film the band. Born in Santa Monica in 1927, Anger had a fascination with the occult, and his work was influenced by the life and philosophy of Aleister Crowley, the British occultist who preached a life of hedonism and "sex magick." Since his youth, Anger had also been friends with Anton LaVey, who in 1966 founded the Church of Satan.

In 1969, LaVey published *The Satanic Bible*, a collection of essays, rituals, and invocations that outlined the core principles of LaVey's church. Despite its provocatively dark title, LaVey's bible was not so much an invocation of evil as it was an argument against all "religionists," and an argument for an ideology of base human gratification as influenced by Crowley's occultism, the Social Darwinism of Ragnar Redbeard, and Ayn Rand's Objectivism. LaVey, dubbed the "Black Pope," laid out the core teachings of his church in his "Nine Satanic Statements":

1) Satan represents indulgence, instead of abstinence!

2) Satan represents vital existence, instead of spiritual pipe dreams!

3) Satan represents undefiled wisdom, instead of hypocritical self-deceit!

4) Satan represents kindness to those who deserve it, instead of love wasted on ingrates!

5) Satan represents vengeance, instead of turning the other cheek!

6) Satan represents responsibility to the responsible, instead of concern for public vampires!

7) Satan represents man as just another animal, sometimes better, more often worse than those that walk on all-fours, who, because of his "divine spiritual and intellectual development," has become the most vicious animal of all!

8) Satan represents all of the so-called sins, as they all lead to physical, mental, or emotional gratification!

9) Satan has been the best friend the church has ever had, as he has kept it in business all these years!

In 1967 during the Summer of Love, Anger had filmed LaVey during a "satanic mass" at his church in San Francisco for a project that carried the working title *Lucifer Rising*. One of the other actors Anger had cast in the film was Bobby Beausoleil, who would later find himself auditioning for a role in Helter Skelter. Anger included scenes from this footage in *Invocation of My Demon Brother*. Jagger wrote the music for the film, and his dissonant and unsettling synthesizer track perfectly matched the demonic mood of Anger's work.

After holding rehearsals on the set of *They Shoot Horses, Don't They?* at Warner Bros. Studios, the Stones began their 1969 American tour on November 7 at Colorado State University. It was their first tour of the States in three years, and a Stones concert was a hot ticket. The rock concert scene had changed since 1966. Concerts were no longer spectator events at which audience members were content to sit or stand and passively watch the performance. By 1969, American crowds had become a *part* of the performance, and they wanted a piece of their favorite bands. More and more, the compressed groups of humanity seemed to lead to violence. After Blind Faith's well-received Hyde Park debut, the band's U. S. debut at Madison Square Garden on July 12 was marred by a half-hour-long riot, during which Ginger Baker was clubbed on the head by a cop and Winwood's piano was destroyed. "Somehow," said Keith Richards, "in America in '69 . . . one got the feeling they really want to suck you out."[15] When they got to America in late 1969, the Stones found that fans really did want to suck as much out of them as they could.

Author Stanley Booth reflects, "The tour had been different from any of their previous ones. Up until then their performances in the U. S. had been brief, incandescent explosions of desecration, attended almost exclusively by shrieking adolescent girls. On the 1969 tour they played longer sets than they'd done since playing English clubs, and the American fans—people their own age, many of them—listened."[16]

Stanley Goldstein, who collaborated with the Maysles brothers in their filming of the Stones's American tour, remembered the sparks in the air for the shows at Madison Square Garden at the end of November:

> The feeling at Madison Square Garden was quite extraordinary. The Stones hadn't toured in a number of years . . . and were the most eagerly awaited of groups except possibly for a reunion of The Beatles. So there was just great excitement. The tickets were in extraordinary demand. It was a phenomenal crush. It started with a crush toward the front of the stage that you would have normally expected near the end of a concert, and then it simply grew from that . . .[17]

With demand for their tickets running high, the Stones had charged as much as $15 per ticket, something for which Ralph Gleason took them to task in the pages of *Rolling Stone*. The Grateful Dead's manager, Rock Scully, suggested to the Stones that they play a free concert in San Francisco, and the band took to the idea. Plans went into motion for a "Woodstock West" to be held at Golden Gate Park on Saturday, December 6, with the Stones to headline a free festival that also included popular bands from the Bay area: Santana, Jefferson Airplane, The Flying Burrito Brothers, Crosby, Stills & Nash, and the Grateful Dead. Reports differ on whether or not a permit had yet been secured for the Park, but when Jagger made a public announcement about the band's planned "surprise" performance, Golden Gate officials either denied or revoked the permit. The organizers turned to the Sears Point Raceway in the Sonoma Mountains, and a construction crew began setting up stage facilities there. There was a dispute over film rights to the show between the Stones—who were already filming their tour—and the owners of Sears Point, Filmways, Inc., and once again plans fell through.

It would be a busy season for Mel Belli. In addition to his involvement in the Zodiac media spectacle—and working with the defense in the Manson case—the "King of Torts" led a group that represented the Stones in their hectic search to find the West Coast version of Yasgur's Farm. Just two days before the scheduled festival, an agreement was reached with Dick Carter, the owner of the Altamont Speedway, who offered free use of his grounds. "I want the publicity," Carter told Belli.[18] The organizers quickly packed up and moved everything downstate to Carter's speedway in Livermore.

Michael Lang, who was brought in to spin his Woodstock magic on the West Coast, was asked if there was enough room at the new site for the anticipated influx of humanity. "I think we have the room, sure. I think we can hold as many people as want to come," he said in his laid-back way. But could they get everything set up in

time? "Well, we had a much bigger operation to change at Woodstock.
I don't think we'll have much problem."[19]

✽ ✽ ✽

As volunteers worked through Friday night in the 30° weather setting up the makeshift stage and scaffolding, thousands of kids from
across the country had already begun arriving and setting up camp
on the barren hillscapes near the speedway. "All day Friday, the Bay
Area radio stations were telling people to stay away, that you wouldn't
be able to get in anyway . . ." remembered author and photographer
David Dalton. "By early Saturday morning when the gates were
opened, the surrounding hills were covered with people, encamp-
ments and cars. Down on the highway, traffic was backed up six
miles in either direction."[20]

In flooded carfuls of kids in their teens and twenties, somewhere
between 300,000 and 350,000 of them, all hopeful witnesses to the
last big happening of the year. "You have no idea what goes on here,"
concert promoter Bill Graham had told Belli's group. "It's an amazing phenomenon. It's like the lemmings to the sea."[21] They converged
like they had at Woodstock, but this was no bucolic summer setting.
Dalton wrote:

> You couldn't have a more apocalyptic theater. . . . from
> the air there seemed to be something ominous about such a
> massive gathering on these bald hills. . . . the bleached-out
> hills around Altamont looked metallic in the haze and glare
> of the morning sun. . . . And there was something swarming
> and ominous about this gathering—kinetic energy zinged
> through the air like psychic pellets. The place was a war zone.
> The state of the Altamont site was unimaginably appalling, a
> mini Vietnam of garbage and old car wrecks. This, com-
> bined with the steep grade of the canyon slope, resulted in
> stoned people rolling downhill onto the stage.[22]

And then in came the Hells Angels. The Angels existed on the darker fringes of the West Coast counterculture and had earned the status of outlaw heroes in the popular culture from Hunter Thompson's nonfiction novel, *Hells Angels*, and B movies like *Hell's Angels '69*, which featured such legendary real-life Angels as Sonny Barger and Terry the Tramp in the role of outlaw motorcycle gang members. They showed up at Altamont from all over northern California, the hard-core, self-touted "one-percenters" from local chapters like Oakland and Frisco.

In a vague agreement that would be debated endlessly by both parties, Stones tour manager Sam Cutler apparently told representatives of the Angels that they could congregate near the stage in exchange for $500 worth of beer. Up until then, Angels had had a prominent presence in the San Francisco concert scene. According to Stanley Goldstein:

> [T]he Hells Angels had traditionally had an area that they established at these outdoor venues and that they were asked to establish or agreed to establish around the techie equip, around the generator, around the equip truck, and so forth, and that just by their presence they kind of ensured security of those areas; they weren't hired security, but they were there, that was Hells Angels territory. . . . and in return for their presence, a few cases of beer would be presented to them by the concert promoter or whoever the group was that was putting on the show, and so this was an arrangement that had become, it was an unspoken agreement that had been worked out over the years—that an area offstage right or stage left would be screened off, and would be Angel land, and within Angel land, house security didn't go; people that went into Angel land went in at their own risk and came out however they came out.[23]

What Cutler didn't understand, though, was that Hells Angels in America were a different type altogether from the Angels he'd seen in Hyde Park. "English Hells Angels at their best or at their worst certainly bore only the faintest resemblance to Hells Angels from California," Goldstein remembered.[24] The ones that showed up at Altamont were the real thing, and since there was an officers' meeting of area Angels Saturday during the day, the brigade of Angels who showed up first at Altamont Speedway were the pledges and newer Angels—the ones who were most eager to show they had what it took.

In an issue devoted to Altamont in January, *Rolling Stone* reported:

> Mid-morning on Saturday, Berkeley people laid what looked like a thousand tabs of sunshine acid on the Angels— not good sunshine: it had a lot of speed in it—and this was being dispersed both at the Angels' bus thirty yards uphill and on the stage. At one point, 500 reds were scattered on the front portion of the stage. The Angels were downing tabs of acid/speed and reds in huge gulps of red Mountain wine.[25]

Angels and hippies and alcohol and drugs—it was a combustible mix. Sonny Barger, a founding member of the Oakland Hells Angels, would later write:

> The people who were the most fucked up on drugs were the ones who got to Altamont first—the so-called Friday-nighters—the ones who camped a day earlier to get a good seat. They'd been exposed to the open air and hot sun for hours on end. They'd staked their territory up front. When we came in on our bikes, they wouldn't give up their space. But . . . they moved. We made sure of that. We pushed them back about forty feet.[26]

The day had evolved into barely organized chaos. The eerie silhouettes of fans climbing the hastily constructed scaffolding might have reminded one of the Tower of Babel just before the confusion of tongues. Cutler spoke into the stage mic in his polite, authoritarian British accent and asked them to climb back down from the scaffolding, but he had less success in getting people off the stage. Unlike the natural amphitheater of the Woodstock stage, the stage at Altamont was only a few feet high and easily accessible to anyone who felt the need to climb onto it. Crew members, Angels, hangers-on—they surrounded the musicians during their sets and created a sense of pandemonium throughout much of the day. "The concert's like the proscenium of a theater. It's like an excuse for everyone to get together," Mick Jagger had said on the eve of Altamont, but now the proscenium had been torn down, and the crowd had become part of the performance.[27]

Jefferson Airplane took the stage amid the confusion and bad vibes. The group had released the album *Volunteers* in November, and just as *Surrealistic Pillow* embodied the spirit of 1967, *Volunteers* captured the kaleidoscope of forces shaping America in 1969. *Rolling Stone*'s David Fricke writes, "It took just two years for the folk-rock shimmer and Camelot optimism of *Surrealistic Pillow* . . . to harden into the black and temper of *Volunteers*, the band's requiem for an America under Nixon."[28] Jim Newsom for *AllMusic* called the album "a powerful release that neatly closed out and wrapped up the '60s" on which the band "presents itself in full revolutionary rhetoric, issuing a call to 'tear down the walls' and 'get it on together.'"[29]

Woven within the sweet San Francisco–style harmonies of the opening track, "We Can Be Together," is an anthemic statement of class war, lawlessness, and anarchy. It's the band's call to join the revolution, a self-righteous statement of social anarchy ("We are all outlaws in the eyes of America . . . and we are very proud of ourselves") and a neo-Marxist warning ("All your private property is target for your enemy"), peppered with the late-sixties radical motto, "Up against the wall, motherfucker." The album's closer, "Volunteers," announced "Got a revolution, got to revolution," and drew the battle lines down the middle of the generation gap: "One generation got old / One generation got soul." In between these bookend anthems were standout tracks like the back-to-the-land hippie fantasy of "The Farm," "Eskimo Blue Day" (described by Fricke as a "prophetic eco-drama" in which Grace Slick's voice is "shivering with apocalyptic dread"), and the postapocalyptic "Wooden Ships," a song cowritten by Paul Kantner, David Crosby, and Stephen Stills. (Crosby, Stills & Nash also recorded it for their debut album). The song summons up the ecological despair of an imagined barren landscape after a future war. "Can you tell me please who won?" the singer asks someone from the "other side."

As Jefferson Airplane performed their set at Altamont, they must have wondered what side everyone was on. Angels began scuffling with non-Angels at the front of the stage. Grace Slick stopped singing and yelled "No! No!" at the combatants, then tried to mollify those in the pit by hypnotically saying, "*Please* be quiet . . . *please* be quiet*." A heavy and bearded Semitic-looking man tried to talk some sense into the Angels, and they beat him to the ground. Vocalist Marty Balin, wearing a cowboy hat and red bandana, grew incensed as he looked down from the stage at the fighting. First he threw a tambourine at someone in the ruckus, probably an Angel, and then he made the decision to jump offstage and into the fray. Once down in "Angel land," he ceased being a rock star and became just another non-Angel—in other words, fair game. The next thing the crowd heard was Paul Kantner speaking into his mic: "Hey, man, I'd like to mention that the Hells Angels just, uh, smashed Marty Balin in the face and knocked him out for a bit. I'd like to thank you for that."[30]

It was a verbal challenge to the Angels. One of the hairier, scarier-looking ones walked onstage. "Is this on?" he said as he grabbed a mic, and then he challenged Kantner: "You're talking to me, I'm gonna talk to you."

"I'm not talking to you," Kantner said. "I'm talking to the people who hit my lead singer in the head."

"You're talking to my people. Let me tell you what's happenin'. *You* are what's happenin," said the Angel. "You know what's happenin'? We're partying like *you*."

Marty reappeared onstage dazed from the blow he'd taken to the head. The Airplane had to cut things short. The Flying Burrito Brothers' set was also interrupted by violence, and Graham Parsons had to beg those in front of the stage, "Please stop hurting each other." When the Grateful Dead got wind of what was going on, they canceled their performance and got the hell out of Livermore.

❁ ❁ ❁

Shortly after Mick Jagger arrived by helicopter and was making his way to the trailer, a young guy, most likely on a bad trip, ran up to him through the crowd and hit the singer. "I hate you!" the kid said as he was restrained by security. Mick looked at him dazed, wondering how this stranger at a free concert could have such contempt toward him. He remained in the safety of his trailer, joined by then-girlfriend Marianne Faithfull.

As soon as Bill Wyman showed up, the band took the stage at night courtesy of a path that the Angels cleared with their bikes. The crowd had endured the scene at Altamont all day, and now they looked to move front and center. Barger remembered, "When the Stones came out onstage, people moved back in toward the roped-in area where our bikes were parked, trying to jump on the stage. In response, we began pushing them off the stage. Plus, they were messing with our bikes."[31]

Jagger, in his plush pants and red-and-black satin shirt with long, streaming sleeves, performing flamboyant gestures as he primped and pranced around stage during the band's set, looked part pirate, part Gypsy, part peacock—the perfect antithesis to the burly bikers in leather vests around him. After "Jumpin' Jack Flash" and "Carol," the Stones launched into "Sympathy for the Devil." It was during the band's Satanic epic that violence in front of the stage was incited once again.

A fan was kneeling on the seat of a Frisco Hell's Angel's bike, causing the seat springs to come into contact with the battery posts and shorting it out. The battery was right next to the oil tank.

Staney Booth writes, "As Mick sang, 'I was around when Jesus Christ had his moment of doubt and pain,' a motorcycle near the right side of the stage suffered a small explosion. Oily blue-white smoke swirled up, and a space opened almost instantly, the people moving away from the trouble. You could see violent movement in the darkness, but no details."[32]

Angels went out into the crowd and began pushing and beating people. Barger recalled, "While we secured the stage, some of the people who had been hit and pushed got mad and started throwing bottles at us and really started messing with our bikes." He continued: "Big mistake. That's when we entered the crowd and grabbed some of the assholes vandalizing our bikes and beat the fuck out of them."[33]

Jagger, performing in the role of Satan, stopped singing and looked out at the chaos in the darkness. One Angel yelled something angrily at drummer Charlie Watts, as if he was blaming the band for the mess. Jagger addressed the crowd: "Hey, people. Brothers and sisters. Brothers and sisters. Come on now. That means everybody just *cool out*. Will you cool out, everybody?"

"Something very funny happens when we start that number," he observed, and then they started the song again from the beginning. To highlight the chaos, a dog (a hound of hell?) walked across the stage in front of Jagger. The band made it to the instrumental bridge, and then the fighting started up once again. Jagger momentarily stopped his dancing and watched helplessly. One guy near the front of the stage shook his head and stared at the singer, as if looking for Jagger to take control of the chaos. A girl sitting on the front of the stage looked up at him with tears streaming from her eyes.

Unsure of what to do, Jagger broke into a rooster dance until the end of the song, when the fighting began again. Finally, he said, "Uh, people, who's fighting, and what for? Who's fighting and what for. Why are we fighting? Why are we fighting? We don't want to fight, come on. Do we want—Who wants to fight?"

Keith Richards pointed at someone down below and yelled, "Look, that guy there, if he doesn't stop it, man—Listen, either those cats cool it, man, or we don't play." Then an Angel yelled into the mic and threatened to turn the whole bus around: "Hey, if you don't cool it, you ain't gonna hear no music! Now you wanna all go home or what?"

"Don't let's fuck it up, man," Jagger urged. "Come on, let's get it together. I can't do any more than just ask you, than to beg you to keep it together. You can do it; it's within your power. Everyone, Hells Angels, everybody. You know, if we *are* all one, then let's *show* we're all one," he pleaded.

The scuffling subsided until "Under My Thumb," the Stones comically misogynistic hit from 1966. As the band ground out a slow and fierce version of the song, a man standing next to the head of the Frisco Angels chapter started writhing in the throes of a bad acid trip. In retrospect, his demonic facial contortions seemed to be warning the crowd of impending doom.

At the end of the song, another scuffle began down in front.

"We're splitting, man, if those cats don't stop beating up everybody in sight," said Keith Richards. "I want 'em out of the way, man."

An Angel ran over to tell Richards, "A guy's got a gun out there. He's shooting at the stage."

What the band couldn't see—but what viewers of the documentary *Gimme Shelter* would see in chilling detail—was that a man had just been killed. While no one seems to remember a gun actually being fired, what is known is that Meredith Hunter, an eighteen-year-old black man who was at the concert with a white girlfriend, Patty Bredahoff, and a group of Angels got into a scuffle. As the rest of the crowd in the immediate vicinity stepped back and formed a sudden clearing, Hunter reached within his lime-green suit jacket and drew out a pistol. Alan Passaro, a twenty-one-year-old Hells Angel, came flying at Hunter, swinging a knife in a lethal, over-handed motion, and stabbed him in the right shoulder blade. Passaro wrestled him to the ground and stabbed him again, this time in the back. Hunter's body was ushered off to the side, much like the bodies of other injured parties from the violence of earlier in the day.

The Stones, unaware of what had just happened, continued their set, debuting the song "Brown Sugar" while Hunter lay dying. When doctors arrived, Hunter was pronounced dead at the scene, and his corpse was flown away by helicopter.

Hunter was just one of four people who died at the Altamont. Around midnight, festivalgoers Mark Feiger and Richard Savlov were killed when the driver of a Plymouth sedan plowed into a campfire and hit them and several others. Meanwhile, the body of a "John Doe" was found after he slid down an irrigation canal on the speedway grounds and drowned. By one estimate, 850 suffered injuries in the fighting and chaos. As Cutler would recall nearly four decades later, the scene at Altamont "got completely out of hand. It was a peculiar version of American madness."[34]

Immediately afterward, the media rushed to make sense of what had happened. Stefan Ponek of KSAN Radio in San Francisco hosted a show the following day to report on the deaths and violence and mayhem. Sam Cutler called in, trying to defuse the situation, but Barger's call to the station resulted in a rambling diatribe against the Stones ("This Mick Jagger, like, he used us for dupes, man"), and the hippie fans who had not given the Angels a wide-enough berth: "Ain't nobody gonna kick my motorcycle. . . . When you're standing there looking at something that's your life, and everything you've got is so much invested in it, and you love it more than anything else in the world, and you see somebody kick it. . . . you're gonna get him. And you know what? They got *got*."[35]

Rolling Stone magazine would help create the infamy of Altamont, errone-ously reporting that Hunter was killed during the perfor-mance of "Sympathy for the Devil." Its description of the scene ren-dered it into something out of the Dark Ages: "Flickering silhouettes of people trying to find warmth around the blazing track reminded one of the medieval paintings of tortured souls in the Dance of Death. . . . It was in this atmosphere that Mick sang about how groovy it is to be Satan. Never has it been sung in a more appropriate setting."[36] The *Berkeley Tribe* bemoaned, "Bringing a lot of people together used to be cool. But at Altamont . . . the locust generation came to consume crumbs from the hands of an entertainment industry we helped to create. . . . Everybody grooved on fear."[37] Michael Lydon's article in *Ramparts* concluded, "At Altamont in December, the dark side snarled its ugly answer to Woodstock's August joy. . . . We all seemed beyond the law at Altamont, out there willingly, all 300,000 of us, Stones and Angels included, and on our own."[38]

Passaro was indicted for the murder of Meredith Hunter but acquitted on the grounds of self-defense. In 2007, former FBI agent Mark Young revealed in a BBC documentary that the Angels had plotted to assassinate Jagger on the property of his Long Island home in December 1969 as "retribution" for the Altamont incident. According to Young, the murder plot involved the Angels rowing out to Jagger's home by the Long Island Sound, but a storm short-circuited their attempt. "As they gathered the weaponry and their forces to go out on Long Island Sound, a storm rolled up, which nearly sunk the watercraft that they were in, and they escaped with their own lives."[39]

❀ ❀ ❀

Was Altamont, as some have written, the death of the sixties? David Dalton writes, "Altamont has become the apocalyptic moment known as the end of the sixties, the moment when the termite-riddled walls of the New Jerusalem finally came tumbling down." The free concert held in Livermore has come to represent the antithesis of Aquarian Exposition at Bethel. But like most labels, this is a huge oversimplification. "Woodstock was no more peace and love than Altamont was. They were the result of the same disease: the bloating of late sixties mass bohemia. At that point, Mercury, the patron saint of merchants and thieves, takes over, all hell breaks loose, and the Devil starts setting up his bleachers out on Highway 61."[40]

The seeds of Altamont had been sown throughout the year, if not throughout the entire decade. The Airplane had sung of anarchy and the Stones of violent revolution, and in the last month of the last year of the decade, they came face-to-face with the culture that they had helped to create. Rockers, bikers, lovers, radicals, peaceniks, and psychedelic stoners—they had been at Woodstock, too, had been there in one form or another throughout the sixties. These were The People, the people who were all one, the people who would never be all one again.

EPILOGUE: FUTURE SHOCK—THE SEVENTIES AND BEYOND

The world did not end. The modern American society that we know today was just beginning.

In 1969, the first Automatic Teller Machine (ATM) was installed in the wall outside of a Chemical Bank in Rockville Center, New York. Don Wetzel conceived of the idea while waiting in line at a bank in Dallas, and he patented the design with mechanical engineer Tom Barnes and electrical engineer George Chastain. This first machine was designed for account holders to only make withdrawals, but it was the prototype for the full service ATMs of today that allow transactions twenty-four hours a day.

The world was about to get smaller, more connected. The ARPANET would—with time—expand exponentially. The ARPANET would not evolve into the commercial Internet for another generation, but since then, the technology that it foreshadowed has influenced the day-to-day lives of people throughout the world more than any other modern invention or innovation.

Techno-urban legend would hold that the ARPANET emerged as a way to keep computer systems connected in the event of nuclear war. Looking to avoid a global apocalypse, Washington and Moscow entered into negotiations in November 1969 for the first in a series of summits known as the Strategic Arms Limitation Talks (SALT). The Americans and Soviets forged the Anti-Ballistic Missile Treaty that

1969

Nixon and Leonid Brezhnev signed in May 1972—the first important step toward easing tensions in the Cold War. Following Sino-Soviet border clashes in 1969, Nixon would also take a huge step in normalizing diplomatic relations with China during his weeklong visit in February 1972.

The United States launched a joint incursion with South Vietnamese forces into Cambodia in 1970, this time with Nixon announcing the operation to the American public. Antiwar activism continued on the home front. During a campus protest at Kent State University on May 4, 1970, four students were killed and nine wounded by Ohio National Guardsmen. The following year, RAND employee Daniel Ellsberg leaked a top-secret Department of Defense study dubbed "The Pentagon Papers" that documented a history of public deceptions and unconstitutional acts on the part of the White House.

Although support for the war continued to erode, Nixon rode a wave of popularity following his trip to China and swamped Democratic nominee George McGovern, the candidate of "amnesty, abortion and acid," to win reelection in 1972. In January 1973, Nixon announced the suspension of operations against North Vietnam, and the U. S. signed the Paris Peace Accords later that month. An American presence remained in the region until April 1975, when the last Americans departed from the embassy in Saigon just hours before North Vietnamese troops poured into the city. That year, Pol Pot and the genocidal Khmer Rouge, one of the most abhorrent regimes in human history, came to power in Cambodia amid the political volatility that the war had brought to the country.

By then, Nixon had left office in disgrace. The White House tapes that he had recorded secretly, in part to monitor leaks following press reports of Operation Menu, came back to bite the president during the Watergate hearings. Americans squirmed when they saw their president ineloquently announce on television, "People have got to know whether or not their President is a crook. Well, I'm not a crook." But to avoid impeachment he resigned as president and left the White House on April 22, 1974. The imperial presidency was over.

In the last week of December 1969, the Weathermen held a "War Council" meeting in Flint, Michigan, to draft a new platform that consisted of orchestrated acts of sabotage against government and law enforcement. Operating now under the name of the Weather Underground Organization, the group began to stockpile explosives for a campaign of bombings throughout the nation. On March 6, 1970, WUO members were constructing a nail-bomb in a Greenwich Village townhouse when the device went off, killing three members. That May, the underground group released a communiqué to the media entitled a "Declaration of a State of War," read by Bernardine Dohrn. In the coming years, the WUO claimed responsibility for the bombing of military and police buildings, courthouses, financial and corporate institutions, the United States Capitol Building, the Pentagon, and the State Department. The same month that Nixon left office, another urban guerrilla group, the Symbionese Liberation Army, made news when a UC Berkeley undergraduate that the group had kidnapped, magazine heiress Patty Hearst, recorded a statement announcing that she had joined the ranks of her captors. She was caught on surveillance camera participating in a bank robbery in the Sunset District of Los Angeles.

The 1970s would be a hallmark era for the "Women's Lib" movement and the second wave of feminism. In 1969, while the *New York Times* was still listing engagement notices for young women who had been "affianced to" their future grooms, both Yale and Princeton admitted their first class of female students. Further underlining the move toward coeducational opportunities, "Seven Sisters" school Vassar College admitted males for the first time. In 1973, the

Supreme Court under Warren Berger, whom Nixon had appointed in 1969, passed *Roe v. Wade*, a landmark decision in the feminist movement.

The Black Panther Party collapsed in the early 1970s as a result of the FBI's systemic campaigns and infighting among competing leaders within Panther ranks. But black American culture would rise in the American consciousness, and a generation of blacks would gain prominent positions on college campuses and in the corporate sector.

Richard Nixon announced an end to the policy of termination in favor of "self-determination" for Native Americans. He appointed Louis Bruce, a Mohawk-Sioux, to the post of Commissioner for Native American Affairs; Bruce's first order of business was to help reclaim tribal land. The Department of the Interior took over Alcatraz Island and turned it into a national park, and the federal government gave the deed to several hundred acres of land near Davis, California to American Indians and Mexican Americans to establish Deganawidah-Quetzalcoatl University. The American Indian Movement gained momentum and staged the Trail of Broken Treaties campaign in 1972. In 1973, a seventy-one-day standoff at the Pine Ridge Reservation at Wounded Knee, South Dakota, between Oglala Sioux and federal lawmen was marked by gun battles that led to the death of two Sioux and the paralysis of a U. S. marshal. The Oglala Incident would stand as a rallying cry for the movement. With the Self-Determination and Education Assistance Act of 1975 and the Indian Child Welfare Act of 1978, tribal governments gained added jurisdiction over Native American policies.

The back-to-the-land movement peaked in the early 1970s but then began to wane. Almost invariably, communes fell prey to the most fundamental of human flaws—jealousy, which came hand in hand with the sharing of property, lovers, and offspring. Many counterculturalists transferred their activism to environmental concerns as the Green Power movement was strengthened by the

Environmental Protection Agency and the Clean Air Act of 1970, along with a nationwide antilittering campaign most memorably symbolized by the famous "Crying Indian" television spots.

The oil crises of 1973 and 1979, the toxic contamination of Love Canal, and the Three Mile Island nuclear accident in 1979, inspired erstwhile hippies to lead the search for alternative forms of energy, including solar power. As an elementary school student in upstate New York, I met a group of long-haired students from the local college who came to our classroom to encourage us to write letters to our local assemblyman in protest of a planned nuclear power plant. They took us on a field trip to see the collective they had established in a solar-powered A-frame on campus.

Science fiction had me daydreaming of interstellar wars, but by then, man's journey to other points in the solar system had taken a backseat to other NASA programs. The *Apollo 12* mission in November 1969 had been an enormous *technical* success. Despite the *Saturn V* rocket having its computer systems knocked offline shortly after liftoff—it was later discovered the spacecraft had been hit by a bolt of lightning!—astronauts Dick Gordon, Pete Conrad, and Alan Bean were able to continue on their mission and achieve a pinpoint landing on the moon's *Oceanus Procellarum* (the "Ocean of Storms"), just 600 feet from the *Surveyor 3* probe that had landed there in 1967. But in a culture where finishing second is often equated with finishing last, Americans' interest was not as great in the second mission to the moon. NASA lost a huge public relations opportunity when a special camera that had been designed to transmit color images for television broadcast was ruined when, during its installation, Bean inadvertently pointed it directly into the unfiltered rays of the sun.

With the lofty goal of a moon landing having already been achieved, the federal government reevaluated the program. There had been twenty planned Apollo missions, but in early January 1970, NASA announced that *Apollo 20* had been canceled so that its *Saturn*

V rocket could instead be used in the Skylab program. Two additional Apollo missions were canceled later in the year. In December 1972, *Apollo 17* became the final manned lunar mission. To this day, Gene Cernan remains the last astronaut to walk on the surface of the moon. After three manned missions to the space station, *Skylab* came crashing back down to earth in 1979.

A science fiction movie for the ages would spell the end of the American New Wave in cinema. Directors from the New Hollywood School produced such hits as *The Last Picture Show, The Godfather, Mean Streets, Badlands*, and *Dog Day Afternoon*. But summer hits like *Jaws*, and, more famously, *Star Wars*, showed movie studios just how many viewers they could reach with huge, special-effects-laden films surrounded by vast promotional campaigns and merchandising.

The music industry grew into an album-oriented culture that yielded megahits like *Led Zeppelin IV, Dark Side of the Moon, Born to Run, Frampton Comes Alive!, Rumours*, and *Hotel California*. The indulgences of arena rock and progressive "art" rock spawned reactionary movements in the burgeoning punk scene, highlighted by Patti Smith, the Ramones, and the Sex Pistols. Vincent Furnier, a theatrically outrageous singer from Detroit, adopted the name of his own band, Alice Cooper, whose debut album barely broke the Top 200 in 1969. Along with Mott the Hoople, whose first release (also from 1969) did little better than Alice Cooper's, they helped propel the glam-rock movement that David Bowie famously adopted in his alter-ego character Ziggy Stardust. *Hair* spawned *Godspell* and *Jesus Christ Superstar*, the rock operas of the Jesus Movement.

On New Year's Eve 1969 and New Year's Day 1970, Jimi Hendrix and his Band of Gypsys trio (with Billy Cox and Buddy Miles) played an historic series of four shows at the Fillmore East. Selections from these shows were captured on the *Band of Gypsys*, the last Hendrix album to be released during his lifetime. On September 18, 1970, he was found dead in a London flat. Within ten months, both Janis

Joplin and Jim Morrison had followed Hendrix and Brian Jones into rock 'n' roll heaven.

Despite the ugliness of Altamont, the outdoor festivals of 1969 spawned more and more music fests in the 1970s, the biggest of which was the Summer Jam at Watkins Glen, in which an estimated 600,000 people—the largest recorded crowd at a concert to that date—gathered in upstate New York on July 28, 1973, to see the Grateful Dead, the Band, and the Allman Brothers. The daylong event was an exercise in jam-band endurance: the Dead played for five hours, the Allmans for four, the Band for three, plus a half-hour break during a thunderstorm. But there was something missing. As Robert Santelli records: "At Watkins Glen a feeling of monotony and tedium constantly challenged the viewers' interest in the music and the proceedings onstage. Long, winding solos were frequent. . . . Many of the 600,000 could barely see the stage, let alone the musicians. Many in attendance were often too busy doing and seeing other things to bother to listen seriously to the music for extended periods of time."[1] As the decade progressed, outdoor festivals morphed into the bloated excesses of corporate rock. The music industry—the erstwhile voice of the counterculture—had become Big Business. The Sexual Revolution and 1960s counterculture evolved into the "Me" decade of "key parties" and Studio 54.

Professional sports became big business, too. Following the first postmerger season of professional football in 1969, the Kansas City Chiefs scored a second consecutive upset victory for an original AFL franchise by soundly defeating the Minnesota Vikings, 23–7, in Super Bowl IV. Nielsen ratings of the Super Bowl and *Monday Night Football* climbed steadily in the 1970s as fans flocked to support teams like Don Shula's Miami Dolphins, Minnesota's "Purple People Eaters," Pittsburgh's "Steel Curtain," and "America's Team," the Dallas Cowboys (and their cheerleaders).

On December 24, All-Star outfielder Curt Flood, whom the St. Louis Cardinals had traded to the Philadelphia Phillies following the

1969 season, declared his intentions to challenge baseball's "reserve" clause and file as a free agent. After Flood consulted with Marvin Miller of the players' union, Miller and attorney Dick Moss drafted a letter to Bowie Kuhn, edited by former Supreme Court justice Arthur Goldberg and approved and signed by Flood. In the letter, he stated, "After twelve years in the major leagues, I do not feel I am a piece of property to be bought and sold irrespective of my wishes. I believe that any system which produces that result violates my basic rights as a citizen and is inconsistent with the laws of the United States . . ."[2]

Flood v. Kuhn went all the way to the Supreme Court, where it was argued and decided in 1972. By a 5–3 vote, the Court upheld the sport's antitrust exemption. Althought he had lost his bid to become baseball's first free agent, his case opened the door for future challenges to the reserve clause, which was overturned by an arbitrator in 1975 after pitchers Andy Messersmith and Dave McNally both played a season without a contract. The era of the big-money free agent was just around the corner, and the economics of America's national pastime would never be the same.

In the 1970s, Major League Baseball also entered into an era of Astroturf, the designated hitter in the American League, Cincinnati's "Big Red Machine," the colorful Oakland A's dynasty, and two classic World Series battles between the Los Angeles Dodgers and New York Yankees. The Mets, for their part, almost pulled off a repeat miracle in 1973. Sitting in last place at the end of August, the team went on another late-summer hot streak, led by Tug McGraw and his rallying cry of "Ya Gotta Believe." After narrowly winning a five-team race in the National League East with a record of just 82-79, the team then upset the heavily favored Reds, setting the mark for the lowest winning percentage of any team to go to the World Series, and then came within one game of beating the A's in the World Series. Two years later, Game Six of the 1975 World Series between the Boston Red Sox and Cincinnati Reds produced the timeless image of Boston's Carlton's Fisk's game-winning home run. Along with the story of the 1969 Miracle Mets, the 1975 World Series helped to return baseball to its rightful place as the national pastime.

In 1975, Gerald Ford, the unelected president, was the target of a halfhearted assassination attempt by former Manson Family member Squeaky Fromme. He survived—she had emptied the firing chamber before the attempt—but following Ford's unpopular pardoning of Nixon and his declaration of amnesty to Vietnam draft dodgers, he lost the 1976 presidential election to Washington outsider Jimmy Carter. The former governor of Georgia's one term in office was marred by double-digit inflation, the energy crisis, and the Iranian hostage situation. America entered the Days of Malaise. Ted Kennedy attempted a comeback and challenged Carter for the Democratic nomination, but the legacy of Chappaquiddick, coupled with a flubbed interview with CBS's Roger Mudd, derailed his campaign and ended his presidential hopes once and for all.

American voters resoundingly sent Ronald Reagan to the White House. In his inaugural speech, he declared, "We are a nation that has a government—not the other way around. And this makes us special among the nations of the earth." Said the man who once lectured college officials during the People's Park riots: "Our government has no power except that granted it by the people." The days of sex and drugs were replaced by the era of abstinence and "Just Say No."

Whether American society had come full circle or had simply circled back on itself, the ripples of 1969 continued to emanate throughout the rest of the century and into the next.

BIBLIOGRAPHY

Books

Ambrose, Stephen. *Nixon, Vol. 2: The Triumph of a Politician 1962–1972*. New York: Touchstone, 1990.

Anderson, David L., ed. *Facing My Lai: Moving Beyond the Massacre*. Lawrence, KS: University Press of Kansas, 2000.

Anderson, Terry H. *The Movement and the Sixties: Protest in America from Greensboro to Wounded Knee*. New York: Oxford, 1995.

Ashe, Penelope. *Naked Came the Stranger*. New York: Dell, 1969.

Bass, Paul and Douglas W. Rae. *Murder in the Model City: The Black Panthers, Yale, And the Redemption of a Killer*. New York: Basic Books, 2006.

Bordowitz, Hank. *Bad Moon Rising: The Unauthorized History of Creedence Clearwater Revival*. Chicago: Chicago Review Press, 2007.

Boyd, Brian. *Vladimir Nabokov: The American Years*. Princeton, NJ: Princeton University Press, 1991.

Braunstein, Paul and Michael William Doyle, eds. *Imagine Nation: The American Counterculture of the 1960s & '70s*. New York: Routledge, 2001.

Breslin, Jimmy. *The Gang That Couldn't Shoot Straight*. New York: Viking, 1969.

Buck, Jack, with Rob Rains and Bob Broeg. *Jack Buck: That's a Winner*. Champaign, IL: Sports Publishing, 1999.

Bugliosi, Vincent, with Curt Gentry. *Helter Skelter: The True Story of the Manson Murders*. New York: W. W. Norton, 1974.

Cannato, Vincent. *The Ungovernable City: John Lindsay and His Struggle to Save New York*. New York: Basic Books, 2001.

Carson, David A. *Grit, Noise and Revolution: The Birth of Detroit Rock 'n' Roll*. Ann Arbor: University of Michigan Press, 2006.

Carter, David. *Stonewall: The Riots That Sparked the Gay Revolution*. New York: St. Martin's, 2005.

Chaikin, Andrew. *A Man on the Moon: The Voyages of the Apollo Astronauts*. New York: Viking, 1994.

Charters, Ann, ed. *The Portable Sixties Reader*. New York: Penguin, 2003.

Cheever, John. *Bullet Park*. New York: Alfred A. Knopf, 1969.

Churchill, Ward and Jim Vander Wall. *Agents of Repression: The FBI's Secret Wars Against the Black Panther Party and the American Indian Movement.* Cambridge, MA: South End Press, 1990.

Cohen, Stanley. *A Magic Summer: The '69 Mets.* San Diego: Harcourt Brace Jovanovich, 1989.

Crichton, Michael. *The Andromeda Strain.* New York: Ballantine, 1969.

Cross, Charles R. *Room Full of Mirrors: A Biography of Jimi Hendrix.* New York: Hyperion, 2006.

Dallek, Robert. *Nixon and Kissinger: Partners in Power.* New York: HarperCollins, 2007.

Damore, Leo. *Senatorial Privilege: The Chappaquiddick Cover-Up.* Washington, DC: Regnery, 1988.

Deloria, Vine, Jr. *Custer Died for Your Sins: An Indian Manifesto.* New York: Avon, 1969.

Densmore, John. *Riders on the Storm: My Life with Jim Morrison and the Doors.* New York: Dell, 1991.

Didinger, Ray, ed. *The Super Bowl: Celebrating a Quarter-Century of America's Greatest Game.* New York: Simon & Schuster, 1990.

Doggett, Peter. *There's a Riot Going On: Revolutionaries, Rock Stars, and the Rise and Fall of the '60s.* New York: Canongate, 2008.

Downs, Donald Alexander. *Cornell '69: Liberalism and the Crisis of the American University.* Ithaca: Cornell University Press, 1999.

Duberman, Martin. *Stonewall.* New York: Plume, 1994.

Dylan, Bob. *Chronicles: Volume One.* New York: Simon & Schuster, 2005.

Echols, Alice. *Scars of Sweet Paradise: The Life and Times of Janis Joplin.* New York: Holt, 1999, 2000.

Feldmann, Doug. *Miracle Collapse: The 1969 Chicago Cubs.* Lincoln, NE: University of Nebraska Press, 2006.

Fuller, R. Buckminster. *Utopia or Oblivion: The Prospects for Humanity.* New York: Bantam, 1969.

Golenbock, Peter. *Amazin': The Miraculous History of New York's Most Beloved Baseball Teams.* New York: St. Martin's Griffin, 2002.

Gordon, Alastair. *Spaced Out: Radical Environments of the Psychedelic Sixties.* New York: Rizzoli, 2008.

Graysmith, Robert. *Zodiac.* New York: Berkley, 2007.

Haldeman, H. R., with Joseph DiMona. *The Ends of Power.* New York: Times Books, 1978.

Harris, Thomas A. *I'm OK—You're OK: A Practical Guide to Transactional Analysis.* New York: Harper & Row, 1969.

Helm, Levon, and Stephen Davis. *This Wheel's on Fire: Levon Helm and the Story of the Band.* Chicago: Chicago Review Press, 2000.

Hersh, Seymour. *My Lai 4: A Report on the Massacre and Its Aftermath.* New York: Random House, 1970.

Heylin, Clinton. *Bob Dylan: The Recording Sessions 1960–1994.* New York: St. Martin's Griffin, 1995.

Horn, Barbara Lee. *The Age of Hair: Evolution and Impact of Broadway's First Rock Musical.* Westport, CT: Greenwood, 1991.

Isaacson, Walter. *Kissinger: A Biography.* New York: Simon & Schuster, 1992.

1969

"J." The Sensuous Woman. New York: Dell, 1969.

Jorgensen, Ernst. Elvis Presley: A Life in Music—The Complete Recording Sessions. New York: St. Martin's, 1998.

Kelleher, Michael D. and David Van Nuys. "This Is the Zodiac Speaking": Into the Mind of a Serial Killer. Westport, CT: Praeger, 2002.

Kimball, Jeffrey. Nixon's Vietnam War. Lawrence, KS: University Press of Kansas, 1998.

Kirkpatrick, Rob, ed., The Quotable Sixties. Guilford, CT: The Lyons Press, 2006.

Kopit, Arthur. Indians: A Play. New York: Hill & Wang, 1969.

Kramer, Eddie, and John McDermott. Hendrix: Setting the Record Straight. New York: Warner, 1993.

LaVey, Anton Szandor. The Satanic Bible. New York: Avon, 1969.

Lax, Eric. Woody Allen: A Biography. New York: Da Capo Press, 2000.

Lazar, Zachary. Sway: A Novel. New York: Little Brown, 2008.

LeGuin, Ursula K. The Left Hand of Darkness. New York: Walker, 1969.

Lewis, Miles Marshall. There's a Riot Goin' On (33 1/3). New York: Continuum, 2006.

Lytle, Mark Hamilton. America's Uncivil Wars: The Sixties Era from Elvis to the Fall of Richard Nixon. New York: Oxford, 2005.

Maier, Thomas. The Kennedys: America's Emerald Kings: A Five-Generation History of the Ultiate Irish-Catholic Family. New York: Basic, 2003.

Makower, Joel. Woodstock: The Oral History. New York: Doubleday, 1989.

Mann, Robert. A Grand Delusion: America's Descent into Vietnam. New York: Basic Books, 2001.

Matteo, Steve. Let It Be (33 1/3). New York: Continuum, 2004.

McDonough, Jimmy. Shakey: Neil Young's Biography. New York: Random House, 2002.

McGinniss, Joe. The Last Brother: The Rise and Fall of Teddy Kennedy. New York: Simon & Schuster, 1993.

McLeese, Don. Kick Out the Jams (33 1/3). New York: Continuum, 2005.

McNally, Dennis. A Long Strange Trip: The Inside Story of the Grateful Dead. New York: Broadway Books, 2002.

McNeil, Legs, and Gillian McCain. Please Kill Me: The Uncensored Oral History of Punk. New York: Grove, 2006.

Miller, Timothy. The 60s Communes: Hippies and Beyond. Syracuse, NY: Syracuse University Press, 2000.

Momaday, N. Scott. House Made of Dawn. New York: Signet, 1968.

Morris, Desmond. The Human Zoo. New York: McGraw-Hill, 1969.

Nabokov, Vladimir. Ada or Ardor: A Family Chronicle. New York: Vintage, 1969, 1990.

Nixon, Richard. RN: The Memoirs of Richard Nixon. New York: Grosset & Dunlap, 1978.

Oberdorfer, Don. Tet! The Story of a Battle and Its Historic Aftermath. Garden City, NY: Doubleday, 1971.

Peary, Danny. Super Bowl: The Game of Their Lives—The Definitive Game-By-Game History as Told by the Stars. Darby, PA: Diane Publishing Company, 1997.

Perone, James E. *Woodstock: An Encyclopedia of the Music and Art Fair.* Westport, CT: Greenwood, 2005.

Peter, Laurence J., and Raymond Hull. *The Peter Principle: Why Things Always Go Wrong.* New York: Morrow, 1969.

Puzo, Mario. *The Godfather.* New York: Putnam, 1969.

Rivers, J. E., and Charles Nicol, ed. *Nabokov's Fifth Arc: Nabokov and Others on His Life's Work.* Austin, TX: University of Texas Press, 1982.

Rosenblatt, Roger. *Coming Apart: A Memoir of the Harvard Wars of 1969.* Boston: Little Brown, 1997.

Roszak, Theodore. *The Making of a Counter Culture.* Garden City, NY: Doubleday, 1969.

Roth, Philip. *Portnoy's Complaint.* New York: Random House, 1969.

Reuben, David. *Everything You Always Wanted to Know About Sex But Were Afraid to Ask.* New York: Bantam, 1969.

Safire, William. *Before the Fall: An Inside View of the Pre-Watergate White House.* Garden City, NY: Doubleday, 1975.

Sale, Kirkpatrick. *SDS.* New York: Random House, 1973.

Sanders, Ed. *The Family.* New York: Signet, 1990.

Shamsky, Art. *The Magnificent Seasons: How the Jets, Mets, and Knicks Made Sports History and Uplifted a City and the Country.* New York: Thomas Dunne, 2004.

Shapiro, Marc. *Carlos Santana: Back on Top.* New York: St. Martin's Griffin, 2004.

Sherrill, Robert. *The Last Kennedy: Edward M. Kennedy of Massachusetts Before and After Chappaquiddick.* New York: Dial, 1976.

Sinclair, John. *Guitar Army: Rock & Revolution with MC5 and the White Panther Party.* Port Townsend, WA: Process, 2007.

Snyder, Brad. *A Well-Paid Slave: Curt Flood's Fight for Free Agency in Professional Sports.* New York: Viking, 2006.

Spinrad, Norman. *Bug Jack Baron.* New York: Berkley, 1969.

Swingrover, E. A. *The Counterculture Reader.* New York: Pearson Longman, 2004.

Tamarkin, Jeff. *Got a Revolution! The Turbulent Flight of Jefferson Airplane.* New York: Atria, 2003.

Toffler, Alvin. *Future Shock.* New York: Bantam, 1970.

Turner, Steve. *Van Morrison: Too Late to Stop Now.* New York: Viking, 1993.

Updegrove, Mark K. *Second Acts: Presidential Lives and Legacies after the White House.* Guilford, CT: The Lyons Press, 2006.

Vecsey, George. *Joy in Mudville: Being a Complete Account of the Unparalleles History of the New York Mets from Their Most Perturbed Beginnings to Their Amazing Rise to Glory and Renown.* New York: McCall, 1970.

Vonnegut, Kurt. *Slaughterhouse-Five or The Children's Crusade: A Duty-Dance with Death.* New York: Dell, 1969, 1991.

Walker, Michael. *Laurel Canyon: The Inside Story of Rock-and-Roll's Legendary Neighborhood.* New York: Faber & Faber, 2007.

Wallace, Irving. *The Seven Minutes.* New York: Simon & Schuster, 1969.

Weddle, David. *If They Move . . . Kill 'Em!: The Life and Times of Sam Peckinpah.* New York: Grove, 2001.

1969

Whitburn, Joel. *The Billboard Book of Top 40 Hits* (8ᵗʰ Edition). New York: Billboard Books, 2004.

Witcover, Jules. *The Year the Dream Died: Revisiting 1968 in America*. New York: Warner Books, 1997.

Yorke, Ritchie. *Van Morrison: Into the Music*. London, England: Charisma Books, 1975.

Zaffiri, Samuel. *Hamburger Hill: May 11–20, 1969*. Novato, CA: Presidio, 1988.

Zebrowski, Ernest and Judith A. Howard. *Category 5: The Story of Camille*. Ann Arbor: University of Michigan Press, 2005.

Zimmer, Dave. *Crosby, Stills & Nash: The Authorized Biography*. Cambridge, MA: Da Capo, 2000.

Periodicals

Life
Look
The Los Angeles Times
Newsweek
The New York Times
Playboy
Rolling Stone
The San Francisco Chronicle
Time
The Washington Post

Web Sites*

All Music Guide
  http://www.allmusic.com
Badcat Records (Blind Faith)
  http://www.geocities.com/badcatrecords/BANNEDblindfaith.htm
Baseball Almanac
  http://www.baseball-almanac.com
BaseballLibrary.com
  http://www.baseballlibrary.com/homepage
BBC News
  http://news.bbc.co.uk
Berkeley Daily Planet
  http://www.berkeleydailyplanet.com
Book@rts
  http://www.cafecancun.com
Detroit Metro Times
  http://www.metrotimes.com
DGA (Directors Guild of America) Quarterly
  http://www.dga.org/news
The Doors—Official Site
  http://www.thedoors.com

Federal Judicial Center ("The Chicago Seven")
    http://www.fjc.gov
FindLaw
    http://www.findlaw.com/casecode/index.html
Gadfly
    http://www.gadflyonline.com
glbtq: an encyclopedia of gay, lesbian, bisexual, transgender, & queer culture
    http:///www.glbtq.com
The Harvard Crimson
    http://www.thecrimson.com
Haskell Home Page
    http://haskellwexler.com/HaskellWexler.Com/Haskell_Home_Page.html
A History of American Indians in California
    http://www.nps.gov/history/history/online_books/5views/5views1.htm
Images: A Journal of Film and Popular Culture
    http://www.imagesjournal.com
Led Zeppelin: Official Web Site
    http://www.ledzeppelin.com
Miles Beyond: The Electric Explorations of Miles Davis 1967–1991
    http://www.miles-beyond.com
Mr. Pop History
    http://www.mrpophistory.com
Museum of Hoaxes
    http://www.museumofhoaxes.com
NASA—Apollo 11: Lunar Surface Journal
    http://history.nasa.gov/alsj/a11/a11.landing.html
National Hurricane Center
    http://www.nhc.noaa.gov
National Oceanic and Atmospheric Administration
    http://www.publicaffairs.noaa.gov
The New York Times
    http://www.nytimes.com
Old School Reviews
    http://www.oldschoolreviews.com
The Progress Report
    http://www.progress.org
Public Broadcasting Service
    http://www.pbs.org
rogerebert.com
    http://rogerebert.suntimes.com
Rolling Stone Magazine
    http://www.rollingstone.com
Salon
    http://www.salon.com

1969

SixtiesCity
http://www.sixtiescity.com
Sound Portraits
http://www.soundportraits.org
The Sporting News
http://www.sportingnews.com
The Sydney Morning Herald
http://www.smh.com.au
Thinkexist.com
http://www.thinkexist.com
Time Magazine
http://www.time.com/time
TreeO.com ("The Jim Morrison Story")
http://www.treeo.com
truTV Crime Library: Criminal Minds and Methods
http://www.trutv.com/library/crime/index.html
UCLA—Henry Samueli School of Engineering and Applied Science
http://www.engineer.ucla.edu
UC Santa Barbara Department of Geography
http://www.geog.ucsb.edu
University of Colorado at Boulder—Center for Science and Technology Policy Research
http://sciencepolicy.colorado.edu
University of Missouri-Kansas City School of Law
http://www.law.umkc.edu
U. S. Centennial of Flight
http://www.centennialofflight.gov/index.cfm
The Villager
http://www.thevillager.com
Where Were You: Stories of the Most Amazing Day on Earth, July 20, 1969
http://www.wherewereyou.com
Wikisource
http://en.wikisource.org/wiki/Main_Page
Woodstock to Watkins Glen: The Rockfest Archives
http://www.chronos-historical.org/rockfest/articles/WG1.html
YouTube
http://www.youtube.com
1969 Woodstock Festival & Concert
http://www.woodstock69.com

*All sites accessed October 2008.

Albums
Alice Cooper. Pretties for You. Bizarre, 1969.
The Allman Brothers. The Allman Brothers. Polydor, 1969.

The Band. The Band. Capitol, 1969.
The Beatles. Abbey Road. Capitol, 1969.
_____. Let It Be. Capitol, 1970.
Blind Faith. Blind Faith. Polydor, 1969.
Blood, Sweat & Tears. Blood, Sweat & Tears. Columbia/Legacy, 1969.
Walter Carlos. Switched-On Bach. Columbia, 1969.
_____. The Well-Tempered Synthesizer. Columbia, 1969.
Johnny Cash. At San Quentin. Columbia, 1969.
Chicago. Chicago Transit Authority. Chicago, 1969.
Creedence Clearwater Revival. Bayou Country. Fantasy, 1969.
_____. Green River. Fantasy, 1969.
_____. Willie and the Poor Boys. Fantasy, 1969.
Crosby, Stills & Nash. Crosby, Stills & Nash. Atlantic, 1969.
Desmond Dekker. This Is Desmond Dekkar. Trojan, 1969.
The Doors. Soft Parade. Elektra, 1969.
Bob Dylan. Nashville Skyline. Columbia, 1969.
Easy Rider: Music from the Soundtrack.
Duke Ellington. 1969: All-Star White House Tribute. Blue Note, 2002.
The Grateful Dead. Aoxomoxoa. Warner Bros., 1969.
_____. Live/Dead. Warner Bros., 1969.
Hair: The American Tribal Love-Rock Musical. Original Broadway Cast Recording. RCA
    Victor, 1968.
Isaac Hayes. Hot Buttered Soul. Stax, 1969.
Jimi Hendrix. Jimi Hendrix: Woodstock. MCA, 1994.
_____. Live at the Fillmore East. MCA, 1999.
_____. Live at Woodstock. MCA, 1999.
Jefferson Airplane. Volunteers. BMG, 1969.
Jethro Tull. Stand Up. Chrysalis, 1969.
Janis Joplin. I Got Dem Ol' Kozmic Blues Again Mama! Columbia, 1969.
King Crimson. In the Court of the Crimson King. EG, 1969.
Led Zeppelin. Led Zeppelin. Atlantic, 1969.
_____. Led Zeppelin II. Atlantic, 1969.
MC5. Kick Out the Jams. Elektra, 1969.
Mott the Hoople. Mott the Hoople. Atlantic, 1969.
Elvis Presley. From Elvis in Memphis. RCA, 1969.
The Rolling Stones. Get Yer Ya-Ya's Out. ABKCO, 1970.
_____. Let It Bleed. ABKCO, 1969.
_____. Sticky Fingers. Virgin, 1971.
Santana. Santana. Columbia, 1969.
Dusty Springfield. Dusty in Memphis. Mercury, 1969.
The Stooges. The Stooges. Elektra, 1969.
The Who. Tommy. MCA, 1969.
Woodstock: Music from the Original Soundtrack and More. Cotillion, 1970.
Yes. Yes. Atlantic, 1969.
Neil Young. Neil Young. Reprise, 1969.

1969

Neil Young and Crazy Horse. Everybody Knows This Is Nowhere. Reprise, 1969.

Films

100 Rifles. Directed by Tom Gries. Twentieth Century Fox. 1969.
Alice's Restaurant. Directed by Arthur Penn. United Artists. 1969.
Berkeley in the Sixties. Directed by Mark Kitchell. PBS. 1990.
Bob & Carol & Ted & Alice. Directed by Paul Mazursky. Columbia. 1969.
Butch Cassidy and the Sundance Kid. Directed by George Roy Hill. Twentieth Century Fox. 1969.
Easy Rider. Directed by Dennis Hopper. Columbia. 1969.
Easy Riders, Raging Bulls. Directed by Kenneth Bowser. Freemantle/Submarine. 2003.
From the Earth to the Moon. HBO. 1998.
Gimme Shelter. Directed by David Maysles, Albert Maysles, and Charlotte Zwerin. Cinema 5/Maysles Films. 1970.
I Am Curious (Yellow). Directed by Vilgot Sjöman. 1967.
In the Shadow of the Moon. Directed by David Sington. Discovery Film Channel. 2007.
John & Yoko: Give Peace a Song. Canadian Broadcasting Corporation. 2006.
Midnight Cowboy. Directed by John Schlesinger. United Artists. 1969.
The Murder of Fred Hampton. Directed by Howard Alk. MGA. 1971.
Once Upon a Time in the West. Directed by Sergio Leone. Paramount. 1968.
Putney Swope. Directed by Robert Downey, Sr. Cinema 5/Herald. 1969.
True Grit. Directed by Henry Hathaway. Paramount. 1969.
The Weather Underground. Directed by Sam Green and Bill Siegel. Creative Capital/Entertainment Television Service, 2003.
The Wild Bunch. Directed by Sam Peckinpah. 7 Arts/Warner Bros. 1969.
Woodstock: 3 Days of Peace and Music-The Director's Cut. Directed by Michael Wadleigh. Warner Bros. 1970.

NOTES

Introduction to the 2019 Edition

1. Hill, Michael, "Dig It: Archaeologists scour Woodstock '69 concert field", Associated Press, *Times Herald-Record* (Middletown, NY), June 21, 2018.
2. *Bridge Over Troubled Water*, Simon and Garfunkel: liner notes, Bud Scoppa, 2001 edition; *Songs of America and The Harmony Game* (documentaries), 2011 deluxe CD/DVD edition.
3. "Independence Day," *Journal Gazette* (Fort Wayne, IN), July 4, 2010
4. Witz, Billy, "Pinstripes, Meet Rainbow: Yankees Plan a Pride Event," *New York Times*, August 10, 2018
5. "Mister Rogers Neighborhood: 1969 Senate Hearing," PBS Kids YouTube channel.

Prologue

1. Theodore Roszak, *The Making of a Counter Culture*, xi.

Chapter 1

1. *RN: The Memoirs of Richard Nixon* 366.
2. *RN: The Memoirs of Richard Nixon*, 366; Stephen Ambrose, *Nixon, Vol. 2*, 245.
3. William Safire, *Before the Fall: An Inside View of the Pre-Watergate White House*, 121.
4. William Safire, 121.
5. H. R. Haldeman, *The Ends of Power*, 82–83.
6. Haldeman, 81.
7. Ambrose, 256.
8. Ambrose, 256.
9. Ambrose, 257–258.
10. Ambrose, 258.
11. Robert Dallek, *Nixon and Kissinger*, 119.
12. Dallek, 258.
13. Dallek, 119; Jeffrey Kimball, *Nixon's Vietnam War*, 135.
14. Kimball, 135.
15. Kimball, 136.

Chapter 2
1. "Men of the Year," *Time*, time.com, January 3, 1969.
2. *Newsweek*, January 20, 1969, 59.
3. *Time.com*, February 21, 1969.
4. *Newsweek*, May 5, 1969, 26.
5. *Life*, May 9, 1969, 76C.
6. *Life*, May 9, 1969, 76D.
7. *Life*, May 9, 1969, 76A–76D.
8. *Newsweek*, February 10, 1969, 53.
9. *Newsweek*, January 20, 1969, 59.
10. *Time.com*, January 24, 1969.
11. "The Playboy Panel: Student Revolt," *Playboy*, September 1969, 92, 96.
12. *Newsweek*, February 24, 1969, 22–23; *Time.com*, February 14, 1969.
13. *Newsweek*, March 3, 1969, 78.
14. Kirkpatrick Sale, *SDS*, 512–513.
15. *FindLaw*, caselaw.lp.findlaw.com, *Tinker v. Des Moines School Dist.*, 393 U. S. 503 (1969).
16. Vincent Cannato, *The Ungovernable City*, 456.
17. Cannato, 156–157.
18. *Time*, February 7, 1969, 68.
19. *Newsweek*, January 20, 1969, 52.
20. *Mr. Pop History*, mrpophistory.com, "Week of June 1, 1969."
21. *Newsweek*, January 13, 1969, 62.
22. *The Weather Underground*, Bill Siegel and Sam Green, dir., DVD.
23. *Newsweek*, March 17, 1969, 106.
24. Sale, 509.
25. *Newsweek*, January 13, 1969, 62.

Chapter 3
1. Ernst Jorgensen, *Elvis Presley: A Life in Music—The Complete Recording Sessions*, 72.
2. Jorgensen, 75.
3. Jorgensen, 79.
4. Bob Dylan, *Chronicles: Volume One*, 120.
5. Erlewine, AllMusic.com, "Nashville Skyline."
6. *Rolling Stone*, January 4, 1969, 16.
7. Don McLeese, *Kick Out the Jams*, 84.
8. *Time*, January 3, 1969, 49.
9. Legs McNeil and Gillian McCain, *Please Kill Me*, 48.
10. McLeese, 85.
11. McLeese, 91–92.
12. David A. Carson, *Grit, Noise and Revolution*, 215.
13. Carson, 215.
14. Carson, 215.
15. Qtd. by Brian Smith, *MetroTimes.com*, May 1, 2002.

16. Mark Demig, *All Music Guide*, allmusic.com, *The Stooges* (review).
17. Brian Smith, *MetroTimes.com*, May 1, 2002.
18. *All Music Guide*, allmusic.com, "The Stooges."
19. McDonough, 301.
20. Qtd. in McDonough, 302.
21. McDonough, 299.
22. *Newsweek*, February 3, 1969, 90.
23. "The Making of *The Complete Bitches Brew Sessions*," *Miles Beyond*, http://www .miles-beyond.com/bitchesbrew.htm.
24. Greg Kot, *Rolling Stone.com*, *Led Zeppelin* (review).
25. Stephen Thomas Erlewine, *All Music Guide*, allmusic.com, "Led Zeppelin" (biography).

Chapter 4

1. *U. S. Centennial of Flight Commission*, www.centennialofflight.gov/essay/Aerospace /Boeing_747/Aero21.htm.
2. Art Shamsky, *The Magnificent Seasons*, 55.
3. Danny Peary, *Super Bowl: The Game of Their Lives*, 39–50.
4. Shamsky, 58.
5. *Sportingnews.com*, "History of the Super Bowl."
6. Shamsky, 55.
7. Shamsky, 58.
8. Shamsky, 56.
9. Peary, 39–50.
10. Peary, 39–50.
11. Shamsky, 70.

Chapter 5

1. Joseph Geringer, "The Assassination of Robert F. Kennedy," *Crime Library: Criminal Minds and Methods*, www.crimelibrary.com/terrorists_spies/assassins /kennedy/7.html.
2. *Newsweek*, January 27, 1969, 27–28.
3. *Newsweek*, February 24, 1969, 33.
4. Geringer.
5. *Wikisource*, http://en.wikisource.org/wiki/Image:Sirhan3.jpg.
6. "The Ascent of Ted Kennedy," *Time*, time.com, January 10, 1969.
7. "Upheaval on the Hill," *Time*, time.com, January 10, 1969.
8. Qtd. in Joe McGinniss, *The Last Brother*, 505.
9. McGinniss, 511.
10. *Life*, January 31, 1969, 8.
11. "His Life and Crimes," *Time*, time.com, January 17, 1969.
12. Jules Siegel, "Saying Goodbye to Mario Puzo,"*Book@rts*, cafecancun.com, July 1999.
13. Eric Lax, *Woody Allen: A Biography*, 243–244.
14. Lax, 244.

15. Lax, 261.
16. Thomas Maier, *The Kennedys: America's Emerald Kings*, xvi.

Chapter 6

1. Playboy, "Sex in Cinema 1969," November 1969, 168–169.
2. "How to Deal with Four-Letter Words," *Time*, time.com, March 7, 1969, 63; *New York Times*, February 23, 1969.
3. *Newsweek*, October 13, 1969, 112-113.
4. *Newsweek*, April 14, 1969, 69.
5. http://www.geocities.com/badcatrecords/BANNEDblindfaith.htm
6. *Newsweek*, April 14, 1969, 67.
7. Gary Giddins, "Still Curious" (essay), *I Am Curious (Yellow)*, dir. Vilgot Sjöman, (DVD, Special Features).
8. *Newsweek*, April 14, 1969, 67.
9. John Nesbit, *Old School Reviews*, oldschoolreviews.com, "I Am Curious (Yellow)" (review).
10. Giddins.
11. Nesbit.
12. Roger Ebert, *roger ebert.com*, rogerebert.suntimes.com, "I Am Curious (Yellow)" (review).
13. Giddins.
14. *Playboy*, "Sex in Cinema 1969," 169.
15. *Newsweek*, March 3, 1969, 80.
16. *Rolling Stone*, September 6, 1969, 4.
17. Barbara Lee Horn, *The Age of Hair: Evolution and Impact of Broadway's First Rock Musical*, 84.
18. Horn, 61.
19. Horn, 61.
20. Horn, 59.
21. "Oh! Calcutta!" *Playboy*, October 1969, 167.
22. "Faking It," *Time*, time.com, April 4, 1969.
23. John Densmore, *Riders on the Storm*, 214.
24. The Doors Infamous 1969 Miami Concert Part 2 of 9," *YouTube*, youtube.com.
25. Densmore, 215.
26. Jan Morris, "The Miami Incident," *The Doors—Official Site*, doors.com.
27. Morris.
28. Densmore, 219.
29. *Mr. Pop History*, mrpophistory.com, "Week of April 20, 1969."
30. Densmore, 231.
31. Densmore, 247.

Chapter 7

1. "The Return of No. 9." *Time*, time.com, May 2, 1969.
2. "Mantle of Greatness," *Time*, time.com, March 14, 1969.

3. Doug Feldmann, *Miracle Collapse*, 49.
4. Feldmann, 67.
5. "Inside Man," *Time*, time.com, February 14, 1969.
6. Feldmann, 50.
7. Jack Buck with Rob Rains, *Jack Buck: That's a Winner*, 7.
8. Feldmann, 44.
9. Feldmann, 47.
10. "Strike One."
11. Stanley Cohen, *A Magic Summer*, 159.
12. Cohen, 158.
13. "Ernie Banks Quotes," *Baseball Almanac*, baseball-almanac.com.
14. Feldmann, 68.
15. Feldmann, 76.
16. Feldmann, 95.
17. Shamsky, 108.
18. Feldmann, 121.

Chapter 8

1. Roger Rosenblatt, *Coming Apart: A Memoir of the Harvard Wars of 1969*, 9–10.
2. Rosenblatt, 13.
3. Rosenblatt, 23–25.
4. Rosenblatt, 26–27.
5. Rosenblatt, 30–33.
6. Rosenblatt, 16.
7. "Harvard and Beyond: The University under Siege," *Time*, time.com, April 18, 1969.
8. Rosenblatt, 88–89.
9. Rosenblatt, 18.
10. Rosenblatt, 19.
11. Rosenblatt, 46.
12. Rosenblatt, 38.
13. *Life*, April 25, 1969, 31.
14. Sale, 522.
15. Rosenblatt, 41.
16. Rosenblatt, 32.
17. *Life*, April 25, 1969, 35.
18. Donald Alexander Downs, *Cornell '69: Liberalism and the Crisis of the American University*, 169-170.
19. Downs, 179.
20. "The Agony of Cornell," *Time*, time.com, May 2, 1969.
21. "The Playboy Panel: Student Revolt," *Playboy*, September 1969, 92.
22. "The Playboy Panel," 91.
23. "The Agony of Cornell."
24. *Newsweek*, May 5, 1969, 26.
25. *Newsweek*, May 5, 1969, 26.
26. *Newsweek*, May 5, 1969, 26.

27. *Newsweek*, May 5, 1969, 26.
28. "The Agony of Cornell."
29. "Harvard and Beyond: The University under Siege," *Time*, time.com, April 18, 1969.
30. "The Campus Upheaval: An End to Patience," *Time*, time.com, May 9, 1969.
31. "The Campus Upheaval: An End to Patience," *Time*, time.com, May 9, 1969, editorial.
32. *Newsweek*, May 12, 1969, 31.
33. "The Campus Upheaval: An End to Patience," *Time*, time.com, May 9, 1969.
34. Newsweek, May 19, 1969, 42.
35. *Newsweek*, May 19, 1969, 42.
36. *Newsweek*, May 19, 1969, 42.

Chapter 9

1. Jeffrey Kimball, *Nixon's Vietnam War*, 142.
2. *Life*, February 7, 1969, 14B-22.
3. Walter Isaacson, *Kissinger: A Biography*, 182.
4. Isaacson, 181.
5. Kimball, 111.
6. Kimball, 101.
7. *New York Times*, May 20.
8. "The Battle for Hamburger Hill,"*Time*, time.com, May 30, 1969.
9. *New York Times*, May 23, 1969, 2.
10. Samuel Zaffiri, *Hamburger Hill*, 246.
11. Zaffiri, 248–249.
12. Zaffiri, 250.
13. *New York Times*, May 21, 1969, 5.
14. *New York Times*, May 23, 1969, 3.
15. Zaffiri, 249.
16. *Life*, May 9, 1969, 38.
17. Sale, 513.
18. Zaffiri, 250.

Chapter 10

1. "The Cities: The Price of Optimism," *Time*, time.com, August 1, 1969.
2. "The Cities: The Price of Optimism."
3. *Life*, February 7, 1969, 38–50.
4. "Environment: Tragedy in Oil, *Time*, time.com, February 14, 1969.
5. "Environment: Tragedy in Oil."
6. "Environment: Tragedy in Oil."
7. "1969 Oil Spill," UC Santa Barbara Department of Geography, http://www.geog.ucs .edu/~jeff/sb_69oilspill/69oilspill_articles2.html.
8. Ernest Zebrowski and Judith A. Howard, *Category 5: The Story of Camille*, 152.
9. *The Los Angeles Times*, http://www.latimes.com/news/local/la-santa_barbara1969 _oilspill-pg,0,7401384.photogallery?index=1
10. "Environment: Tragedy in Oil."

11. Mark Hamilton Lytle, *America's Uncivil Wars*, 328–329.
12. *Berkeley in the Sixties*, Mark Kitchell, dir. (DVD).
13. Lytle, 329.
14. *Berkeley in the Sixties*.
15. "Postscript to People's Park," *Time*, time.com, February 16, 1970.
16. *Berkeley in the Sixties*.
17. *Berkeley in the Sixties*.
18. *Berkeley in the Sixties*.
19. *Berkeley in the Sixties*.
20. *Berkeley in the Sixties*.
21. Lytle, 329–331.
22. *Berkeley in the Sixties*.
23. *Los Angeles Times*, January 28, 1989, I23.
24. *New York Times*, November 30, 1969.
25. Adam Jon Monroe, "When Is the Real Earth Day?" *The Progress Report*, progress.org.
26. Thinkexist.com, "Gaylord Nelson quotes."
27. *Playboy*, September 1969, 209.

Chapter 11

1. David Carter, *Stonewall: The Riots That Sparked the Gay Revolution*, 77.
2. Carter, 114.
3. Carter, 115.
4. Carter, 123.
5. Lincoln Anderson, "'I'm sorry,' says inspector who led Stonewall raid," *The Villager*, thevillager.com, June 16–22, 2004.
6. Anderson.
7. Martin Duberman, *Stonewall*, 198.
8. "Remembering Stonewall," *Sound Portraits*, soundportraits.org,
9. "Remembering Stonewall."
10. Carter, 123.
11. Duberman, 208–209.
12. Duberman, 208.
13. "Gay Liberation Front," *glbtq: an encyclopedia of gay, lesbian, bisexual, transgender, & queer culture*, glbtq.com.
14. *Newsweek*, August 11, 1969, 36.
15. *Newsweek*, August, 18, 1969, 36.
16. *The Weather Underground*. dir. Sam Green and Bill Siegel, DVD.
17. Sale, 570.
18. Sale, 574.
19. Sale, 560.
20. *The Weather Underground*.
21. *The Weather Underground*.
22. *The Weather Underground*.
23. *The Weather Underground*.
24. *The Weather Underground*.

1969

Chapter 12

1. Andrew Chaikin, *A Man on the Moon*, 141.
2. Chaikin, 142.
3. Chaikin, 144.
4. Chaikin, 158.
5. Chaikin, 159.
6. Chaikin, 173.
7. *Apollo 11: Lunar Surface Journal*, ed. Eric M. Jones, http://www.history.nasa.gov/alsj/a11/a11.landing.html.
8. *From the Earth to the Moon*, Tom Hanks and Michael Grossman, dir., DVD.
9. Chaikin, 183.
10. Chaikin, 186–188.
11. *In the Shadow of the Moon*, David Sington, dir., DVD.
12. *Apollo 11: Lunar Surface Journal*.
13. *In the Shadow of the Moon*.
14. *Apollo 11: Lunar Surface Journal*.
15. *In the Shadow of the Moon*.
16. *In the Shadow of the Moon*.
17. *In the Shadow of the Moon*.
18. "I Am Buzz Lightyear!" Salon.com, http://www.salon.com/news/feature/1999/07/20/aldrin/index1.html.
19. John Markoff, "An Internet Pioneer Ponders the Next Revolution," *The New York Times*, December 20, 1999, http://partners.nytimes.com/library/tech/99/12/biztech/articles/122099outlook-bobb.html.
20. Chris Sutton, "Internet Began 35 Years Ago at UCLA with First Message Ever Sent between Two Computers," September 2, 2004, *UCLA: Engineering*, http://www.engineer.ucla.edu/stories/2004/Internet35.htm.

Chapter 13

1. William Safire, *Before the Fall: An Inside View of the Pre-Watergate White House*, 149.
2. Joe McGinniss, *The Last Brother*, 531.
3. Leo Damore, *Senatorial Privilege: The Chappaquiddick Cover-Up*, 6–7.
4. *Life*, August 1, 1969, 16B.
5. Damore, 21.
6. *Life*, August 1, 1969, 16B.
7. *Life*, August 1, 1969, 17.
8. *Life*, August 1, 1969, 17–18.
9. Robert Sherrill, *The Last Kennedy: Edward M. Kennedy of Massachusetts Before and After Chappaquiddick*, 96.
10. Sherrill, 65.
11. Damore, 9.
12. McGinniss, 539.
13. Damore, 77.
14. Damore, 77.

15. Damore, 77–78.
16. Damore, 77.
17. Damore, 83.
18. Damore, 83.
19. Damore, 13.
20. Damore, 18.
21. McGinniss, 544.
22. "Chappaquiddick," *Federal Bureau of Investigation*, foia.fbi.gov.
23. Sherrill, 63.
24. Sherrill, 63.
25. Damore, 40.
26. Sherill, 102.
27. Qtd. in Sherrill, 87.
28. *Life*, August 1, 1969.
29. Sherrill, 111–112.
30. Damore, 201.
31. *Life*, August 1, 1969, 25.
32. Sherrill, 96.

Chapter 14

1. *Newsweek*, August 18, 1969, 89.
2. Timothy Miller, *The 60s Communes: Hippies and Beyond*, 153.
3. Alastair Gordon, *Spaced Out*, 185.
4. Gordon, 204.
5. Gordon, 107, 111.
6. Roszak, 2, 7, 22.
7. *Woodstock: 3 Days of Peace and Music*, dir. Michael Wadleigh, DVD.
8. *Life*, July 18, 16B.
9. *Life*, July 18, 1.
10. *Life*, July 18, 1.
11. "Easy Rider: Shaking the Cage" (documentary), *Easy Rider* [35th Anniversary Edition Deluxe Edition], DVD (2004).
12. *Life*, July 18, 16B.
13. "Easy Rider: Shaking the Cage"; *Easy Riders, Raging Bulls*.
14. *Alice's Restaurant*, Arthur Penn, dir., DVD (commentary).
15. *Alice's Restaurant*.
16. *Playboy*, April, 1969, 149–150; 216.
17. Nancy Kapinatoff, "Under the Influence of Paul Mazursky's *Bob & Carol & Ted & Alice*," *DGA* Quarterly, http://www.dga.org/news/e_expand.php3?type=archives &UID=16.
18. *Newsweek*, May 12, 1969, 104.
19. *Bob & Carol & Ted & Alice*, Paul Mazursky, dir., DVD (commentary).
20. Ebert, *Bob & Carol & Ted & Alice* (review).

1969

Chapter 15

1. "Easy Rider: Shaking the Cage."
2. "The Book of Revelation (Chapter 9) and the Ideology of Charles Manson," http://www.law.umkc.edu/faculty/projects/ftrials/manson/mansonrevelation.html.
3. Graysmith, 33.
4. Ed Sanders, *The Family*, 25.
5. Sanders, 207.
6. "Zodiac Killer letters," Wikisource, http://en.wikisource.org/wiki/Zodiac_Killer_letters#July_31st_1969.
7. *San Francisco Chronicle*, August 2, 1969, 4.
8. Graysmith, 53–54.
9. "Zodiac Killer letters."
10. Michael D. Kelleher and David Van Nuys, *"This Is the Zodiac Speaking": Into the Mind of a Serial Killer*, 62.
11. Bugliosi, 276.
12. Bugliosi, 275–276.
13. Bugliosi, 277.
14. Bugliosi, 3.
15. Sanders, 243.
16. Bugliosi, 177.
17. Sanders, 246.
18. Bugliosi, 178.
19. Sanders, 249.
20. Bugliosi, 179.
21. Bugliosi, 180.
22. Bugliosi, 85.
23. Bugliosi, 85.
24. Sanders, 263.
25. Sanders, 273.
26. Sanders, 276–280.
27. Qtd. in Bugliosi, 20.
28. Bugliosi, 55.
29. Michael Walker, *Laurel Canyon: The Inside Story of Rock-and-Roll's Legendary Neighborhood*, 124.
30. Walker, 125–126.
31. Walker, 125.

Chapter 16

1. Feldmann, 164-165.
2. "Wayne Garrett," Baseball Library.com.
3. Cohen, 152.
4. Qtd. in Feldmann, 162.
5. Qtd. in Feldmann, 162.
6. Feldmann, 163–164.

7. Feldmann, 164.
8. Qtd. in Feldmann, 165.
9. Cohen, 117.
10. Cohen, 165–166.
11. Cohen, 117.
12. Feldmann, 170.
13. Qtd. in Cohen, 145.
14. Cohen, 146.
15. Qtd. in "The Little Team That Can," *Time*, time.com, September 5, 1969.
16. *Life*, September 26, 1969.
17. "The Little Team That Can."
18. Feldmann, 229.
19. Feldmann, 232–233.

Chapter 17

1. Qtd. in James E. Perone, *Woodstock: An Encyclopedia of the Music and Art Fair*, 7.
2. Robert Santelli, qtd. in Aquarius Rising, http://www.chronos-historical.org/rockfest /Woodstock/01.html
3. "Pop Drugs: The High as a Way of Life," *Time*, September 26, 1969.
4. "Pop Drugs: The High as a Way of Life."
5. *Life*, August 22, 1969, 20B.
6. "Pop Drugs: The High as a Way of Life."
7. Elliot Tiber, "How Woodstock Happened," *Woodstock69*, woodstock69.com.
8. Joel Makower, *Woodstock: The Oral History*, 113.
9. Makower, 115.
10. *Saratogian*, July 19, 1969; Qtd. in Makower.
11. Michael J. Fairchild, *Jimi Hendrix: Woodstock* (CD), liner notes, 7; Elliot Tiber.
12. Fairchild, 9.
13. *Rolling Stone*, September 20, 1969, 16.
14. *Woodstock: 3 Days of Peace and Music.*
15. Makower, 201.
16. Tiber.
17. *Times Herald-Record*, August 16, 1969, qtd. in Makower.
18. *Woodstock: 3 Days of Peace and Music.*
19. Elliot Tiber.
20. Zebrowski and Howard, 70.
21. Zebrowski and Howard, 63.
22. Qtd. in Perone, 149.
23. Marc Shapiro, *Carlos Santana: Back on Top*, 86.
24. *Woodstock: 3 Days of Peace and Music.*
25. "Jerry Garcia & Bob Weir—Letterman 1987 Part Two," *YouTube*, youtube.com.
26. Dennis McNally, *A Long Strange Trip: The Inside Story of the Grateful Dead*, 332–333.
27. Hank Bordowitz, *Bad Moon Rising: The Unauthorized History of Creedence Clearwater Revival*, 64.

28. Alice Echols, *Scars of Sweet Paradise, The Life and Times of Janis Joplin*, 266.
29. Miles Marshall Lewis, *There's a Riot Goin' On* (33 1/3 series), 67.
30. Qtd. in Lewis, 67.
31. *Rolling Stone*, July 12, 1969, 16.
32. "The Who - Abbie Hoffman incident - Woodstock 1969," *YouTube*, youtube.com.
33. Jeff Tamarkin, *Got a Revolution! The Turbulent Flight of Jefferson Airplane*, 206.
34. Zebrowski and Howard, 65–66.
35. Elliot Tiber.
36. *Woodstock: 3 Days of Peace and Music*.
37. Levon Helm and Stephen Davis, *This Wheel's on Fire: Levon Helm and the Story of the Band*, 199.
38. Dave Zimmer, *Crosby, Stills & Nash: The Authorized Biography*, 11.
39. Zebrowski and Howard, 90.
40. Zebrowski and Howard, 94.
41. Zebrowski and Howard, 109.
42. Zebrowski and Howard, 118–119.
43. Fairchild, 15.
44. Fairchild, 11.
45. Eddie Kramer and John McDermott, *Hendrix: Setting the Record Straight*, 216.
46. Kramer and McDermott, 216–217.
47. David Fricke, *Jimi Hendrix: Live at Woodstock* (CD), liner notes, n.p.
48. Al Aronowitz qtd. in Charles R. Cross, *Room Full of Mirrors: A Biography of Jimi Hendrix*, 287.
49. Fairchild, 20.
50. Center for Science and Technology Policy Research, University of Colorado at Boulder, http://sciencepolicy.colorado.edu/about_us/meet_us/roger_pielke/camille/figures/fig1a.jpg.
51. Zebrowski and Howard, 127.
52. Zebrowski and Howard, 122.
53. Zebrowski and Howard, 149.
54. "Hurricane Preparedness: Hurricane History," National Hurricane Center, http://www.nhc.noaa.gov/HAW2/english/history.shtml#camille.
55. Rob Kirkpatrick, ed., *The Quotable Sixties*, 179.
56. Qtd. in Echols, 265–266.
57. *Rolling Stone*, September 20, 1969, 1.
58. Bob Dylan, *Chronicles: Volume One*, 116–117.
59. *Melody Maker* qtd. in Steve Turner, *Van Morrison: Too Late to Stop Now*, 105."
60. Qtd. in Makower, 296.
61. *Woodstock: 3 Days of Peace and Music*.

Chapter 18
1. Peter Golenbock, *Amazin': The Miraculous History of New York's Most Beloved Baseball Teams*, 243.
2. Cannato, 396.
3. "A Trumanesque Comeback," *Time*, time.com, October 31, 1969.

4. Cohen, 285.
5. Cohen, 289.
6. Golenbock, 258.
7. Cohen, 301.
8. George Vecsey, *Joy in Mudville*, 247.
9. Cohen, 305.
10. Cannato, 436.
11. Cannato, 436.
12. Cannato, 437.

Chapter 19
1. William Safire, *Before the Fall: Inside the Pre-Watergate White House*, 171.
2. "Strike Against the War," *Time*, time.com, October 17, 1969.
3. Charles Mann, *A Grand Delusion: America's Descent into Vietnam*, 638.
4. Mann, 637.
5. Kimball, 165-166.
6. Mann, 640.
7. "Strike Against the War."
8. Safire, 172.
9. "Strike Against the War."
10. Mann, 635, 642.
11. Mann, 628.
12. Safire, 175.
13. Mann, 644.
14. Safire, 175.
15. Safire, 180.
16. *John & Yoko: Give Peace a Song*, Canadian Broadcasting Corporation.
17. *John & Yoko: Give Peace a Song*.
18. Mann, 648.
19. "Incident in Song Chang Valley," *Time*, time.com, September 5, 1969.
20. Hersh, 134.
21. Seymour Hersh, *My Lai 4: A Report on the Massacre and Its Aftermath*, 87.
22. Don Oberdorfer, *Tet!*, 158.
23. Hersh, 13.
24. Hersh, 11.
25. Hersh, 105.
26. Hersh 125
27. Hersh, 54.
28. Hersh, 140.
29. *New York Times*, November 25, 1969; transcript of CBS Network Radio interview of Paul Meadlo by Mike Wallace, November 24, 1969.
30. David L. Anderson, ed., *Facing My Lai: Moving Beyond the Massacre*, 57.
31. Anderson, 61.
32. Walter Lippman, *Newsweek*, December 1, 1969, 27.

33. Mann, 650.
34. Safire, 179.
35. Mann, 650.

Chapter 20

1. Vincent Canby, "Real Events of '68 Seen in 'Medium Cool,'" *The New York Times*, movies.nytimes.com, August 28, 1969.
2. Ann Hornaday, *Washington Post*, March 2, 2008, M04; haskellwexler.com
3. Canby.
4. Douglas O. Linder, "The Chicago Seven Conspiracy Trial," http://www.law.umkc .edu/faculty/projects/ftrials/Chicago7/Account.html.
5. *The Weather Underground.*
6. Doggett, 207.
7. *The Weather Underground.*
8. *The Weather Underground.*
9. Doggett, 308.
10. Qtd. in Doggett, 295.
11. *Newsweek*, November 10, 1969, 41.
12. Peter Doggett, 295.
13. Linder.
14. Doggett, 236.
15. Doggett, 236.
16. Ward Churchill and Jim Vander Wall, *Agents of Repression: The FBI's Secret Wars Against the Black Panther Party and the American Indian Movement*, 42.
17. Paul Bass and Douglas W. Rae, *Murder in the Model City: The Black Panthers, Yale, And the Redemption of a Killer*, 3.
18. Ahern qtd. in Bass and Rae, 33.
19. Bass and Rae, 9-10.
20. Bass and Rae, 17.
21. Bass and Rae, 35.
22. Bass and Rae, 104.
23. Bass and Rae, 69.
24. Churchill and Vander Wall, 65.
25. Peter Doggett, 248.
26. *Eyes on the Prize: America's Civil Rights Movement 1954–1985* (transcript), http:// www.pbs.org/wgbh/amex/eyesontheprize/about/pt_206.html..
27. Churchill and Vander Wall, 65.
28. Churchill and Vander Wall, 69.
29. *Eyes on the Prize.*
30. *The Murder of Fred Hampton*, Howard Alk, dir.
31. *Eyes on the Prize.*
32. *The Murder of Fred Hampton.*
33. *The Murder of Fred Hampton.*
34. Churchill and Vander Wall, 84.

35. Linder.
36. *The Murder of Fred Hampton.*
37. *The Murder of Fred Hampton.*

Chapter 21
1. David Weddle, *If They Move . . . Kill 'Em!: The Life and Times of Sam Peckinpah*, 334.
2. Weddle, 332.
3. Weddle, 356.
4. Weddle, 334.
5. Weddle, 342.
6. *Life*, July 11, 42.
7. *Life*, July 11, 40.
8. *Life*, July 11, 41.
9. *Life*, July 11, 1.
10. Ann Barrow, "In Search of Masculinity: Martin Ritt's *Hud* and John Schlesinger's *Midnight Cowboy*," *Images: A Journal of Film and Popular Culture, 2004*, http://www.imagesjournal.com/2004/features/masculinity/text.htm.
11. Sherman Alexie, "Because My Father Always Said He Was the Only Indian Who Saw Jimi Hendrix Play 'The Star-Spangeled Banner' at Woodstock," qtd. in *The Portable Sixties Reader*, Ann Charters, ed. 317.
12. Philip Deloria, Counterculture Indians and the New Age," qtd. in *Imagine Nation: The American Counterculture of the 1960s &'70s*, Peter Braunstein and Michael William Doyle, 162.
13. "N. Scott Momaday: Keeper of the Flame," *New Perspectives on* The West, http://www.pbs.org/weta/thewest/program/producers/momaday.htm.
14. *Newsweek*, October 27, 1969, 81.
15. *Alcatraz Is Not an Island*, http://www.pbs.org/itvs/alcatrazisnotanisland/nativeland.html.
16. *Newsweek*, December 8, 1969, 52.
17. *Newsweek*, December 8, 1969, 52.
18. *Alcatraz Is Not an Island.*
19. *Alcatraz Is Not an Island.*
20. *Alcatraz Is Not an Island.*

Chapter 22
1. Graysmith, 65.
2. Graysmith, 68.
3. Graysmith, 71.
4. Graysmith, 76–77.
5. Kelleher and Van Nuys, 70.
6. Sanders, 345.
7. Walker, 125–126.
8. Kelleher and Van Nuys, 77.
9. Kelleher and Van Nuys, 78.

1969

10. *Wikisource*, http://en.wikisource.org/wiki/Zodiac_Killer_letters#October_13th_1969.
11. Graysmith, 116.
12. Graysmith, 121.
13. Graysmith 122–123.
14. "Paul Is Dead," *The Museum of Hoaxes*, http://www.museumofhoaxes.com/hoax/Hoaxipedia/Paul_Is_Dead/.
15. David Dalton, "Altamont: End of the Sixties," *Gadfly*, http://www.gadflyonline.com/archive/NovDec99/archive-altamont.html.
16. Stanley Booth, "The True Adventures of Altamont," *Gimme Shelter* (DVD liner notes), 14.
17. *Gimme Shelter*, David Maysles, Albert Maysles, Charlotte Zwerin, dir. (DVD bonus features).
18. *Gimme Shelter*.
19. *Gimme Shelter*.
20. David Dalton.
21. *Gimme Shelter*.
22. David Dalton.
23. *Gimme Shelter* (DVD bonus features).
24. *Gimme Shelter* (DVD bonus features).
25. *Rolling Stone*, January 21, 1970, 28.
26. *Gimme Shelter* (DVD liner notes).
27. *Gimme Shelter*.
28. *Rolling Stone*, rollingstone.com, *Volunteers* (review).
29. All Music Guide, allmusic.com, *Volunteers* (review)
30. *Gimme Shelter*.
31. Sonny Barger, "From 'Let It Bleed: No Sympathy for the Devils of Altamont,'" *Gimme Shelter* (liner notes), 32.
32. Barger, 32–33; Booth, 14.
33. Barger, 32–33.
34. Bruce Elder, "The Day the Music Died," *The Sydney Morning Herald*, December 11, 2006, http://www.smh.com.au/news/film/the-day-the-music-died/2006/12/10/1165685550250.html?from=rss.
35. *Gimme Shelter* (bonus features).
36. *Rolling Stone*, January 21, 1970, 22.
37. George Paul Csicsery qtd. in Peter Doggett, 313.
38. Michael Lydon, "The Rolling Stones—At Play in the Apocalypse," qtd. in *The Portable Sixties*, Ann Charters, ed., 314.
39. "Jagger 'escaped gang murder plot,'" *BBC News*, http://news.bbc.co.uk/2/hi/entertainment/7274829.stm.
40. Dalton.

Epilogue

1. Robert Santelli qtd. on *Woodstock to Watkins Glen: The Rockfest Archives*, www.chronos-historical.org/rockfest/articles/WG1.html.
2. Snyder, 94–95.

INDEX

1969

television
  ABC, 47, 71–72, 160, 189
  Melvin Belli and "Sam," 331–332, 338
  Brady Bunch, The, 189–190
  CBS, 160, 275–276, 358
  CBS Evening News, 275, 279
  "Crying Indian" public service
    announcement, 354
  David Frost Show, The, 68
  Elvis (NBC broadcast), 23
  Love, American Style, 71–72, 111, 190
  moon landing, 159–160, 161–162, 177
  NBC, 23, 40, 160, 253, 334
  "Silent Majority" speech, 271–272
  Ted Kennedy's address, 177–179
Teller, Thomas, 176
Ten Years After, 242–243
Tennant, William, 211
"termination" policy, 318
Terry the Tramp, 340
Tet Offensive, 119, 276
theater
  Arena Stage (Washington, DC), 315
  Broadhurst Theater, 60
  Broadway, 60, 77–78, 80
  Carnival, 159
  Che! 84
  Dionysus in '69, 83
  Eden Theater, 82, 83
  Geese, 84
  Hair, 60, 77–82, 86, 355
  Hamlet, 77
  Indians, 314, 315–316
  Jesus Christ Superstar, 355
  Living Theatre, 85
  Oh! Calcutta! 82–83
  Play It Again, Sam, 60–61
  sex and nudity in, 77–78, 80, 82–84
  Sex. Y'all Come, 228–229
  Shaftesbury, Theatre (London), 81
  Shubert Theater (Chicago), 81
  Theater of Cruelty, 29, 84
  Tony Awards, 315
Thieu, Nguyen Van, 8
Third World Liberation Front, 12
Third World Nations, 138
Thomas, B. J., 304

Thompson, Hunter, 340
Thornton, Big Mama, 223
Three Dog Night, 80, 223
Three Mile Island, 354
Thunderclap Newman, 26
Tiant, Luis, 90
Tingen, Paul, 34
Toll, John, 17
Topanga Canyon, 31, 184, 198
Toronto, Canada, 81, 272, 293
Torre, Joe, 221
Townshend, Pete, 239, 240, 251
Trail of Broken Treaties, 353
Transactional Analysis, 190
Treacher, Evelyn, 72
Tretter, Charles, 169
Trouille, Clovis, 82
Trudell, John, 324
Turner, Jim, 44, 45
Twentieth Century Fox, 303, 305
Tynan, Kenneth, 82
Tyner, Rob, 26, 27–28

Udall, Morris, 277
Udall, Stewart, 125
Union Oil, 125–127
Unitas, Johnny, 41, 45
United Artists, 66
United Nations, 133
United States Army Corps of Engineers, 322
United States Chamber of Commerce, 111
United States Coast Guard, 321, 324
United States Congress, 2, 10, 115, 146, 269, 275, 277, 285
United States Court of Appeals, 74, 75
United States Customs Service, 74
United States Department of Defense, 104, 351
United States Department of Justice, 55, 319
United States Department of State, 104, 189, 352
United States Department of the Interior, 125, 322, 353
United States Geological Survey, 125
United States House of Representatives, 277
United States Navy, 115, 116